The Birth of Chinese Feminism

WEATHERHEAD BOOKS ON ASIA

WEATHERHEAD EAST ASIAN INSTITUTE, COLUMBIA UNIVERSITY

WEATHERHEAD BOOKS ON ASIA

WEATHERHEAD EAST ASIAN INSTITUTE, COLUMBIA UNIVERSITY

FOR A LIST OF TITLES IN THIS SERIES, SEE PAGE 309

The

Birth of

Chinese

Feminism

ESSENTIAL TEXTS IN TRANSNATIONAL THEORY

Lydia H. Liu, Rebecca E. Karl, and Dorothy Ko, editors

Columbia University Press   *New York*

Columbia University Press
Publishers Since 1893
New York   Chichester, West Sussex
cup.columbia.edu
Copyright © 2013 Columbia University Press

Library of Congress Cataloging-in-Publication Data
The birth of Chinese feminism : essential texts in transnational theory / edited by
Lydia H. Liu, Rebecca E. Karl, and Dorothy Ko.
    p. cm.
Includes bibliographical references and index.
ISBN 978-0-231-16290-6 (cloth : alk. paper)—ISBN 978-0-231-16291-3 (pbk.)—
ISBN 978-0-231-53326-3 (electronic)
1. Feminism—China—History. 2. Feminists—China—Biography. I. Liu, Lydia He.
II. Karl, Rebecca E. III. Ko, Dorothy, 1957–

    HQ1767.B57 2013
    305.420951—dc23

                                                            2012021352

Columbia University Press books are printed on permanent
and durable acid-free paper.

This book is printed on paper with recycled content.
Printed in the United States of America

Cover image: Detail from an image of Lin Tianmiao's art installation,
   Meishenme haowande (known as "There is no fun of it"); white cotton thread,
   embroidery frame, and one needle, 1998. Courtesy of Lin Tianmiao.
Cover design: Rebecca Lown

References to websites (URLs) were accurate at the time of writing.
Neither the author nor Columbia University Press is responsible for URLs
that may have expired or changed since the manuscript was prepared.

Contents

Acknowledgments *vii*
List of Chinese Dynasties and a Note on Translation *xi*

Introduction: Toward a Transnational Feminist Theory 1

The Historical Context: Chinese Feminist Worlds
at the Turn of the Twentieth Century 27

He-Yin Zhen

Biography 51

"On the Question of Women's Liberation" 53

"On the Question of Women's Labor" 72

"Economic Revolution and Women's Revolution" 92

"On the Revenge of Women" 105

"On Feminist Antimilitarism" 169

"The Feminist Manifesto" 179

Contents

Liang Qichao

Biography   187

"On Women's Education"   189

Jin Tianhe

Biography   205

"The Women's Bell"   207

Bibliography 287
Index 293

Acknowledgments

This volume is the culmination of a series of gatherings and discussions among the three editors. In December 2007, a workshop called "Living Texts: Rethinking China and the World in the Late Qing" was organized by Lydia Liu at Columbia University. (In April 2004, a related workshop on "Rethinking the Nineteenth Century: China and the World in Transition" had been held at the Center for Chinese Studies of the University of Michigan.) The Columbia workshop focused on the late-Qing intellectual legacy in modern China. It brought He-Yin Zhen to light again, as if for the first time, leading us to this collective project of translation and theorizing. In the course of the preparation and production of this volume since then, we have incurred, personally and collectively, many debts.

Our work has been collaborative in the most positive and truest sense of that practice: we have worked together by sharing and creating to achieve a goal. The three editors have each other to thank for a most pleasurable process. We also wish to thank our fellow translators, whose hard work and efforts we, and all readers of this volume, must appreciate: Michael Gibbs Hill and Tze-lan D. Sang; Jeremy Tai; Meng Fan and Cynthia Roe; Robert Cole and Wei Peng. The latter four were graduate students in a seminar on He-Yin Zhen and her feminist worlds that the editors co-taught at Columbia University in spring 2010; we are delighted that they wished to translate even after the semester was over. At our request, Michael translated Jin Tianhe, and he did so in a remarkably short amount of time and with a great deal of erudition; Tze-lan generously offered to edit and review that translation. We, the editors of the volume, have gone through all the translations and endeavored to make them consistent with one another, to the extent possible. Interpretive choices made in the process of translation have been approved by all three coeditors, and we alone are responsible for any errors that may remain.

In the summer of 2009, the three coeditors presented a preliminary version of this project to a conference held at Fudan University in Shanghai. We thank Wang Zheng and Chen Yan for inviting us to organize the session and Gail Hershatter for chairing it. In October 2009, the coeditors held a workshop at Columbia self-servingly organized around our translations of He-Yin Zhen's three major essays as well as Hill's translation of Jin Tianhe's pamphlet. We invited scholars whose specializations included many non-China-related geographical zones and asked each participant to read the translated texts carefully, along with some background materials, and to come to New York prepared for two days of intensive conversation. Everyone in attendance took the invitation seriously and contributed immeasurably to our understanding of He-Yin Zhen's significance, resonance, and importance in transnational feminist and intellectual theorizing. Our participants were Swapna Banerjee, Marilyn Booth, Amy Dooling, Janet Jakobsen, Michael Gibbs Hill, Lila Abu-Lughod, Yukiko Hanawa, Viren Murthy, Mae Ngai, Joyce Liu, Anupama Rao, Neferti Tadiar, and Elizabeth Weed. They will each recognize their contributions to the overall shape of the project. We cannot thank them enough for their seriousness of purpose and for the fun we had discussing, debating, and dining together. A special thanks to our graduate students: Zhang Li for being so helpful with the organizing and Annie Shing for designing a beautiful poster. We especially want to thank Amy for being such a great reader for the press and advising us throughout; the anonymous second reader for the press; Neferti, for reading our introductions and providing commentary; Lisa Rofel, for reading and commenting at the last minute; the Feminist Reading Group at Columbia, for giving the introductions a critical reading; Yukiko Hanawa, for helping track down obscure Japanese sources; and Myra Sun, for her assistance in the research and preparation for the book manuscript. For their encouragement and support, we are deeply grateful, although none of those named herein is responsible ultimately for what we made of their contributions.

In addition, we are full of gratitude to Mr. Wan Shiguo, independent scholar from Yangzhou, who punctuated many of the essays we have translated here, even though he had them published in the collected works of Liu Shipei. Mr. Wan also answered many of our questions. We thank Wang

Fan-sen from the Institute of Philology and History at the Academia Sinica in Taiwan for sending us copies of essays from *Natural Justice* missing from the Japanese facsimile edition of the journal. Our gratitude also goes to Liu Huiying, who made her own and Xia Xiaohong's work available to us and whose lone voice in demanding the reevaluation in Chinese academia of the work of He-Yin Zhen has been inspiring. And to Gabriele von Sivers-Sattler from Heidelberg, we express our admiration for her pioneering work, which confirmed our sense that He-Yin Zhen's preferred name was indeed He-Yin Zhen.

A special note of thanks is due to Li Tuo, who helped resolve many interpretive conundrums with his informed feminist readings of He-Yin Zhen's prose.

Michael Gibbs Hill wishes to thank Tze-lan D. Sang for her many corrections and suggestions for the initial draft of the Jin Tianhe translation and Jie Guo, a colleague at South Carolina, who also helped improve the translated text. He is grateful as well to Colin Barr, Melissa Haynes, Tze-Ki Hon, Mark Kellner, Dorothy Ko, Alexander Ogden, Wang Daw-hwan, and Xia Xiaohong for providing assistance and advice.

Numerous institutional debts were also incurred as this volume took shape. Our workshop, held at Columbia University's Institute for Research on Women and Gender, was funded in large part by a generous grant from the Weatherhead East Asian Institute of Columbia University. A grant from the Middle East Institute of Columbia, facilitated by Lila, allowed us to bring Marilyn Booth from Edinburgh. In addition, we received a much-appreciated publication subvention from Lauren Benton, dean of humanities at NYU, and another from the NYU Humanities Initiative. Finally, Jennifer Crewe and Columbia University Press have been wonderful partners in this project; we thank her and the whole team at the Press for moving efficiently and sensitively through the production of this volume.

The three coeditors have lived on and off with He-Yin Zhen for the past three or more years; as we launch her into the English-speaking world, we hope our readers will find her as astonishingly fresh, consistently challenging, and intellectually stimulating as we have.

List of Chinese Dynasties and a Note on Translation

Dynasties

Many dates for the earlier dynasties are at best approximations. As He-Yin Zhen prolifically references dynastic histories, we provide the following as a rough guide. There are many differentiations within these dynastic spans, as China was often not unified; we have eliminated most of those divisions.

Three Dynasties: Xia, Shang, and Zhou dynasties
   (ca. 21st–3rd century B.C.E.)
Zhou dynasty (1046–256 B.C.E.)
Spring and Autumn period (772–476 B.C.E.)
Warring States period (475–221 B.C.E.)
Qin dynasty (221–206 B.C.E)
Han dynasty (202 B.C.E.–220 C.E.)
Former or Western Han: 202 B.C.E.–24 C.E.; Later or Eastern Han:
   25–220 C.E. (We count the Western Han from Liu Bang's founding
   and include Wang Mang's Xin dynasty to simplify matters.)
Three Kingdoms (220–280 C.E.)
Jin, Western and Eastern (265–439 C.E.)
Northern-Southern dynasties (420–581 C.E.)
Sui dynasty (581–618 C.E.)
Tang dynasty (618–907 C.E.)
Five Dynasties: Liang, Later Tang, Later Jin, Later Han, Later Zhou
   (907–960 C.E.)

Song dynasty (960–1279 C.E.)
Yuan dynasty (1279–1368 C.E.)
Ming dynasty (1368–1644 C.E.)
Qing dynasty (1644–1911 C.E.)

Note on Translation

Chinese names are ordered surname first, given name last, without a comma in between. Thus, He-Yin Zhen is Ms. He-Yin; Liang Qichao is Mr. Liang; Jin Tianhe is Mr. Jin. We have retained this order in our translations and in our referencing. However, if a Chinese scholar is known by the Western order of his or her name, we have retained that preference.

All references to personal age are by Chinese reckoning, which considers a person one year old when born.

All notes in the translations are original to the text, unless marked "Tr:," which indicates annotations added by the translators. Dates added into the texts by the translators are in parentheses ( ); all other matter not original to the texts is in brackets [ ]. The translators have striven for comprehensibility and readability in English, at the same time retaining the distinctive voices of the originals and the flavor of the usages of that time.

The Birth of Chinese Feminism

Introduction

TOWARD A TRANSNATIONAL FEMINIST THEORY

I n 1903, Jin Tianhe (aka Jin Yi; male), a liberal educator and political activist, published in Shanghai what historians have commonly called a feminist manifesto entitled *The Women's Bell* (*Nüjie zhong*). In the preface, Jin contrasts his own pathetic existence with that of an imaginary counterpart in Euro-America:

> The muggy rainy season with its endless drizzles is stifling. Lotuses droop in the torpid hot breeze. The trees are listless and the distant hills dormant. On the eastern end of the continent of Asia, in a country that knows no freedom, in a small room that knows no freedom, my breathing is heavy, my mind gone sluggish. I want to let in the fresh air of European civilization, draw it in to restore my body.
>
> I dream of a young, white European man. On this day, at this hour, with a rolled cigarette in his mouth, walking stick in hand, his wife and children by him, he strolls with his head held up high and arms swinging by his sides through the promenades of London, Paris, Washington. Such happiness and ease! I wish I could go there myself.[1]

This extraordinary confession of racial melancholy by a young man is an odd opening to what is touted as the first Chinese feminist manifesto. The desire to emulate an upper-class white European man in his marital bliss reflects the painful situation of Chinese *men* and their psychic struggles in

---

[1] Jin Tianhe, *The Women's Bell*, translated in this volume, p. 207.

relation to white European men. But what does this have to do with Chinese women and, more important, with feminism? Must racial melancholy mask itself in the image of subjugated gender and civilization? Were women readers of *The Women's Bell* in China troubled by such mental projections?

He-Yin Zhen (1884—ca.1920), a preeminent feminist theorist and founding editor of an anarcho-feminist journal *Natural Justice*, was among the first women readers of Jin Tianhe's manifesto. In 1907–1908, she published a perceptive critique of Jin and other contemporary male feminists in an essay called "On the Question of Women's Liberation." She writes:

> Chinese men worship power and authority. They believe that Europeans, Americans, and the Japanese are civilized nations of the modern world who all grant their women some degree of freedom. By transplanting this system into the lives of their wives and daughters, by prohibiting their practices of footbinding, and by enrolling them in modern schools to receive basic education, these men think that they will be applauded by the whole world for having joined the ranks of civilized nations. . . . I am inclined to think that these men act purely out of a selfish desire to claim women as private property. Were it not so, why would a woman's reputation, good or bad, have anything whatsoever to do with them? The men's original intention is not to liberate women but to treat them as private property. In the past when traditional rituals prevailed, men tried to distinguish themselves by confining women in the boudoir; when the tides turn in favor of Europeanization, they attempt to acquire distinction by promoting women's liberation. This is what I call *men's pursuit of self distinction in the name of women's liberation*.[2]

He-Yin Zhen's attack on the progressive male intellectuals of her time—men who championed women's education, suffrage, and gender equality and who would have been her allies—opens up a vast space for a new interpretation of the rise of feminism in China and in the world. The current volume makes this interpretive space accessible and available to scholars and students of feminism for the first time.

He-Yin Zhen 何殷震 is better known to Chinese historians as He Zhen 何震. In her published works, the author prefers to sign her name He-Yin Zhen so as to include her mother's maiden name in the family name. This was a decision grounded in her theoretical work published in *Natural*

---

[2]He-Yin Zhen, "On the Question of Women's Liberation," translated in this volume, p. 60.

Justice. As she makes clear in her own "Feminist Manifesto" (translated in this volume), the history and politics of the patrilineal surname were of crucial importance to grasping how a feminist space for activity and practice in the social and political worlds of her time could be claimed and shaped. Out of respect for her decision to attach her maternal surname to her paternal one, we adopt her preferred name He-Yin Zhen throughout this volume.[3]

A long-suppressed intellectual figure in modern Chinese history, He-Yin Zhen is an original thinker and powerful social theorist often identified as an anarcho-feminist. Her writings, some of which were selected for inclusion in this volume, suggest an impressively broad awareness of women's suffrage movements in Europe and in North America. They address not only the oppression of women in China, past and present, but also the conditions of women's livelihood in industrializing Japan as well as the anarchist and socialist struggles around the world. Her objective was to develop a systematic global critique of the political, economic, moral, and ideological bases of patriarchal society in critical response to the social agendas of progressive Chinese men who also promoted women's rights. The strength and richness of her critique, in particular her discovery of the analytic category of *nannü* 男女 (literally, "man and woman" or "male/female"), and its relevance to our own feminist theory making will be elaborated in later discussions in the present introduction.

By initiating this work of translation and reinterpretation of He-Yin Zhen's works, we do not imply that women have a more authentic feminist voice than do men. Rather, we want to resuscitate the voice of a preeminent female theorist who has largely been ignored for as long as a century.[4] The absence of

---

[3]For a discussion of the naming issue, see Gabriele von Sivers-Sattler, "He Zhens Forderungen zur Namensgebung von Frauen im vorrevolutionären China: Untersuchungen zur anarchistischen Zeitschrift *Tian Yi* („Naturgemäße Rechtlichkeit") (1907–1908)," in *Cheng—In All Sincerity*, ed. Denise Gimpel and Melanie Hanz, 275–284, Festschrift in Honour of Monika Übelhör (Hamburg, Germany: Hamburger Sinologische Gesellschaft, 2001).

[4]Peter Zarrow's study of He-Yin Zhen (aka He Zhen) is one of the few published studies in English. See his article "He Zhen and Anarcho-Feminism in China," *Journal of Asian Studies* 47, 4 (November 1988): 796–813. See also Liu Huiying, "Feminism: An Organic or Extremist Position? On *Tien Yee* as Represented by He Zhen," *Positions* 11, 3 (Winter 2003): 779–800. He-Yin Zhen is virtually ignored in Chinese scholarship, with the exception of Beijing-based scholars Liu Huiying and Xia Xiaohong. For Liu's attempt to reevaluate her role in early Chinese feminism, see her article "Cong nüquan zhuyi dao wuzhengfu zhuyi—guanyu He Zhen yu Tianyi" [From feminism to anarchism: On He Zhen and *Natural Justice*], *Zhongguo xiandai wenxue yanjiu congkan* 2 (2006): 194–213; and Xia Xiaohong, "He Zhen de wuzhengfu zhuyi 'nüjie geming' lun" [On He Zhen's anarchist "Women's Revolution"], *Zhonghua wenshi luncong* 83 (2006): 311–350.

He-Yin Zhen's voice in feminist theorizing in and out of China has meant a tremendous loss for feminist movements in general. In this introduction, we outline the rationale and goals of our translations and explain the relevance and significance of He-Yin Zhen, in particular, to the theoretical endeavors of our own time. For a detailed account of the historical context in late-Qing China that gave rise to the texts of He-Yin Zhen, Jin Tianhe (1874–1947), and another important male thinker, Liang Qichao (1873–1929)—whose major feminist texts are included in this volume of translation—we refer our readers to the chapter that immediately follows this introduction.

Early Chinese Feminisms

The birth of Chinese feminism was an event of global proportions that is yet to be properly grasped and analyzed as such. As editors and translators of this volume, we hope that an appreciation of this event will cast new light on the limitations of our current feminist struggles and point us in new directions. Initially, we undertook the translation of the representative works of He-Yin Zhen and those of her male contemporaries Jin Tianhe and Liang Qichao in order to fill a lacuna in the knowledge of Chinese feminism. For few translations or studies of early Chinese feminists and their writings exist in English, and whatever there is of published studies, English or Chinese, has presented little systematic engagement with the possible theoretical contributions of early Chinese feminism to worldwide feminist thought. In making the writings of early Chinese feminists available to the English-speaking world, we are trying not merely to rescue the voice of non-Western feminists—a worthwhile project in itself—but to engage contemporary feminist theoretical discourse in broader terms than the well-known debates over the theoretical priorities of gender, sex, sexuality, sexual difference, identity politics, or intersectionality that have dominated contemporary Euro-American feminist discussion over the past few decades.

Our goal in translating the texts of early Chinese feminist theorists, and in highlighting He-Yin Zhen, is threefold: First, we aim to bring to light—for the first time in English or Chinese—the vital contributions of early Chinese feminists to global feminist thought and theory. *Tien Yee* (*Tianyi bao*) or *Natural Justice*, in which all He-Yin Zhen's extant writings first appeared, was an anarchist-leaning Chinese feminist journal published by the Society for the

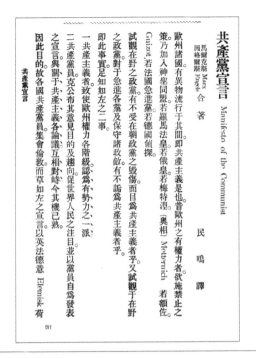

The first Chinese translation of *The Communist Manifesto*, chapter 1, in *Natural Justice*, 1908.

Restoration of Women's Rights in Tokyo in 1907–1908.[5] Although short-lived, this journal, which He-Yin Zhen edited with the support of her husband, Liu Shipei (1884–1919), has a vital contribution to make to our understanding of the revolutionary and internationalist fermentations of the time in its rejection of the facile opposition of tradition and modernity.[6] The journal offers some rare early feminist critical analyses in Chinese of political economy, capitalism, the modern state, and patriarchal systems; indeed, we cannot go without pointing out that the earliest Chinese translation of *The Communist Manifesto*, the first chapter, was published in *Natural Justice*

[5]Both *Tien Yee* and *Natural Justice* are original titles of the journal; *Tianyi* is a modern rendition of 天義 in the pinyin system. In the first two issues, the qualifier *bao* (meaning "journal" or "newspaper") follows *Tianyi*; it was dropped from the title beginning in the third issue.
[6]The journal itself is well known as an anarchist publication and is frequently cited in Chinese scholarship. What is most often suppressed is that this journal was the official organ of the Society for the Restoration of Women's Rights; hence its feminist origin.

in 1908. The significance of this detail has heretofore been overlooked: it was Chinese feminism that first translated communist thought, among other radical ideas, and introduced it to China (by way of Japan), not the converse.[7]

The second goal of this volume is to reassess the birth of Chinese feminism in a series of global intellectual developments at the turn of the twentieth century that culminated in the publication of Jin Tianhe's *The Women's Bell* in 1903 and in the inauguration of He-Yin Zhen's feminist journal *Natural Justice* in 1907. These developments—spurred on by the accelerated expansion of modern capitalism and imperialism into Asia and elsewhere—involved a simultaneous spread of the ideas of liberalism, Christian evangelism, evolutionism, socialism, anarchism, feminism, and Marxism to Japan, China, and other parts of the world. The arrival of feminism under these historical circumstances raised vital stakes not only for Chinese women but also for Chinese men, and especially for such men of the educated gentry class as Jin Tianhe and Liang Qichao. These progressive thinkers—and educated Asian men in general—were confronted on the one hand with the assault on their self-image as men by the hypermasculinity of the military powers of Western colonialism and imperialism; on the other hand, they were bombarded with accusations of their enslavement of women—footbinding, concubinage, and sati being cited as chief examples—which became one important moral justification for the imperialist assault on societies classified as "barbarous" and "half-civilized."

As the civilizational status of the gentry class—coded "male"—came under increased threat by the superior military and discursive forces of the West, a number of contradictory social conditions began to emerge and prepare the ground for the rise of feminism in China. The movement began with a kind of protofeminist rhetoric and activism led by Chinese men alongside the responses of Chinese women at the turn of the century. The enthusiastic support for women's right to education by male reformers like Kang Youwei (1858–1927), his student Liang Qichao, Jin Tianhe, and Chinese women in the last decades of the Qing dynasty (1890s–1911) must be grasped in that light. Through our translation of the conflicting voices of such pioneering figures as He-Yin Zhen, Jin Tianhe, and Liang Qichao, the

---

[7]He-Yin's essay "What Women Should Know About Communism" has previously been translated in *Sources of Chinese Tradition: From 1600 Through the Twentieth Century*, compiled by Wm. Theodore de Bary and Richard Lufrano, 2nd ed., vol. 2 (New York: Columbia University Press, 2000), 389–392.

reader will appreciate the important role played by the early feminists, men as well as women, in the advent of Chinese modernity.

Jin Tianhe's *The Women's Bell* was a popular text in the first quarter of the twentieth century. Because of the important role this text played in the history of Chinese feminism, we have chosen to include its first English translation in our volume. We hope to spark discussion among readers who encounter this text along with the texts by He-Yin Zhen. Reprinted in several editions in China and Japan, with expanding numbers of prefaces by prominent feminists and readers, it exerted a significant impact upon the Chinese feminist movement over the next decades.[8] For this reason, the text is taken by some historians to be the beginning of a specifically Chinese-articulated feminism, even though prior to its publication, there had been many discussions in Chinese journals devoted to various aspects of what came to be called "the woman question" by women as well as men. *The Women's Bell* may well have been the first systematic championing of women's rights to education, to suffrage, to employment and livelihood, and to human dignity. Yet, as far as Jin Tianhe was concerned, women's emancipation was part of a larger project of enlightenment and national self-strengthening, coded either "male" or "patriarchal."

For He-Yin, by contrast, the feminist struggle was not to be subordinated to struggles that advanced the nationalist, ethnocentric, or capitalist modernization agendas; rather, it was the beginning and outcome of a total social revolution that would abolish the state and private property to bring about true social equality and the end to all social hierarchies. Thus, by reading He-Yin Zhen alongside and in comparison to Jin Tianhe and Liang Qichao, readers may come to appreciate the plurality of and contradictions within Chinese feminisms, which indicate, reflect, and articulate the diversity of global feminisms at the turn of the twentieth century.

Our third goal in preparing this volume is to reconsider the rise of Chinese feminism in the face of what Gayatri Chakravorty Spivak has critically termed "the ironclad opposition of West and East" and its inescapable logic.[9]

---

[8]Among the first scholars to study this text outside China is Louise Edwards. See her "Chin Sung-ts'en's *A Tocsin for Women*: The Dextrous Merger of Radicalism and Conservatism in Feminism of the Early Twentieth Century," *Research on Women in Modern Chinese History* (Jindai Zhongguo funüshi yanjiu) no. 2 (June 1994): 117–140.

[9]Gayatri Chakravorty Spivak, "French Feminism in an International Frame," *Yale French Studies*, no. 62 (1981): 155.

This opposition and logic prevail in European and American societies but not exclusively there, for they are also accepted by nearly all modern societies, including China. We seek to undo that universal oppositional logic by taking the reader through the numerous counterpoints and often irreconcilable conflicts between the works of Jin Tianhe and Liang Qichao and that of He-Yin Zhen. Neither position can neatly be mapped onto any preconceived ideas of what Chinese feminism was or should have been in opposition to the fiction of a totalized Western feminism.

On the one hand, Jin Tianhe's *The Women's Bell* approaches the question of women's liberation through the lens of enlightenment discourse and a mix of paternalism, liberalism, nationalism, and women's suffrage. He-Yin Zhen's critique of liberalism and capitalism, on the other hand, is partly directed against the programs of the women's suffrage movement endorsed by such progressive men in China as Jin or Liang. She also saw the limitation of such movements in Europe and America and insisted on developing a feminist socioeconomic analysis that illuminated the patriarchal foundation of capitalist modernity and the capitalist extensions of patriarchy. These discursive struggles over the terms through which one may understand women's relationship to the modern state and to the capitalist mode of production while conceptualizing women's liberation suggest that Chinese feminism did not originate from a single standpoint, nor did it form a one-way relationship with women's struggles in Europe and North America.

Ultimately, aside from introducing a little-known feminist theorist to a wider audience, we hope with this volume to initiate a discussion among English-language scholars and students of how He-Yin Zhen's work and concerns can help enrich feminist scholarship and pedagogy in our academic and teaching lives; how, through her, we can link China and the world in the past and the present; and how, with her insights, we can enhance ongoing feminist theoretical engagements with the gendered body, gendered labor, and gendered knowledge.

The Basic Tenets of He-Yin Zhen's Feminist Theory

He-Yin Zhen wrote a series of critical essays about her contemporary world in 1907–1908. These critiques encompassed a spatial and temporal totality through which she understood all hitherto existing social relationships. Her analytical totalization was utterly unlike that of her male or female contemporaries, whose analyses usually mobilized "woman" to speak to supposedly larger sociopolitical problems, whether these "larger" concerns were economic modernization, nationalism, state rationality, international relations and imperialist imposition, the threatened loss of masculine authority as a result of the diminished political utility of classical scholarship, and so on.

In contrast to many of these analyses (including Jin Tianhe's and Liang Qichao's), one of He-Yin Zhen's major points in her intellectual practice was to elucidate how "woman" as a transhistorical global category—not of subjective identity but of structured unequal social relations—had been constituted through scholarship, ritual, law, and social and labor practices over time, in China as elsewhere. Indeed, not only did He-Yin Zhen lament that categorical constitution in its multiple guises, but she also understood those guises as themselves constitutive of her past and her contemporary moment. In this totalizing way, she arrived at a prescient critique of the world as it appeared to her at that time.

In her long major essay "On the Revenge of Women," as well as in her other writing, He-Yin Zhen made little distinction between China's imperial (pre-nineteenth-century) past and the situation characterizing her more globally integrated imperialist-capitalist present. Rather, she argued that the past and the present formed a constant reiteration of inherent and inexorable injustice. The historicity of injustice was not merely perpetrated upon women by men (the past and the present, in other words, did not uniquely victimize women); instead, in He-Yin Zhen's theoretical idiom, history is formed by a continuously reproduced injustice in the manner of what the Annales school of French historians would come to call the *longue durée*, whose generalized contours of uneven wealth and property as well as its specificities of embodied affect could be made visible through the figure of "woman."

In this analytical mode, "woman"—rendered by He-Yin Zhen in various incommensurable but related semantic forms—was far from a naturalized figure of biological or cultural subordination.[10] Rather, she was the product

---

[10]The terms we have rendered "women" (or "female") include *nüzi* 女子, *funü* 婦女, *furen* 婦人, and, on occasion, *nüxing* 女性 (see the later discussion in this introduction). In the cases of her essay titles, 女子非軍備主義 ("On Feminist Antimilitarism") and 女子宣告書 ("The Feminist Manifesto"), we gloss *nüzi* 女子 not as "women's" but as "feminist." He-Yin also uses *wunüzi* 吾女子, which we render "we women." The term *nüjie* 女界 is rendered "women," "womanhood," and "women's world." We use "man" or "men" to render *nanzi* 男子 and *zhangfu* 丈夫.

of historical social relations. In that sense, "woman" was a political ontology, or an endlessly reproduced principle of politicized and social practice *in* and *through* time. In her analysis, whereas the form of the injustice could and did shift, the logic of injustice was historically reinscribed and, in that sense, continuous. Defining "woman" through and embedding her into endlessly reproduced historicized social relations, thence to reconceptualize the past and the present in a historical mode, was the principle through which He-Yin Zhen perceived her contemporary world and conceived her own analytical and activist pursuits.

This analytical category is what she named *nannü* (man and woman; male/female), a mostly untranslatable conceptual totality that signifies not only gendered social relations between man and woman but also, more broadly, the relationship of the past to the present, of China to the world, of politics to justice, of law and ritual to gendered forms of knowledge, interaction, and social organization. In short, *nannü* is the category through which He-Yin Zhen understood her world as an always-already gendered time-space of social activity, production, and life. Although the valences of *nannü* changed over time, in its historical connection to another of He-Yin Zhen's key terms, *shengji*, or what we have translated as "livelihood," *nannü* is nevertheless the central logic through which an uneven and unjust world can be perceived and understood. In the sections that follow, we discuss the centrality of *nannü* and *shengji* to her feminist critique of the political economy of her time and analyze the ways in which this intertwined mode of thinking can enrich contemporary feminist discussion of gendered bodies, labor, and social reproduction. *Nannü*, we propose, is a more comprehensive rubric than "sex-gender," whereas *shengji* is a more enabling rubric than "class."

Translating *Nannü* as Analytical Category

Nannü is the most crucial term in Chinese feminist discourses in the twentieth century. The key slogan for the feminist movement throughout the century has been *nannü pingdeng*, the standard translation of which is "gender equality" (in legal status, access to education, right to vote, social benefits, and so on). In this context, the equation of *nannü* with "gender" as a shorthand for male-female is most appropriate. But He-Yin Zhen's use of the term is different and singular. From early on in the translation process, the editors were struck by how He-Yin's notion of *nannü* exceeds and resists facile rendition into "man and woman," "gender," "male/female," or other familiar English concepts. A brief explanation of our theory and practice of translation is in order here before we go on to explore the potential theoretical contributions of He-Yin Zhen's categories to Anglophone feminist theories in the twenty-first century.

Interpreting *nannü* as a kind of "gender" has the advantage of assimilating He-Yin Zhen's work into the discourse of late-twentieth-century feminism familiar to Anglophone readers. By the same token, it could ensnare us in conceptual traps. Translating *nannü* literally word for word—*nan* for "man" and *nü* for "woman"—into two or several English words, "man and woman" or "male/female," is just as unsatisfactory because the literal translation could contradict He-Yin Zhen's theoretical project, which takes *nannü* as a single conceptual mechanism, used as both noun and adjective, that lies at *the foundation of all patriarchal abstractions and markings of distinction.* These abstractions and markings apply to both men and women but are by no means limited to socially defined men and women. In the end, we decided to leave *nannü* untranslated in some situations, whereas in others we allowed it a full range of semantic mobility when contextually appropriate—"gender," "man and woman," and "male/female." This decision was based on our understanding that the issue here was not so much about the existence or nonexistence of verbal equivalents as it was about the translingual precariousness of analytical categories as they pass or fail to pass through different languages and their conceptual grids.

In this sense, we understand our critical task as translators and scholars as not merely to find an approximate term to render He-Yin's expanded meanings but to make sense of the analytical valences of *nannü* as a category in Chinese *and* English. In the interest of maintaining interpretive openness, we determined it would be wrong to begin by asking if the concept of "gender" or "woman" exists in a non-Western language; neither would it be fruitful to ask if the category of *nannü* exists in English. The issue at stake is not linguistic incommensurability, which could be self-contradictory if we had to rely on English to make an argument of incommensurability through the act of translation.[11] But rather, we understand

---

[11] In *The Invention of Women: Making an African Sense of Western Gender Discourses* (Minneapolis: University of Minnesota Press, 1997), Oyeronke Oyewumi makes such an argument while trying to problematize the category of "gender" in Western feminist discourse.

our challenge to be to put He-Yin Zhen's category in comparative terms and in so doing, to question not only Chinese usage but also theoretical categories used in the English language as well.

This undertaking is a two-pronged process. First, it requires us to focus on the analytical and historical valences of *nannü* in the Chinese language and in He-Yin Zhen's writing. It involves, in particular, taking into account the translingual inventions of neologisms and supersigns in He-Yin Zhen's own time when the Chinese language, yet to be codified into its modern form, was open to exposures to foreign languages.[12] The difficulty we have encountered in trying to translate *nannü* and other key concepts is matched only by the fluidity that He-Yin Zhen's own generation confronted in working with the novel translations and neologisms derived from Japanese, English, and other mediated foreign language sources. At the same time, while wrestling with this slippery semantic slope, a second challenge we face is to be vigilant lest the concept of "gender" catches us unawares as a hidden or naturalized English term of reference in our translations.

The difficulty of making epistemic leaps across languages notwithstanding, we are careful not to reduce an intellectual problem to the incommensurable differences between a Chinese term and an English term, or to a problem of "influence" of the West over China. Far more productive is to tease out the theoretical resonances in the spaces opened up between *nannü* and "gender" or any other such categories in contemporary feminist theories, which have always passed back and forth through a multiplicity of modern languages. To acknowledge linguistic proliferation and discursive multiplicity in the global making of feminist theory is to allow the analytical categories to play against one another and to illuminate the limitations of each term in its historical interconnectedness to other terms.

For this reason, we believe that the historical valences of "gender" as an analytical category in contemporary feminist theory should itself be reevaluated in this comparative light. Joan W. Scott has observed in her classic essay "Gender: A Useful Category of Historical Analysis" that "gender" was not part of the social theories in Europe in the eighteenth through the early

---

[12]The concept "supersign" refers not to a self-contained word unit but to a heterocultural signifying chain that cuts across the semantic fields of two or several languages, which makes an impact on the meaning of a native word. It identifies the bonding of heterolinguistic elements through the act of translation that typically renders that process invisible. For a theoretical elaboration in semiotic terms, see Lydia H. Liu, *The Clash of Empires: The Invention of China in Modern Worldmaking* (Cambridge, MA, Harvard University Press, 2004), 12–13.

twentieth centuries. The earlier social theories had drawn on the male and female opposition to build their logic or to discuss the "woman question" or sexual identities, but "gender as a way of talking about systems of social or sexual relations did not appear."[13] When it did appear in the late twentieth century, feminists found the category tremendously useful—albeit fraught with ambiguities and contradictions—for analyzing "social relationships based on perceived differences between the sexes" and examining gender as "a primary way of signifying relationships of power" (Scott 1067).

Gender historians, in particular, have allowed the category of "gender" to range across cultural and linguistic divides and across historical time. "Gender" is extended to the study of a historical past in which the category itself is missing while the epistemological distance between the subject and object of analysis is guaranteed. This cannot but pose a series of intellectual as well as political challenges to feminist theorists. Should a category that purports to analyze history remain itself ahistorical? Does its historicity from the time of Latin grammar belong only to our world and not theirs, i.e., the world of the past and that of the foreign? Why are we anxious about maintaining the distance between the subject and the object of knowledge, a distance that feminists have long identified as a patriarchal prerogative that defines the modern subject? He-Yin Zhen's concept of *nannü* is helpful in suggesting ways out of these binds.

Nannü: Beyond the Sex-Gender Problematic

In "On the Question of Women's Liberation" (1907), He-Yin posits that men have created "political and moral institutions, the first priority of which was to separate man from woman (*nannü*). For they considered the differentiation between man and woman (*nannü youbie*) to be one of the major principles in heaven and on earth."[14] This use of *nannü* performs a kind of analysis that the category of gender also does, but it does more. For *nannü* is simultaneously

---

[13]Joan W. Scott, "Gender: A Useful Category of Historical Analysis," *American Historical Review* 91, 5 (1986): 1066.

[14]The mapping of the cosmology of heaven and earth onto a male-female hierarchy was accomplished by Confucian scholars in the Han dynasty (202 B.C.E.–220 C.E.). He-Yin Zhen developed a thorough critique of the resulting misogynist tradition in her "On the Revenge of Women."

an object of analysis and an analytical category, which confounds the need for "distinguishing between our analytic vocabulary and the material we want to analyze."[15] Like all other terms of the vocabulary we inherit from the past, the concept of *nannü* is a historical elaboration and a normative distinction internal to patriarchal discourse itself. He-Yin Zhen identifies this concept as central to and ubiquitous in Chinese patriarchal discourse over the past millennia and treats it as a highly developed philosophical and moral category that has legitimated men's oppression of women.

What, then, can we learn from He-Yin Zhen's approach to the category of *nannü*? Inasmuch as *nannü* is a well-established concept in Chinese philosophical discourse, He-Yin Zhen's method is to turn it inside out and against itself, making the term bear the burden and evidence of its own patriarchal work. Her critique demonstrates that the normative function of *nannü* is not only to create "gendered" identities (which it also does) but also to introduce primary distinctions through socioeconomic abstraction articulated to metaphysical abstractions, such as the external and the internal, or to such cosmic abstractions as yang and yin. He-Yin Zhen sees *nannü* as a mechanism of distinction or marking that has evolved over time, capable of spawning new differences and new social hierarchies across the boundaries of class, age, ethnicity, race, and so on. This is in part why, at the end of her "Feminist Manifesto" (1907), He-Yin argues that "by 'men' (*nanxing*) and 'women' (*nüxing*), we are not speaking of 'nature,' but the outcome of differing social customs and education. If sons and daughters are treated equally, raised and educated in the same manner, then the responsibilities assumed by men and women will surely become equal. When that happens, the nouns *nanxing* and *nüxing* would no longer be necessary."[16] Here, she clearly calls for the end of philosophical dualism and its naming practice, for that practice, she observes, is neither neutral nor innocent but, rather, creates and spawns insidious social hierarchies that make a claim to social truth and historical reality.

Did He-Yin's critique of *nannü* anticipate what poststructuralist feminists of the 1980s–1990s have termed the "social constructivist" view of gender? Yes, and no. Superficial similarities notwithstanding, the problem here is that no fixed biological views of sex or sexual difference existed in the Chinese context with which He-Yin Zhen contended, as it did for

---

[15]Scott, "Gender," 1065.
[16]See He-Yin Zhen, "The Feminist Manifesto," translated in this volume, p. 184.

Euro-American poststructuralist feminists many decades later. Indeed, as Michel Foucault and many others have shown, the biological concept of the body was also a recent invention in Europe; thus it is important to keep in mind that "the facile mapping of anatomy onto sexual difference, or the conflation of 'sex' and 'gender' was in fact a peculiar dynamic in the formation of the modern rational and individual subject."[17] If the patriarchal discursive tradition critiqued by He-Yin Zhen relied on something other than a biological concept of the body or the sex-gender problematic as we know it today, there was hardly a need for her to advance a counterargument to establish a constructivist view.

Rather, He-Yin constructed her feminist critique from within—and against—the indigenous Confucian tradition, especially its theories of human nature. Specifically, her critique of the dualism of *nanxing* and *nüxing* was two-pronged. It was directed on the one hand at the Confucian concept of *nannü* and on the other at the reinvention of the Confucian concept of *xing* in the late Qing—known variously as *renxing or benxing*—often rendered as "human nature" or "personhood." Both *xing* and *nannü* were highly developed and fundamental philosophical concepts in the millennia-long evolution of the Confucian scholarly and ethical discourses, but it was not until the late nineteenth century that *nanxing* and *nüxing* began to emerge as concepts, first in Japanese and then in Chinese popular media.

In modern Chinese usage, the term *xing* has acquired a new meaning of sex-gender, and even of biological sex. *Nanxing* (man/men) and *nüxing* (woman/women) came to connote a new way of construing male-female differences on the basis of modern understandings of the sexualized human body. These modern meanings were not yet prevalent in He-Yin's time when she was publishing and editing *Natural Justice* in 1907–1908. Although she was among the first to use the terms *nanxing* and *nüxing*, the meanings she imparted to them are neither the modern ones of sex-gender or biological sex nor the classical Confucian one of the nature/character of a person or a thing.[18] To illuminate what He-Yin meant by the

---

[17]Dorothy Ko, "Gender," in *A Concise Companion to History*, ed. Ulinka Rublack, 203–225 (Oxford: Oxford University Press, 2011), 221. Katharine Park has argued that in northern Italy in the 1490s, medical treatises began to identify male bodies as surfaces, whereas "the woman is identifiable by a visualizable inside." Katherine Park, *Secrets of Women: Gender, Generation, and the Origins of Human Dissection* (New York: Zone Books, 2006), 27.

[18]The classic treatment of the Confucian view of human nature is Donald J. Munro, *The Concept of Man in Early China* (Stanford, CA: Stanford University Press, 1969).

terms, the question we must ask is, When and how did the concept *xing* begin to acquire its new meaning of "sex-gender" in modern Chinese? Our answer is that like numerous other Japanese invented neologisms written in kanji characters, the indigenous concept *xing* began to acquire the connotation of "sex/gender" through a process of roundtrip translation involving Japanese, Chinese, and European languages at the turn of the twentieth century.[19]

In He-Yin Zhen's time, *nanxing* and *nüxing* were still unfamiliar neologisms imported from Meiji Japan when the Japanese had coined the kanji Chinese compounds 男性 and 女性—read *dan-sei* and *jo-sei* in Japanese—to translate European concepts for "man (men)" and "woman (women)." What the neologisms did was to conjoin *nan* and *nü* each to the character *xing* (nature/character) to produce the modern concept "sex-gender" in modern Japanese and Chinese. For this reason, scholar Tani Barlow renders *nüxing* back into English as "female sex," and she dates the invention of this neologism to the 1920s. Although we agree with her analysis of *nüxing* as a unique signifier of Chinese modernity, we should point out that on the evidence of a large number of late-Qing texts and He-Yin Zhen's essays in this volume, the neologisms *nanxing* and *nüxing* began to appear in Chinese publications as early as the turn of the twentieth century and, more importantly, they were not taken to signify "male sex" and "female sex" at that time.[20]

In "On the Question of Women's Liberation" and "The Feminist Manifesto," He-Yin Zhen refers to *nüxing* as something malleable that can be molded and developed with education or distorted with the lack of it, just as one's character or personhood can be developed or underdeveloped in a Confucian sense. To avoid the anachronism of imputing modern meaning to an earlier usage, we decided to render He-Yin's use of *nüxing* as the "character of woman (women)" or "woman (women)" rather than the modern sense of "female sex," "female nature," or "femininity," which was foreign to her. In short, in our interpretive view, *nüxing* was still coded by the Confucian understanding of *xing* in the late Qing although the neologism was

---

[19]For a study of translingual self-fashioning and the invention of the modern Chinese language, see Lydia H. Liu, *Translingual Practice: Literature, National Culture, and Translated Modernity—China, 1900–1937* (Stanford, CA: Stanford University Press, 1995).

[20]See Tani E. Barlow, *The Question of Women in Chinese Feminism* (Durham, NC: Duke University Press, 2004), p. 52.

on its way to becoming something else: "female nature" and later "female sex" (even as the earlier connotations and ambiguities have not disappeared completely from today's usage). The transvaluation of concepts from the late-Qing period to modern Chinese discourse was a lived moment for He-Yin Zhen's generation, and we have striven to capture that moment of change and becoming in our translations.

More central even to He-Yin Zhen's critique of patriarchy and the late-Qing invention of neologisms *nanxing* and *nüxing* is her powerful analysis of the category of *nannü*. What does *nannü* signify? Before translating her use of *nannü* into other terms, we must try to follow its echoes and metamorphosis in the historical unfolding of Chinese patriarchal discourse, as we hope the readers of this volume will do. We will then discover that the specific kinds of marking or distinction He-Yin Zhen identified in the power of *nannü* are both metaphysical and physical—literally physical in the sense of cloistering, corseting, prostituting, punishing, enslaving, maiming, and abusing the body. Poor women, young girls, slaves, and lower-class boys were all susceptible to such marking and exploitation, as she argues in her essay "On Women's Labor." The production of normative heterosexuality is but part of the problem—homosexuality was "tolerated" to a certain extent by traditional Chinese society which would not, however, permit the free movement of its gentry women[21]—and only a symptom of the structure of power she analyzes in her work.

For this and for other reasons, He-Yin Zhen refuses to take the notions of "class" (in the Marxian sense) and *nannü* as separate terms. She asks instead that we approach *nannü* as always already a kind of class making, one that is more originary and primary than any other social distinctions. She coined the concept *nannü jieji*, or "*nannü* class," with which to analyze and critique such a highly integrated and elaborated hierarchal system as the Chinese patriarchal family. This powerful notion of "*nannü* class," which sees *nannü* as an originary and primary category in the division and subdivision of social group and as a primary division in the global political

---

[21]This situation began to change with the introduction of European sexology and medicine to China, precisely as the Confucian concept of human nature *xing* came to be equated with "sex-gender" in medical discourse. For a historical study, see Tze-lan D. Sang, *The Emerging Lesbian: Female Same-Sex Desire in Modern China* (Chicago: University of Chicago Press, 2003). See also Wenqing Kang, *Obsession: Male Same-Sex Relations in China, 1900–1950* (Hong Kong: Hong Kong University Press, 2009).

economy, cannot otherwise be thought in a juxtaposition of gender, class, and race as distinct, parallel, or even intersecting terms, as is common in the contemporary Anglophone discourses of intersectionality.

Beyond Intersectionality

The multidimensionality of marginalized subjects was first articulated as "intersectionality" in the work of legal scholar Kimberlé Crenshaw.[22] Since the late 1980s, this approach has drawn a great deal of attention amongst feminist social scientists and legal scholars for whom gender, sexuality, and race can no longer be taken as mutually exclusive categories.[23] Crenshaw's work strives to explain how "race and gender intersect in shaping struc-tural, political, and representational aspects of violence against women of color."[24] Others who share her critique of single-axis studies of gender, sexuality, race, class, and nationality have sought to conceptualize the mul-tidimensionality of social identities in terms of "transnational connectivity" or "co-formation."[25] It is interesting that "women of color" has evolved into a general prototype in many studies informed by intersectional and post-intersectional approaches. This historically inflected politics of identity in the United States, France, the United Kingdom, and other European coun-tries has no doubt animated much progressive thinking on the complexity of contemporary society and its legal problems. This is especially true of the minority and diasporic communities in these countries. However, we can-not help but ask what He-Yin Zhen, who lived a hundred years ago in China

---

[22]See Kimberlé Crenshaw, "Demarginalizing the Intersection of Race and Sex: A Black Femi-nist Critique of Antidiscrimination Doctrine, Feminist Politics and Antiracist Politics," *Uni-versity of Chicago Legal Forum 1989*, 139–167.
[23]Michel Foucault's analysis of sexuality and biopolitics has inspired fruitful scholarship on the interrelations of race and sexuality in colonial history that is framed in terms other than "intersectionality." See Ann Laura Stoler, *Race and the Education of Desire: Foucault's History of Sexuality and the Colonial Order of Things* (Durham, NC: Duke University Press Books, 1995).
[24]Kimberlé Crenshaw, "Mapping the Margins: Intersectionality, Identity Politics, and Violence Against Women of Color," *Stanford Law Review* 43, 6 (1991): 1241–1299.
[25]See Inderpal Grewal, *Transnational America: Feminisms, Diasporas, Neoliberalisms* (Dur-ham, NC: Duke University Press, 2005); and Paola Bacchetta, "Sur les spatialités de résistance de lesbiennes 'of color' en France," *Genre, Sexualité & Société* 1 (June 2009): 2–18.

and Japan, would have thought of today's intersectionality or postintersectionality studies and their symptomatic silences.[26]

We imagine her asking, first, if it is true that gender, sexuality, and race intersect to produce "women of color," do the same categories produce "white men" as privileged subjects of the modern liberal state or "white women" as "women" unmarked by race or class?[27] If the answer is yes, then how do the same categories produce simultaneously the oppressor and the oppressed? How do they help us understand the structure of oppression, which seems universal and yet also quite historically specific? Where are the points of intersection among gender, sexuality, and race in the *nannü* structure?

Second, He-Yin Zhen would have been surprised to find that "race" is deemed more fundamental than "class" as an analytical category. She would have doubted that a historically specific and inflected politics of identity, based on gender, race, or national origin, could seriously challenge the systemic roots of oppression that feminists and critical race theorists aim to uproot, insofar as identity-based analyses often, if not always, acquiesce in the liberal-legal conception of the state, its politics, and its preconstituted subjecthood. This conception, He-Yin Zhen would insist, is grounded in capitalist relations, private property ownership, and its political and legal regimes—those very regimes that underpin and reproduce injustice—rather than providing a way out of structuring forms of inequality.

As readers will see in "On the Question of Women's Liberation" and He-Yin's other essays, her critique of *nannü* in patriarchal discourse is a theoretical wager, one that is more thoroughgoing than "gender," "sexuality," or "intersectionality." She allows us to see *nannü* as the originary term of distinction or abstraction, one that is philosophically, philologically, and historically more grounded than anything we can possibly illuminate with "gender" as an analytical category or "intersectionality" as method. The *nannü* distinction is philosophically grounded. It is so grounded because

---

[26]For critiques of methodological weaknesses in intersectionality studies, see Jennifer C. Nash, "Re-thinking Intersectionality," *Feminist Review* 89 (2008): 1–15; and Leslie McCall, "The Complexity of Intersectionality" *Signs* 30, 3 (Spring 2005): 1771–1800.

[27]The point here is not whiteness studies but, rather, the continual production and universalizing of modern racial categories. See Ruth Frankenberg, *White Women, Race Matters: The Social Construction of Whiteness* (Minneapolis: University of Minnesota Press, 1993); and Robyn Wiegman, *American Anatomies: Theorizing Race and Gender* (Durham, NC: Duke University Press, 1995).

abstraction wields a tremendous power by inducing a certain conception of ontological difference and incommensurability as uncontestable truth. That is, as if prior to any articulation of social difference, the philosophical abstraction of *nannü* is already justified by cosmic principles or the laws of nature. From He-Yin's standpoint, such abstraction—the ontology of *nannü*—is first and foremost a concretely embodied and constantly reproduced political act that needs to be unpacked and historicized as such.

He-Yin's argument that the *nannü* distinction is also philologically and historically grounded is supported by her debunking of the millennia-long classical textual scholarship and Confucian commentarial traditions as well as legal, ritual, and social institutions in China. In her essays, she takes these traditions and institutions to be chiefly responsible for the sociohistorical ramifications and enduring reiterations of the *nannü* category. Her analysis of the origins of political and social power in that sense leads her to grasp the *nannü* distinction as a more abstract, more fundamental, and more operational category in patriarchal discourse than what we take to be "sex," "gender," "sexuality," or "sexual difference" in English.

Now, what does it mean for her, as well as for us today, to push the *nannü* distinction, rather than "gender" or "sexual difference," as a fundamental analytic rubric for feminist theory? He-Yin Zhen insists that feminists must take *nan* and *nü* together as a single conceptual dividing mechanism rather than focusing on "*nü*-woman" or on "difference" per se. The notion of *nü* cannot possibly be captured outside of the originary structural distinctions introduced by the binary opposition of *nannü*, which produces both *nan* and *nü* as meaningful concepts and social categories. From a structural viewpoint, woman is the problem of man. The articulation of *nannü*, therefore, is not so much about biological or social differences, which can never be settled, as it is about reiterating a distinction that produces historically a political demand for social hierarchy. On this view, we can see that when Jin Tianhe issued his manifesto for women's rights and spoke about women's equality, he did not question the *nannü* category and he failed to see the *nan* side of the *nannü* distinction as operational and central to the philosophical and ideological production and reproduction of social domination. By contrast, He-Yin Zhen's questioning of this category enabled her to identify the sources of that domination and trace the conditions of women's oppression to the category of distinction itself. In this sense, the solution to *nannü* is not for "woman" to become "man," nor for "man" to be the standard against which "woman" and social justice are measured; rather, the solution is the elimination of this category of distinction as a metaphysical-political principle.

In *Undoing Gender,* Judith Butler does something very interesting to the idea of "sexual difference," which parallels what He-Yin Zhen did nearly a hundred years before to the operational power of *nannü.* Butler writes: "Understood as a border concept, sexual difference has psychic, somatic, and social dimensions that are never quite collapsible into one another but are not for that reason ultimately distinct. . . . Is it, therefore, not a thing, not a fact, not a presupposition, but rather a *demand for rearticulation that never quite vanishes—but also never quite appears?. . .* What does this way of thinking sexual difference do to our understanding of gender?" (Emphasis added.)[28] We must press Butler's questions further by asking, What can the thinking of *nannü* do to our understanding of "sexual difference" as well as "gender"? Does it have something to do with "a demand for rearticulation that never quite vanishes—but also never quite appears?"

The answer lies in He-Yin Zhen's understanding of *nannü,* which, as we have seen, is not about the positive or negative marking of gendered identities but about something more totalizing and foundational. To summarize her main argument: First, the *nannü* category—as elaborated and reinvented by philosophers and scholars in the millennia-long discursive traditions of China—was the foundational material and metaphysical mechanism of power in the organization of social and political life in China. The prestige of that category was reinforced by the Confucian philological exegesis of classical scholarship and by the imperial patriarchal system supported by its ideology. This argument is made in the most concentrated fashion in her long essay "On the Revenge of Women," whose incantatory style will surely strike readers, as it struck us, with its comprehensive erudition and scholarly reach.

Second, as an operational category of distinction, *nannü* is first and foremost political because its function is not only to generate social identities but also to create forms of power and domination based on that distinction. Such domination is reiterated through lived social life by maintaining the divisions of the inner (domestic) and outer (public) in terms of how labor, affect, and the value of human life should be organized. As He-Yin Zhen argues repeatedly, the Chinese written character for "slave" (*nu* 奴) is inflected by the stem-radical *nü* 女, suggesting that the body is *nannü*'ed

---

[28]Judith Butler, *Undoing Gender* (New York: Routledge, 2004), 186.

and thus "enslaved" in a political-material discursive prison even before it is "sexed." This argument is clearly made in her essay "On the Question of Women's Liberation."

Finally, armed with that insight, she moves on to discern new forms of distinction, discrimination, and domination that have emerged in the capitalist reorganization of life and labor. Her essays "On the Question of Women's Labor" and "Economic Revolution and Women's Revolution" rehearse this argument in full. There, she observes a rearticulation and reiteration of the *nannü* distinction in the modernizing societies of Europe, America, and Japan, which becomes the basis for her vigorous rejection of the liberal argument on behalf of women's suffrage. He-Yin Zhen is thus a feminist theorist in the most fundamental sense of the word.

Shengji: A Critique of the Political Economy of Gender

If *nannü* is a totalistic rubric that names the unevenness and hierarchies in all social relations, including but not limited to that between man and woman, the idea of *shengji* 生計 (livelihood) supports the all-encompassing gendered lens with a radical critique of capitalism, modernity, coloniality, the state, and imperial traditions. As a more enabling category than "class," the concept of *shengji* is the second of He-Yin Zhen's key theoretical innovations that deserves close attention.

He-Yin Zhen takes property relations as the key to social life. She views the legal institution of private property—and women as private property—as the origin of the uneven accumulations of wealth that lead to the perpetration and reproduction of social injustice. In "Economic Revolution and Women's Revolution," she says, "The beginning of the system of women as private property is also the beginning of the system of slavery."[29] The key historical and contemporary questions for feminist struggle, therefore, must revolve around the social, national, and global accumulations of capital and wealth underpinned by the system of private property protected by the national state and the international state system. In this sense, no state could be the guarantor of social justice; it could merely be

---

[29]See He-Yin Zhen, "Economic Revolution and Women's Revolution," translated in this volume, p. 92.

the guarantor for the reproduction of social hierarchies at local, national, and global scales simultaneously.

For this and other reasons, He-Yin Zhen was uncompromising in her attacks on the state, any state, and on the illusion that the state could be anything but a realm for securing the reproduction of the powerful and the wealthy in society. This stance was a radical departure from that of the majority of Chinese revolutionaries and reform-minded intellectuals who wanted to replace the old dynastic regime with a new republic. For example, in the eyes of Sun Zhongshan (Sun Yatsen), Liang Qichao, and Jin Tianhe, among most others of their generation, freedom, in the liberal sense of national and individual liberty underpinned by the state, had to be the dominant component and goal of any postdynastic social life. For He-Yin Zhen, however, equality and the conditions for its material realization in the world had to form the most important goal of any future social arrangement. In her view, equality could be realized only in a radically reconfigured social and cultural sphere, where *nannü* equality was no longer hierarchically subordinated to any other form of equality but was, rather, the very social and material basis for all equality. For that reason, she was deeply suspicious of the liberal idea of freedom that subordinated women's emancipation to the general logic of the state. This fundamental conflict between women's demand for equality and that for freedom would reverberate throughout the history of feminist struggles in modern China and elsewhere. The conflict could never be resolved as long as the state, liberal or otherwise, served as the sole conceptual framework for progressive politics.

In this sense, anarchism was as important for He-Yin Zhen as was feminism: they were inseparable and intertwined modes of analyzing and thinking history and the present. Unlike most of her contemporaneous compatriots, male or female, He-Yin Zhen's anarcho-feminism tempered any advocacy of statist theory with a huge skepticism toward any and all institutions of social hierarchy. Indeed, the anarchism of her time—discussed in our essay "The Historical Context" following this introduction—targeted for critique not only the tsarist state in Russia and its associated despotism, nor just the Qing state as a dynastic tyranny (irrespective of the fact that the ruling house was the alien Manchu, an ethnic minority).[30]

---

[30]The contemporaneous anarcho-feminist who comes closest to He-Yin's positions is Emma Goldman, who was being translated into Chinese and Japanese. There is evidence that He-Yin was aware of Goldman and that Goldman knew of He-Yin's journal. See footnote no. 19 in the next essay.

It also took aim at the liberal state *qua* state for its production and reproduction of hierarchical and unjust social relations of property, law, and rule.
Unimpressed by the freedom and the limited amount of gender equality
attained in liberal societies in Europe and the United States, calling these
"false freedom and sham equality," she was also critical of suffrage movements and men's advocacies for women's education as a boost for citizenship of the propertied class, calling them no more than "empty rhetoric of
emancipation."

Indeed, Liang Qichao's argument in favor of women's education—
translated and included in this volume—may be taken to represent the
voice of progressive liberal male Chinese intellectuals at the turn of twentieth century. These men saw women's education and participation in nation
building as conducive to the state's welfare and the goal of national survival.
For example, Liang points out:

> In China, even if we consider only the men, the number of those who only
> consume comes to roughly half of those who produce. According to phi-
> losophers [of political economy], this situation alone already makes a stable
> national government impossible, let alone the fact of the nation's two hun-
> dred million women, among whom all are consumers and none are produc-
> ers. Owing to women's inability to support themselves and their dependence
> on other people, men raise women as livestock or slaves. Thus women can-
> not but live harsh lives.[31]

Liang attributes the suffering and debasement of women to their economic
dependence on men and to women's lack of education and survival skills, a
view that male feminists as well as progressive women of his time shared. It
was in response to such blatant erasure of women's labor and their poorly
understood situation of economic dependency that He-Yin Zhen developed a rigorous feminist analysis of labor, livelihood, and property ownership in "On the Question of Women's Labor" and "Economic Revolution
and Women's Revolution."

From the very beginning of her essay "On the Question of Women's
Labor," for example, He-Yin Zhen insists that labor must be understood as a
basic human activity, or what philosopher Bruno Gulli calls an ontology of

---

[31]See Liang Qichao, "On Women's Education," translated in this volume, pp. 190–191.

"organic, creative labor."[32] This is not labor as an economic concept: it does not harbor within it a fundamental antagonism, an instrumentalization, or a historical abjection. He-Yin Zhen's concept of labor is a materialist ontology that proposes labor not as an always-already appropriable power for private gain but, rather, as organic to life itself; whereas for classical and neoclassical political economy and the states associated with it, just as for the advocates in the late-nineteenth-century Chinese "Study of Wealth and Power" (*Fuqiang xue*) based upon those principles, labor is a purely economic category in analytical separation from the remainder of human life. He-Yin Zhen's articulation of a distinction between labor as an autonomous ontological practice and labor as an enslaved or commodified form encodes within it her important vision of the possibility for a historical potential to reground labor in a human ontology rather than in human capital.

This vision emerges in her analysis of female-embodied labor, for it is only when women can reclaim their laboring bodies for the basic human ontology of labor that all humankind will have been liberated from the instrumentalization of themselves by the wealthy and the powerful. This is what she calls the problem of *shengji*, the securing of which forms the necessary condition for the liberation not only of women but of humankind. For He-Yin Zhen, then, the point is to explore how the commodification of women's bodies over the long course of Chinese (and human) history has effectively crushed the possibility for any reimagining of the futurity of labor as genuinely free and autonomous. Indeed, it is at the cusp of the final suppression of autonomous labor with the global advent of textile factories and collectivized wage labor that He-Yin Zhen sees the possibility for an alternative to commodified labor slipping away. Hinging her understanding of labor in history on the figure of the subjected and abjected female body—the very body that makes starkly visible the enslaved form of all commodified labor—He-Yin Zhen's is a historical argument about the reiteration of forms of enslavement legally underpinned by the property form of inequality and injustice. It is, thus, only with what she sees as the imminent disappearance of the enduring possibility of autonomous labor that the supremacy of commodified labor appears now to be secured. And this

---

[32]Bruno Gulli, *Labor of Fire: The Ontology of Labor Between Economy and Culture* (Philadelphia: Temple University Press, 2005), 25. Gulli recuperates the theory of labor in early Marx, especially in the "Economic and Philosophical Manuscripts," before Marx's full theorization of the labor theory of value, which, Gulli argues, reduces labor to the problem of value-creation.

supremacy is being secured through the spread of the new form of enslaved labor called industrial waged work as a global form of injustice.

Conclusion

At its birth at the turn of the twentieth century, Chinese feminism in the voice of He-Yin Zhen—responding to and extending the analyses of her contemporary male feminists as represented in this volume by Jin Tianhe and Liang Qichao—achieved a radical and comprehensive critique that in our opinion remains unmatched to this day. It is our hope that her entirely original concepts of *nannü* and *shengji*, in all their complexity, will be taken up by feminists and radical theorists around the world. It is high time, then, that we savor He-Yin Zhen's incisive and uncompromising engagements with her worlds in her own words.

The Historical Context

CHINESE FEMINIST WORLDS AT THE TURN OF THE TWENTIETH CENTURY

From its birth at the turn of the twentieth century, feminism in China was enmeshed and engaged in many worlds simultaneously. As the literary scholar Amy Dooling points out, "[A] narrow definition of feminism as about sexuality and rights (basically, the liberal position) will not be sufficient given the historical framework in which the politics of gender were lived and written about in China at the time."[1] This narrow insufficiency is nowhere better illustrated than through a study of the works of He-Yin Zhen, in juxtaposition to contemporaneous male writers on feminism, Jin Tianhe and Liang Qichao, presented in this volume. This historical introduction locates He-Yin Zhen in her many overlapping worlds by tracing in outline the worlds of her thinking: her textual and linguistic worlds; her domestic and global historical worlds; and her worlds of translation and conceptualization, among others.

By "worlds of thinking" we mean the texts and contexts, including the languages and concepts of the contemporary moment to which He-Yin Zhen was responding, in which she was operating, and through which she understood her own lived experience as a Chinese woman at the turn of the twentieth century. We wish to emphasize the open-ended nature of He-Yin's dialogue with the texts and contexts of her time and of her past.

---

[1] Amy Dooling, *Women's Literary Feminism in Twentieth Century China* (New York: Palgrave, 2005), 28. What Dooling and we are pointing to here is a certain strong trend in some scholarship that singles out rights and sexuality as being the privileged content of gender studies and the mapping of that assumption onto China and elsewhere.

In this sense, we avoid speaking of "influence" because that connotes a more mechanical process of interaction and distorts the interpretive processes of intellectual work. By contrast, we stress that He-Yin actively constructed a historical perspective and a reality through and with the texts she encountered. There is a politics to her reading, a very radical politics that we can register only by noting the asymmetry between her theory and her history, as well as by paying attention to her mode of argumentation. Recognizing the historical moment of her knowledge production through her active practice of reading is more important, we feel, than simply tracing the sources she cited. It is for this reason that we evoke "worlds of thinking" rather than the notion of influence.

Late-Qing China in a Global World

The world of late-Qing China (1860s–1911) was suffused by political, economic, cultural, and military crises. Beginning with the Opium Wars in the mid-nineteenth century (1839–1842; 1856–1860), China's historically self-sufficient economy was forced by war and treaty to open to a free flow of commodities manufactured in the burgeoning industrial sites of Britain, France, Prussia, and the United States. Thus although China had traded with foreign countries for many centuries and links with its southern neighbors had become particularly dense by the nineteenth century through immigration and consequent family-entrepreneurial connections, the new forms of commerce and of foreign relations demanded by the incorporation of China into the global capitalist world were now directed into an international system dominated by Euro-America.

From the 1840s onward, China's economy, society, culture, and politics increasingly came under pressure either to submit or to adapt to these new global realities. Internal social rebellions, such as the massive Taiping uprising of 1850–1864, were sparked as much by imported and adapted ideologies as by internal dislocations. Missionaries from various countries flooded into the country along with the gunboats, converting few but creating ideological and social fissures through their translation efforts and promotion of different sociocultural values.

Among the more momentous changes was that in the Chinese language itself, with classical usages giving way and adapting to new vocabularies and new concepts demanded by the incorporation of China into the inter-state capitalist system of trade, governance, and politics. Just as salient were transformations in conceptualizations of domestic and international hier-archies, with racialized understandings of human difference becoming a structuring system of thought. In this new view, not only was the white world of Euro-America pitted against the yellow world of Asia, for exam-ple, but also the Manchu Qing dynasty (1644–1911) came to be designated by Han Chinese revolutionaries as an alien colonizer of China, whereupon their centuries-long rule was rendered illegitimate because of their racial-ized otherness.

As the pace of change quickened from the mid-nineteenth century onward, successive waves of educated men, many of whom served in the dynastic bureaucracy as officials, tried to think their way through and out the other side of the multisided catastrophes facing China through these decades. Initiating new industrial manufactures, translation bureaus, schools, and institutes where new forms of knowledge were disseminated; going abroad to study the ways of the dominating powers; critiquing the mores and cus-toms of their own society, these educated and sometimes even moneyed men came to understand, in the space of less than a generation, that the old ways of the integrated Chinese sociocultural and political-economic system could not and would not last. When the newly built Chinese navy was sum-marily destroyed by the Japanese in the Sino-Japanese War of 1894–1895—a war the Chinese humiliatingly lost to their historically weaker neighbor—the sense of accumulated crises came to a climax.

In the heady years of 1895–1898, the critical energies of many concerned and educated men—now joined by an intrepid few educated women, often family members—centered on reforming the dynastic structures of rule so as to allow for a fuller flexibility in political, social, cultural, commercial, and military organization and development. This push culminated in the Hundred Days' Reform period in 1898, during which the young Guangxu emperor was petitioned and agreed to a series of political reforms. His reform-mindedness was soon suppressed by the Empress Dowager Cixi and her faction of conservatives. This last best chance for total dynastic reform soon yielded to a revolutionary movement organized by the Chinese who were now in exile (mostly in Japan, Hong Kong, and the United States). By late 1911, this revolutionary movement succeeded in toppling the Qing dynasty and replacing China's age-old dynastic system with a republican form of government. Full of revolutionary ferment, the first decade of the twentieth century also witnessed the birth of feminism in modern China, which spoke to and was informed by the sociopolitical upheavals.

From the explosive reform movement of 1898 to the establishment of the Republic of China in 1912, the intertwined foundations of Chinese society, politics, economics, and culture crumbled. Educated elites had to rethink the entire premise of the Chinese civilization, and in a radically new global context.[2] However the rethinking was ordered, whether all the issues separately or in relation to one another, the problem of reimagining China in the world was widely acknowledged as one of *the* great problems of the early twentieth century. For many, China's geographically incomplete but politically and economically disastrous subjugation to foreign powers meant that China had to compete with the rapacious colonizers on the latter's terms, whether militarization, enlightenment thought, or "free market" capitalist-driven industrialization. The pregiven nature of the terms of engagement and competition—forced upon China through wars, unequal treaties, and imperialist-capitalist aggression—led to a simultaneous acceptance and questioning by Chinese elites of the premises dictated by the invading powers. The various types of adaptations and accommodations they espoused generally included the technological, capital, institutional requisites, and labor mobilizations for the beginnings of industrialization. These efforts, called "self-strengthening" in the second half of the nineteenth century, later became known as "modernization" (*jindai/xiandai hua*).

An adequate discussion of the socioeconomic thinking of the late-Qing period falls outside the scope of this introduction; suffice it to say, therefore, that one of the primary schools of thought to emerge to deal with this question was called the "Study of Wealth and Power" (*Fuqiang Xue*). This school in large part derived from the translation and popularization of Herbert Spencer's sociological reworking of Charles Darwin's biological survival of the fittest as then adduced to explain the manifest military and commercial superiorities of the Euro-American powers.[3] It stressed the urgent necessity for technological militarization and institutional-bureaucratic

---

[2]For an extended discussion of this global context, see Rebecca E. Karl, *Staging the World: Chinese Nationalism at the Turn of the Twentieth Century* (Durham, NC: Duke University Press, 2002).

[3]James Pusey, *China and Charles Darwin* (Cambridge, MA: Harvard University Press, 1983); Benjamin Schwartz, *In Search of Wealth and Power: Yen Fu and the West* (Cambridge, MA: Harvard University Press, 1964); Andrew Jones, *Developmental Fairy Tales: Evolutionary Thinking and Modern Chinese Culture* (Cambridge, MA: Harvard University Press, 2011).

rationalization, as well as the socioeconomic industrialization of coastal China, or those areas most susceptible to Euro-American and Japanese invasions, colonial territorial concessions, and manufacturing strength. The source of labor to fuel these semipublic or semiprivate endeavors would be the vast population of China's rural interior, whose land, though not expropriated outright, was becoming more and more difficult to cultivate so as to produce for the increasing burdens of landlord surplus extraction and imperial taxation.[4]

Particularly affected by the combination of land squeeze, rural labor intensification, and steady collapse of home-based handicrafts in the face of foreign industrial imports and foreign-owned coastal manufactures were women, whose economic activities had always been—in times and places of plenty as in times and places of scarcity—crucial to household economic viability. No mere "supplement" or "sideline" (as many economists and economic historians continue to call it) to a preexisting supposedly proper male-dominated economy, female-dominated spinning and weaving activity was a central and necessary element of the functioning of any rural household economy.[5] As the self-sufficient rural economy steadily deteriorated through the nineteenth century, there was an accelerating subordination of rural to urban space. In consequence, there formed a lopsided competition in textile production between the rural producers, on the one hand, and, on the other, producers in urban-based, highly capitalized, and foreign-owned industries or foreign-imported manufactures protected

---

[4]There is debate in the economic history of China about whether there was absolute or even relative rural immiseration through these years. What is clear, despite the disputes, is that intensification of land use was proceeding very rapidly; that the dynastic accommodation with landlords was inimical to rural land adjustments in favor of agricultural labor; that handicraft manufacture, particularly in the realm of the traditional women's work of spinning and weaving, was severely impacted by the industrial competition in silk and cotton from Japan, British-colonized India, and the revival of the American South after the civil war as well as by the recovery of the silk industry in France and Italy after the midcentury silkworm plagues, among others. For example, see Kathy Le-Mons Walker, *Chinese Modernity and the Peasant Path: Semicolonialism in the Northern Yangzi Delta* (Stanford, CA: Stanford University Press, 1999); Ken Pomeranz, *The Great Divergence: China, Europe, and the Making of the Modern World Economy* (Princeton, NJ: Princeton University Press, 2000); Philip Huang, *The Peasant Family and Rural Development in the Yangzi Delta, 1350–1988* (Stanford, CA: Stanford University Press, 1990).

[5]Hill Gates, *China's Motor* (Ithaca, NY: Cornell University Press, 1996); Le-Mons Walker, *Chinese Modernity and the Peasant Path*.

through tariff inequalities maintained by British colonial power. The dynastic state was powerless to ameliorate the livelihoods of the vast majority of China's inhabitants, even had it wanted to try.

Women, whose family livelihoods were being ruined, bore the brunt of the impending crisis: they had to labor more intensely for lower returns within the family; were increasingly subjected to being sold as brides, concubines, servants, or even prostitutes; and were increasingly induced to leave their families either voluntarily (that is, forced by poverty) or in coerced fashion. These women worked long and hard hours in the families of the urban or rural elites, in the factories of the many foreign and few domestic industrialists, and in the streets and byways of the cities, towns, and villages; they were mortgaged to "owners"—whether in the factory and brothel or in families to men who had bought them as servants, brides, or concubines—often for a lifetime. The conditions of these laboring women enraged He-Yin Zhen and formed one important point of departure for the radical feminist critiques translated in this volume and originally published in 1907–1908.

The anarchist He-Yin Zhen was virtually alone in her critiques of labor because for most liberal feminist and other commentators of the late Qing, be they male or female, laboring women and rural economic hardship remained largely invisible.[6] A reading of the male intellectual Liang Qichao's essay "On Women's Education" makes clear that such women did not even enter his field of vision. Indeed, it was not until the late 1910s and into the 1920s that these issues formed a major part of the daily journalistic fare and widespread editorializing as well as causes for organized political activism. Instead, the major part of editorial commentating in the newly founded periodic journals at the turn of the twentieth century revolved around reported news from abroad (diplomatic affairs as well as revolutions and anticolonial uprisings, among others) and around lamenting the decline of the Chinese state; many editorials offered suggestions and opinions on how to forestall the national state's total collapse or total colonization and

---

[6]As Ming K. Chan and Arif Dirlik point out, "It was . . . Liu Shipei and his associates in Tokyo who first introduced the necessity of labor as an integral component of anarchist revolution." They indicate specifically Liu's 1907 *Natural Justice* essay "On Equalizing Human Labor" (*Renlei junli shuo*). We would note that He-Yin was perhaps far more vigorous in her advocacy for the centrality of labor than even her husband, Liu Shipei. See *Schools Into Fields and Factories: Anarchists, the Guomindang, and the National Labor University in Shanghai, 1927–1932* (Durham, NC: Duke University Press, 1991), 26–27.

domination by Euro-America or Japan. New knowledge derived from new sources along with new practices of citizenship and of economic production were promoted as antidotes to the generalized decline and as methods of saving the state and saving the nation.[7] Education, citizenship involvement, and the rate of statistically measurable economic production became key indicators of the health of the national people and thus of the prospects for the Chinese nation and the state. For example, in "On Women's Education," Liang argues for the benefits of female education in terms of the enhancement of national productivity and nurturing of male citizens in the family.

The problem of suffrage was broached, and various examples of electorates from around the world were promoted. Other than in Finland, Norway, England, and Italy (the examples that He-Yin Zhen cites in "On Women's Liberation"), none advocated women's suffrage and very few advocated universal male suffrage; almost all the global examples had some version of a property and race requirement while also being restricted to men. In China, as in many other places, feminist advocates loudly proclaimed the fitness of elite women to join elite men in the proposed electorate. However, prior to the Republican Revolution of 1911, very few of these advocacies gained much traction, although as elite men made advances into electoral politics at the provincial levels, elite women also staked a claim to fitness for political participation, a claim they continued to press relentlessly through the 1910s and onward.[8]

Meanwhile, issues of education and bodily wholeness also came to the fore. New forms of education were promoted for men, where the emphasis on classical textual analysis, formulaic writing styles, and rote memory started to wane. The prestige of the Confucian canon, which had been used as sanction and guide for the dynastic system through its mobilization as the textual foundation for the civil service exams, also began to falter, particularly after

---

[7]The very form of the state was a contentious issue that became entangled with efforts to "save" it. Widespread calls for reform of state structures and institutions became an insistent clamor in journals published in China and among overseas Chinese populations in Japan, the South Seas, and the United States. By 1906, even the Qing dynasty itself was tepidly supporting parliamentary elections so as to address rising provincial discontent over dynastic policies and state impotence.

[8]See Louise Edwards, *Gender, Politics, and Democracy: Women's Suffrage in China* (Stanford, CA: Stanford University Press, 2008), for a complete survey of Chinese women's suffrage movements in the early twentieth century.

1905, when the exam system was terminated. Girls' educational institutions were founded alongside boys' schools, first by Euro-American missionaries and then soon enough by Chinese merchants, entrepreneurs, and local educated elites in shifting alliances and espousing shifting priorities. For some of the girls' schools, the effort was said to be about educating women for motherhood and the more efficient raising of sons to be good citizens (the pithy phrase used here was imported from Japan: "good wives, wise mothers"); in others, education was aimed at basic literacy and the beginnings of what soon came to be called home economics or home management.[9] A strong linkage was made between freeing the mind through education and freeing the feet from the constraints of footbinding.[10] These schools and efforts were either urban-based or aimed at the upper elites of rural society. Little if any of this filtered into the larger population.

For the critically minded educated women of the late-Qing period, the problems they perceived within their own elite lives took center stage in their analyses of China's ills and the consequent challenges facing "women." Their concerns, represented then and now as concerns for the analytical totality of women *as such* (*nüzi*), tended to concentrate on such socially reformist solutions to women's and China's problems as educational opportunities, limited marriage freedom, footbinding, social and cultural equality with men, independence from crushing family norms that suppressed "female personhood" (*renge*), and participation in newly emerging forms of governance.[11] These grievances and advocacies filled those journals of the day that specialized in promoting women's issues and/or state reforms.

---

[9]For more on the debates over female education of the time, see Joan Judge, "Talent, Virtue and the Nation: Chinese Nationalisms and Female Subjectivities in the Early Twentieth Century," *American Historical Review* 106, 3 (June 2001): 765–803. For home management, see Helen Schneider, *Keeping the Nation's House* (Vancouver: University of British Columbia, 2011).

[10]As Dorothy Ko has written in this regard, the "end" of footbinding was a tortured affair, pitting missionaries and state bureaucrats, as well as male and female elites, against the common practice and against the pain of the unbinding process. Ko comments: "In the tug-of-war footbinding shrank in stature. It was not so much outlawed as outmoded; footbinding came to a virtual death when its cultural prestige extinguished. To put it another way, the end came when the practice exhausted all justifications within the existing repertoire of cultural symbols and values." Dorothy Ko, *Cinderella's Sisters: A Revisionist History of Footbinding* (Berkeley: University of California Press, 2005), 13–14.

[11]Rebecca E. Karl, *Staging the World* and "The Violence of the Everyday in Early Twentieth-Century China," in *Everyday Modernity in China*, ed. Madeleine Yue Dong and Joshua L. Goldstein, pp. 52–79 (Seattle: University of Washington Press, 2006).

The most well known of the late-Qing feminists who wrote in this idiom was Qiu Jin (1875–1907), the cross-dressing revolutionary martyr, who left her husband and children behind to seek education in Japan and who, upon her return to China, was executed by the Qing state for her advocacies of dynastic overthrow. In her essays, songs, poetry, and short stories, Qiu tirelessly wrote of the nationalist political need for female emancipation.[12] Although He-Yin Zhen makes no direct reference to Qiu Jin, it is most likely that they knew each other (they both resided in Japan from 1905 to 1907).[13] Whatever the personal case, He-Yin Zhen was clearly familiar with the type of nationalist-feminist analysis exemplified by Qiu Jin in its most revolutionary form; for although a supporter of the nationalist revolution, He-Yin had no illusions that it would bring about women's liberation.

This late-Qing Chinese historical context of national humiliation, global economic unevenness, and nascent nationalist and feminist stirrings as well as revolutionary fervor forms one "world of thinking" to which He-Yin Zhen responded and in which she was deeply embedded.

Textual and Ideological Worlds

In our annotations to He-Yin Zhen's comprehensive critique of the Chinese scholastic tradition, "On the Revenge of Women," and in her shorter essay on feminist antimilitarism, we address more specifically He-Yin Zhen's complicated relationship with the androcentric tradition of Confucian learning. Here, we simply wish to mention that the classical texts that incurred the most concerted attack by He-Yin in her critical essays were those of the New Text Confucian tradition popularized and spread through the revived Han school of learning of nineteenth-century China. Indeed,

---

[12]For an introduction to Qiu Jin's life and an extended translation of an excerpt from her political story, "Stones of the Jingwei Bird," see Amy Dooling and Kris Torgeson, eds., *Writing Women in Modern China* (New York: Columbia University Press, 1998), 40–78. Also see Hu Ying, "Writing Qiu Jin's Life: Wu Zhiying and Her Family Learning," *Late Imperial China* 25, 2 (December 2004): 119–160.

[13]Immediately after Qiu Jin's martyrdom, *Natural Justice*, under He-Yin Zhen's editorship, printed Qiu's biography to commemorate her life (no. 5, August 1907). The same issue also included Zhang Taiyan's preface to a posthumous collection of poetry by Qiu Jin that was scheduled to be published.

these were the very texts that such male reformers as Liang Qichao and his teacher Kang Youwei resorted to in an attempt to legitimize their political program for the radical reform of the Qing dynasty.[14] In constructing her critiques, moreover, He-Yin used the precise repetitively citational philological method her male counterparts deployed in their erudite and defensive commentaries. As readers encounter her "On the Revenge of Women," they will find that He-Yin cites fragments of classical texts and submits them to interpretive scrutiny. Her method of recitation—piling on examples—will perhaps strike readers as obsessive, but it is well to remember that textual authority had been cited precisely this way for millennia to argue in defense of the very ritual, social, and political institutions of injustice at which He-Yin Zhen was taking aim.

We might even note here that He-Yin's attack on Confucianism—as textual practice, as a system of ethics and thought, and also as a structure of sociopolitical and economic arrangement—is one of the first such comprehensive attacks in Chinese history, analogous perhaps to Elizabeth Cady Stanton's shocking feminist attack on biblical scholarship in America just a decade before or Simone de Beauvoir's dissection of the antiwoman biases of Western thought in mid-twentieth-century France. In the Chinese case, this type of totalistic rejection might be familiar from the later May Fourth period (1919–1925); He-Yin Zhen was prescient in this and other regards.

In addition to her deep familiarity with the classical heritage, He-Yin was also completely conversant with the newer texts and ideologies circulating in China and among Chinese educated elites at the turn of the twentieth century. This complex textual and ideological context forms another "world of thinking" to which He-Yin Zhen responded and in which she was deeply embedded. We next elaborate on these newer texts and discourses under four broad rubrics: liberalism, statism, anarchism, and socialism.

The conventional view of the birth of Chinese feminism is that it is a by-product of the introduction of liberalism. Many accounts of early Chinese feminism trace the beginnings of its systematic textual articulation to the separate translations by Liang Qichao and Ma Junwu (both men) of sections of J. S. Mill's famous mid-nineteenth-century tract *On the Subjection*

---

[14]For more on the New Text scholarship in the late Qing, see Benjamin Elman, *Classicism, Politics, and Kinship: The Ch'ang-chou School of New Text Confucianism in Late Imperial China* (Berkeley: University of California Press, 1990).

of Women and Herbert Spencer's "The Rights of Women" section of *Social Statics* in the early twentieth century. Liang's translations and commentary on Mill in his 1902 "On the New Citizen" (*Xinmin shuo*) and Ma's commentary on and translation of Spencer in 1903 form the backdrop to a conceptual language for almost all discussions of "women" in China's early twentieth century; indeed, many of the subsequent key male and female texts of Chinese feminism make direct or indirect reference to these foundational texts.

These texts present the scholar of Chinese feminism with several problems. The first is the male and European philosophical origins of early Chinese feminist discussions. In other words, Mill and Spencer are both European men whose language juxtaposing emancipation, independent personhood, and rights against domestic enslavement, dependent play object for men, and servitude widely informed the articulated expression of much early as well as later Chinese feminism, along with most feminisms globally. It was the language and conceptual frame used by most male intellectuals of the early period in China to advocate not only for women but on their own behalf as well (see Liang's essay, translated in this volume). It forms the foundation for the liberal narrative of the origins of Chinese feminism.

The Taiwanese feminist scholar Liu Jen-p'eng summarizes the problem from the vantage of the late 1990s attempt to assert an authentic Chinese female feminism: "The reappearance of so-called 'native feminism,' when placed in the framework of the nation, creates the problem of 'male' origins (as in: Chinese feminism originates in male intellectuals' promotion); yet, placed in the framework of imperialist colonization, then the origins are in 'the West' (as in: Chinese feminism originates in Western feminism). That is to say, if one wants to reconstruct a history of 'native feminism,' then whether in asking questions or posing answers, these inevitably emanate from the 'outside,' regardless of whether that 'outside' is construed as women opposed to men, or China opposed to the West."[15]

---

[15]Liu Jen-p'eng, "'Zhongguo de' nüquan, fanyi de yuwang yu Ma Junwu nüquanshuo yijie" ['China's' feminism, translation's desire, and Ma Junwu's translation of feminism], *Jindai zhongguo funüshi yanjiu* [Research on women in modern Chinese history] 7 (August 1999): 1–42; cited on p. 13. Also see Xia Xiaohong, *Wanqing wenren funü guan* [Late-Qing elite views of women] (Beijing: Beijing daxue chubanshe, 1995).

This historical and historiographical problem does indeed appear in much scholarship, current and past, on the issue of Chinese feminism. We argue, by contrast, that we can move beyond the Western or male problem of origins by framing He-Yin Zhen's and our own concerns differently. We appeal to such alternative framing not because He-Yin Zhen fails to reference these foundational male European philosophical texts: she does reference them, directly and indirectly and quite critically. But it is crucial to recognize that in He-Yin's analytical strategy, the world cannot be dichotomized into native and nonnative, Chinese and non-Chinese, male and female. For He-Yin, history cannot be seen in such dichotomous terms; the world is Chinese and global at the same time, and it is always already gendered, or *nannü*'ed (see the introduction to this volume).

Indeed, instead of looking to Euro-America or Japan as models for the future of gender equality for China to follow, as many feminists and other critical intellectuals of the time did, He-Yin Zhen saw Euro-America and Japan merely as representing more advanced ways in which newly emerged and now-globalizing forms of oppression—industrial waged labor, democratic polities and female suffrage, enlightenment knowledge—could attach themselves to native forms of subjection, to reconfigure and deepen these extant forms on a larger scale and in less detectable ways. And unlike, for example, Jin Tianhe (see his text, translated in this volume), who marveled at the "ideas shipped in crates across the Pacific," He-Yin Zhen was ambivalent about what she called the "empty rhetoric" of ready-made concepts and terminology from the imperialist metropolitan center. She preferred to conceptualize and think through problems in her own way. In this regard, for He-Yin Zhen, Euro-America functioned not as a hierarchical comparative but, rather, as part of a global conversation on feminism and modernity, a conversation in which she was as fully participant as anyone else. Here, then, the West-versus-China distinction is simply inoperative; it is, rather, entirely insufficient for the purpose of addressing the problem of gender-class (*nannü*) and livelihood (*shengji*) in the world (see the introduction to this volume).

A second, albeit less noted problem presented by the Mill and Spencer "origins" of Chinese feminism is that both Mill and Spencer were responding to and discussing problems encountered by the mid-nineteenth-century liberal state in Britain specifically and Europe more generally. In China, with the crisis in dynastic rule accelerating through the Boxer Rebellion (1899–1901) and beyond, for many male intellectuals at the turn of the twentieth century, most prominently for the journalist and political philosopher Liang Qichao as well as his nemesis, the revolutionary Sun Zhongshan (Sun Yatsen, 1866–1925), the liberal state (republican or parliamentary-monarchical) was a paradigm of a not-yet-achieved form of state worth striving for. The liberal state, Liang believed, could be attained through reformist policies aimed at opening governance and institutions of rule to a wider section (yet to be determined) of the populace; meanwhile, Sun advocated the revolutionary overthrow of the Qing dynasty altogether. More the philosopher than Sun, Liang found in Rousseau's concepts of the social contract, general will, and popular sovereignty a possible route away from what he called the Chinese servile character toward a more virile practice of citizenry. He discovered in what he understood to be the natural rights theory promoted by Rousseau and Mill the sanction for educated elites such as himself to oppose their own government peacefully and loyally.

After 1903, however, along with the rise of more radical and revolutionary ideas and actions in the Chinese and global context, Liang turned away from Rousseau's and Mill's natural rights theories toward a far more statist approach to the national collective. Taking on a more explicitly Darwinian conceptualization of society and state as forms in constant political struggle, Liang abandoned liberal theories of individual rights (or of the rights of society against the state), deeming them now too dangerous to indulge; he began strongly to favor German statist thinking, most prominently that promoted by the political theorist and jurist Johann Kaspar Bluntschli.[16]

Aside from statism, there were also two currents of anarchism (both profoundly antistatist, albeit in different ways) that took hold among Chinese intellectual circles in exile at the turn of the twentieth century. One was headquartered in Paris and another in Tokyo. He-Yin Zhen's circle in Tokyo was significantly informed by Japanese author Kemuyama Sentaro's book *Modern Anarchism*.[17] Much of this book was devoted to a discussion of Russian despotism and the revolutionary movement against it. Yet, of

---

[16]For more on Liang's political thought, see Hao Chang, *Liang Ch'i-ch'ao and Intellectual Transition in China, 1890-1907* (Cambridge, MA: Harvard University Press, 1971).
[17]The following account of anarchism among Chinese intellectuals at the turn of the twentieth century substantially derives from Arif Dirlik, *Anarchism in the Chinese Revolution* (Berkeley: University of California Press, 1991), chap. 2.

most concern to Chinese interpreters of anarchism in Tokyo was the crushing of "natural freedom" (*tianran ziyou*) by institutions of the state, law, religion, and formal education.[18] Broadly critical of institutions of the state and formal social hierarchies, Tokyo anarchists were also aware of the nihilism and violence promoted by some Russian anarchists (particularly by Sofia Perovskaya, one of the assassins of Tsar Alexander II in 1881). This anarchist literature directly informed He-Yin Zhen's critique of state institutions. In her conceptualization, state institutions themselves reproduce social injustice, in large part because of the state's defense of the very system of private property that gives rise to inequality. This perspective lends import to her concept of livelihood (*shengji*) for feminist theory. For, in this perspective, the securing of *shengji*, just as the securing of women's and social liberation, cannot be dependent upon the state; rather, genuine liberation and livelihood would be a new form of social life that eliminated economic and political dependences of all sorts. This view is clearly illuminated in the essays "On Women's Labor" and "Economic Revolution and Women's Revolution," translated in this volume.[19]

By 1906, the Paris-based and Tokyo-based anarchists had diverged in their advocacies. Those in Paris read Peter Kropotkin's work and were becoming more enamored of the futuristic promise of technology to overcome social injustice. Meanwhile, those in Tokyo favored Tolstoy's agrarian utopian work and focused on the nihilism of antitsarist Russians. The Tokyo group was convinced that freedom from the state and all hierarchical social institutions was the only plausible path away from endlessly reproduced social injustice. We could speculate that the violence-inflected version of anarchism popular in the Tokyo circle could be one source for the overt violence of He-Yin Zhen's language, particularly in her "Revenge" essay, whose uncompromising depictions of classical texts call out the brutal truths of social life hidden in plain sight.

[18]See in particular Ma Xulun, "Ershi shijizhi xin zhuyi" [The new "ism" of the twentieth century], in vol. 1 of *Wuzhengfu zhuyi sixiang ziliao xuan* [Selection of materials on anarchist thought], ed. Ge Maochun et al., 1–13, 2 vols. (Beijing: Beijing daxue chubanshe, 1984). Ma was affiliated with Sun Zhongshan's Revolutionary Alliance.
[19]There is a notice provided in Tianyi bao (#6; January 1, 1907) of Emma Goldman's *Mother Earth* and of her attendance at the World Anarchist Society meeting in Amsterdam. Kotoku Shusui, the Japanese anarchist, was the conduit through which He-Yin received this information. It is thus evident that He-Yin at least knew of Goldman's work, although their perspectives are quite different.

Unlike Sun Zhongshan and other supporters of an antidynastic revolution who specifically targeted the Qing *as Manchus*, for He-Yin Zhen and other anarchists, it made no difference if the rulers were Manchu, Han, Mongol, or any other race or ethnicity. All rulers, just as all states, were equally invested in the preservation of social injustice and its material underpinning—unequal property relations. Despite these ideological differences, she and others made common organizational political cause with Sun Zhongshan for his promotion of a revolutionary movement aimed at toppling the dynastic system of rule in China. He-Yin Zhen stopped short of ever joining the Revolutionary Alliance even though her husband Liu Shipei was a prominent member.

Anarchism was only one of several radical currents of thought among late-Qing Chinese intellectuals that also included embryonic understandings of socialism and Marxism. Indeed, as noted in the introduction to this volume, He-Yin Zhen's journal, *Natural Justice*, was the first to publish in Chinese excerpts from Marx and Engels's *Communist Manifesto*. Pioneering as that was, Marxism was not to receive systematic articulation in China until after the 1911 revolution, and more specifically, until after the 1917 Russian Revolution. It certainly did not attract in the pre-1911 period any sustained interest among Chinese, unlike among Japanese radical circles, where vibrant Marxist study societies were beset by state censorship and police repression. Nevertheless, various socialist or quasi-socialist currents were of some interest to Chinese intellectuals in exile, particularly among those who promoted the importance of the social redistribution of land wealth as a complement to and accompaniment for political revolution. Chinese intellectuals'—including He-Yin Zhen's—personal connections to the political organizations involving Japanese radicals of various political persuasions helped refine and hone understandings of these crucial resources for a critique of China and the world at the turn of the twentieth century.

Most prominent of these currents was Sun Zhongshan's advocacy for socialism as a fulfillment of the promise of republicanism. For Sun, socialism was not inherently in opposition to republicanism; instead, socialism would help to forestall the violence produced by class division in the industrialization process, even as it would help to realize the republican ideals of equality and democracy.[20] Sun's land redistribution advocacies were

---

[20]See Dirlik, *Anarchism in the Chinese Revolution*, 134–135.

informed not by Marx or even continental European utopian socialists such as Proudhon; rather, they were informed by American social reformer Henry George's promotion of the equalization of land ownership.[21] In George's view, as in Sun's, the premise of individual wealth is in the wealth of society as a collective (unlike in Adam Smith's version, where individual wealth is the premise of the wealth of nations). In the non-Smithian view, the task for the state is to enhance the growth of social wealth, where land is the basis of all wealth-producing activity. In this version of social life, the state's role was thus not the protection of private property as an individual right but, rather, the protection of private property as a collective right and as the premise for the production of national wealth.

These explicitly radical revolutionary or more ameliorist statist political philosophies and social ideologies were of critical importance to He-Yin Zhen and her circles in Tokyo, as well as to those educated critics of the Qing dynastic state who remained in China or traveled elsewhere in the world. They formed a vital world of thinking at the time.

Media Worlds of Thinking

Discursive and organizational interactions among sometimes geographically diffused groups of critics were facilitated by the rise of journals and print media around the turn of the twentieth century. Chinese-language print media sprang up in Tokyo, Paris, China, Hawaii, and elsewhere. Those journals started by critics of the Qing dynasty to promote their critiques were often ephemerally supported by the wealthy family or entrepreneurial connections of individuals who wished to publish their views. This lends the critical journalistic world of the time an unstable yet ubiquitous presence: journals pop up with grand statements of purpose and then suddenly disappear only to reappear several months later under new names with new pseudonyms attached; meanwhile, some journals remained in publication for multiyear runs. Pseudonyms were often needed to evade Japanese and Chinese police censorship, although the use of pen-names was also a time-honored practice among Chinese intellectuals, male and female.

[21]See Henry George, *Progress and Poverty* (New York: Robert Schalkenbach Foundation, 1955), first published in 1880, republished in 1905.

The combination renders the question of who wrote for which journals and who wrote what essays a topic of great contention that has preoccupied scholars ever since the turn of the twentieth century; unraveling the connections, pseudonyms, unfamiliar pen-names, ephemerality of publishing, and the financial disguises of the various critics and their supporters is no simple task. The specifics of that need not detain us, although we should mention that our claims for He-Yin Zhen's authorship of the essay "On Women's Labor" is enmeshed in this type of uncertain contention; suffice it to say that we have established to a degree of certainty that she is indeed the author of that essay, and not her husband, Liu Shipei, who is usually credited with its composition.

More generally, the rise of journalism, and particularly the rise of women's journals, is a crucially important material aspect of the flow and circulation of information and ideas in the late-Qing. Women's journals occupy a vital position in the publishing world of the time, in part because they were a new phenomenon: women writing and publishing for direct circulation in the public sphere fundamentally transformed the earlier history of women writing for circulation by their male kith and kin. But perhaps even more important, women's journals gave late-Qing women access to a medium through which they could directly critique the intertwined patriarchal systems of politics, culture, and social life *at the very moment* those systems were coming to be recognized as sources of oppression. That is, journalistic writing, particularly in its editorial and essay forms, allowed women writers to tease out and articulate, for the first time, the *systemic* sources of gendered life in China at the time. It is through these editorial efforts that a language and a history of gendered oppression were established and popularized among members of the small but disproportionately influential sector of literate female and male society. Aside from the editorial writing, journals also reprinted news from abroad, speeches, educational and didactic materials, anti-footbinding ditties and songs, and encouragements to women wishing to think beyond the horizons of their domestic lives—in addition to advertisements for potions, lotions, and pink-pill medicines that promised miraculous cures and recoveries for putative ailments as well as newly identified modern cosmetic needs of all types. This explosion of incipient capitalist journalism formed a crucial media world of thinking for He-Yin Zhen.

Female writers of essays, political critiques, and editorials (both Chinese and Japanese), into whose discussions He-Yin Zhen's conceptualizations intervened, were consequently of major importance in helping shape the environment through which He-Yin's sensibilities and writing were contextualized and informed. We mentioned earlier one such famous writer, Qiu Jin. In addition, however, was a host of other female voices bursting into the field of print media at the turn of the twentieth century. On the Japanese side, perhaps most important was the radical political and social figure Fukuda Hideko (1865–1927), whose career spanned the liberal movement of early Meiji Japan (1868–1911) through to the birth of a socialist movement in the early twentieth century and beyond. Editor and publisher of the journal *Women of the World* (Seikai Fujin) from 1907 to 1909, when it was forcibly shut down by Japanese authorities in a general crackdown against socialist voices, Fukuda was committed to women's emancipation, albeit not within the confines of the state. A fierce critic of the Japanese Women's Patriotic Association, Fukuda was also associated with the most famous Japanese literary feminist journal of the early twentieth century, *Bluestocking* (Seito), which began publication in 1911. Although no direct personal relationship between Fukuda and He-Yin Zhen can be established, they operated in the same radical circles in Tokyo and would have known of each other; indeed, in *Women of the World* (number 13, July 1907), for instance, Fukuda reprinted "The Regulations of the Society for the Restoration of Women's Rights" from the first issue of He-Yin's journal, *Natural Justice*.[22] We can also mention one other important Japanese feminist, with whom He-Yin would have been familiar, either personally or by reputation: Kanno Suga (1881–1911), an anarchist and feminist activist who, along with her partner Kotoku Shusui, was executed by the Meiji state in 1911 for political crimes (Kanno was the first woman in modern Japanese history to be dealt with so harshly). Kanno was a frequent author of political essays and editorial commentary, with which He-Yin was most likely familiar.

---

[22]See Ono Kazuko, *Chinese Women in a Century of Revolution, 1850–1950* (Stanford, CA: Stanford University Press, 1989), 65–66. The Japanese editor appended a commentary to the reprint. It goes: "Among the revolutionary youths from the Qing state who currently reside in Japan, a number of people have recently formed a 'Society for the Restoration of Women's Rights' and are publishing a journal called *Natural Justice*. . . . Although there are some idiosyncrasies, as is often the case with the Chinese (*Shinajin*), and there are some clauses we cannot fully endorse, these [Chinese youth] are incredibly strong-willed and spirited. This is something we ought to have observed more among the Japanese" (*Seikai Fujin*, no. 13 [July 1907]: 100).

Among the host of Chinese female writers for the political press of the time were such prominent figures as Lin Zongsu (1878–1944), Chen Xiefen (1883–1923), and Luo Yanbin (1869–?), writers He-Yin Zhen undoubtedly knew of and whose essays she most probably read. Lin, an early advocate for female political participation, wrote one of the many prefaces to and commentaries on Jin Tianhe's *The Women's Bell* (Lin's work is not translated in this volume),[23] commending it as an exemplary text on the historical oppression of women in China. A founding member of the Fujian Women's Study Society, Lin also was among the first batch of women to join Sun Zhongshan's Revolutionary Alliance (Tongmeng Hui) soon after its establishment in 1905 in Tokyo. After 1911, Lin's was a leading voice for female suffrage. Chen Xiefen, for her part, was the founder of one of the earliest Chinese-language women's journals, *The Woman's Paper* (*Nübao*), originally published as a supplement to her father's radical nationalist paper *Subao* and then resumed, under a different name, as an independent publication after *Subao* was banned by the Qing government and Chen broke with her father over her impending sale as a concubine to a rich merchant. Along with Lin Zongsu and Qiu Jin, Chen Xiefen lived and worked in Tokyo in the first decade of the twentieth century, publishing political essays that promoted the concept of female citizenship based upon opposition both to imperialism and patriarchy. Nationalist in orientation, Chen and Lin (as well as Qiu) insisted on an equal place for (elite) women within a just-evolving notion of national-state social life and governance.[24]

Luo Yanbin, older by a decade than Lin and Chen, was also a vigorous advocate for female citizenship. As the founding editor of the journal *China's New Woman's World* (*Zhongguo Xin Nüjie*), Luo focused more than Lin and Chen on the problem of the paucity of female education, even as her narrative of the history of women's oppression was also different from Chen's and Lin's. Where the latter two argued that women's inequality had been a fact of life since the distant past, Luo insisted that women had been equal to men earlier in history but had been relegated to second-class citizenship somewhere along the line. Her strategic focus, then, was often to argue

---

[23]Her commentary was published in the journal *Jiangsu* 5 (1903).
[24]See Mizuyo Sudo, "Concepts of Women's Rights in Modern China," trans. Michael Hill, *Gender & History* 18, 3 (November 2006): 472–489. For other women writers, see Nanxiu Qian, Grace S. Fong, and Richard J. Smith, eds., *Different Worlds of Discourse: Transformations of Gender and Genre in Late Qing and Early Republican China* (Leiden: Brill, 2008).

for the *recovery* of lost rights, rather than on the newness of the advocacy for women's rights in the present.[25] With different but compatible perspectives on the problems of women's oppression and on the mechanisms for amelioration, Chen, Luo, and Lin were some of the more influential mainstream voices in the burgeoning world of women's journalistic writing and its articulation of the sources and systems of patriarchal domination.[26]

In addition to the journalistic worlds in which He-Yin Zhen and many other late-Qing educated people were enmeshed was the world of book publishing which took on, among many other things, the task of translating and publicizing works from abroad. In addition to political philosophies, international relations treatises, miscellaneous histories, and hosts of other types of texts, such as didactic children's literature and adult educational books, a huge and influential sector of publishing in the first decade of the twentieth century concentrated on the translation of novels and stories from abroad. In fact, one of the most prolific promoters of foreign fiction of the time, Lin Shu, "translated" from French, German, English, and so on, without knowing a single foreign language, by collaborating with those who knew one of the languages. Lin Shu's classical-Chinese renditions (they are translations only in the loosest sense) of Euro-American works—Shakespeare as well as Dumas, H. Rider Haggard, and Sherlock Holmes and Harriet Beecher Stowe, among many others—took the reading public by storm.

The new plots, romantic twists, semi-independent women, heroic roles, political intrigues, and vast mobility of characters over time and space provoked debates and large-scale rethinking about the role of fiction in sociopolitical life. Previously less valued as a form of writing, fiction in the guise of short stories and novels now became acknowledged as a key popular textual form for promoting new ideas, new senses of community, and new modes of social being in the world. He-Yin Zhen's numerous references to the translated fiction of her time, either in Lin Shu's renditions or in

---

[25]For the derivation of some of this material, for more on all these figures, and for an extended discussion of each, see Dooling, *Women's Literary Feminism*, chap. 1.

[26]We should also note Lü Bicheng (1884–1943), pioneering journalist at Tianjin's *Dagong bao*; like Chen, Luo, and Lin, Lü advocated for female education and equal rights, and she helped raise funds for the founding of Beiyang Women's Public School in 1904. See Grace S. Fong, "Alternative Modernities, or A Classical Woman of Modern China: The Challenging Trajectory of Lü Bicheng (1883–1943): Life and Song Lyrics," *Nan Nü: Men, Women & Gender in Early & Imperial China* 6, 1 (2004): 12–59.

renditions available in Japanese, demonstrate the huge importance of fiction in shaping her understanding of the Euro-American world.

Conclusion

Many overlapping worlds of thinking and of practice informed He-Yin Zhen's historical moment. By 1907, she was joining an increasingly crowded discursive and activist fray, where the question of the modern transformation of political, social, cultural, and economic life in China and the world, as well as the relationship of such transformations to women in general and Chinese women in particular, was just being articulated systematically and systemically for the first time. Although He-Yin Zhen was thus not an isolated case of a woman protesting against injustice, she nevertheless stands out as a unique social and political critic whose basic worldview was gendered from the outset.

It is our contention in publishing this volume of her translated texts in juxtaposition to the texts of two prominent male liberal feminists of her time that He-Yin Zhen's feminist and anarchist radicalism allows us to complicate today's received narrative about the origins of Chinese feminism in a borrowed male liberal worldview. That is, to the extent that the existing narrative of the origins of Chinese feminism, found in contemporary Chinese as well as American scholarship, continues to focus on the "influence" of Euro-American male liberal philosophy on the articulation of feminist concerns in China, the genuinely new analyses of the gendered nature of the modern world offered by He-Yin Zhen will remain buried.

We are confident, therefore, that in the essays that follow, readers will discover new perspectives from He-Yin Zhen's systemic thinking about the historical instantiations of gendered oppression, made with reference to her interpretation of the social totality of the early-twentieth-century world and China, and specifically to the intertwined systems of scholarly knowledge, female bodily subjugation, and juridicopolitical practice. These intertwined systems, she claims, not only had resulted in the subjection of Chinese women in the past but also would continue to provide the basis of women's subjection in the "civilized" present and future. In other words, for He-Yin Zhen, these misogynist practices were not by-products of history but, rather, constitutive of the very stuff of history. Thus, for her, women were not absent in history, as many feminists have claimed; rather, they were a ubiquitous presence as the very principle of history.

Finally, then, because of the complexity of her overlapping worlds of thinking and yet also because of her radical contestation of those worlds, He-Yin Zhen insisted that all social life needed to be viewed through the lens of *nannü* in conjunction with *shengji*, those two all-important analytical categories (discussed fully in the introduction to this volume) that materially grounded and ideologically shaped for her the forms of domination and of distinction, past and present, through which she lived and to which all critique, she believed, had to answer.

He-Yin Zhen, first left in front row, 1908, in Shanghai, from *Liu Yazi xuanji* [Selected works of Liu Yazi], ed. Wang Jingyao et al., vol. 1. Beijing: Renmin chubanshe, 1989.

He-Yin Zhen 何殷震 (aka He Ban 何班, He Zhen 何震, ca.1884–1920?)

was born and raised in Yizheng, Jiangsu Province, at a time of great transition in China. Married in 1904, she and her husband, Liu Shipei, a renowned classical scholar, went to Tokyo in 1907, where they joined Chinese revolutionaries in exile in Japan and became acquainted with anarchist perspectives and leaders. In the same year, He-Yin Zhen and her fellow travelers in Tokyo formed the Society for the Restoration of Women's Rights and created the official journal of the society, which they called *Tien Yee* (*Tianyi*), or *Natural Justice*. This journal, though only published between 1907 and 1908, became the foremost and the most influential medium for the articulation and spread of such radical ideas as feminism, socialism, Marxism, and anarchism in the last decade of the Qing dynasty.

He-Yin Zhen and Liu Shipei published numerous articles, both single authored and collaborative, during the two years the journal was in print. Since they both adopted pen-names, He-Yin Zhen's editorial role and authorship are often misattributed by historians to Liu Shipei. The couple's fallout with renowned scholar Zhang Taiyan and other revolutionary nationalists in 1908 on charges of collusion with the Manchu regime led to their ostracism after the overthrow of the Qing dynasty in 1911. Following the death of her husband in 1919, at age thirty-five He-Yin Zhen is rumored to have entered a Buddhist order of nuns and become ordained as Xiao Qi; others claim that she died of a broken heart and psychic disorder soon thereafter. No one has found reliable information about the end of her life.

"On the Question of Women's Liberation"

He-Yin Zhen (1907)

For thousands of years, the world has been dominated by the rule of man. This rule is marked by class distinctions over which men—and men only—exert proprietary rights. To rectify the wrongs, we must first abolish the rule of men and introduce equality among human beings, which means that the world must belong equally to men and to women. The goal of equality cannot be achieved except through women's liberation.

The social system in China has enslaved women and forced them into submission for many thousands of years. In ancient times, men acquired proprietary rights over women to prevent them from being claimed by other men. They created political and moral institutions, the first priority of which was to separate man from woman (*nannü*). For they considered the differentiation between man and woman (*nannü youbie*) to be one of the major principles in heaven and on earth.[1] Men thus confined women to the inner chamber and would not allow them to step beyond its boundaries. *The Book of Rites* states, "When a married aunt, or sister, or daughter returns home (on a visit), no brother (of the family) should sit with her on the same mat or eat with her from the same dish." It goes on to state that "[m]ale and female, without the intervention of the matchmaker, should not know

---

[1] Tr: The compound *youbie* refers to the marking of difference or the act of making something distinct or different. This act of primary injunction is prior to the appearance of difference as such. We emphasize this important point because He-Yin Zhen is attacking the act of marking *nannü* difference rather than how people consider or think about the perceived or already established difference.

each other's name. Unless the marriage presents have been received, there should be no communication or affection between them."[2] Boji of the state of Song said that "a woman does not venture out at night without the company of her teacher or senior female companion."[3] The Han dynasty Confucian scholar Zheng Xuan wrote, "[A] woman should not concern herself with the outside world."[4] This is what they meant by distinguishing man from woman. Whenever people describe an age of prosperity in China, they invariably speak of how men and women walk different paths. What can they mean by the different paths but an extreme case of differentiation?

In ancient times, the separation of the inner from the outer was originally instituted to prevent illicit sexual affairs. Unfortunately, this has led to a situation where a woman's lifelong responsibility has been restricted to the double task of raising children, managing the household, and nothing else. These tasks are relegated to women out of a widespread belief that a man's offspring embodies his soul and that the art of defying death lies in the perpetuation of his own seed. The socioeconomic system of China treats a man's children and grandchildren as his own property, which should explain why every man regards multiplying his progeny as the way of becoming wealthy. Men take advantage of this socioeconomic system and the moral teachings that sanction their indulgence in sexual gratification, all the while regarding women as nothing more than instruments that make and nurture human seeds. Moreover, Chinese men never bother to attend to small things, and they expect women to take care of all the details in the management of the household. Women serve and toil for them and devote their whole lives to the two tasks of raising children and running the household.

How far back can we trace the conditions of such an arrangement? I suppose that one explanation is that it began when men started to treat women as their private property. The other explanation is that the cost of living before modern times was low, so it was relatively easy for men to find employment to feed their parents and their immediate family. The income based on men's employment alone could support a family of moderate means and above, so their wives could afford to stay home and do nothing

---

[2] Tr: *The Li Ki (The Book of Rites)*, trans. James Legge, book 1: "Quli," part 3, section 6:30.

[3] Tr: This quotation is from the *Gongyang zhuan* (Gongyang commentary on the Spring and Autumn Annals), 30th year of Duke Xiang (d. 637 BCE).

[4] Tr: This quotation is from Zheng Xuan's commentary on the *Zhou Li* (The Rites of Zhou), juan 8.

more than raise the children and run household affairs.[5] But this has inadvertently instilled a habit of idleness and a slave mentality among some women, whereas men are mostly content with this state of affairs.

Chinese men refer to their wives as *neiren*, "person of the inner chamber," or *neizi*, "the inner one." The word *nei* is opposed to the word *wai*, or "outer." By keeping woman as his own property, a man cloisters his wife within the walls and deprives her of her basic freedom. When we get closer to the present age, it seems that women are not the only ones who have lost their freedom. Men, too, have lost their freedom by taking on the burden of supporting their families, for a man is solely responsible for the cost of caring for his mother, [maintaining] his wife, and [providing] the dowry of his daughter.[6] Despite all these hardships, men prefer to abide by traditional rituals and laws, remaining hostile to the liberation of women.

Families below middling means, however, can hardly depend on men's labor alone for support; women have no choice but to go out to earn their own keep. These women either work on farms or sell their labor as bondservants. Women further down the social ladder might become prostitutes. Even though lower-class women need not suffer the hardship of being cloistered at home, and even though their bodies are in that sense liberated, this liberation has nothing to do with the liberation of the mind. Not to mention that those who enjoy a modicum of freedom of the body are the kind of women who suffer the most strenuous forms of labor, the most ruthless exploitation, and the most shameful humiliation. Is this not very sad?[7]

We must consider further whether the idea of cloistering women in the home can effectively be put into practice. Young women from wealthy families or families of moderate means are supposed to be sheltered and secluded,

---

[5]In ancient times, even women from aristocratic families were expected to do some weaving and textile work, but today's [elite] women are habitually lazy and seldom work.

[6]Because of their idleness, some [elite] women gain in vanity and expend more on the extravagant care of their appearances than do men. The situation is aggravated by traditional ritual requirements for such ceremonial occasions as weddings. Thousands of gold pieces are spent on vain appearances, and even poor families strive to emulate these practices. An untold number of families in Fujian Province and in Jinde County of Anhui Province have been reduced to poverty by the need to marry off their daughters. The husband resents his wife for the same reason as a father resents his daughter. These men are reacting to the same burden.

[7]In terms of physical confinement, young Japanese women seem to enjoy more freedom than do their counterparts in China, but Japanese women in fact suffer more oppression than do Chinese women: Japanese men hoist upon them the most laborious, degrading, and humiliating tasks.

but the seclusion cannot but lead to desire and fantasy, which is the natural tendency of human beings. A man may spend months and years traveling in distant lands, or he may devote his attention to a favored concubine. His wife might get angry but dare not tell him her feelings. Her pent-up sexual desire might smolder and burn; it cannot be suppressed by traditional ethics and laws. When a young widow is forbidden to remarry after the death of her husband, her cloistered life consists of eating and sleeping, and there is nothing in the daily routine of her life that occupies her heart's desire, nothing to prevent her from indulging in sexual fantasy. As we reflect on the situation of wealthy households, it seems that the wife's devotion to one man is in name only; in actual practice she may end up having more than one husband. In the case of young widows who do not remarry, they remain chaste in name only but not in practice. There is no need to cite examples from the remote past. In recent years, when Wu Yinsun was promoted to be the prefecture chief and was posted to Ningbo and Shaoxing, his fifty-year-old wife engaged in illicit sex with one of her handsome male servants at home.[8] Another well-known example is Liang Dingfen's wife, who had a smattering of learning. She was seduced by Wen Tingshi and went to live with him for several years.[9] The cases of Sheng Xuanhuai's daughter and that of Fei Nianci's wife indicate that the former engaged in illicit affairs after she became a widow, whereas the latter indulged in all kinds of incestuous relationships with male members of her own clan.[10] Did these acts of transgression not take place in prominent families?

In arranged marriages, the parents make all the decisions and the young woman has absolutely no say. When a woman is not allowed to marry her lover, she either resorts to eloping like Zhuo Wenjun or plots secret rendezvous with her lover as in the case of Cui Yingying.[11] If we conduct an annual

---

[8]Tr: Wu Yinsun (1851–1920) was a renowned scholar and official from the city of Yangzhou who was posted to Ningpo in 1888–1898.

[9]Tr: Liang Dingfen (1859–1920) was an important historical figure in late-Qing reform and worked in the office of the viceroy Zhang Zhidong. Wen Tingshi (1856–1904) was a renowned poet and Hanlin scholar.

[10]Tr: Sheng Xuanhuai (1844–1916) was a leading industrialist and a high-ranking official in the late-Qing reform government. Fei Nianci (1855–1905) was a renowned poet, calligrapher, and scholar.

[11]Tr: Zhuo Wenjun was a Han dynasty woman who eloped with Sima Xiangru. Cui Yingying is the young woman in Yuan Zhen's much-adapted piece of the Tang dynasty called "The Story of Yingying." In the story, Yingying falls in love with the narrator, who first seduces her and then regrets the entanglement. He eventually abandons her in order to pursue a successful career.

survey of the number of cases of sexual transgression committed by women from county to county across China, we would discover dozens of them, not including the countless unexposed cases. Infamous capital crimes involving the murder of husbands or children are usually the outcomes of these circumstances. The foregoing analysis proves that confining women to the boudoir does not prevent them from conducting illicit affairs with other men. This obviously contradicts the stated goal of cloistering women within walls. The unintended consequence, as we have seen, is to encourage women to indulge freely in sexual fantasies even though the original intention was to deny them freedom. In other words, the prohibition of sexual transgression exists in name only; it encourages sexual transgression in practice.

The main reason that men object to women's liberation is that they are concerned that once women obtain their freedom, they will become sexually promiscuous. In fact, the stricter the controls, the more eager women are to break down such controls, jumping at the slightest opportunity to find an outlet for their sexual fantasy. It is not unlike the act of hiding something, which precisely alerts a thief to its value and therefore intensifies his desire to steal it. I argue that women's sexual transgression is caused by their cloistering rather than by their freedom. And it makes no sense to say that women's liberation itself leads to sexual promiscuity. Not understanding this, the people of China are wary of liberating women. We must realize that the more women are cloistered, the further women's virtue deteriorates, thus hindering the character of women [nüxing] from developing.[12]

In China, the sanctioning authority behind a marriage is Confucian ritual. In Europe and America, marriage was sanctioned by religion in the past. In recent years, the role of religion has been overtaken by legal institutions, and this system is deemed superior to the practices in China. We are told that first, individuals [in the West] are free to marry, divorce, and remarry; second, they practice monogamy; third, both men and women are educated, and they can associate with one another in the same social space. As we scan the surface of that system, we may conclude that Western women are liberated individuals. Yet, in my view,

---

[12]If there are some Chinese women who share the same fallacy about liberation, it is not because women are naturally content with being cloistered but because they are bound by their blind faith in traditional ethics and laws.

their system may have set the physical body free but their minds are still far from free. Why so?

Liberation means setting [the body and the mind] free from bondage. The problem with the marriage systems in Europe and America is that individuals remain constrained by three bondages: power/privilege and self-interest/profit (*quanli*), morality, and law.[13] They talk about freedom in marriage and so on. But do individuals in Europe and America get married purely out of free love? What often happens is that a man may lure a woman with his wealth, or a woman's family fortune may cause a man to admire her and propose marriage. The rich and the powerful can coerce the weak into such relationships. And this is what I call the bondage of self-interest and the desire to profit (*li*). Conversely, when a woman is from a prominent family, a man may propose marriage out of his desire to use the status and power of her family to climb up the social ladder. It may happen that a man of wealth and social status falls in love with a poor woman and they want to get married, but this desire can be thwarted by the social divide and concerns about reputation. This is what I call the bondage of power/privilege (*quan*). How can anyone claim that there is free marriage [in Europe and America]?[14]

The system of monogamy is rooted in nothing other than the bondage of religion; it is patrolled by law and a sham morality. There are women in Europe and America who remain unmarried for life; but even if they are unmarried in name, they can still have more than one husband in practice. There are men in Europe and America who also remain unmarried for life and who may have numerous wives in practice. In a monogamous relationship, which allows a woman to have only one husband, she may have illicit affairs with other men. A man, too, is legally allowed to marry only one woman; but in married life he may have many affairs with other women. The dance floors of the metropole populated by fashionable women provide but thin cover for illicit affairs among men and women. The so-called bonds

---

[13]Tr: The Chinese word for "rights," *quanli*, is made up of two characters: *quan* and *li*. The original translation of this English concept occurred in the first Chinese translation of Henry Wheaton's *Elements of International Law* by W. A. P. Martin and a group of Chinese scholars. For a discussion of the curious neologism *quanli* and why the English word "rights" is equated with "power/privilege and self-interest/profit" in the Chinese translation, see Lydia H. Liu, *The Clash of Empires* (Cambridge, MA: Harvard University Press, 2004), 125–129.

[14]Tr: For a fuller discussion of these issues, see He-Yin's essay "Economic Revolution and Women's Revolution," translated in this volume.

of a monogamous relationship are in fact coerced by law and whitewashed by a packaging of morality.[15]

As for equality between man and woman, it is likewise often a sham. Although men and women are both now educated [in Europe and America], they live in a world supremely ruled by man. Women seldom study politics or law and are completely barred from acquiring knowledge in the fields of the military and the police. It is true that women and men may socialize freely; but when the world is controlled by governments that systematically exclude women from their governing bodies, so-called gender equality can exist only in name.

To liberate women means letting women enjoy equal rights and sharing the fruits of all freedoms. If we decided to follow the model of the current European and American systems, we would get our freedom in name but not in substance and also would have equal rights in name only. A sham equality deprived of true freedom is not equality at all. I argue that the lack of true freedom has led to the underdevelopment of the character of women (*nüxing*) and the lack of true equality has led to the state of inequality insofar as human rights (*renquan*) [of men and women] are concerned.[16] Asian women have been greatly impressed by the advances in the civilizations of Europe and America. They believe that European and American women have already achieved the goal of liberation and are enjoying the equality and freedom whose precedents they are content to follow. There is no reason why in the age of women's liberation our women should be satisfied with sham freedom and sham equality. I want them to pursue, and attain, true freedom and equality.

In recent times, calls have been issued to promote women's liberation in Chinese society. Some are active calls and some passive calls. By active calls, I mean the ones initiated by women themselves as they struggle to free themselves. Passive calls are those that are acted upon women and initiated by men who dangle the promise of liberation before their eyes. As we survey the Chinese situation, it seems that active calls for women's liberation are few as compared with passive ones. As men are more motivated, it stands

---

[15]For example, Queen Victoria's marriage to the German prince did not prevent her from having affairs with one of her horse grooms. When we look at the marriages among members of German, British, Russian, and other aristocratic families, the men nearly all have affairs outside of wedlock.

[16]Tr: For an analysis of the historical meanings associated with *nüxing* and our translation of *xing* as "character," see the Introduction.

to reason that they, rather than women, will benefit far more from the fruits of such work than might women. It is interesting that in the past, men took it upon themselves to confine women within the boudoir and regarded the oppressive treatment of women as their given duty. They now turn around and call for women's liberation and for a system of equality between man and woman. When I ponder this striking reversal in attitude, I can think of the following three reasons.

First, Chinese men worship power and authority. They believe that Europeans, Americans, and the Japanese are civilized nations of the modern world who all grant their women some degree of freedom. By transplanting this system into the lives of their wives and daughters, by prohibiting the practice of footbinding, and by enrolling them in schools to receive basic education, these men think they will be applauded by the whole world for having joined the ranks of civilized nations. Not only would the man enjoy such a reputation, his entire family would as well, and he himself would be credited as a pioneer. For instance, when a man brings his wife and daughters to a social gathering in a public square filled with crowds, he wants to draw people's attention so they marvel at him with such comments as "Aren't these So-and-So's wife and daughters? They are certainly more enlightened than your ordinary Chinese women!" But my question is whether this kind of liberation has any benefits for women themselves; perhaps men merely take advantage of it to promote their own name. I am inclined to think that these men have acted purely out of a selfish desire to claim women as private property. Were it not so, why would a woman's reputation, good or bad, have anything whatsoever to do with them? The men's original intention is not to liberate women but to treat them as private property. In the past, when traditional rituals prevailed, men tried to distinguish themselves by confining women in the boudoir; when the tides turn in favor of Europeanization, they attempt to acquire distinction by promoting women's liberation. This is what I call *men's pursuit of self-distinction in the name of women's liberation.*[17]

Second, the general decline of people's livelihood (*shengji*) in China has caused families of moderate means to become mired in poverty; many of them are experiencing a hard time providing food and shelter for their women and children. Since men are responsible for supporting their families,

---

[17]Tr: We would note that this is a pointed critique of Jin Tianhe. See Jin's *The Women's Bell*, translated in this volume.

they are beginning to feel pressure and realize that confining their women in the household not only brings no real benefit but can in fact cost them dearly and inflict tremendous damage [to the household economy]. Men are now promoting women's autonomy and argue that women should not depend on men for their livelihood.[18] They ask that women study at women's school and that even the lowest degree of education for women should include at least craftsmanship or skills for making embroidery, knitting, sewing and tailoring, cooking, and so on. The more advanced can specialize in a teacher's college, while the brightest may receive a college education and study professional subjects (such as medicine and sciences). I wonder if this plan to send women to school was designed with the goal of advancing women's own interest or if the objective of turning women into teachers or skilled workers is not to help alleviate men's burden. In large families with many mouths to feed, circumstances often force women to earn the means of supporting the elderly and feeding the young. When such is not the case, men can travel and roam in distant places and choose not to concern themselves with the management of the household. They squander the family budget on concubines and brothels and indulge themselves in all kinds of carnal pleasures, leaving their women to suffer loneliness at home. When the men say that women ought to be liberated, they are thinking of how they themselves may profit from this. This is what I call men's *pursuit of self-interest* in the name of women's liberation.

Third, Chinese men view the family as their personal property and treat having progeny as a top priority, but the task of running the household and raising the children is not something they can bear. They then turn it instead into the responsibility of women. A quick survey suggests that women's schools in China uniformly emphasize the field of household management and that modern political parties always discourse on how family education forms the backbone of all educational efforts. What do they mean by this language? They are actually saying that barbaric women are inferior to civilized women in the running of the household—namely, providing services to men—and that barbaric women are equally inferior to civilized women in the education of children. Nonetheless, the family is still a man's family—an example being the continued adoption of the father's family name and the dropping of the mother's surname. It shows that men

[18]Tr: This implies a critique of Liang Qichao. See Liang's "On Women's Education," translated in this volume.

have promoted the liberation of women out of a secret desire to make use of women [and their labor] so that the men can escape from such responsibilities and enjoy themselves.[19] This is what I call men's *pursuit of self-comfort* in the name of women's liberation.

The three points I have outlined suggest that the project of liberating women in today's discourse sprang from the self-serving interests of some men. They talk about helping women achieve their autonomy or leading them toward a more civilized existence, but what this empty discourse of women's liberation does is drive women toward even harsher conditions of work.[20] The old system granted social prestige to men and put women down by relegating them to lower ranks. But the irony is that men worked harder than women. In today's world, however, women partake of men's hard work, even as men enjoy a share of women's leisure; but this has not brought the slightest improvement in the kind of social prestige that is due to women. Why should women take pleasure in thus being used by men? Unaware of the true situation, there are those who foolishly believe that Chinese women are indebted to those men for setting them free and that they should be deeply grateful for the wonderful things that men have done for them. This manner of reasoning is not unlike the argument made by those within the Manchu regime who advocate constitutional reform.[21] Just as the constitutional reform instrumentalizes the idea of a constitution and has no real intention to confer rights on all citizens, so does the male project of liberating women makes similar use of the idea of liberation with no intention of conferring real rights on women.[22] I am not suggesting that men's obligations should be fulfilled by men only and never be shared by women, nor am I opposed to the expansion of women's

---

[19]Tr: We would note again that this is a critique of Liang Qichao's advocacies. See his "On Women's Education," translated in this volume.

[20]Women used to suffer the pains of cloistering, but their bodies were more at leisure. Today, as women are becoming more liberated, they are forced to accept more work obligations. As their bodies must take on a heavier load of work, the situation cannot but bring more hardships to women.

[21]Tr: For more on the historical context of which He-Yin Zhen is speaking here, see "The Historical Context" in this volume.

[22]To the outside world, the constitutionalists in the Manchu regime try to present their country as a civilized nation even as they try to win the trust of their own people to help sustain the government with financial support. Their argument bears striking resemblances to how men promote women's liberation for their own selfish purposes.

suffrage.[23] All I am saying is that women's obligations ought to be fulfilled by women rather than be imposed upon them by men.

The cause of women's rights must be won through women's own efforts. It must not be granted by men. If we allow women's rightful role to be imposed by men, we are renouncing our freedom; and if we allow ourselves to look up to men and ingratiate ourselves to them, whatever rights we obtain in this way are handed to us from above. As we continued to be instrumentalized and remain men's appendages, we would be liberated in name only and our rights could never really be our own. I argue that we women must rely on ourselves to find the joy of liberation and should never expect men to be our liberators. Today, Chinese women still expect men to come to set them free; we are content with playing a passive role. We have not risen to the level of self-consciousness. Not only do we fall easy prey to men's manipulation, we also pay homage to them. Is this not a disgrace?[24]

So far I have pointed out the undesirable consequences of the passive role that women play in the cause of women's liberation. I should admit that in recent years a few women are so completely inebriated with the idea of freedom and equality that they want to break down all ethical and legal restraints. On the surface, these women appear to be liberated and are by no means passive, but I wonder if these women are not just taking cover under freedom and equality to seek self-gratification and the fulfillment of sexual desire. These women construe the notion of liberation much too narrowly and believe that liberation means simply self-indulgence. They do not understand that the joy of liberation lies in the development of the character of women and that this will in turn help us win rights to change society. But if self-gratification were to be our objective, our goal to save the world would be thwarted and nothing could be accomplished. Of course, free love is an exception. When I look around, it seems that cases of free love in sexual partnerships are extremely rare. What I do observe is that some liberated women are driven by blind passion and some are seduced

---

[23]Tr: The Chinese neologism *nüquan* is rendered "women's suffrage" here and, in other contexts, *nüquan* is taken to be a translation of "feminist," "feminism," and "women's rights." This broad spectrum of meanings in *nüquan*—paralleling the other neologism *nüxing* discussed in the introduction to this volume—was introduced through modern Japanese translation and was first established in late-Qing prose when He-Yin Zhen's generation came of age.

[24]In recent years, some men have written for newspapers and magazines to promote women's rights. It seems that they do so either out of curiosity or out of self-interest; they are not doing it for the love of women.

by men and fall into their snare; worse still, there are women who become enamored of men's money. They prostitute themselves to obtain money and property, currying favor with the wealthy. What could be more degrading in the world than exploiting your own body for profit?[25] How can we call those who behave this way liberated women? The idea of liberation is utterly opposed to any system of enslavement. How is it possible for a woman to refuse to be enslaved otherwise yet to be content with prostituting her body? When liberation is mistaken for self-indulgence, a woman cannot think of a nobler task than sexual pleasure, not knowing that she might have fallen into prostitution unwittingly. These are some of the weaknesses of Chinese women.[26]

Today, white women have increasingly become aware of the harmful effects of the inequality that exists between man and woman. They attribute inequality to the fact that men hold political office whereas women do not. These women, therefore, decided to form their own organizations and societies to struggle for women's suffrage. Rather than dwell on the remote past, let me mention some recent events. Finnish women, for example, are renowned for their courage and fearless acts. They established the Finnish Women's Association (Suomen Naisyhdistys) in 1884 to mobilize efforts for women's participation in politics. In 1898, the entire country left gender distinction and hierarchy behind as they threw themselves into the resistance movement against the Russian empire. The movement soon evolved into violent struggle and continues to this day. In Finland, as many as nineteen women have been elected to parliament, unprecedented in the world.

Next to Finnish women are women of Norway, where the feminist struggle has focused on universal suffrage. The Norwegian parliament sets the limits to woman's right to vote, stipulating that women below age twenty-five and below a certain threshold of taxable income are not qualified to vote. Even so, up to three hundred thousand women in Norway have obtained the right to vote. In England, women have come to frequent clashes with the police forces at the parliamentary building; and in Italy, women form broad alliances to fight for universal suffrage. All this testifies

---

[25]The shame of a prostitute lies not in her having sex with many men but in the degrading of her body for money. Women who exploit their bodies for profit are not that different from prostitutes.

[26]Women's longtime cloistering may help explain their headlong rush into sexual freedom. As men are inclined to lust, they may have bestowed some of this trait to their daughters.

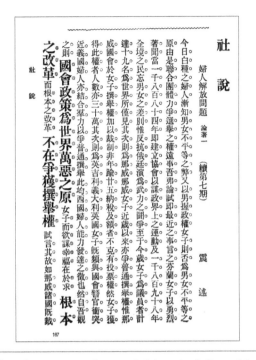

He-Yin Zhen, "On the Question of Women's Liberation," *Natural Justice*, nos. 8–10, October 1907.

to the well-developed capabilities of Western women. But in my view, parliamentary politics has been the source of many inequities in the world, and women who seek happiness must take their aim at the roots [of social injustice]. I doubt that the struggle for women's suffrage can bring about a fundamental transformation of society.

Let us consider the Norwegian case. Parliament circumscribes women's right to vote and sets the age limit and the threshold of annual tax payments. Although one could argue for the merit of the age limit, the requirement of a certain level of tax payment indicates that those who pay taxes at the stipulated level would have to be property owners. Rich taxpayers come from the aristocracy, wealthy families, or medium-income households and above. Should women's right to vote be concentrated in the hands of a few rich ladies? My understanding of gender equality implies equality among all human beings, which refers to the prospect of not only men no longer oppressing women but also men no longer oppressed by other men and women no longer oppressed by other women. If gender equality simply means that a minority of women may take political office and maintain an equilibrium of power with a minority of men who hold similar office, we should try to explain how the following happens among men: namely, in today's world where there is difference between men who rule over other men and men who are ruled by them, the majority of the ruled in the world of men are demanding a revolution. As for the idea of equal division of power between men and women, most people seem to believe that since there are power holders among men, there should be among women as well. But did such powerful female sovereigns as Queen Victoria of the British Empire or Empresses Lü Zhi and Empress Wu Zetian in the dynastic history of China ever bring the slightest benefits to the majority of women?

A minority of women holding power is hardly sufficient to save the majority of women. In the case of Norway, for instance, the few aristocratic women who occupy political office do little in the way of bringing benefits to the general population. And as representatives of women from the upper classes and gentry families, these women have gained political rights and are assisting men from the upper classes in perpetrating damages even further. If their legislative work benefits upper-class women only, it deepens the suffering of lower-class women. Norway is not the only country where this has happened. A good number of women in Australia are able to participate in political governance. But have they tried to improve the condition of working-class women? And when working-class women do not go to the polls to vote, where is gender equality?

As we go from limited suffrage to universal suffrage, it would seem that we could arrive at a more equitable legislation. But I cannot but notice that a great number of men in Europe and America do not enjoy universal suffrage and that the electorate mainly consists of propertied classes. Since the rich control the basic livelihood of the poor, the poor are often compelled to ingratiate themselves to the rich, and this situation prevails among men as well as among women. Moreover, the poor, be they workers or bondservants, make up the majority by far among women; and these women depend upon the rich for food and clothing. How can we be sure that a working-class woman would not vote according to the desires of the rich lady on whom she depends for her livelihood? Having followed the ways in which countries where universal suffrage has taken effect choose their parliamentary members from among the affluent classes, we may predict what would happen when women begin to participate in universal suffrage. There is little doubt that female members of parliament would originate from the upper classes. My examples make it abundantly clear that the roots of social inequities reside in the system of parliamentary representation itself.

Some may hasten to point out that the women's movement in Finland has been driven to a large degree by ordinary people. As the first elected female member of the parliament[27] puts it, women who come to occupy political office should never play the role of assistants to men who perpetrate social inequities; where women's own interests are concerned, it is reasonable [for female members of parliament] to serve the majority of women. However, reality may well contradict her statement. In the beginnings of the French Revolution and the American Revolution, idealistic revolutionaries wanted to overthrow the Crown to establish a republic. They, too, assumed that the [French] parliament or [U.S.] Congress was created by the people and, therefore, it would never engage in a politics of domination. The people's elected representatives did follow through on their promises and endeavored to help the people and oppose dictatorships. They persevered courageously and admirably in tending to the happiness of the people, and their power of resistance was by no means inferior to that of Finnish women. But as time passed, the politics of parliamentary representation began to erode and became an oppressive force. Its troubles are deeply felt and are revealed by the manifestos of the Social Democrats and by the numerous oppositional publications of labor movements. It is clear that in recent years, government officials have become the most oppressive force in both France and the United States and seem much worse than the people's party[28] in the past. The progressive force that had once rejected the Crown to empower the people to participate in national politics has become itself the exact double of what it used to oppose. This suggests that oppression is bound to emerge from where power is born as long as the rule of man is not abolished.

The admirable courage of Finnish women members of parliament must be commended. But I am afraid that it will not take many decades

---

[27]Tr: The Finnish MP's name is transcribed as Bu-li-bai-er-ke, but we have been unable to identify this person. Of the list of nineteen female Finnish parliamentarians of the period, none has a name that fits this phonetic transcription.

[28]Tr: We are not sure to what He-Yin is referring here: the Democratic Party? Perhaps some other party.

before their absolute reliance on the politics of parliamentary representation converts elected women into the oppressors of women at large. The mirrors of France and the United States will help us understand this process. Some may also observe how contemporary European and American women have joined the Social Democratic Party to promote women's suffrage, thereby concluding that women's suffrage is becoming a worldwide trend. The idea derives from the assumption that by securing women's universal rights to vote with the help of the Social Democrats, the majority of women can hope to obtain freedom. But the truth of this claim can hardly be substantiated. The Social Democrats insist on parliamentary representation, and their political movements have gained the support of ordinary citizens. The Social Democrats hold sway among the working class and are amply qualified to be elected members of parliament or even to occupy the seats of the majority party, as has been the case in Australia this year. Before being elected, Social Democrats had vowed to reform the economic order by opposing the interests of the rich and seeking liberation on behalf of the majority of ordinary citizens. Now that Social Democrats have joined the ranks of parliamentary representation and more than one of them has been elected, the opportunity to promote the interest of the common people has finally arrived. But let us look at what has happened. The laboring classes find themselves caught up in the same wage system as before, and they are enslaved by the rich and suffer the same exploitation as before. With increased participation in electoral politics, which has strengthened the hand of a political party and allowed the Social Democrats to manipulate politics the way they want, one would expect the work of reform to be less formidable than before; yet how much longer are we supposed to wait before the goal of reform is achieved? The record of the Social Democratic Party has demonstrated that the successful entrance into the politics of parliamentary representation cannot guarantee the welfare of the majority of poor people. By the same token, we cannot expect the women within the Social Democratic Party to work on behalf of the majority of working-class women. What may very well happen is that a handful of women will earn the empty title of political representation and nothing more. Those who are deluded by it may think that women's liberation must be preceded by their participation in the politics of parliamentary representation. As we reflect on the situation of those countries where the Social Democrats have participated in parliamentary representation, we should ask if the laboring masses have been liberated as they were promised. This may provide further evidence, for no sooner do Social Democrats throw themselves into this politics than their original goal gives way to a politics whereby they flatter ordinary citizens from below and curry favor with those in power from above. They take advantage of the majority vote from the poor people to benefit themselves and can seldom avoid being caught up in insidious politics. Why should women be an exception to this?

Clearly, fundamental reforms must be introduced if universal equality is to be achieved for the majority of women. It would be far better to relinquish the struggle for universal suffrage lest we lend a hand to the small minority of women who may win political office. The majority of women used to be oppressed by two major forces in the world: the government on the one hand and men on the other. Today, women are being subjected to a third force next to the oppressive forces of the government and men, and this third force is upper-class women who inflict yet another layer of oppression upon them. Even if the oppression has not tripled, they are still taken advantage of by upper-class women. And what do the majority of women gain? Is this what the women's liberation movement amounts to?

When the women's suffrage movement first began in Finland, women agitated for their cause, raised funds, published pamphlets, made rounds in towns and villages, and condemned social oppression. Those who followed their teaching jumped into action and dedicated themselves to the social cause. These women risked their lives in the struggle for freedom. Some carried out undercover activities, and others openly attacked the government. Acts of assassination and violent uprisings in those days were not infrequent. They defied the dangers of being exiled to Siberia or being sentenced to life in prison. In their exemplary bravery and fearless spirit of struggle, Finnish women stood at the head of European and American women. Had they persevered in this struggle, they might have been able to effect fundamental changes in society and to overturn the rule of man and masculine domination completely. But when they saw how difficult it was to reach the goal, they began to develop a faith instead in parliamentary representation, with the sole objective of obtaining equal rights for women. There is no doubt that these women knew how to oppose the violent rule of the aristocracy and of government, but they had no way of freeing themselves from the trap of government. It is extremely foolish of them to commit this grave policy error. My fervent hope is that women of the world would not regard the Finnish women as their sole model.

In sum, the question of women's liberation is one of enabling each and every woman to partake in the joys of freedom. The current discourse of women's liberation means the following: first, professional independence for women; and second, women's equal rights to participate in political office. It is not clear whether so-called professional independence means the independence of individuals or of women as a collective. If one individual achieves her professional independence, it does not follow that the majority of women will achieve the same independence. If they are referring instead to the professional independence of women as a collective, then a more appropriate description would be professional enslavement; for in the organization of today's economy, a handful of rich people monopolizes the means of production, whereas the unemployment of ordinary citizens goes up day by day. If women's profession can be said to be independent, so-called independence only means their submission to economic exploitation. How can women obtain their freedom and liberation in these circumstances? So rather than insisting that professional independence can lead to women's liberation, it is far better to suggest that women can be liberated only when common property (*gongchan*) is established.

As for equal rights, we must understand that men have held such rights for many centuries and that rights cannot easily become equal in haste. Even if equal rights could thus be effected, it would not allow everyone to participate equally in politics; in effect, a small minority of women in political office would occupy positions of domination. They would rule the majority of powerless women and not only would the disparity between man and women continue, a disparity among the different classes of women would also emerge. Does it look likely that the great majority of women who reject the rule of men would submit to the rule of other women? So rather than wrest power from men, modern women should aim to overturn the rule of man by compelling men to renounce their privileges and power and humble themselves so man and woman can achieve equality on woman's terms.

In my view, the ultimate goal of women's liberation is to free the world from the rule of man and from the rule of woman. Herein lies fundamental reform: how not to allow the struggle for universal suffrage as stipulated by parliamentary representation to limit our efforts? I would be gratified to see women renounce their desire to mobilize with the objective of governmental rule and to begin to look toward the eventual abolition of government.

Originally published in *Tianyi*, no. 7 (September 1907): pp. 5–14; triple issue nos. 8–10 (October 1907): pp. 187–192. Signed Zhen Shu (authored by Zhen). Reprinted in Wan Shiguo, ed., *Liu Shenshu yishu buyi* [Supplementary additions to collected works of Liu Shipei] (Yangzhou, China: Guangling Press, 2008), pp. 776–785. Translated by Lydia H. Liu from the Chinese original "Nüzi jiefang wenti 女子解放問題." (The title in the combined issue nos. 8–10, "Furen jiefang wenti" 婦人解放問題, varies slightly from that of no. 7, in which *nüzi* is used for "women" instead of *furen*.)

"On the Question of Women's Labor"

He-Yin Zhen (1907)

From ancient times to the present, China has had an unequal system with regard to women. It is called slave girl keeping (*xu bi*).

From the most ancient of eras, men have looked upon all women with the same gaze they use to contemplate slaves and servant girls. With the exception of wives, all other [women] are named as slave and servant girls. This began as early as the Three Dynasties. The [second-century dictionary] *Analysis and Explication of Written Characters* (*Shuowen*) states flatly that in ancient times slaves were criminals by another name. The *Rites of Zhou* (*Zhou Li*) concurs: "Slave—punish a man with charges of indictment; punish a woman by servile labor of husking grain." The gloss by scholar Zheng Sinong (d. 83 C.E.) elaborates: "This is called punishing people by enslaving them. Of old, those who were condemned with charges of indictment or to surveilled grain husking were precisely those who were named slaves." It is thus clear that "slave girls" (*bi*) in ancient times were women who had committed an offense; their punishment of servile labor is entirely similar to the Western legal device of commitment to hard labor.

When the well-field system was in practice, the common people began to accrue property, with one husband and one wife jointly occupying land consisting of a hundred *mu*.[1] At that time, unemployed women were a small

---

[1] Tr: The well-field system is commonly understood to have been in effect during the Western Zhou dynasty; it was a system of equal land distribution. A *mu* is a measure of land (.16 acres). The translator has omitted interlinear notes from the *Rites of Zhou* and the official histories.

minority and most were saved from having to serve wealthy families. It was only after the Warring States period [and] Qin and Han dynasties (after 220 c.e.) that ordinary people were subjected to being bought as slaves and that women began to be employed as servants in increasing numbers, and not only as punishment for a crime. In this way, they lost the right to their bodily freedom. Then, in the Han dynasty, selling people came to be strictly regulated. To kill a slave girl became a punishable offense. Branding a slave with a hot iron was banned. And, in 108 c.e. Emperor An of the Later Han dynasty announced that slave girls sold into an official household were to be reverted to commoner status. By the Tang dynasty, men and women of decent families were prohibited by the text of the law from presenting themselves as slaves. Although oblivious to the principle of the equality of humankind, these laws are in fact compatible with our respect for human rights (*renquan zhi dao*).[2]

In the midst of the Mongol conquest of China, an unequal system treating Han people as enslaved prisoners of war was established by the so-called system of transfer sales [of such prisoners], by so-called promotional distribution [of such prisoners], and by so-called occupation and confiscation. Even worse, there were codes equating slaves with cows and horses. The Ming dynasty inherited the defects of Mongol law, whereby the households of officials and scholars frequently inflicted cruel corporeal punishment on their slaves. As the Manchus moved into the interior, in the provinces of Zhejiang, Fujian, Yunnan, and Guangdong, they openly kidnapped men and women in numbers reaching the tens of thousands so as to distribute [the prisoners] to their loyal bannermen; even women of decent families whose husbands were accused of crimes were bestowed upon the armored troops as slaves. It could be that the above system originated in ethnic or racial issues (*zhongzu*) or that it originated for political reasons. Today, it is impossible to say. However, what we can say is that in China, from the time of the Mongols, the number of elite families enslaving female servants rose exponentially. How can it be that this is entirely due to the invasion and robbery by alien peoples? Or, some may argue that the Mongols and Manchus established the system of slavery and the wealthy and prominent Han families emulated and appropriated this practice. Although plausible at first glance, this explanation is ultimately wide of the mark.

---

[2]Tr: Each of the above statements is followed by a relevant citation to a classic. Those have been omitted. Emperor An's measure of leniency was enacted in a year of widespread famine.

For the system of slavery does not originate in the class system; rather, it originates in the problem of livelihood (*shengji wenti*). It is for this reason that from the time of the Three Dynasties onward, the problem of rich-poor differentiation has become exasperated by the day. For the wealthy, land is consolidated from adjoining fields. They accumulate wealth either as merchants or officials. Whereas the interest of the poor is gradually expropriated by the rich by forcing them to cultivate land and then collecting their harvest at the rate of five parts for every ten units, [so] there is no surplus left over. Or, in the case of the desperately poor [literally, those who have no ground on which to stick an awl], they cannot even dream of supporting their families.[3] They look at their hovels and misery grows; the more ignorant they are, the more children they have; they give birth to more and more girls—even in good years they teeter on the verge of not making ends meet, and in lean years the parents themselves are starving to death. They want to save themselves from perishing: because the love felt for girls is no match for the love felt for boys, thence comes the extensive practice of selling daughters to the wealthy for a pittance.

This is why the custom of keeping slave girls spread widely after the Qin-Han period. The Han philosopher Xu Gan (170–217) says in his *Balanced Discourses* (*Zhonglun*): "The families of the elite and merchants within the seas [in the empire] who possess myriad wealth employ servant-slaves; their numbers can be as high as the hundreds, or as low as the tens." Hence, sage thinkers in the past have long criticized this slave system. With the Mongol invasion of China, the number of households that came under its occupation numbered in the hundred thousands. They enslaved people to enrich themselves. In addition, because of the fertility of the soil of the Jiangnan region, the division and conferral of private taxing authority to ministers of the state grew many times over from the Han and Tang dynasties. Those people who lost their land as a consequence either died or migrated. In the "Biography of Zhang Dehui" of the *Yuan History* it says, "If weak people wish to protect themselves and their families, it is unavoidable for them to commandeer themselves to the rich and powerful; in due time they degenerate into household slaves."

The *Yuan History*'s account details only the reasons for the establishment of the system of slave keeping. Yet, the system of rearing female servants

---

[3]Tr: Here, she uses a line from Mencius: "Looking up, they have sufficient with which to serve their parents; looking down, they have sufficient with which to support their wives and children."

must arise from this period. When a man became a slave, it is likely that he also sold his daughters. In the Ming dynasty, half of the dry arable land belonged to the families of ministers who aided the founding emperor; and in Jiangsu and Zhejiang, land tax was particularly heavy. As a result, the poor lost work at a rate not unlike that of the Mongol dynasty.

Since modern times, those without any land have become the majority: one out of ten is a landlord, and nine out of ten are tenant farmers, resulting in the landlord getting richer and the tillers getting poorer. If by accidental misfortune there is the disaster of a drought or flood, then the tillers must flee and lose everything. I heard that one year some time ago in Shanxi, a drought covered more than a thousand *li*; more recently, there were disasters in Xuhai, northern Anhui, Hunan, and Yunnan, where the number of people who had to flee was in the millions. When they came upon a slightly more well-off area, weak little girls vied to sell themselves to the rich. Some thus garnered several thousand cash.[4] Extending this logic, over the past several centuries, the people have suffered from innumerable random calamities, so we can only imagine the number of daughters sold through this time. And then, in the Huaiyang region of Jiangsu, the agricultural population is large; they till the soil for others, and their incomes are insufficient. When their daughters reach the age of ten, they are routinely sold to the families of gentry and merchants. Although this is an evil practice of one small region, its logic can certainly be extended to cover the more than ten provinces of [central] China, from which we can see that when people's livelihood is threatened, they will most likely act in the same way as those of Huaiyang and sell their daughters in huge numbers.

In this sense, the selling of daughters originates in poverty; poverty originates from the fact that property is not equally distributed. People tend to blame only the rich for keeping slave girls, but do they ever realize that the misery of the people who are forced to sell their daughters is also the fault of the rich? The poor have the bitterness of selling daughters; the rich have the joy of keeping slave girls. Does this not contradict principles of common justice?

When poor daughters are sold to the wealthy, the amount of bitterness they suffer is too much even to mention. The capacity [of a slave girl] to live or die lies in the hands of the mistress of the house: either they [the slave girls] can

---

[4]Tr: Money was volatile at the time. "Cash" refers to an amount of copper, although precisely how much is not clear. The amount will not have been sizable, however.

be flogged with a whip; or they can be branded; or their skin can be pierced with sharp instruments; or their bodies can be doused in boiling water. If they want to escape, they cannot; even if they want to die, they have no way to make a plan. There are some who are killed through illegal torture; some who die from suicide; and those who die off in epidemics are too numerous even to record. Aside from this, the harsh industriousness with which they must serve is not at all different from that of the black slaves of the southern United States. They can all be considered those who have lost the right both to freedom and to life. The philosopher Xu Gan says: "Although slave girls are mean and worthless, they embody the five constant virtues.[5] When the emperor's commoners (*liangmin*) are turned into the demeaned (*xiaoren*), alas, pity the poor for losing everything, and yet there is no recourse." And isn't it just so?! Thus, the system of female enslavement is a huge tragedy for girls. Outside of the American South where black slavery existed, in Europe the system was curtailed earlier. Hence today, Chinese officials and commoners all deeply deplore the crime of enslaving girls, and yet families of middling means and higher continue to implement this system. Is this not the bitterest part of women's labor? Is not the reason that women lose the right to their bodily freedom and the freedom of their lives because they must labor?

Even though China's system of enslaving girls is harsh and oppressive, the benefits that the wealthy obtain from this enslavement are the use of the [slave girls'] service without the accruing of wealth. Hence, the reason that poor girls become slaves originates in the problem of livelihood and has nothing to do with the class system. But on the part of the rich who keep slaves, the problem of livelihood never enters their minds. [For them it is a matter of class.][6] Thus although there is a class system in China, the motive for self-enrichment is weaker than that among slave-owners in the American South.[7]

---

[5]Tr: These are *ren* (benevolence), *yi* (righteousness), *li* (propriety), *zhi* (knowledge), *xin* (sincerity). It is another way of saying that slave girls were human too.

[6]Tr: The argument He-Yin is making is that there is not a particular "class" of people who are enslaved; rather, slavery is contingent on poverty—although, from the perspective of the rich, poor people *constitute* a class of potentially enslavable labor. The analytic distinction she draws between "class" (*jieji*) and "livelihood" (*shengji*) is significant. For an elaboration, see the introduction to this volume.

[7]In the American South, the slave system used black slaves to produce profit [by growing cash crops], specifically the exhausting tasks of growing cotton and planting crops, which could not do without the labor of black slaves. The slave-owners themselves rested in leisure.

When we consider the modern situation of the various countries of Euro-America and the use of girls as instruments of wealth, then the system is even more unjust. From the nineteenth century onward, the wealthy have embraced capital in order to accumulate more wealth. And yet wealth cannot be generated from one person; it must grow from the employ of the services of others in one's own interests and for one's own gain. In a word, it is poor people's labor power that is offered so the wealthy can accumulate more wealth. In the beginning they used only men but later extended the practice to female labor. We can surmise that women's service began for two primary reasons: one is that in premodern times, machine industry was not yet developed and women had to spin and weave in their homes. This can be seen as free or voluntary employment. The materials that they produced were sold in the market. This was the condition for the freedom of labor and the condition for the freedom of trade. However, as factories arose, wealthy people used the black arts of pursuing profit to gain a victory over the poor. Then, mechanization flourished and the poor were not well-placed to take advantage of it. As a consequence, the means of production soon fell into the exclusive hands of the rich, such that the industries undertaken by poor girls were the first to be monopolized, and [the poor girls] could not but work for the rich.

The Japanese Tazoe Tetsuji's book *Economic Evolution* says: "Before the flourishing of mechanized industry, the world of women's production was limited to the labor used to serve the family and she was the family production queen. This was a glorious labor service; a sovereign and independent labor service. When family production changed into factory production, the sphere of women's productive employment was increasingly diminished. Day by day women became oppressed by poverty. It reached the point where women could but rely upon capitalists for a living, catering to their every whim. They had to throw their bodies into the factories, and the olden days of being the queen of family production were thus incorporated into the wage system. Women were rendered into laborers for this system." Although his words are a little brief, they are useful to examine two of the reasons that women became waged laborers.

The first reason is that the increase in factories led to an increase in the production of goods; items that were not useful for the everyday lives of regular people became more numerous, and more people were engaged in producing meaningless items (such as luxury items). As a consequence, the items of daily use required by the people became scarcer by the day and their prices became dearer by the day. As the price of items became costlier, then the wages of men became insufficient to cover them and the survival of the family came to depend upon women, who had no choice but to go out to seek food for the morrow. [The second reason is as] the American labor secretary[8] says: "In olden times, the livelihood of a family was generally dependent upon a man's income. When he becomes a waged laborer, he has to use his wages to provide for his family. But he tends to be constantly short of two thirds of his family's needs. This forces women and children to earn an income as a supplement. Even children under fifteen years of age have to contribute to the family income; the least they contribute is up to one-eighth, the most they are able to contribute is up to one-sixth. This is a general tendency for children, not to mention women." Even though this is a description of America, this kind of situation is hardly limited to America. The various countries of Europe are not dissimilar in this regard. This is the second reason.

From these two perspectives, who cannot see that the reasons for women's labor are unequal distribution of property as well as the crime of capitalists?

Currently, the number of women laborers is increasing daily. For example, in 1870, of the laboring people in North America, 8,600 in 10,000 were men and 1,400 were women; in 1880, 8,500 of 10,000 were men and 1,500 were women; in 1890, 8,200 in 10,000 were men and 1,700 were women [sic]. And from 1841 to 1891 in England, the number of male laborers increased only by three-fifths, whereas the number of female laborers doubled twice over. From this we can assume that in recent years in the various countries of Euro-America, female labor has increased by a good deal over the levels of a decade ago. In Japan alone, according to a Meiji 32 [1900] survey, there were 2,752 factories nationwide and they employed 392, 902 people of whom around 138,115 were men and 254,787 were women. The number of women laborers was hence almost two times the number of male laborers.

That the most strenuous labor was all being heaped onto the bodies of women—how can this not be a major tragedy of the world? How is this not the case of the society of the wealthy *using women as instruments of wealth accumulation*?

---

[8]Tr: He-Yin gives the name Xi-de-la-yi-tu, which is likely to have been transliterated from Japanese katakana. The secretary of commerce and labor at the time was Oscar S. Straus, who served from 1906 to 1909.

In the various Euro-American countries, one can find no more cruel and strict regulations on women's work than those of the factory. For example, if one is five minutes late, one is locked out of the factory for a half day and one's wages for that time are thus forfeit. In addition, inside the factory, even though women and men have their own work areas, yet they have to share sanitary facilities, which is extremely embarrassing to women. These two examples suffice to show that in the hearts of the wealthy there is only self-interest and there is no consideration for the female workers.

An American newspaper from New York[9] published an item entitled "Record of a Woman's Lot." It says: "Married women stay in the home as wives and mothers and they also are the major caretakers of the family. As soon as they leave their beds in the morning, they begin their labor, which only ends when they go back to bed in the evening. Further, even after a wife has gone to bed her work is still not done—for example, if her child is suffering from some illness, then she may not rest for the whole night. The next morning, at eight she must again get up to expend her labor." And the Japanese author Kaneko Kiichi says: "A woman's labor is society's crime. The words 'the problem of women's labor' have an incredibly cruel sound." He also says: "After a laboring woman gets married, her horizons are still more tragic; she is trapped in a narrow well where she spends her life. This is the fate of women laborers." The book *Economic Evolution* by Tazoe Tetsuji says: "In the contemporary industrial world, examining the major trends in women's labor reveals that women are constrained by the wage system. I'm afraid there is no hope for freedom [from it]." He continues that "as long as the responsibility of a family's livelihood is shared by both men and women, the bitterness of competing for survival will permeate family relations. Between wife and husband, between sons and their elders, as well as between parents and children, all will vie with one another on the basis of the wages each pulls in. When income sinks, not only will the livelihood of the family be endangered, the family's happiness and harmony also might be jeopardized." Then, for the reasons stated, women's labor will not only harm the woman's own body, but the family's happiness and harmony will also be ruined. If we seek an explanation, how can this not be because of the capitalists? If the women of the whole country are driven to the edge of poverty, is this not because capitalists monopolize the profits of the market?

[9]Tr: He-Yin gives the title of the newspaper as *Xi-yu-nuo-jie*. Could it be the *Syracuse Herald*?

However, there are those who say that women are free to seek waged work or otherwise. But if they were not on the verge of poverty, why would they beg for food from factories? What the capitalists have done to women is tantamount to first stealing clothing and food from them so as to force them to take the one-way trip into the factories to labor. Some say that a woman is free to enter the factory just as she is free to resign from the factory; hence factory work is different from being sold into servitude. But how is it different when, aside from working, there is no way for the woman to survive? This is no less than forcing innumerable women to sell their bodies in reality if not in name. [The capitalists] use others' labor power to accumulate wealth for themselves. They force people into poverty and use that poverty to pile up riches for themselves. What does this exhibit other than a perspective on laborers as more worthless than used-up goods? In ancient times, people treated women as playthings; today, people treat women as instruments. Seeing women as playthings degrades women's bodies; yet seeing women as instruments not only degrades [a woman's] body but also exhausts her labor power. The crime of the capitalists can be said to reach up to high heavens.

The good thing is that recently, in Europe and America, one can read in the newspapers of many countries about women's unions and strikes. As for Japan, groups of laborers, encouraged by socialism, often decry inequality. Women laborers there support unions and strikes. Take, for example, the silk workers of Gunma Prefecture. On July 6, 300 female workers at the silk-reeling factory there rose up in struggle protesting the imposition of overtime, the disgusting food, and the lasciviousness and violence of the management. They shattered the factory windows. After a few days, once the fulfillment of the women's demands had been promised, they went back to work. For another example, take the copper mine at Kaga Prefecture. The mine is in the Yusenji Temple and employs one hundred women as miners. Because of the lowering of wages, on July 7 they demanded a raise. The managers acceded, averting much chaos. Aside from these two incidents, in Yokohama there was a garment factory that stopped production because Chinese and Japanese women united together into a large chaotic riot against it. It is evident from this that the thinking of these working women is quite progressive. If these workers build on their achievements and move forward to effect fundamental reform, then they are likely to demand the equal distribution of property. This would expropriate the power and profits of the wealthy, and the workers would no longer have to labor for others. If this happens, it would be a great blessing to the world's women.

In contrast, in China from past to present, some poor women have lowered themselves to become maids, concubines, and prostitutes; whereas others have constantly striven to support themselves. For example, the silk-reeling workshops of Western Zhejiang and cotton-spinning and -weaving workshops in northern Jiangsu have both relied on women's labor. Other tasks such as embroidery and sewing have also been common occupations for poor women. The most miserable fact is that their survival depends entirely on their ten fingers. From morning 'til night, they industriously engage in needlework. Hence a Tang poem laments, "Bitterly I loathe the gold threads year after year,/ Expended in making wedding dresses for others."

As for recent times, livelihood is even more difficult to secure, and women who undertake this line of work are especially numerous. For [the traditional livelihood of] weaving cloth and selling silk for food is far preferable to serving others. It all has changed today. The government and the people alike are abandoning the basic [principles of livelihood] and chasing after the peripherals. They exaggerate the benefits of industrial enterprise. Every province is now gradually building factories and employing poor people. As this trend grows stronger by the day, the silk and cotton industries will soon be monopolized by the wealthy; they are likely to expand their companies so as to block the people's interest. The poor women who had relied on weaving and sewing for their livelihood in the past are likely to see the prices of their goods plummet, and they will become poorer and poorer. If we add in the fact that the weaving industry is now switching over to machines, which are not within the reach of poor people's pocketbooks, and that Western skills are being transmitted as specializations in schools and that poor women have no money for tuition, then we can know that from this time onward, those women who will lose employment will increase exponentially by the day. As those who lose their livelihood become more numerous and as the factories operated by the wealthy become more numerous, inevitably poor women will have to sell their bodies to the factory and be employed by them. The wages they will derive will necessarily be much lower than those of Westerners.

The history of our Chinese women sinking into bodily slavery is very long! Today, they are the slaves of capitalists, whereas of old they only were being ordered around as servants. Today, in addition, they are the instruments of the production of wealth. The so-called "Study of Wealth and Power" (*Fuqiang Xue*) is a kind of learning that forces people into bitter lives.[10] The system of buying and selling labor power emerges from this. If today we wish to prevent this from happening and to save our compatriot women, inevitably we must eliminate the approach proposed by the wealth and power reformers; inevitably, we must kill all capitalists.

Today, there are four types of difficulties into which women can fall. The lowest is prostitution, next is concubinage, next is bond servitude (those whose bodies are sold into service), and highest are those who are hired domestic servants and factory workers. The lives of women in these four categories are quite different, and yet the reasons they fall into these situations *come from absolutely the same conditions*: this reason is nothing but *the problem of livelihood*; or, *the unequal distribution of wealth*. The circumstances of bondservants, regular servants, and factory girls were described earlier. Here we must discuss the circumstances of prostitutes and concubines.

The practice of taking concubines is most widespread in China. If one investigates where these concubines come from, there are those who were prostitutes but who were able to escape the brothel quarters and their registration [as prostitutes]; there are those who had been bondservants but who became favored by their masters; and there are those who were bought from poor people's families.[11] Prostitutes and bondservants all emerge from poor families, meaning that the evil ways of concubinage and prostitution all are created from reasons of poverty.[12] And yet, this can under no circumstances be blamed upon poor people. The wealthy grow wealthier as they expropriate common people's interests or benefits, which leads to increasing poverty among common people. Because they are poor, they sell their daughters; because they sell their daughters, the number of prostitutes and concubines rises daily. Hence, instead of saying that the systems of prostitution

---

[10]Tr: *Fuqiang Xue*, what we translate as "The Study of Wealth and Power," was a school of thought deriving from classical nineteenth-century European political economy, specifically Herbert Spencer's sociological study of the "survival of the fittest" as filtered through Yan Fu's translations. See "The Historical Context," in this volume, for background.

[11]Aside from these three types, there are also those who were prisoners captured during wars or those abducted by aristocratic families. But each of these is quite a minor percentage of the total, so they are left out of the discussion.

[12]Prostitutes of ancient times came from families convicted of crimes and thus were entered into prostitute registration; today is not the same.

and concubinage originate from poor families, it is better to say that they originate in rich families. The result is that *poor girls suffer the bitterness of concubinage and prostitution while wealthy people savor the joys of owning concubines and patronizing prostitutes.*

As such, it is the desires of the wealthy that encourage poor families to rear prostitutes and concubines in preparation for the indulgence of such desires. When people say, "To be rich and mean," isn't that what they have in mind? I observe that in China, prostitutes might emerge from decent families (*liangjia*) where either the father is dead and the mother survives or the mother is dead and the father survives, where the family owns nothing but the four walls of the house, where survival and debt inevitably force them to sell their bodies so as to alleviate their parents' difficulties. Or, they are driven by starvation to go on the road but have no means to return home. Then they sell themselves to the wealthy, and afterward they are either subjugated to the first wife or eventually become estranged from the man because of the failure to produce a son. If the man dies, even though the widow might still be young, she will never marry again for the rest of her life. The bitterness she will suffer is more than can be narrated aloud or in writing.

As for reasons a woman becomes a prostitute, [she may do so because of] either her family being poor and her parents selling her or her having been seduced and raped by a procurer and then sold.[13] Thereby the prostitute not only suffers from the shame of having her body insulted, she is also subject to being flogged, which is no different from being a bondservant. In the lyrics composed by poets of the Tang and Song dynasties, the resentment felt by prostitutes is often palpable. Hence, we know that they did not submit to prostitution willingly.

New York City is one of the cities in which prostitution thrives. Recently, some people in New York began to inquire why women became prostitutes. They conducted a survey of 2,000 women, of whom over 520 said it was because of poverty. In addition, there was a newspaper in America that published a prostitute's record of her life in which she narrated the story of poverty leading to the bitterness of prostitution. In China, newspapers often tell of the affairs of famous prostitutes, mourning the misfortunes that they

---

[13]The crime of the procurer stinks up to high heavens, but he does this only because of the profit motive. In a world of communal property one would not find this kind of procurer in any country.

encounter while deeply sympathetic to their plight. What other cause is there beside poverty? Indeed, the disgrace of prostitution and concubinage is brought on by the wealthy people who ensnare women. *It is not just the fault of women.* Unaware of this, people of the world often call prostitutes and concubines insulting names—aren't they pathetic?

How can the crimes of the wealthy be said to be limited to forcing women into the bitterness of prostitution and concubinage? In every well-trafficked or major city, where the rich and big merchants reside, the number of prostitutes is many times greater than in other places. In the homes of high officials or large extended families, the number of concubines can reach more than ten. Thus, it must be that the majority of those who keep concubines or patronize prostitutes are the wealthy. As for the women, they become prostitutes in return for a pittance; they become concubines in the hopes of obtaining abundant clothes and food; they cannot help but vie among themselves to coddle the wealthy. As for the wealthy, [prostitution and concubinage amount to using] an indirect method of seizing the property of the poor as well as an indirect method of raping the daughters of the poor. In this world, only those who wallow in idle indolence and ignorance tend to indulge in pleasures of the flesh. Ji of Lu[14] has a saying: When the people are idle, they become lewd. Today in China, there is an analogous saying that goes: Once people's stomachs are full and bodies warm, they will think of debauchery and licentious pleasure. So, are not those who enjoy debauchery the wealthy? It is clear: a country's trends in dissoluteness originate in the places where the wealthy live in large numbers. Daily, the wealthy encounter prostitutes and sometimes take them as concubines. The daughters to whom they give birth receive the inheritance [of their lewd nature]. Even though these daughters come from wealthy families, they openly act like prostitutes. How could this be the natural tendency of women? Not only have these women inherited lewd behavior, they also are exposed to the lewd behavior [of their parents]. So, those daughters born of licentiousness embody the shame of the wealthy. Indeed, they are the fruits of the wealthy, who debauch poor women. This is one indirect means through which the wealthy ruin the virtue of women.

Some say that the large number of prostitutes is attributable to the fact that there are more girls than boys. [It is said that] if there were no

---

[14]Tr: Ji of Lu, or Lu Jingjiang, was a virtuous woman listed in the *Biographies of Exemplary Women.*

prostitution and concubinage, then in the outer world there would be no unmarried men but in the inner chambers there would be many spinsters. Indeed, in the mountains there are more men and in the damp climes there are more women; in a world in which communication is underdeveloped and migration has yet to become a trend, the numbers of men and women [in a population] would not be equal. In the Americas there are more women, and in Tibet and Gansu there are more men; each place provides clear evidence of this fact. This is especially true in China. The number of women in the regions south of the Yangzi River [Jiangnan] is relatively large, whereas in the north, the number of men is not fewer than that of women: it is entirely dissimilar to the situation in America, where the number of women exceeds the number of men. So why are there so many prostitutes and concubines in China? In fact, in the region between Jiangsu and Anhui, women are not especially numerous. Yet in the various cities of the southeast, half of the prostitutes come from Huiyang. And those wealthy people who purchase concubines often choose them from Yangzhou. In such places as Yancheng, Xinghua, and Gaoyou, among the lower classes one woman belongs to many men; or younger and older brothers share a wife. In Yangzhou, peasants who have many sons always provide a wife for the eldest, whereas the sons next in line can never marry. One more example will suffice to illustrate the point sufficiently: a country with a system of one man and many wives has to have a system of one woman and many husbands. Moreover, there have to be a certain number of men who have no wives, and those without wives are sure to be the poor.

Although all are equally parts of humanity, some indulge in pleasures of debauchery, whereas others suffer from living alone. Out of the gap between having and not having money emerges as the distinction between bitterness and joy. Thus the evil of the wealthy lies not only in raping the daughters of the poor but also in tacitly stealing the wives of the poor. Instead of saying the rich are the enemy of women, might it be better to say that the rich are the enemy of the poor? If one wishes to save poor women, what other ways are there but to get rid of the rich?

In contemporary Euro-America, many believe that prostitution is detrimental to social customs and advocate its abolishment. At the same time, they attack the concubine systems of both China and Turkey. Knowledgeable people in China also want to substitute monogamy for concubinage. Surely, it is not a bad thing to do away with the systems of prostitution and concubinage. However, the proliferation of prostitutes and concubines is not a question of customs; it is a problem of livelihood. As long as there is income inequality between rich and poor, neither prostitution nor concubinage can disappear quickly. Even if one were suddenly to pronounce them dissolved, perhaps the names would be gone, but the reality would persist.

In Euro-American countries, the concubine custom does not exist. There is freedom of marriage and divorce. Yet their so-called marriages are no different from the property-based marriages of savages. According to Western people's newspaper reports and the narratives of novels, the majority of marriages among the rich and aristocratic are primarily based upon property: if a woman is rich, many men desire her; if a man is rich, many women fall in love with him. There are women's families whose fortunes fall, and the man quickly ends the engagement; there are men who use their wealth to bully hapless women into marrying them. In a word, today's system of marriage is one that weds the desire for flesh to the lust for money. The most miserable cases involve talented and intelligent orphan girls. A rich man falls in love with her, but she is not interested. He uses his money to win over her relatives and then coerces her to marry him. Concerned that he will lose face with other prominent families for marrying a poor daughter, he keeps the wedding a secret. And as she becomes old, the man's love also falters. Hence, incidences of divorce are too numerous to count. This is most prevalent in America.

According to the Japanese author Kaneko Kiichi: "The divorce problem in America originates in the fact that women are monopolized by the wealthy. What are marriages among the wealthy like? Their marriages with one another are in reality unions of flesh. If they love each other, they marry; if not, they divorce. There are seventeen- and eighteen-year-old girls who marry geezers over sixty years old. How is this a girl's desire? For women see themselves as a tool and offer their sex for a man's use; men see women as hired hands: yesterday he loved her, today he transfers his love to another. It is as if he is firing one and hiring another, and this is the reason why divorces and remarriages are so numerous." He also says, "The contemporary American wealthy and gentry are so amoral that they can be married twice, and there are those who even marry three and four times and also engage in adultery; where is society's censure?" From these words, we can see that the situation of poor women marrying rich men— which amounts to pawning their bodies—is no different from the system of selling daughters to become concubines in China. What would be the distinction?

Meanwhile, in Japan, concubinage is prohibited. But among those of moderate means and above, no one knows how many men take their servant girls as concubines or house concubines under separate roof. There is even a system of hiring concubines. So even though the name "concubine" might be erased, concubinage in reality persists. As for the issue of prostitutes, one could abandon the name and, although public prostitutes might be eliminated, private prostitution nevertheless would flourish by the day.

Now take a look at the countries of Europe, where the ages of men and women upon marriage for the wealthy is relatively young, whereas for the poor, it is later. Moreover, as for the law, those who debauch virgins are immune from punishment. Those women of the poor whose talent and appearance are relatively pleasant are often coerced or forced [to have sex] by the rich and aristocratic. The widespread nature of adultery and debauchery is also written about by an American author in "History of Prostitution." This author says that in the one city of New York, in 1895, there were thirty thousand private prostitutes, which means that approximately one of fifty-five city residents had to be a private prostitute. This number has risen to over fifty thousand in recent years. Could it be that all metropolitan centers in civilized countries are thus corrupt to the extreme? Also look at women in Japan: the number of private prostitutes is far greater than that of public ones. There are women who conduct this immoral business in their homes; there are those who, though married, do not stop their adultery. And as for women from decent families who were defiled by aristocrats and officials, they are impossible to keep records of.[15] When one goes to an inn or restaurant, one comes across several waitresses who are also selling themselves. How are they different from prostitutes? Not a few commentators say that Japan is a country of prostitutes. But do they know that Japanese women have fallen into such straits because of poverty?

Therefore, unless the system of communalized property is in place, there is no way to effect major reforms to improve people's livelihood. Simply reforming customs will not help. *Although eliminating prostitution and concubinage is spoken of all over the country*, neither public opinion nor

---

[15]As for the debauched conduct of Prince Ito, the whole country knows. But a Japanese paper published in America defended him by saying that Ito is extremely honest with women. How can they twist and conceal the truth like this? Tr: Prince Ito Hirobumi (1841–1909) was a noted politician in Meiji Japan who was assassinated in 1909 by a Korean nationalist. His womanizing was the topic of many cartoons and political comedies in the papers of the day.

legislative prohibition can stop poor women from becoming prostitutes and concubines. Nor can they stop the rich from patronizing prostitutes and keeping concubines. Even if the systems of prostitution and concubinage were eliminated in name, they would persist in reality.

Some say that in any place where wealthy people are numerous, they are likely to employ numerous service people. The women of the poor can seek employment as maids or factory girls to support themselves without resorting to becoming prostitutes or concubines. Little do they know that hired maids and factory girls are both subject to control by others and have lost their freedom; they are no different from prostitutes and concubines. In addition, as the number of factories increases, prices of life's necessities also soar. The wages of the factory girls are not sufficient to support even [the girls] themselves, and [the girls] cannot but help sink into a semiconcubine, semiprostituted state. According to American standards of employment, the daily hours of employment stretch from nine in the morning until ten at night; the wages are five florins [dollars] per week. This means that for every day, for thirteen hours of work, the wages are not even one dollar. No wonder they are poor and destitute!

An American newspaper in New York[16] published the honest words of a waged maid: "A worker's room and board costs three dollars a week; if it is raining or snowing, one needs to take a bus instead of walking. Although I do all my laundry myself, if we add up expenses for clothes, shoes, handbags, and other miscellaneous items, one cannot get by for less than two dollars per week." The fact that wages are not sufficient for sustenance is proven by this account. To prepare for the possible misfortune of losing one's employment, or falling physically ill, one needs to stow away some savings in advance. As a consequence, apart from working in one's main job, one needs to take on supplementary work prostituting oneself to make up the difference. Indeed, if there is insufficient provision for the necessities of life, one cannot help but sink into the immoral professions in order to survive. And the wealthy take advantage of poverty to indulge their own fleshly lust for a pittance. Therefore, accounts of hired maids also working as prostitutes frequently appear in New York newspapers.

By the same token, in Japan the wages for female housemaids are particularly meager. But even if one doubled the pay, there would still be prostitution. Why is this? Consider that a family must rely on their daughters'

---

[16]Tr: The transliterated title of the newspaper is *Bai-la-er-bu*.

supplementary income to make ends meet, and there is no money for her schooling; so, in Japan many sell themselves into a debauched life in order to save up enough to go to school. Can one blame women for this? It is the evil crime of society! Hired maids are for all intents and purposes half concubine and half prostitute.

The system of factory girls is particularly pitiful! In a newspaper in Kumamoto, Japan, there is an article entitled "Humble Voices of the Miserable." It reports on the state of violence in the Kanebo Textile Mill. It says: "[T]hey constrain factory girls like caged animals. They can be flogged with a whip or they can be denied food and drink." The paper also published an anonymous factory girl's letter, which said: "Hidden behind the textile company there are some very cruel and oppressive phenomena. Managers take workers into a separate room in order to enjoy debauched desires. Worried that they would escape, girls are absolutely forbidden from leaving the factory even when their fathers have fallen seriously ill or died. This is similar to the rules that govern prostitutes in brothels." Although in name the place is a bona fide textile corporation, in reality it is a field of misery. This is only one case [of many] in Japan.

Yet, extending this logic, one can surmise that in countries other than Japan, the number of girls hired in factories is huge. In these factories, there are bound to be those who use [the factory] as a cover for prostitution. Yet this is neither seen nor heard by most people. This is what the capitalists do to factory girls: they harm their eyesight, damage their health, diminish their happiness, and steal their virginity with their evil and dirty deeds. Therefore, that women lose their virtue is entirely perpetrated by the wealthy. Is the bitterness factory girls suffer any less than that of prostitutes? In China especially, wealthy families hire a lot more maids than do Westerners. Even when concubinage is condoned in broad daylight, maids are still susceptible to being raped. How much worse it would be if concubinage were outlawed! Those who want concubines would surely attain them under the cover of hiring maids. Indeed, there is simply no difference between servants and concubines.

In addition, in China wages are much lower than in Europe, America, or Japan. In due time, the silk and cotton industries will develop. This means they will have to hire more women, and yet the women will not receive enough wages to support themselves. It is entirely natural that they will make the same mistakes as the mills in Kumamoto. The more industrial establishments are formed, the more prostitutes there will be. If one just looks at the past situation in Euro-America and Japan, one can clearly know that *in a world of rich-poor inequality, the systems of prostitution and concubinage can never be eliminated.*

In sum, *in a world where property is not equal, those who escape being a concubine may not escape being prostitutes; those who escape being a prostitute may not escape being a factory girl or a servant. Even if one is a factory girl or a servant in name, prostitution is the hidden reality.* In addition, before the modern period, for those who were concubines and prostitutes, it was their bodies but not their labor power that were swallowed up; for bondservants, it was their labor power and not their bodies that was swallowed. But in today's system, *the bitterness of having both labor power and the body swallowed up is concentrated on the bodies of women of the poor.* The bodies of poor women cannot enjoy even an iota of freedom. Is it not the case that the misery of selling her body is already foretold in the buying and selling of her labor power? This is the foremost tragedy of women who labor. Women who wish to avoid this tragedy might want to promote all over the world the Fujianese custom of female infanticide; this would deny life to girls, thus sparing them a lifetime of bitterness. This is passive [resistance]. Yet aside from this, there is a form of active [resistance] that calls for the implementation of communalized property, where there is no differentiation between the wealthy and the poor. *This would allow poor women not to seek money by sacrificing their bodies and would prevent the rich from using their wealth* to satisfy their desires. It would also eliminate the system of women's employment, *thus overturning the trend toward semiprostitution and semiconcubinage.* In this way, one could save women from hardship.

Some argue that although the systems of prostitution and concubinage are surely evil, the employment of servants and factory girls—or an exchange of wages for labor—cannot be dismissed as unjust, so why is it necessary to abolish the system of women's employment? Little do they know that today we live in a world of mutual dependence. The wealthy depend upon the poor for their service and labor; the poor depend upon the wealthy for their clothing and food. The wealthy employ the labor of the poor; the poor employ the riches of the wealthy. If all of a sudden the wealthy were to lose their riches, or the poor to lose their capacity for labor, neither could stand autonomously. Indeed, the poor rely upon others to eat and have already thereby lost their right to independence; since the wealthy rely upon others for labor, can it not be said that they have also lost their right to independence? In this mutually dependent world, the wealthy cannot but sink into arrogance and indolence, and the poor cannot but sink into inferiority and cowardliness; morality is thus debased for all. Thoroughly uprooting the systems of servitude and working girls would go a long way toward correcting this culture of mutual dependence.

Labor is a natural calling for women. But everyone, not just poor women, should labor. When labor is borne only by some poor women, then it is a kind of subservient labor. So, in our opinion if there were the implementation of a system of communalized property, then everyone, whether man or woman, would labor equally. Those who expended a certain amount of labor toward [the production of] things of daily necessity to the people would enjoy the right of free use [of these products]. When employed labor is transformed into equal labor, then some people would no longer be dependent on other people; everyone would be independent—no one would have to rely on others, and no one would have to serve others. This would indeed be fortunate for the world. How could it be fortunate only for women?

This essay was originally split into two parts. As the break appears only to have been for publishing convenience, we present the essay without the break. Originally published in *Tianyi*, no. 5 (July 10, 1907): pp. 71–80; *Tianyi,* no. 6 (August 10, 1907): pp. 125–134. Editorial, signed Wei Gong 畏公. Reprinted in Wan Shiguo, pp. 744–755. Translated by Rebecca E. Karl; edited by Dorothy Ko from the Chinese original "Nüzi laodong wenti 女子勞動問題."

"Economic Revolution and Women's Revolution"

He-Yin Zhen (1907)

P ower in ancient times survived on brute force; from the Middle Ages
forward, power has survived on money. If in ancient times women
were controlled by brute force, then from the Middle Ages onward,
they have been controlled by money. This is a common and general principle the world over.

From the beginning of the earliest times, in addition to the communal
system (*gongchan zhidu* 共產制度) under which people lived, there also
was a system of shared wives and husbands. There was no private property,
and women were not controlled as anyone's possession. With the growth of
desires, some began to wish to take other people's things for their own; this
included wanting to turn the women of other tribes into private possessions.
Lust for sex and things gradually spread. Those with good weapons and the
strength to do so attacked other tribes; in addition to pillaging property, the
attackers also would plunder the best men and strongest women: men to
provide labor service (to increase production to the point of supplying others) and women to be the receivers of [sexual] favors. This is chronicled in
the ancient records of many countries and is recognized by all scholars of
society. It marks the beginning of the system of women as private property
as well as the beginning of the system of slavery; it is also the era in which
the communal system collapsed.

Hence, just as the systems of communal marriage and common property were linked, so were the systems of pillaging women for marriage and
slavery also linked at their very birth. And so it was that brute force became
the way to rule: separating the strong from the weak, creating division into

two classes. Both women and men were the objects of brute force, suppressed by those men with strength and power. Henceforth, slavery became the mode of production: whereas the weak expended their strength, the strong enjoyed their successes without effort; and the extremes of wealth and poverty gradually became more severe. Along with the severity of the extremes between wealth and poverty, some men were transformed from being slaves into being agrarian serfs;[1] today, they have entered the system of daily employed labor. Meanwhile, women went from a system of marriage through plunder and entered into a system of marriage by purchase; today, they have gone from the system of marriage by purchase to the system of one husband–one wife.

But the crux of the matter is that laboring people and women are all basically in a position of weakness. Since the Middle Ages, wealthy people have generally accepted the trend of the slave system and made others produce for them; they have expended their unproductive money to seduce laborers and women, forcing them to obey without choice. In this way, power by brute force has been transformed into power by money. If we look more closely, the system of daily employed labor is no different from agrarian serfdom, as both are slavery by another name. By the same token, today's one husband–one wife system is also no different from the system of marriage by purchase: it merely represents an apparent transformation from the system of marriage through plunder. I explain below.

In ancient times, the system of plundered marriage arose because of the desire to possess women as one's own. Today's system of marriage similarly is about women being possessed privately. Women can be privately possessed because men have power over money and can thus control the fate of women. Today's marriage, hence, is exactly marriage based on money. It would be no exaggeration to call it a form of property-marriage. In his story *The Lady from the Sea* (1888, *Hai zhi nü*), the European author Henryk Ibsen (1828–1906) writes: "Marriage in recent times is nothing but a woman selling her body to a man in order to escape a lifetime of difficulty and to provide for herself a livelihood. A man calculates his economic situation and buys a woman to marry. This is called marriage for purchase."[2] We can

---

[1] Tr: This corresponds to what would now be called feudalism, which He-Yin calls agrarian serfdom.

[2] Tr: This Ibsen play was not translated into Chinese until the 1920s. However, there was a Japanese translation by 上田敏訳 (Ueda Bin) under 海の夫人 and printed in the journal *Kokoro no Hana* in 1905. This translation was included in the "Anthology of Translated Literature of Meiji."

see from this passage that the relationship between men and women develops from an economic relationship. In accordance with this meaning, I will adduce the evidence for China next.

1. When parents select a match for their daughter, they first ask about the family's economic circumstances. Why is this? Is it not because in order to secure the livelihood of their daughter for her lifetime, they have to see if the man is able to provide for her or not?[3]

2. Women of poor families or those without parents often are raised in the families of their husbands before they marry. This is called child bride marriage. It means being tortured by one's mother-in-law. If one doesn't suffer to death, is one not provided insufficient food and clothing by one's in-laws?

3. Men with ample wealth manage to find a wife even before entering adulthood. When a man is not provident enough to obtain a wife [through purchase], either he goes for a lifetime without marrying or only after the prime of life does he gain a wife; or else, for a long time after being employed, he remains unmarried. As a result, out in the world there are plenty of lonesome men; inside, resentful women abound. In some remote villages, several brothers share one wife. Hence, if there is no money to obtain a wife or even to rear a child bride at home, where are poor people to get wives from?

4. Women of wealthy families are often endowed with talent and wisdom. They might fall in love with good-looking and talented sons of poor families, but their parents and brothers will hatch schemes and conspiracies to make [the girl] change her mind. The girl thus has to resort to suicide or to elopement. Is it not because the parents worry that if their daughter marries into a poor family, she will suffer from want of food and clothing, and hence they have no choice but to disrupt their love?

We thank Yukiko Hanawa for tracking this citation down for us. The play is about a woman living by the sea who forsakes her first love (a criminally accused sailor, who must flee the premises to escape prosecution) to marry a man who is more stably employed; the marriage becomes unhappy, whereupon the sailor reemerges, forcing the woman to decide whether to leave her husband or to stay in the unhappy but financially stable marriage. She chooses the latter, but reluctantly.

[3]They may ask about appearance, and this is to ascertain if the [man's] appearance is sufficient to attain an official position and to get rich. Of course, if a man can become an official and get rich, after the woman marries him her survival and comfort will be assured.

5. Beautiful girls from poor families are often forcibly preyed upon by the good-for-nothing sons of the wealthy. Although the girl is steadfast in her refusal, her parents and brothers, greedy for bribes from the wealthy family, will force the girl to comply. She is then pressed to kill herself or else be condemned to a lifetime of unhappiness. Is it not the case that the relatives are so greedy for money that they have no qualms about harming a girl of their own family?

6. The sons of wealthy families privately dishonor or use violence to rape the girls of poor families, but [the girls'] relatives do not dare make any fuss. The reasons and consequences are as described earlier.

7. The marriage contract between a girl and a boy is concluded in their childhood by parents. After the contract is settled, if the boy's family becomes poor, then the girl's parents renounce the contract or else conclude a marriage contract with someone else for the same daughter. In common speech this is called "disliking poverty, loving wealth." Legal actions in many provinces are brought over this issue.

8. Recently, many girls' schools have been established, and most require tuition. Philandering men are willing to lay out the money to help, but in exchange they force the girls to become engaged to them.[4] More than a few girls have been seduced in this manner.

9. If, after marriage, there is no love lost between husband and wife, the woman can only wallow in sorrow and sob bitter tears; she would never dare to leave for another. She might even try to hasten her own death. To the extent that the woman's only support might be the man, she must allow herself to be trapped.

10. When the husband dies, the wife often kills herself (to signal her resolve to remain faithful to him). This has nothing to do with love; she has no choice. This stems completely from the necessity to secure her livelihood. Because once the man dies, if the woman has no financial support, she will fall into terrible difficulty and it would be just as well for her to die.[5]

---

[4]Tr: "become engaged" means here to have sex with the promise of marriage to come.

[5]Some blame this kind of chaste martyrdom on blind adherence to tradition or custom. This may well be true. But the very reason why suicides are so prevalent that they have become customary is because after a woman marries she is supported by her husband's family,[and] she is thus obliged to remain chaste as an expression of gratitude for the favor [of having been supported]. But preserving a lifelong chastity is really difficult for a widow unless she has the financial means. It is easier to die a martyr to chastity. Those who kill themselves out of love are a minority. If one looks, one would realize that widows from wealthy families seldom choose to kill themselves; those who do all come from families with no resources. This is the reason why.

One can conclude from the above that this thing called money is the common enemy of love. Whenever the tragedy of love suicide occurs, it always stems from money. One can know how common the occurrence is from novels or stories and operas. It [money/marriage] not only shackles women in fetters, but it is the knife that cruelly murders women as well. Women in China today are controlled by money and by the brute force that grows directly out of money.

When money is the essence of things, not only does marriage lose all the joy of freedom, but it actually sinks women into bond-servitude. Concubines in wealthy families, if numerous, can number in the tens or more; and if not so numerous, there are still a few. Do these women really want to give up their emotions and just prostrate themselves? They do so only as a way to secure food and clothing for their bodies or just so that their parents can obtain some wealth. Those bullies, whose number of servile underlings grows along with their wealth, coerce or openly capture women of the common folk who exhibit some charm, regardless of whether they are married or single. When the girl's parents take the case to court, officials are paid off by bullies and return a verdict of false complaint. Or then there are the really wealthy families that employ slave girls and maids;[6] it is commonly recognized that married or otherwise, maids can be the target of the master's lustful desire. If the maid does not submit, then she will be punished severely. If her kinfolk find out about the affair, they do not dare publicly make an issue of it in order to avoid incurring the master's wrath. In recent times, one often hears of cases of rape among factory girls. The most egregious story is the one about parents and brothers who forced a girl to become a prostitute in order to pocket the money from the sale.[7]

Therefore, poverty is the root cause of prostitution, just as wealth is the root cause of lustful indulgence. The more money a man has, the more numerous are the women he violates. When a man sees a woman, what appears before him is merely a commodity that money can buy; a woman's body for a man is nothing but a display in the market awaiting a purchase. When a man and a woman unite, this can only be called the buying and selling of flesh; it can only be a transaction founded upon money. If one

---

[6]Tr: *Binü* (slave girl) can cover any number of different relationships, from outright slavery to maid-servant.
[7]Tr: In other words, the family enacted the equivalence between factory labor and prostitution as selling of one's body.

looks at the rape cases of recent times, they seldom come from families of relatively modest or middling means; they come either from the wealthiest families or from the poorest. The wealthy are those who have money to burn; the poor are those whose money is scarce. Those with money to burn expend a bit of money to buy what they lust after; those whose money is scarce have little choice but to sell perversion for a living, so as to gain their livelihood (*shengji*). Therefore the selling of lewdness and obscenity is usually caused by economic inequality.

The early-Qing female poet Shao Feifei[8] wrote: "May I ask, my dear mother,/ How much money is left from pawning your daughter back then?" One can see from this poem that it is no fault of the woman when she sinks into dissolution; rather, it is the fault of money. But let's not speak just of those women who fall into dissolute situations. What of wives? Because women who are wives are provided for by men, they offer their flesh as a playground, as if between a man and a woman there is nothing but a contract of indentured servitude: I sell you my body in exchange for your consideration and support. What a high-class way of selling bodies! The wife exclusively pawns her body to the man, and thus she initiates a loan into perpetuity. This is why I say that marriage system in China today is not founded on love; it harbors within it the fundamental character of "a woman selling her body to a man."

Every day that money is not forsaken is another day that economics become more unequal; in this situation, there is no hope of attaining free marriage between a man and a woman. Is this not something that we can safely predict today?

Customs of the countries of Euro-America in recent times are slightly different from those of China: there, marriage has evolved into a system of mutual prostitution on the parts of both men and women. There are two reasons for how this came about. First, there is the issue of property inheritance for women. If a father dies, he can leave his property to his daughter, unlike in China, where, when a father dies without sons, a relative's son is installed as the heir and inherits the wealth. Second, women can find independent employment. For example, some women, such as those in Belgium, can join the police; those in Finland can be members of parliament;

---

[8]Tr: Shao Feifei was a seventeenth-century poetess from Hangzhou; she grew up near West Lake. Beautiful, talented, and from a déclassé family, she was purchased by an official to become his concubine and then later sold by his jealous wife to another.

those in France and the United States can be employed either as drivers or in agriculture. And in each country, female teachers are particularly numerous. If we just look at factory girls: in the United States in 1900, of 10,000 workers, 1,722 of them were women; in Japan in Meiji 33 [1901], there were over 254,790 girls among factory workers. This all is evidence of women's independent employment.

From these two factors, we arrive at the situation that if a man wants to gain access to a woman's wealth, he must sell his body to the woman; likewise, if a woman wants to gain access to a man's wealth, she has to sell her body to him. The two sides work out to be about even in number. Let me give a few examples below to show how this works.

- A girl of a wealthy family whose fortune is great: Numerous young men struggle to crowd at her doorstep, fabricating stories and flattering her in a million ways in an effort to get their hands on her wealth by inducing her to marry them. This is the most common situation.
- A girl from a wealthy family who has many admirers: Because of jealousy, the men fight with each other when they realize that she will marry another man and that her wealth will belong to another. A large number of murder cases in Euro-America stem from this issue.
- A young man wishes to marry a girl from a wealthy family: this man is from a poor background, so he goes to borrow money in a number of ways to indulge in luxuries, all in an effort to win the girl's affection. This is an attempt to cheat the girl out of her wealth. A good example of this is in the Englishman Shakespeare's story *Yinbian yanyu* [*The Merchant of Venice*] in the part about the Englishman who brings the money to the Jew.[9]
- An aristocrat's poor cousin: His kinfolk help him gather sufficient wealth to marry, in order to prime the well of wealth. In this case, even if the boy loves another girl, he must end the affair, just as in the Englishman [H. Rider] Haggard's *Story of Jiayin* [*Joan Haste*] when Henry Graves is

---

[9]Tr: According to Alex Huang, by the early twentieth century in China there were several adaptations and translations of *The Merchant of Venice*, one by Lin Shu (see next footnote), none of which bore the original title and all of which were based upon the Lambs' *Tales of Shakespeare*. The title He-Yin Zhen uses here, *Yinbian yanyu* 吟邊燕語, does not correspond to any of the titles Huang mentions for early-century China but was Lin Shu's translation published in 1906. See Alex Huang, *Chinese Shakespeares* (New York: Columbia University Press, 2009), 74–75ff.

forced to marry Emma.[10] Or, recently in the United States, a girl from a wealthy family wanted to marry a European aristocrat and the aristocrat demanded a large sum of money. Just a few days ago, an American girl named Ke-lan Di-si-en-bi-er took 1,200 fu [florins] to marry the Hungarian aristocrat Di-au-yi. The American Mr. Si-ha-si (a congressional representative from Shi-e-gu) said: "Turning her back on the spirit of the American Republic and forgetting her station as a commoner, she gets married to an aristocrat and takes with her a huge amount of wealth out of the country. Our people will become vain. Unless we impose a heavy tax, we cannot stop this harmful behavior."[11] Mr. Wuyin (also a congressman) said: "European aristocrats are like geese.[12] To marry them is like shacking up with livestock."[13] This provides evidence for the phenomenon of poor aristocrats marrying girls with wealth.

- Boys of middling means marrying wealthy girls: After marriage, the girl starts to indulge in luxuries and lust after others instead of staying calmly in her home. She insults her husband and has an affair with another, but her husband dare say nothing. Because he lusts after her property and wealth, he can do nothing but endure the insults and the dishonor.[14]

- A widow who commands a fortune: Profligate men vie to have affairs with her, and so man and woman alike forget about marriage altogether.

---

[10]Tr: At first glance, it appears that He-Yin is referring to the translation of *Joan Haste* by Lin Shu, the prolific "translator" of Euro-American literature in the late-Qing period, who introduced more than 180 different titles into Chinese (see the historical introduction in this volume for more on Lin Shu and translation). However, He-Yin must be making reference to a different translation, which is Pan Xizi's (pseud. for Yang Zilin) of 1900, as Lin's version only came out in 1914. Pan's version omits the second half of the book, when Henry defies his father's wishes and has a child with Joan; in the first half, Henry is being coerced into leaving Joan for Ellen (here rendered Emma). Thus, He-Yin thinks the book is about Henry's coerced marriage to Ellen/Emma, when in fact it is about Henry and Joan defying all social conventions to have a child and live together. This error is not He-Yin's fault, but the fault of the partiality of the translation to which she had access.

[11]Tr: It is entirely unclear to what particular story He-Yin is referring; our efforts to track down some cognate story in the newspapers of this era have failed. The names of the congressional representatives and of the states they may have represented are also unclear from He-Yin's rendition.

[12]This is a way to curse people: it is like the Japanese *bakka* [silly fool; literally, horse-deer].

[13]Tr: If one looks into the newspapers from around the early 1900s, it is true that there appears to be a sudden increase in the number of American heiresses marrying European aristocrats of every description and nationality. There seemed to be a veritable hunt on for aristocratic titles and heiresses, or so the journalists would have had one believe.

[14]Just as the affair between Queen Victoria and her horse groom had to be endured.

They do it only because they all lust after her wealth. Recently, in the U.S. state of Suli [Missouri], in the city of Columbia, a number of very wealthy widowed women seduced unmarried men, thus creating havoc with customary morality. Worse still, countless single women had to defer marriage. The city councilors have proposed a tax on singletons to the effect that those men who have reached maturity and are still bachelors should pay one hundred dollars a year so as to forestall the incidence of illicit sex. This is solid proof [for the corruption of money].[15]

As we can see from the above, when men covet the wealth of women, they try to marry them. To put it plainly, the women, depending on their own wealth, are forcing *men* to prostitute themselves. Because men covet money, they sell their bodies to women. What difference is there between them and the boy actors of Beijing?[16] In China, men are at least embarrassed by having to rely on their wife's wealth.[17] By contrast, in Euro-America, if a man marries into a wealthy family, his kin and friends will be delighted to congratulate him. In reality, this type of man is no better than a common prostitute. Why shouldn't we just call him a male prostitute? What shame and embarrassment this is! As for the more common phenomenon of poor women selling themselves to men in Euro-America, I will adduce some examples next.

- When the sons of wealthy families rape or molest girls from poor families, their kin dare not say anything. This is because of the power of money.
- Poor girls who have talent or who have lofty ambitions are forced into marriage to the good-for-nothing sons of the wealthy. Her [The girl's] kin

---

[15]Tr: See http://multibraries.missouri.edu/collections/documents/mo/x/TaxHistory-pt1.pdf (accessed November 1, 2011) for more information on this bachelor tax. He-Yin Zhen is misinformed, however, about the dates and purpose of this tax: apparently it was repealed as of the mid-nineteenth century, and it had been instituted by the Territory of Missouri as a method of encouraging immigrants to the area to settle with wives so as to permanently populate the territory with white people. He-Yin Zhen's highly creative interpretation is nevertheless interesting.

[16]Tr: In the Qing dynasty, the boy actors of Beijing were famed sodomites, so much so that observers remarked that there were few brothels in the city. See Sophie Volpp, "The Male Queen: Boy Actors and Literati Libertines" (PhD diss., Harvard University, 1995).

[17]In colloquial language, this is called "eating by the skirt."

eagerly reinforce this coercion, forcing her to nurse a grudge for her whole life or to commit suicide. This is brought about entirely because her kin, seduced by money, are too blind to consider the true interests of the girl.

- Wealthy men of an age or who are marrying for a second or third time, marry much younger girls, and their primary marketplace to find such girls is among poor families, who want to secure food and clothing. This type of thing is most evident in the United States.

- A wealthy boy and poor girl get married: when she ruffles his feathers in the slightest, he threatens to divorce her; the girl won't dare to say anything for she worries that she will be unable to be economically independent if divorced.

- A landlord rapes the daughter or even wife of one of his tenants, a situation often seen in Russia: although furious, the tenant dares only to obey because his sustenance comes from the landlord.

- Women employed daily in factories are often raped by wealthy merchants or men in management or higher positions; this is particularly prevalent in the Americas, and Japan also exhibits this trend. (In today's China, this also exists.) Because people are forced by poverty to accept the cash wage system, women cannot avoid such insults for this reason.

- A wealthy family hires a servant girl and offers very little money, forcing her to sell herself for sex to the household head. (This is prevalent in Japan.)

- Aristocratic or middle-class girls, because of poverty, mortgage themselves to a wealthy but lowly family in marriage. (This happens to Ellen in the novel *Joan Haste*.[18])

- Wealthy men, after a formal marriage, privately marry a poor girl in a secret ceremony: they see the poor girl as so lowly that there is no need to receive her with formal gifts and ceremony.

- The women of poor families, no matter whether married or not, often are compelled to sell their bodies for survival.

- In every city, red light districts proliferate; New York in America is a particularly flourishing case in point.

As we can see from the above, generally when women covet the wealth of men, they offer up their bodies. To put it plainly, the men, depending on their wealth, are forcing women to prostitute themselves. A woman who

---

[18]Tr: see note 10 above regarding *Joan Haste*.

sells her body to a man because of her lust for money—no matter whether she actually works in a brothel or not—is still a prostitute by another name. In China, the women are at least bound by the rites of propriety, as epitomized in the teaching, "Starving to death is a small matter; losing one's chastity is a major matter." Even though this goes against common principle, nevertheless because of it one seldom sees a woman selling herself openly in pursuit of wealth. But in Euro-America, where the moral prohibitions are far more lax than in China, it is not shameful to prostitute oneself.

According to a recent American survey, those women who marry with the most ease are nurses, journalists, servant girls, shop clerks, and factory girls; female teachers are next in line, with phone operators and seamstresses next. We can see that nurses, servant girls, clerks, and factory workers are all women of the poor who must get married quickly in order to have a man support them.[19] As for those in the teaching profession, the women make a decent salary and therefore need not rely on men; they are not seduced by men as much and thus marry relatively later. Hence, the poorer the women, the easier it is for men to seduce them. Is this not licentiousness stemming from the desire for wealth? Last year in New York, the wife of a wealthy man by the name of Di-bu-ni demanded 10,000 dollars per year for her wardrobe, saying that if he did not meet her needs, she would divorce him. Is this not a case of using money as the only yardstick for marriage? This wife brings shame on all women.

Thus it is established that our contemporary age is an age in which [marriage takes the form of] mutual prostitution on the parts of both men and women. And yet, this licentiousness is not the fault of the men and women themselves; it is the fault of money. The lack of freedom in marriage today is most often the result of economic inequality. In such a state of economic inequality, the poor desire the money of the rich but have no [legitimate] means to get it. The rich, in turn already luxuriating in comfort, constantly search for better ways to expand their enjoyment and pleasure. The consequence of this is that the wealthy use money to purchase licentious enjoyments, whereas the poor must sell themselves to provide them with these enjoyments.

Therefore, instead of naming this kind of transaction "the [gender] relationship between men and women," it is more accurate to name it "[class]

---

[19]Stenographers and secretaries make a large salary; often talented, they are courted by a large number of men. This is the same thing as men who prostitute themselves.

relationship between poor and rich." In the *Book of Rites*, it says, "When marriage is abandoned and the way of husband and wife becomes difficult, then the error of licentiousness flourishes." Today, I want to turn that phrase around to say, "When the system of money is established, the way of husband and wife is difficult and thence arises the flourishing error of licentiousness." In a phrase, today's marriage is not marriage for love but marriage for money. In the classic texts of China, marriage for wealth is named a custom of the "foreign barbaric peoples."[20] Today, however, marriage for wealth has swept over the whole world; love is no longer an obstacle to the dominance of wealth. Is this not lamentable?

In our contemporary world, if we wish to establish the happiness of freedom for men and women, then all marriages need to be for love. That is to say, we need to move away from a system of marriage for money to one of marriage for love. If we want love to flourish, then we must first abandon money. Once that happens, economic equality would follow; the majority of men and women would no longer be constrained by money, and they could then rely upon their mutual love to unite in marriage. Whatever tendencies toward brutalities or lingering licentious customs remained, these could be rectified expediently. Therefore, a women's revolution must go hand in hand with an economic revolution. If an economic revolution cannot be accomplished, then the common phrase heard today calling for a "revolution between men and women" cannot be said to have touched the essence of the problem.[21]

Today, I want to use one phrase to spread among the women of the world: If you do not desire and demand liberation [for yourself] in order to realize a women's revolution, then so be it. But if you desire to realize a women's revolution, you must begin with an economic revolution. What is an economic revolution? It is to overthrow the system of private property and to replace it with communal property, meanwhile abandoning all monies and currencies.

Today, many commentators speak of love between man and woman as a lie or delusion. They are unaware that love develops from human nature;

---

[20]Tr: For an analysis of the discussion of foreign customs in classical texts, see Chin, Tamara, "Defamiliarizing the Foreigner: Sima Qian's Ethnography and Han-Xiongnu Marriage Diplomacy." *Harvard Journal of Asiatic Studies* 70, 2 (2010): 311–354.

[21]Tr: For the more common contemporaneous expressions of "revolution in the male and female world," see Jin Tianhe's pamphlet, included in this volume. For contextualization, see the Introduction in this volume.

He-Yin Zhen

it arises by itself naturally. But when love becomes entangled with money, only licentiousness is produced. For both men and women, this entanglement brings great shame. When love is induced by money, then it is a fake love born of a fake thing; it is no longer a sentiment that emerges from human nature. After the economic revolution, unions will be born of love. Love marriages are the noblest and purest marriages in the world. How can they be a lie or a delusion?

Originally published in *Tianyi*, double issue nos. 13–14 (December 30, 1907). Editorial, signed Zhen Shu 震述. Reprinted in Wan Shiguo, pp. 902–909. Translated by Rebecca E. Karl from the Chinese original "Jingji geming yu nüzi geming 經濟革命與女子革命."

The weakest essay so far: wild generalisation

"On the Revenge of Women"

PART 1: INSTRUMENTS OF MEN'S RULE OVER WOMEN

He-Yin Zhen (1907)

I address myself to the women of my country: has it occurred to you that men are our archenemy? Are you aware that men have subjugated us for thousands of years? The ancients used to say that those who abuse me cannot but be my enemy. Such is how men have treated women, and there is not a single woman who has not been ill treated by some man. Consequently, there is not a single woman who does not bear a grudge against men. Critics compare this situation to the political subjugation of a subject to his prince, but I beg to disagree. It is true that men can be subjugated and must submit to an alien group, the will of a king, or some capitalists. When that happens, the people who rule and the people who submit to the rule are both men. With women, however, the subjugation takes on a whole different character. One cannot deny that an empress occupies a highly esteemed position, but she never questions her own subjugation to a man (men). At the other end of the hierarchy, one finds beggars whose social position cannot be more degraded, yet even a female beggar would not question her subjugation to a man (men). This situation is by no means confined to the ancient world and is just as prevalent in the modern world as it was in the past; nor is it a uniquely Chinese situation, since the same

The original essay was serialized in three parts. We present it in two parts and add subheadings according to the logic of the argument.

thing happens in foreign lands as well.[1] I would not raise an issue about this if women were regarded as a nonhuman species. [But] suppose we are granted our humanity, how can we tolerate this oppression day after day and not think about resistance?

The level of self-awareness among the women of China is very low, and those who have attained a notch slightly higher rush to pick up the crumbs of men's fallacious discourse of racial revolution. There is no doubt that the Manchu court [of the Qing dynasty] should be overthrown, but I would like to point out that a Han sovereign or regime could be a disaster worse than the ones wrought by foreign rule. I argue that the more successful a Han-dominated regime is, the worse their oppression of women and the worse their injustice against us.

For a long time, the Han have venerated the Yellow Emperor [Xuan Yuan] as the remote ancestor of their people. The Yellow Emperor had nearly a dozen consorts, who gave birth to twenty-five sons. Twelve of them bore different family names, which indicate matrilineal descent. After that, King Shun and King Wen became the ancient sages of China. Shun had three consorts, whereas King Wen allegedly had a hundred sons to his credit. This seems to speak to the prevalence of male-dominated polygamy [among the Han]. Emperor Wu of the Han dynasty (156–87 B.C.E.), renowned for his military prowess, exploited and raped women ruthlessly and was as ferocious as a beast. He did not spare the lives of his own consorts when he established the rule that any queen or royal consort whose son was chosen as direct heir to the throne must be put to death. The founding emperor of the Ming dynasty [Zhu Yuanzhang] built his illustrious career on the successful expulsion of foreign [Mongol] invaders. This man is remembered for making the statement that "[h]ad it not been the fact that I owed my own life to a woman, I would have wiped out womankind."

Does not this history provide enough evidence that there has not been a single Han sovereign who is not the archenemy of women? If we admit the fact that all sovereigns of the Han are women's archenemy, there is no reason why our revolution must stop at abolishing foreign rule. We should

---

[1] For example, the idea of gender equality is often applied to Western Europe, but this is in name only. The fact is that European women are barred from the ranks of the army and police force and that there are hardly any women who have been granted power in the legislative, judicial, and executive branches of the government. This makes me question the reality of their claimed gender equality.

press further and oppose political rule by a Han (male) sovereign and overthrow him as well. The reason that we are now seeking to end Manchu rule is that this foreign people have imposed their tyranny upon us women. They have permitted men to wield power within the government and extend their control throughout the bureaucratic system of the country. That is why the revolution to overthrow the Manchu regime should fall to women. If we let us ourselves be led by a xenophobic language to echo the discourse of some men, we will have acted like Han men who aided the Manchu regime in their campaign against other foreigners. What difference would it make, then? We are fighting a foreign regime mainly because they have ruled us with tyranny (not because they are foreigners).

All despotic regimes must be overthrown. Even when a despotic polity decides to adopt a constitution or to transform itself into a republican state, it is the responsibility of each and every one of us to overthrow the government they attempt to establish. To set up a [republican] government, they would import the machinery of political rule; and the machinery of political rule cannot but fall into the hands of men. This would not be very different from despotism. Even if men and women hold power together, they would not be sharing political power equally, and there is always a distinction between those who rule and those who are ruled. There would be no justice to speak of if women continue to be subjugated by men, nor would it be equitable for some women to submit to the will of other women. Eventually, we must abolish all governments. And only when governments are out of the way can men acquire equal rights with respect to other men, and women be rendered equal to other women, and [thus] men and women finally be on an equal footing. Is this not the universal truth?

To do away with governments, one must consider the possibility of communally owned property. My argument is that the social divide between rich and poor originates from the existence of class structure; contrary to the view that the rich merely abdicate their humanity when they enslave the poor the way they do, we should be looking within the class structure for an explanation. Take the rich in China, for example. Women are generally held in the lowest possible regard by the wealthy. The more affluent a man's family is, the more concubines he owns; the more wealth a man accumulates, the more licentious his behavior becomes. The majority of those who take prostitutes and visit brothels are wealthy men. As long as this class of men exists, women will always suffer from the harm they bring to them. To eliminate the causes of the unequal distribution of wealth between men and women, land and property must be communally owned. This is the only path that will lead toward universal equality for all, so that men may not indulge their licentious desires when their basic needs are satisfied and women need not prostitute their bodies and humiliate themselves in order to feed themselves.

Following this path, all would have their rights restored and women would also see fulfilled their desire to be vindicated. Bear in mind that the goal of women's struggle is no more and no less than the restoration of universal justice for all. Our goal is not to take revenge on men for the wrongs they have done to us, nor is it to subjugate men and make them obey women's rule. Few women in China seem to understand this; many fail to grasp their own situation or to understand how they arrived in such hopeless circumstances. What are the sources of this [subjugation]? Below, I would like to share with my fellow women the results of my own investigation into the causes of women's oppression.

Family Names and the Rise of Patriarchy

In the ancient world, there existed totemic societies in which the system of communal husbands and wives prevailed. British writer Edward Jenks describes the system in his book *A History of Politics* as follows: "[A]ll the women of his marriage totem in the same generation are a man's wives. All their children are his children; all the members of his totem in the same generation are his brothers and sisters (whom he may not marry); all the members of his mother totem are his parents (for descent is nearly always reckoned through females)."[2] This suggests that men in savage societies regarded women as communally shared and women also treated their men as communally shared. Take the etymology of the Chinese written character *fu* 婦. This character is both a term referring to someone's wife and a generic term for an adult woman. The corresponding character *fu* 夫 refers to someone's husband but may also be used as a generic term for an

---

[2]Tr: Quoted from the original, see Edward Jenks, *History of Politics* (London: Macmillan, 1900), 11; for the Chinese translation of Jenks by Yan Fu, see *Shehui tongquan* (Beijing: Shangwu yinshuguan, 1981), 11. Jenks's observation is based on the fieldwork of Baldwin Spencer and F. J. Gillen in *Native Tribes of Central Australia* (1899).

adult male. Do these etymologies not provide the evidence for the fact that a man used to have more than one specific wife and a woman more than one specific husband?

By permitting a man to have multiple wives and a woman multiple husbands, the ancient system recognized nothing like an institution of marriage; not having an institution of marriage in place, there was no need to distinguish between a virgin and a married woman. Herbert Spencer points out in *The Principles of Sociology* that the South African bushmen did not make a distinction among husbands, wives, concubines, spouses, and so on; nor did they make a verbal distinction between "virgin" and "woman."[3] In the Chinese language, the written character *nü* 女 (woman; female) covers the semantic field of married woman and unmarried woman, rather similar to the ways of primitive people.[4] The descent of the family line passed from generation to generation through women, and not through men. Master Gengcang observes: "When the legendary king Jiqu founded his kingdom, all under heaven knew who their mothers were but not their fathers." This observation is supported by the classic *White Tiger Discourse*, which records that "[i]n the remote past, the Three Bonds and Six Threads had not existed and people knew only their mothers and not their fathers."[5] This situation corresponds to Jenks's observation, namely, that matrilineal descent was reckoned through women, whose primacy outweighed that of men, and only when females were valued more than males can it explain why children inherited their family names from their mothers.

Take the written Chinese character *xing* 姓, denoting "family name." This character is composed of the radical *nü* 女, for "female," which is combined with the character *sheng* 生, for "life," to form the word *xing* 姓 (literally,

---

[3]Tr: The translator is grateful to Qiao Zhihang for her assistance in identifying the obsolete coinage *boxiumen* as a Chinese transcription of "bushmen." Apparently, He-Yin's ethnographic reference is drawn from a footnote in Zhang Taiyan's work *Qiushu*.

[4]Although the *Zuo Commentary on the Spring and Autumn Annals* glosses the character *nü* as "unmarried woman," as in the phrase "the *nü* did not measure up to the *fu* code," the *Book of Songs* makes no such distinction. Take the verse "So sad is my *nü* (woman's) heart,/ O that my soldier might return" (*Minor Odes of the Kingdom*) or "The *nü* (woman) says, 'It is cock-crow';/ The husband says, 'It is grey dawn'" (*The Odes of Zheng*). The character *nü* is here applied to a married woman.

[5]Tr: The Three Bonds and Six Threads are the Confucian moral codes that govern the three primary and six secondary moral relationships between ruler and ruled, father and son, husband and wife, as well as siblings, husband and wife, friendship, and so on. See *Baihu tongde lun*, chap. 2, "On Titles."

"woman/life"), which denotes "family name." As a matter of fact, the names of all great families of remote antiquities were written with a female radical, witness Ji 姬, Jiang 姜, Yao 姚, Si 姒, Yun 妘, Gui 媯, Ji 姞, Ying 嬴, Ran 燃, and Niu 妞. Legendary figures like Shennong and the Yellow Emperor were descendants of the king Shaodian, but each bore a different family name, Ji and Jiang respectively. The Yellow Emperor fathered twenty-five sons, who bore as many as twelve different family names; and their descendant Lu Zhong had six sons, who carried six different family names. This suggests that the sons were born of the same father but of different mothers whose family names they bore. Other such illustrious ancients as Tang Yao, Bo Yi, and the founders of the Shang and Zhou dynasties all bore their mothers' family names. Legend has it that the ancient kings who conquered the world were not the sons of men. What could they have meant by that? Evidently, matrilineal descent was the norm, not the exception. The ancients practiced matrilineal descent when the idea of putting men over and above women had not yet occurred. Such was the system of totemic societies.

The customs of totemic societies demanded that men of one totem group marry women of another totem group. But when two totem groups came into conflict in a time of war, one of them eventually prevailed to defeat the other. The victorious would inflict damage and atrocities upon the vanquished and lord it over them by massacring the males and taking their women as prisoners. This must have been the initial stage when women were enslaved.[6] When men captured women and possessed them, they became contemptuous of them, as they were of all slaves, and began to treat them as property. Men made women perform servile jobs and gratify their sexual desires. This would be the beginning of male domination over women and of their appropriation of the female body.

---

[6]Chinese nationality originated in the west. When the Han ethnic group migrated east, they traveled tens of thousands of *li*, but many of their women may not have joined them on the journey. As the Han people reached China, they conquered the native Qiang and Miao peoples and kidnapped their women and then became their masters. In the remote past, the Han males mated with the females of foreign ethnicities as a rule. The family name Jiang 姜 is written with the female radical and is a female name. In antiquity, the characters *jiang* 姜 and *qiang* 羌 were used interchangeably and the family name Jiang 姜 was a name belonging to women of Qiang ethnicity. Take another character, *man* 嫚, which is also written with the female radical and is another one of those family names that passed through women. The character 嫚 was used interchangeably with the character 蠻 (barbarian) in ancient usage and those who bore the family name 嫚 were the women of Miao barbarians. The list could go on, suggesting that Chinese women may not all be traced back to the Han ethnic origins.

As time passed, habits turned into the norm. Because the supply of female slaves could not always be guaranteed to satisfy their desires, men turned their attention to the women of their own community and began to appropriate them by means of monetary transactions. The women they bought with money were held in the same low regard as were slaves; the children born of enslaved women were given the father's family name.[7] Matrilineal descent gave way to patriarchal descent so that not only did the children [of such mothers] have to bear the father's name but women themselves had to drop their own family names and adopt their husbands' instead. What other sense could it make to treat a child as the father's private property when both parents are responsible for bringing the child into the world and nurturing his or her life? Does it make any sense to claim that this mother has a son to depend on when he does not really belong to her?

In the West today, there is a great deal of empty discourse on the equality of man and woman. But the moment a woman gets married, she adopts her husband's family name and allows others to address her by her husband's name. The reverse rarely happens, since one can hardly find a man who does the opposite by adopting his wife's family name. What does it mean for a woman to adopt her husband's name if not to carry on the eternal celebration of men's conquest over women? European and American women pride themselves on being civilized, but why should they obey the old custom and give up their family names by taking on their husbands' family names? Have they not sensed something wrong about this? I lament this folly and am mortified by their lack of awareness of their own humiliation.

The transition from matrilineal rule to patriarchal rule signaled the beginning of a social hierarchy that put men over women, dignifying the former and degrading the latter. Men have long imposed the system of monogamy upon women. A woman is allowed to marry one husband, whereas a man can marry as many wives as he can afford. What could be more unjust under heaven than this system? In Western Europe, where the practice of monogamy is the norm and the laws of the Christian churches prevail, many men engage in extramarital affairs and their number is simply too large to count. In Asia, the system of polygamy has gained the upper hand; and among Asian countries, China is the most notorious in

---

[7]Alas, we may compare the situation with that of Poland. When that country was conquered by a foreign nation, it also lost its written language. What could have been more tragic than such a fate?

this respect. Chinese men feared that a woman would be unfaithful to her husband and invented the dictum that the wife must "remain true to one [man] unto death" in order to guard against women's marital transgression. Women's practice of polygamy was eliminated to allow a male-dominated system of polygyny to flourish. Beginning in the Three Dynasties, men of power and prestige who enjoyed the highest rank owned the largest retinue of wives. The following chart should give us an idea of how that system distributed women according to a man's social rank in the Zhou dynasty (1046–256 B.C.E.):

MEN	WOMEN
Tianzi (the monarch)	One queen, 3 first-rank consorts, 7 second-rank consorts, 27 third-to-fifth-rank consorts, 81 sixth-to-eighth-rank consorts. Total number of women: 121
Zhuhou (feudal lord)	Nine wives
Dafu (grand master)	One wife and two concubines
Shi (third-rank official)	One wife and one concubine
Shuren (commoner)	One wife

This chart indicates that the system of multiple wives can be traced back to antiquity. Feudal lords and grand masters began to aggrandize themselves by increasing the number of consorts and wives to which they were entitled in the period of Warring States (475–221 B.C.E.). By the Han dynasty (202 B.C.E.–220 C.E.), the cap on allotted consorts and wives for men of each official rank was lifted and the emperor allowed himself to have a harem of five to six thousand women. Under the sovereign, his ministers and the aristocracy each had their retinues of concubines, a good example being the Han dynasty minister Tian Fen, who had a harem of hundreds of women. Ministers in the subsequent dynasties did more or less what Tian had done and pushed the patriarchal practice of polygamy to the extreme. These numbers hardly diminished in the Tang dynasty, as is testified by the poet Bai Juyi, who chants in a poem, "[His] love for three thousand [consorts] is now lavished upon a single one [woman]." The number "three thousand" is

112

only approximate, suggesting that women in the harem of the Tang dynasty (618–907 C.E.) probably reached at least three thousand. There is no need to enumerate the even greater number of palace women in the courts of Mongols and Manchus. Now, does this not amply illustrate the gross inequality between husband and wife?

It is only to be expected that not having equality between husband and wife, parents also treat their own children as unequal beings. The *Book of Songs* has this verse:

Sons shall be born to him:
They will be put to sleep on couches;
They will be clothed in robes;
They will have scepters to play with;
. . .
Daughters shall be born to him:
They will be put to sleep on the ground;
They will be clothed with wrappers;
They will have tiles to play with.[8]

Is this not sufficient to show that parents in ancient times valued their sons much more than their daughters? Worse still, not only do parents discriminate between their sons and daughters, but children learn to value their fathers and devalue their mothers. The classic *Etiquette and Rituals* (*Yili*) declares the father to be the "absolute authority" and the mother the "private authority." Scholar Gu Yanwu (1613–1682 C.E.) reiterates that "[t]here can be no two authorities in a family. As long as the father is still alive, the mother must never use her authority in the education of their son." Alas, a female child in China is to be slighted first by her own parents; and as a grownup, she is to be slighted by her own husband; finally in old age, she is to be slighted by her own male children. Reflecting on this situation, I cannot but sigh and feel outrage, but I must elaborate on the other sources of inequality subsisting between man and woman.

---

[8]Tr: As quoted from a poem titled "Si Gan" (These banks) in the *Minor Odes of the Kingdom* (no. 189). Adapted from the translation by James Legge, made accessible online by the Chinese Text Initiative, University of Virginia Library, http://etext.virginia.edu/chinese/shijing. All subsequent translations from the *Book of Songs* are adapted from this edition and cited by number (e.g., no. 189) only. For an insightful gendered reading of the *Book of Songs*, see Tamara Chin, "Orienting Mimesis," *Representations* 94 (2006): 53–79.

He-Yin Zhen

Inscribing Gender Inequality with Writing

Inequality between man and woman is inscribed in the writing system. As evidence for how the ancients treated women as property rather than as human beings, the *Chronicle of Three Kingdoms* cites from the authority of *History of the State of Wei* to say that "the Xiongnu word for slaves and maids is property." The *Cangjie Primer* concurs with this view. In savage societies [such as the Xiongnu's], there was no verbal distinction between slave and property. As we follow the etymologies of the written characters *nu* 奴, for "slave," and *bi* 婢, for "maid," in the *History of the State of Wei,* we will see that both characters refer explicitly to women. And as we turn to the [Han dynasty] *Analysis and Explication of Written Characters,* we are given this explication: "[T]he character 媼 *xi* means 'slave woman'" and "the character 婢 *bi* means 'the lowly (卑) among women (女).'" Zheng Xuan glosses in his *Annotations on the Rites of Zhou*: "What we mean by the words 'slave woman' and 'lowly woman' used to connote 'criminals' in the ancient world." In later days, only those who committed an offense became slaves; whereas in the ancient world, woman and slave were interchangeable terms. Further examples from the *Analysis and Explication of Written Characters* will indicate how this was indeed the case in ancient times:

- 媒 This character, pronounced *wo* and written with the female radical, means "servant" as used, for example, in the phrase "two female *wo*" in the *Mencius.* The character *wo* in this phrase was explicated by Zhao Qi as "servant," indicating that women in the ancient world were expected to wait on men and serve them.
- 婦 This character is pronounced *fu* and written with an ideograph suggesting the figure of a woman holding a broom; the *Book of Rites* (the section on *quli*, or etiquette) explains: when the grand master wanted to take a woman as his wife, he used the expression "getting [someone] to clean and sweep [the house]." This is to assign the responsibilities of a slave to his wife and make her obey him.
- 嬪 This character, pronounced *pin* and written with the female radical, derives from the character for "gift." In the *Rites of Zhou*, the character *pin* is used in the word *pingong* to refer to a woman who was offered to the sovereign as a gift. Woman was treated as one of the exchangeable commodities.

- 奴 This character (pronounced *nu*) combines the female radical and the ideograph denoting the state of being "bent" or "bound" in ancient usage. The way the ancients treated their women was not that different from how they treated prisoners.
- 帑 This character (pronounced *tang*) is glossed as "treasure" or "stored wealth"; and in its alternative form 孥 (pronounced *nu*), the character means "women and children," which implies that the ancients equated property with women and children.
- 妃 This character originally referred to a large quantity of silks and money, and it was also used for "consorts" or "harems"—further evidence that women were treated as "property" in ancient times.

The etymologies of the foregoing characters suggest that in ancient times "woman" was a name for the least respected rank, whereas her responsibilities were more numerous than those of others. Women have been bound and burdened with tasks; they have been exchanged as gifts; and they have toiled and worked for others. They have been used by men as an instrument of wealth. As a man's family becomes more and more prosperous, he increases his collection of women, not unlike the way in which female slaves have been used in the American South. In later days, *pinfei* 嬪妃 was an honorific title for royal consorts. In ancient times, when a woman was called a *pinfei*, the respect it conferred on her was no more than the respect one owed to a piece of goods.

We tend to believe that *furen* 婦人 is a common term for "woman," but the written character *fu* derived from an ideograph for "broom." The term is deeply mired in its own involvement in the history of women's enslavement. This enslavement is stipulated as a woman's proper tasks in the ancient classic the *Book of Rites* (*Liji*), which included the weaving of linen threads, the unwinding and reeling of cocoons to make silks, wine manufacture, and preparations of ritual vessels and food. From the time of the *Book of Songs*, when the preparation of wine was a task assigned to women through the later periods down to the present moment, it has been repeatedly asserted that a woman's entire life must be devoted to preparing food and to [doing] her needlework. This legacy is perpetuated by women's schools of modern times, where household management is given top priority in the school curricula and where food preparation and dressmaking are each taught as special fields in these schools. But what does household management mean? It means that a woman is supposed to assist a man in the management of his household. Does it not echo the way in which men enslaved their women in the distant past? But many women are so accustomed to this role that they are not aware of their own state of enslavement. Is this lack of consciousness unique to them [modern women]?

As early as the Three Dynasties (Xia, Shang, and Zhou dynasties, ca. 21st–3rd century B.C.E.), a lady would speak of herself as "your humble child," and in a later time a woman would address herself as "your humble woman" or "your humble slave." Does this mean that those women were content with their own enslavement? Whenever people reiterate "women and children," they are lumping women and children together in order to put women down. Why do they do that? Confucius made a similar point in the *Analects* when he spoke of "women and petty-minded individuals" [lower-class people]; by his putting women and petty-minded people in the same category, his contempt for women was made clear. Men have tried hard to clamp down on women's speech, and they have not been able to erase the traces of their oppression of women. This is the first aspect of the tyranny of men's rule.

Inscribing Inequality Through Social Institutions

The second aspect of the tyranny of men's rule is rooted in rites or social institutions. By rites, we refer to the symbolic representation of social beliefs and mores in which the system of inequality between man and woman is always embedded. Let us take a few well-documented social institutions as examples, the first being that of marriage and the second being that of funerary rites.

1. On Marriage

Concerning the institution of marriage, we find the following description of the European custom in *A History of Politics*: "Even in polite modern society, the 'best man' is said to be a survival of the friends who went with the bridegroom in ancient days to help him to carry off his bride, while the bridesmaids are the lady's companions, who attempted to defend her from the audacious robber, and the wedding tour is a survival of the flight from the angry relatives of the bride."[9] Edward Jenks argues convincingly that the rites of marriage in modern times have evolved from the primordial custom of bride kidnapping. As we turn to the chapter on marriage in the Chinese classic *Etiquette and Rituals*, we encounter an obligation that the bridegroom should prepare several vehicles and his attending men should ride these vehicles. What was the original purpose of such vehicles and attendants but to help the groom kidnap a bride? The same classic instructs further that when the bride arrives in the home of the groom, she should be accompanied by her nurse and companions. Are these companions not there in order to defend the bride from the impudent robber? Moreover, the wedding ceremony [in China] usually take place at dusk, and this tradition goes back to the ancient time when bride kidnapping had to happen at dusk because the woman's family would not be on the alert at this hour of the day.[10] Generations of people have inherited this tradition and believe that the wedding ceremony is no more than a ceremonial ritual, not knowing that it is actually a legacy of ancient men's kidnapping of brides.

When Fu Xi founded the institution of marriage, he introduced the practice of using deerskin as a wedding present.[11] At that time, animal skin represented wealth and was used as a currency. People bought and sold women using that currency. According to *Etiquette and Rituals*, the initial three stages leading to marriage—the stage of proposal, the stage of birth-date matching, and that of betrothal gifts—all involved the offering of wild geese. The next stage was the presentation of wedding gifts that included black-and-red-tinted linens, bales of silks, and deerskin. For an emperor, the gift would include an imperial jade emblem in addition to the above; and a minister should include a half-size jade emblem as part of his wedding gifts. On the date of the bride's first meeting with the in-laws, a bale of silk should be given, which is a legacy from the ancient ritual of deerskin exchange. As for the custom of presenting wild geese, that seems to reflect the archaic system of exchange when people used animals as a token of value.

The preface to the *Han Tradition of the Book of Songs* mentions a woman from the state of Shen who refused to embark on her journey to the groom's

---

[9]Tr: Quoted from the original. See Jenks, *History of Politics*, 27.

[10]Tr: The written character *hun* in its archaic form stands for both "wedding" and "dusk." The double entendre of this character is what drives He-Yin Zhen's analysis here.

[11]Tr: Fu Xi is said to have lived in the mid-twenty-ninth century B.C.E. and was the first of the Three Sovereigns of ancient China.

family because of their failure to prepare these gifts prior to the wedding. That she did this as a matter of principle provides unmistakable evidence that women were already bought and sold as commodities in the ancient world. In recent years, Chinese society has undergone reforms to eliminate some of the old customs, but there have been cases in metropolitan areas where it is said that a groom carried a palanquin to fetch his bride and when he reached her door, the bride's family guarded the door and refused to let him in. The groom battered the door down to get his bride. This may well have been a remnant of the ancient system of bride kidnapping, since the legacy has survived to this day and is by no means limited to backward areas. Moreover, people continue to abide by the established ways of proposing a marriage and giving betrothal gifts and so on. The bride's family can sometimes get into a dispute with the groom's family when the giving of clothing and jewelry is perceived to be insufficient. To this day, people continue to barter their daughters thus, and the practice is by no means limited to the wealthy, who alone can afford to purchase concubines. We are therefore confronted with a tradition of bride kidnapping that has evolved from situations where women were taken as prisoners and then with the tradition of trafficking in women whereby women were treated as slaves to be bought and sold. The combined humiliation of being both prisoner and slave now concentrates in the figure of woman. Whenever a woman announces that she is going to get married and uses the word *xiajia* 下嫁 (go down and get married), she is essentially equating herself to a prisoner or a slave and does not seem ashamed of being degraded thus. This situation cannot but lead to a point where the idea of woman itself is rendered utterly inhuman.

2. On Funerary Rites

Among the established rites of China, the funerary rites rank foremost. Here fundamental inequalities between man and woman begin with the allotted length of mourning periods for each gender as well as the differential quality of their mourning attire, and this is just as true of the modern age as of the distant past. Philologist Cheng Yichou (1725–1814), the author of *A Comprehensive Study of Funerary Rites*, has compiled some detailed tables to show how mourning practices should be regulated. If I may simplify these tables to three, these are (1) the regulation of mourning periods as distinguished between the paternal line and maternal line; (2) the regulation of mourning periods as distinguished between husband and wife; (3) the regulation of mourning periods as distinguished between male and female deceased in general. Let me cite these tables below:

Differentiating mourning periods between paternal and maternal lines[12]

FOR THE PATERNAL LINE	FOR THE MATERNAL LINE
Observe three years of mourning for the father	Observe one year of mourning for the mother when the father is alive; three years when the father is dead
Do the same for the stepmother as for the mother	One year for the stepfather
One year for paternal grandparents	Five months for maternal grandparents
One year for paternal elder uncles	Three months for maternal uncles
Nine months for paternal aunts	Five months for maternal aunts
Nine months for the son of a paternal uncle	Three months for the son of a maternal uncle

Differentiating mourning periods between husband and wife

HUSBAND	WIFE
Three years for a deceased husband	One year for a deceased wife
One year for paternal in-laws	Three months for maternal in-laws
Nine months for husband's brothers	No mourning for wife's brothers
Nine months for husband's grandparents	No mourning for wife's grandparents

[12]Tr: The observation of mourning periods varied from dynasty to dynasty; these tables correspond more closely to the practices of the Qing dynasty (1644–1911) than those of the earlier dynasties. We should note that each mourning period in traditional Chinese funerary rites is

Differentiating mourning periods between man and woman in general

FOR MEN	FOR WOMEN
The eldest son observes three years	The daughter observes nine months
The daughter-in-law observes nine months	The son-in-law observes three months
The oldest grandson observes one year	The maternal grandson observes three months
The oldest granddaughter observes one year	The paternal granddaughter observes five months
All other grandsons or grandsons by a concubine observe nine months	All other granddaughters-in-law observe three months
Brothers observe one year	Sisters observe nine months.
Uncles observe one year	Paternal aunts observes nine months
Grand-uncles observe three months	Paternal grand-aunts observe three months

When we examine the first table, we learn how much more esteemed the father is than the mother; from the second table, we learn how the husband is placed above the wife; and from the third, we learn how men in general are shown more respect than women. I suppose that the source of these practices may be attributed to one of the Three Bonds, which places the husband over and above the wife. Inevitably, as the wife submits to the patrilineal order of her husband's family, her mourning obligations increase. But when the son mourns members of his maternal family, his

---

correlated with the appropriate mourning attire—usually made of hemp-fiber cloth in various degrees of coarseness—to be worn by the man or the woman who mourns the dead. The cut and style of such clothing is strictly regulated depending on the position the mourner occupies in the hierarchy of the lineage. Our translation of Chen's tables omits a detailed description of each type of mourning attire that comes with the required observation of mourning periods. See footnote 6 on p. 181 for detailed explanation.

mourning obligations decrease, which cannot but cause the son to esteem his father more than his mother and cause the family to value the sons more than the daughters. Is this not a consequence of the husband's domination over the wife? The sole exception in the later age is the observation of three years' mourning for both the father and the mother (as long as the father is deceased), which seems more equitable. Imagine a married woman observing three years' mourning for her maternal uncle or for her paternal aunt, as [her doing] this would disrupt the balance of established rules, which are worse than those of remote antiquity. This is because the rites and social institutions of China were crafted by men who established the system to suppress women's rights. And can we continue to regard this system as the natural embodiment of universal truths?

In addition to the marriage institution and mourning regulations, there is also the rite of ancestral worship to consider. On this subject, the *Book of Rites* states in a section on *quli*, or etiquette, that "a husband does not offer sacrifices to commemorate a deceased wife." The scholar Fang Bao (1668–1749) further opined that women must not preside over the ancestral temple. Is this not clear evidence of inequity between man and woman in the matter of ancestral worship? As for social etiquette, we are told by no less an authority than [the 2nd–3rd century B.C.E. scholar] *Mao's Annotations to the Book of Songs* that women should not interfere with external affairs. The Confucian scholar Zheng Xuan (127–200 C.E.) states that women have no business outside the confines of her household. In the *Book of Rites*, we are told that women should not talk about external affairs and they should not overstep the bounds of their own sphere. The fences are so tightly constructed and policed that women virtually become prisoners, whereas men are left free to explore the wider world and search for friends to support each other. This sort of social etiquette can hardly be deemed equitable. As we reflect on the inequalities in social institutions, it is clear that the relationship between man and woman over the past millennia has evolved into the inequality between social classes. In other words, men have subjugated women and turned them into private property. And this is what I mean by the second aspect of the tyranny of men's rule.[13]

---

[13]Tr: Many of these arguments are more fully amplified in He-Yin's essay "Economic Revolution and Women's Revolution," translated in this volume.

He-Yin Zhen, "On the Revenge of Women," *Natural Justice*, no. 3, June 1907.

Inscribing Gender Inequality in Classical Learning

A third aspect of the tyranny of men's rule is manifest in the entire scholastic tradition of China.[14] In the age of high antiquity, men treated learning as their own private prerogative. No wonder that *every school of thought was*

---

[14]Tr: The term *xueshu* 學術 is an amorphous concept. In rendering it "scholastic tradition" and "scholarship," the translator hews to its meaning in the early twentieth century. What He-Yin Zhen meant by it includes the classical canon, the Confucian hermeneutic tradition and teachings, and also the words and deeds of women exemplars who internalized these teachings. In the sections below, she quotes from a handful of key texts in the Confucian canon and their seminal commentaries to document the beginnings of a misogynist tradition. The most salient ones she cites are commentaries to four of the Confucian "Five Classics": the *Book of Songs*, *Book of Changes*, *Book of Rites*, and *Spring and Autumn Annals* (the fifth being the *Book of Documents*). Most of the texts He-Yin Zhen discussed were codified in the Han period (Former or Western Han, 202 B.C.E.–24 C.E.; Later or Eastern Han, 25–220 C.E.), the foundational period of misogynist thought attributable to the rise of yin-yang cosmology. This period is seminal

founded by men, and every book from the Three Dynasties contains words that degrade women while elevating men.[15]

They are but the biased concerns of men. Since the Qin and Han dynasties (221 B.C.E. to 220 C.E.), all schools of thought more or less traced their roots to Confucianism (literally, the School of Ru 儒), the key concept of which is none other than elevating men and deprecating women. Consider Confucius, the founder of Confucianism, who was known for discarding his wife. His sons and grandsons learned the same from him. But when it comes to inflicting violence onto wives, the followers of Confucius are truly peerless. Consider Mencius, the great Confucian master. Just because his wife failed to greet him when he came into the room, he plotted to get rid of her. What tyrannical control this is!

Later generations of scholars not only revered Confucian words but also modeled their behavior after their Confucian forebears. They therefore privileged men as if they were up in the Ninth Heaven and put women down as if they were in the pits of the Ninth Ravine. *If it is to men's benefit, they would not hesitate to twist words and concoct truth so that the biased interests of men could flourish.* These scholars began by establishing the theory that the husband is the wife's "Bond." They made it sound as though when Heaven gave birth to humans, men were to be valued and women slighted. In order to augment the rights and power (*quan*) of men, they made women their appendages. Worrying that women would not willingly submit, they harped on the virtues of obedience and admonished women to "remain true to one [man] unto death." Still worrying that women would fight back, they made sure that women would have only obligations but not rights and restricted women's comings and goings. In forbidding wives from remarrying and condemning jealousy among women, men ensured that their polygyny could be perpetuated. They also devised the separate roles of "wife" and "concubine" so that women would restrain and compete with each other. Thus it has come to be that men mistreat women and hold them in such low esteem. Isn't it obvious that they are under the spell of Confucianism? Inclined toward despotism, Confucian scholarship has enabled

---

also because it marked the beginning of the consolidation of Confucianism as the leading ideology of the state. The logic of He-Yin Zhen's argumentation is simple and consistent: Identifying the theoretical root makes it easier to understand how misogynist thought became naturalized through time by active state promotion and the sheer sedimentation of culture.

[15]Tr: The italics indicate emphases in the original.

men to cater to their self-interest. It comes as no surprise that polygyny and female chastity are both heralded by Confucianism.

Scholars in the Han dynasty were firm adherents to Confucianism. Whenever they came across mentions of women in the ancient texts, they concocted meanings from the superficial meanings of written words and bent the ancient classics to justify their own biases. An extreme example is the *White Tiger Discourse. But whoever promulgated this book was merely promoting the patriarch's selfish interests.*[16] Song dynasty Confucianists followed with an even more draconian suppression and control of women; women were despised so much that they were cast beyond the pale of humanity. Since then, scholars and officials have held fast to the teachings from the Han and Song dynasties as their golden standard. As these teachings became convention, no one questioned how wrong they were. *The shrewd who knew these teachings were wrong whitewashed them to further their self-interest; the dumb swallowed the teachings without a shadow of a doubt.* In the process, who knows how many of our fellow women were killed because of them! In sum, all Confucian teachings are teachings that kill people. One by one, they can be listed as follows:[17]

- *Book of Changes* (*Yijing*, the Qian hexagram): "[Although there is beauty in yin, it will not accomplish kingly projects.] Neither can the way of the earth, the way of the wife, and the way of the subject."
- *Xunzi* (chapter on "Rulership"): "The Son of Heaven [the ruler] cannot have a wife so as to announce to the world that he is peerless."[18]

---

[16]One example is when the usurper of the Han throne Wang Mang (ca. 25 B.C.E.–23 C.E.) twisted the *Rites of Zhou* to justify his expanding the ranks of his consorts, such scholars as Zhang Yu and Ma Rong followed suit and enlarged their harem. Tr: *White Tiger Discourse* (*Baihu Tong*), a record of discussions about the classics and Confucian philosophy held in the White Tiger Hall during the reign of Emperor Zhang of Han (r. 75–88 C.E.), was compiled by Ban Gu (32–92 C.E.).

[17]Tr: Lost in translation is He-Yin's facility with these texts. All classically educated people of her age, male or female, memorized the canon and its most important early commentaries. He-Yin Zhen sometimes used abbreviated titles or skipped lines in her citations because she knew that her readers, like her, would have committed these passages to memory. She still opted to list the texts one by one for maximum rhetorical force.

[18]Tr: This is a classic play on words with homonyms, since the Chinese word for wife, *qi* 妻, is a homonym of *qi* 齊, "being equal" or "a peer." The consort to the Son of Heaven cannot strictly be called a "wife" because of the homonym situation. She is addressed as *hou* 後 (literally, "after" or "queen").

- *Biographies of Exemplary Women* (citing the *Book of Rites*, chapter 13): "Before a woman marries, she takes her father as heaven. When married, she takes her husband as heaven."

- *Book of Rites* ("Suburban Rites"): "The man goes in person to meet the bride, the man taking the initiative and not the woman, [according to the idea that regulates the relationship between the strong and the weak]."[19]

- *White Tiger Discourse* ("On Marriage"): "The rites of marriage: Why is it that a man takes in a wife and a woman leaves her house to marry? It is because yin, being lowly, cannot have her own prerogatives; she relies on yang to accomplish things. Therefore, the annotations to the *Book of Changes* states: 'Yang initiates, yin responds; man acts, woman follows.'"

- He (Xiu, 129–182 C.E.), *Explications of the Commentary of Gongyang* (Gongyang jiegu): "The rites insist that in a marriage, the man goes in person to meet the bride; this is to demonstrate that men come before women."

- Ma (Rong, 79–166 C.E.), Annotation to *Etiquette and Rituals* (Yili): "The husband of a woman is heaven, therefore he is called 'the most exalted one.'"[20]

- (Liu Xiang, 79–8 B.C.E.), *Biographies of Exemplary Women*:[21] "Docility and obedience constitute the business of a woman; her devotion is to chastity and steadfastness. Therefore a woman serves her husband by paying respect to him at dawn with her hair tied back with a long strip of cloth and secured with hairpins. She thus shows a solemnity like that between a ruler and his minister."

---

[19]Tr: Translation adapted from James Legge, *Li Ki (The Book of Rites)*. See http://ctext.org/liji (accessed February 15, 2012).

[20]Cited in *Comprehensive Institutions* (*Tongdian*). Tr: Compiled by Tang scholar Du You (735–812) in 801 C.E., it is the first comprehensive survey of the political, economic, and ritual institutions from the classical period to his times.

[21]Cited in the *Imperial Readings of the Taiping Era* (*Taiping yulan*, 977–983 C.E.). Tr: *Biographies of Exemplary Women* (*Lienü zhuan*) was compiled by Liu Xiang (79–8 B.C.E.) toward the end of the Former Han dynasty (202 B.C.E.–9 C.E.). It was the earliest extant book devoted solely to the moral education of women. Anne Behnke Kinney translates the title as *Traditions of Exemplary Women*. He-Yin Zhen is such a scrupulous philologist that following conventional practice, she always identifies the section of the book in which her citation appears or she states, as in this selection, that she is citing from a secondary source. The translator has retained this information in this section only.

- Xun Shuang (128–190 C.E.), memorial to [Emperor Huan of Han, 166 C.E.]: "The relationship between husband and wife is the beginning of human ethics and kingly transformation. Therefore King Wen of Zhou began section 1 of his *Book of Changes* with the *Qian* ䷀ and *Kun* ䷁ hexagrams and Section 2 with the *Xian* ䷞ and *Heng* ䷟ hexagrams.[22]

- Confucius opined, "Heaven is as high as the earth is low. The way of husband and wife is subservience." The *Canon of Yao* (Yaodian) describes that King Yao "arranged and sent down his two daughters to the north of the Gui, to be wives in [the family] of Yu."[23] Notice how even the daughters of King Yao were said to be "sent down" (*jiang* 降) to be wives. They had to prostrate and lower themselves in their diligent practice of the wifely way. Likewise, the *Book of Changes* refers to "King Yi's [rule about the] marriage of his younger sister. By such a course there is happiness and there will be great good fortune."[24] We see that for a woman, the word used for marrying is "to return" (*gui* 歸). Yi used the proper rites of marriage to "return" his younger sister to [her true home]. In the Spring and Autumn period (772–476 B.C.E.), the protocol [was strict]. When Wangji [the younger sister of the reigning king of Zhou] married Duke Xiang of Qi, the officiating parent was not the king but a duke from Lu to avoid [Wangji using her dominant rank as the sister of] the Son of Heaven to overpower the lesser Qi.

---

[22]Tr: The descriptions of the four hexagrams are

Qian 乾 [Qian]: Represents what is great and originating, penetrating, advantageous, correct, and firm.

Kun 坤 [Kun]: Represents what is great and originating, penetrating, advantageous, correct, and having the firmness of a mare.

Xian 咸 [Xian]: Indicates that (on the fulfillment of the conditions implied in it) there will be free course and success. Its advantageousness will depend on the being firm and correct, (as) in marrying a young lady. There will be good fortune.

Heng 恒 [Heng]: Indicates successful progress and no error (in what it denotes). But the advantage will come from being firm and correct; and movement in any direction whatever will be advantageous.

Adapted from the translation by James Legge; accessed February 15, 2012 from http://ctext.org/liji.

[23]Tr: The *Canon of Yao* is part of the *Book of Documents*, one of the Five Classics of the Confucian tradition.

[24]Tr: The *Tai* (泰) hexagram.

[Xun continued:] "But our Han house has opted to follow the method of the intervening Qin dynasty (221–206 B.C.E.), whereby a husband of a lower noble rank could marry a princess, making him in terms of ranking a subsidiary of hers.[25] The wife then lords it over her husband; the lowly situates herself above the high. This is an infringement of the way of *Qian* over *Kun* [in the *Book of Changes*], or yang leads and yin follows. Confucius thus said of the origins of *Changes*: 'The sage [Baoxi] had come to the rule of all under heaven, looking up, he contemplated the brilliant forms exhibited in the sky, and looking down he surveyed the patterns shown on the earth. He contemplated the ornamental appearances of birds and beasts and the different suitabilities of the soil. Near at hand, in his own person, he found things for consideration, and the same at a distance, in things in general. On this he devised the eight trigrams, to show fully the attributes of the spiritlike and intelligent [operations working secretly], and to classify the qualities of the myriads of things.' When we look up to contemplate the brilliant forms of the sky, the North Star rules supreme and the four stars surround him like his empress and consorts. When we look down to survey the patterns on earth, Mount Kun symbolizes the husband and the lowly streams and marshes, wife. When we contemplate the ornamental appearances of birds and beasts, the male bird crows and the female obeys; the male animals take the lead and the female follows. Near at hand, in our own body, 'qian' refers to the head of man whereas 'kun' refers to the belly. At a distance, we see how the fruits of a tree belong up high to the sky, and the roots are buried in the ground. It is obvious, then, that in the nature of all things yang is high and yin low. Further, if we ponder the fact that the *Songs* begins with the [conjugal] poem 'Guan Ju' and capping and marriage rites head the *Rites*, we recognize that the correct relationship between husband and wife is paramount. Therefore the natural order in heaven and earth accords with the emphasis in the Six Classics.[26] I, therefore, implore Your Highness to abolish our prevalent custom of allowing a husband of a

---

[25]Tr: The Chinese term for this practice, *shangzhu* 尚主, has a wider range of meaning. In the Tang dynasty, the "one who is shangzhu'ed" (*shangzhu zhe* 尚主者) refers to a man of lesser status who married uxorilocally to a princess.

[26]Tr: The Six Classics refers to the Confucian canon of the Five Classics plus a long-lost *Book of Music*. Alternatively, it refers to the "Six Arts" of the Confucian gentleman.

lower rank to marry a princess so that the nature of 'qian' and 'kun' will be preserved."[27]

These constitute indisputable evidence that the husband was to be the "bond" of the wife. Ancient teaching held that the wife is to the husband as the minister is to his lord, therefore men come first, women last; men are superior and women inferior. On the basis of "men first, women last," such other deviant teachings as "yang initiates, yin harmonizes" or "men act, women follow" were concocted to restrict women's freedom. And, from "men superior, women inferior" such deviant teaching as "the husband is the heaven of the wife" also came into being. The husband is thus made into heaven and the wife earth; the husband becomes identified with yang and the wife yin. *The relationship between men and women thus became one of absolute inequality* [through cosmic abstraction]. I cannot but sigh at this.

- *Commentary of Guliang* [on the *Spring and Autumn Annals*]:[28] "Before a woman marries, she is subservient to her father; when married, she is subservient to her husband; after her husband dies, she follows her first-born son. A woman should not act on her own; she always follows."
- *Records of Rites by Dai Senior* (Da Dai Liji): "To be female (*nü* 女) is to comply (*ru* 如). It means that she complies with the teachings of men in order to develop into a person with righteousness and propriety."

---

[27] *History of the Later Han* [Biography of Xun Shuang, *juan* 62]. Tr: Xun Shuang, like many Han Confucian scholars (such as Wang Ji and Du Qin, cited by He-Yin Zhen below) who attacked the prevalent practice of "man marrying a princess (*shangzhu*)," derived his theoretical position from the yin-yang cosmology formulated by Dong Zhongshu (179–104 B.C.E.). Dong developed the theory of "yang-high and yin-low," and these scholars applied the theory specifically to conjugal relations. The equation of husband with the yang-high position and wife with yin-low was thus an invention by the Han Confucian scholars. Essentially, they did so by adding a new regime of positionality to the existing hierarchy of noble ranks. Even if the wife enjoys a higher noble rank than the husband, in her *subject position as wife* she was made subservient to the husband. The Confucian dicta of "Thrice Following" and "Four Virtues," which became normative for women in posterity, both stem from this theoretical foundation. No wonder He-Yin Zhen cited predominantly Han texts to show how they formed a cultural nexus. Curiously, however, she cited Dong Zhongshu only once (see below).

[28] Tr: Three commentaries to the *Spring and Autumn Annals* circulated in the Han: the Zuo in the Old Text tradition as well as the Gongyang and Guliang in the New Text tradition.

- *Etiquette and Rituals*: "A woman has the responsibility of 'thrice-following.' She does not indulge in her own way."
- *White Tiger Discourse*: "To be female (*nü* 女) is to comply (*ru* 如). It means that she follows and yields to someone else. At home, she follows her father and mother; in marriage she follows her husband; after he dies she follows her son."
- Zheng's *Annotations to the Book of Changes*: "The term '*wu you sui* 無 攸遂' means that a woman dare not make decisions for herself."
- He Xiu, *Explications of the Commentary of Gongyang*: "A *ji* (筓) is a single-prong hairpin. A woman wears this [when she comes of age at 15] to indicate that she will belong to someone. She uses it to cultivate her undivided chastity."
- (Xu Shen, ca. 58–ca. 147 C.E.), *Differing Meanings in the Five Classics* (Wujing yiyi): "A woman's responsibility is to follow. If her husband advances at court, she gains glory in her inner chambers. Therefore after he dies, she will be known by his posthumous titles."
- *White Tiger Discourse*: "The word *yin* (姻) is made up of the woman radical (*nü* 女) on the left and the radical *yin* 因 on the right, which means to comply with or to depend on. *Yin* 姻 connotes the dependence of a woman on her husband; therefore the word has come to mean affinal relations, or more specifically the family of one's son-in-law."
- Jing Fang (77–37 B.C.E.), *Commentary to the Book of Changes*: "For yin to follow yang and for a wife to be compliant to her husband, both are the natural workings of heaven and earth."
- Zheng, *Annotations to the Book of Rites*: "A married woman wears a *ying* 纓 [perhaps a five-colored silk cord] to indicate that she is tied and belongs to someone."

The above provide ample evidence that women are made subsidiaries of men [in the Confucian tradition]. [In life,] men indeed treat women as their subsidiaries,[29] barring them from pursuing independence and freedom. Thus they admonish women not to have their own prerogatives, not

---

[29]The writings of recent scholars are even more extreme. The Qing scholar Chen Li (1809–1869): "The husband is yang and the wife yin. A wife follows her husband—this is what 'following yang' means." Hu Chenggong (1776–1832): "Rites: After a woman is promised in marriage, she wears a *ying* 纓 to show the world that she is tied and belongs to someone. A woman should devote herself to one man only and should not want to wear another cord."

to insist on their own way, not to take any initiatives, to be subservient, and to achieve themselves through their husbands. Is this not a statement of how women cannot be independent? Does this not amount to controlling women so that they cannot be free? This is the origin of the doctrine of "Three Obediences" or "Thrice Following" (*sancong*).

- *Book of Rites* ("The Meaning of Marriage"): "For a wife to be compliant means that she is deferential to her parents-in-law and harmonious with other members in the women's quarters. She then makes a fitting partner for her husband."
- *Records of Rites by Dai Senior*: "A woman (*furen* 婦人) is one who is subservient (*fu* 服) in serving others (*ren* 人)."
- *Mao's Annotations to the Songs* (Mao zhuan):[30] "In ancient times when a lady was matched with her gentleman lord, she did not neglect to be respectful."
- *White Tiger Discourse*: "A woman (*fu* 婦) is the subservient (*fu* 服) one. She is made subservient by the rites."
- Zheng [Xuan, 127–200], *Annotations to the Mao Tradition of the Songs* (Maoshi jian):[31] "The behavior of a woman is distinguished by obedience and deference; she holds herself in cleanliness and purity."
- Zheng [Xuan], *Annotations to the Rites of Zhou*: "'Womanly virtue' means chastity and compliance; 'womanly word' means her speech; 'womanly deportment' means an appearance of grace and docility; 'womanly work' means textile work with silk and hemp."
- [This is repeated in] Zheng [Xuan], *Annotations to Etiquette and Rituals*: "'Womanly virtue' means chastity and compliance; 'womanly word' means her speech; 'womanly deportment' means an appearance of grace and docility; 'womanly work' means textile work with silk and hemp."

---

[30]Tr: *Mao's Annotations to the Songs* (*Maozhuan* 毛傳, or *Maoshi guxun zhuan* 毛詩故訓傳) was attributed to the founder of the *Mao Tradition of the Songs*, the Qin-Han scholar Mao Heng 毛亨 (3rd–2nd century B.C.E.?), who transmitted it to his Western Han disciple Mao Chang 毛萇. The Han edition is lost; the extant version was extracted from Zheng Xuan's *Annotations of the Mao Tradition of the Book of Songs*.

[31]Tr: Four editions of the *Book of Songs* circulated in the Han: the Mao (Old Text) tradition and the Lu, Qi, and Han, all New Text traditions.

- Zheng [Xuan], *Annotations to the Book of Rites*: "The rites of the supplicant lie chiefly in being filial and compliant."
- Zheng [Xuan], *Annotations to the Book of Changes*: "When a woman cultivates the virtue of obedience, her sons will be decent and good."
- *White Tiger Discourse*: "Why does a woman need an instructress? To learn the way of serving others."
- *Garden of Persuasions*: "The marquis went personally to meet his bride. Her mother admonished her: 'You now go! Serve your parents-in-law well, and shelter yourself by obedience as if it were your palace. Do not let your heart be divided, and do not dream of coming back!'"[32]

These, then, constitute evidence that women were made to be subservient to men. Since womanly virtue involves [the woman's] lowering herself into submission, *when women were educated in the past all that they learned was the way of serving others.* Does it not indicate that women were being regarded as maids and slaves? Docility is just another name for lowering oneself into submission. Respect is just another name for docility. To be graceful is just another way of saying appearing docile. For men were loath to have women resisting them; hence *they made docility into a desirable thing* and praised such women who practiced it—those of the ilk of Gongji of the state of Song or Huan Xiaojun and Meng Guang of the Han dynasty—as sagacious women. But when men acted deferentially, they were reprimanded as practicing the Way of a concubine. Therefore, men knew full well that docility was not a good virtue but nonetheless made women abide by it. Does this not imply that they were banishing women from the realm of the human?

- *Book of Rites*: "Once a woman becomes a man's wife, she remains so for life. Therefore, when the husband dies she does not remarry."
- Kuang Heng (fl. 47–36 B.C.E.), on the *Qi Tradition of the Book of Songs*: "The couplet in the *Songs*, 'The modest, retiring, virtuous young lady: —/ For our prince a good mate she,' means that she perseveres with her chastity to the end and that she is undivided in her loyal conduct."

---

[32]Tr: *Garden of Persuasions* (*Shuoyuan*) was compiled by the Former Han scholar Liu Xiang (79–8 B.C.E.) and consisted of anecdotes and discussions of themes with Confucian concerns.

- Preface to the *Mao Tradition of Songs*: "A woman who abides by the protocol is one who can inherit and pass on the ancestors' mantle and partake in ancestral rites."
- *Mao's Annotations to the Songs*: "For a woman, virtue is being chaste, quiet, and abiding by the protocols."
- *Mao's Annotations to the Songs*: "If an empress or consort takes pleasure in the virtue of the prince, she would achieve harmony in everything. Also, he should not indulge in her beauty, and she should hold fast to her concealment. This is the meaning of [the first poem in *Book of Songs*] Guan Ju."[33]
- Ditto [*Mao's Annotations to the Songs*]: "To say that an empress or consort is endowed with 'Guan Ju's virtue' is to mean that a good maid who is retiring, quiet, chaste, and devoted makes a fitting mate for the prince."
- Zheng [Xuan], *Annotations to the Mao Tradition of the Songs*: "A woman should have the virtue of singular devotion—like a turtledove—before she can be mated with the lord of a country."
- Ditto [Zheng Xuan, *Annotations to the Mao Tradition of the Songs*]: "She is like a piece of jade—steadfast, white and pure."
- Xue [Han] (fl. 25–72 C.E.), *Syntactic and Semantic Analysis of the Han Tradition of the Book of Songs* (*Hanshi zhangju*): "The poet [of the Guan-ju poem in the *Book of Songs*] was saying that the osprey, being chaste and clean, chooses its mate carefully. In mating, it sends out the "guan-guan" chirping sound but conceals itself in a place where it cannot be seen."
- He Xiu, *Explications of the Commentary of Gongyang*: "Rites: A new bride offers dates, chestnuts, and dry meat to her in-laws. [This is because the word for dates (*zao* 棗) is homonym for 'without delay' (*zao* 早) and the word for chestnuts (*li* 栗) can also mean 'trembling.'] Therefore, a gift of dates and chestnuts symbolizes her resolve to guard herself without delay. [The words for dry meat (*duan xiu* 股脩) are homonyms of 'guarding the right path' (*duanduan* 斷斷) and 'correcting oneself' (*xiuzheng* 修正).] Therefore, a gift of dry meat symbolizes her desire to adhere to the right path and to correct her behavior."

---

[33]Tr: *Ju* 雎 means "ospreys" and *guan* refers to the sound they make; hence the first couplet: "Guan-guan go the ospreys/ On the islet of the river." He-Yin Zhen quotes the couplet that follows, "The modest, retiring, virtuous young lady: . . ./ For our prince a good mate she" above.

- Ditto [He Xiu, *Explications of the Commentary of Gongyang*]: "In chastity and trustworthiness, she accomplishes the rites of a wife."
- Master Cheng [Yi, 1033–1107]: "To starve to death is a small matter, but to lose one's integrity is a major matter indeed."[34]

These are cases of women being taught to remain faithful to one man unto death. Let me add a telling one. In the Han, a certain Feng Yan told Bao Yong: "There was a man who flirted with the wives of his neighbors. When he approached an elder one, she soundly reprimanded him; when he approached a younger one, she rewarded him. Later the husband of the elder woman died. The man proceeded to marry her. When people asked, 'Isn't she the one who scolded you before?' the man replied, 'When it's another man's wife, I want her to favor me; when it comes to my own wife, I want her to scold others.'" Ha! Didn't all men secretly use this tactic? They practiced polygyny themselves but worried that their wives would follow their example in taking multiple husbands; hence they made chastity, faithfulness, and purity into female virtues. And since they feared that women could not control themselves, they enticed them with teachings of holding fast in concealment, treating women as virtual prisoners. They also fretted that in the end, after they die, their wives would cease to belong to them. So they commended chastity, granting women empty titles, which is *no different from authoritarian rulers rewarding loyalty* in the hopes that their ministers will die for them. Truly there are no words craftier than these.

Consider that in ancient times, women did not shy from remarriage after their husbands died. The *Book of Rites* had to invent the teaching of "When a husband dies, do not remarry." Confucian scholars of the Song pushed it even further, deeming it a minor problem to starve to death but a major problem to lose one's chastity. Isn't it making women into instruments of men's selfish desires? Besides the honored title of "chaste widow" there was also "faithful maiden." Chaste widows are those who remained loyal to their dead husbands, whereas faithful maidens were loyal to men to whom they were betrothed but who died before consummating marriage. Faithful maiden became a category when *Biographies of Exemplary Women* transmitted the deeds of Lady Weixuan and Boji [sic; Mengji] the consort of

---

[34]*Posthumous Writings of Cheng Hao and Cheng Yi* (Er Cheng yishu). Tr: Cheng Yi (1033–1107) was a Neo-Confucian thinker in the Song dynasty. His appearance here is abrupt, as all the other Confucian texts He-Yin Zhen cited were from the classical period about a millennium earlier.

Duke Xiao of Qi under the special heading of "chaste and docile."[35] The Jin scholar Xie Feng held that when a bride performed the ritual of *baishi* 拜時 (picking an auspicious wedding date), it was analogous to a ruler entering the name of an official in his appointment book.[36]

[Many recent scholars have found faithful maidens admirable.] The philologist Jiao Xun (1763–1820), for instance, praised faithful maidens, saying that when they refuse to serve a man of a different surname, it is tantamount to loyal subjects refusing to serve a new dynasty; when wives kill themselves to follow their dead husbands, it is tantamount to a martyr giving his body for his fallen country.[37] Shen Qinhan (1775–1832) wrote, "What is expected of even a single word is constancy, what is invested in one oath is life and death."[38] Thus even daughters whose betrotheds die before marriage are forced to remain chaste.[39] They say that when a daughter receives a marriage letter or betrothal gifts, the proprieties of husband-and-wife are sealed. The philologist Qian Daxin (1728–1804) made it clear: "When a girl pins up her hair and ties on a ribbon [in her coming-of-age ceremony], it means that she is already tied to and belongs to another person." Hu Chenggong (1776–1832), a scholar from Jixi, Anhui Province, opined that "the wedding is finalized with the rite of presenting betrothal gifts to the bride's family," and "since the couple already knows each other's name, even if he dies before the wedding, she can [move to his house to] serve his parents."[40] Further, that "after a daughter is promised in marriage, she belongs to her husband."[41]

---

[35]Tr: The tale of Lady Weixuan was set in the Spring and Autumn period (770–476 B.C.E.). *Biographies of Exemplary Women*, edited by Liu Xiang (79–8 B.C.E.), cited by He-Yin Zhen above, is an important collection that remained popular as a didactic text for women in late imperial times.

[36]*Tongdian*, chap. 59.

[37]Jiao Xun, "Li Zhennü shi," and "Zhenfu bian," in *Diaogulou ji*.

[38]The burial tablet of Chaste Woman Jin, née Long.

[39]Jiao Xun argued that rewards to faithful maidens enjoyed a precedent in the Han by citing from the *Sequel to the History of the Later Han*: "When there is a faithful maiden, the Three Elders of the neighborhood are to put a plaque on her door to promote this excellent behavior." (See Jiao's "Zhennü bian.") Many recent observers have referred to this.

[40]Hu, "Bo shinü buyi shouzhi yi."

[41]Tr: Confucian scholars have debated the propriety of faithful maidens since the sixteenth century. This debate, which involved such major philologists as Qian Daxin in the eighteenth century, took the form of identifying the point at which a marriage was considered ritually finalized during the long process of exchanging names, documents, and gifts (comparable,

So, first they admonish women to remain true to one man, then they expect her to remain true to him even before they are married! How have they fooled and toyed with women! In China, those who adhered to this discourse have kept it up by conferring the title of "the chaste and faithful." Li Chaoluo (1769–1841) reasoned, "If we force a maiden to marry another man after [her] betrothed's death, aren't we teaching [her] to be *un*-chaste?" Isn't this *using the empty name of "faithful maiden" in order to press women to death*? Now we fully realize that the so-called *"rites and propriety" being upheld by Confucian scholars in the past were none other than an instrument for the brutal murdering of women*. Recent scholars such as Wang Zhong (1745–1794) and Yu Zhengxie (1775–1840) have both criticized the faithful maiden cult.[42] Their discourses are rooted in that of Ming scholar Gui Youguang (1506–1571).[43] But detractors only observed that the faithful maiden cult violates classical rituals without pointing out that the two words "chastity and loyalty" could kill. As such they failed to diagnose the root of the problem.

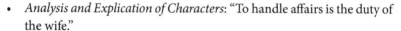

- *Analysis and Explication of Characters*: "To handle affairs is the duty of the wife."
- Zheng, *Annotations to the Rites of Zhou*: "The work of a wife is textile and needlework: to weave, twist thread, and sew."
- Zheng, *Annotations to the Book of Rites*: "To make the wine and to sweep and clean, these are the duties of women."

---

in a way, to identifying the beginnings of human life during conception in the pro-choice versus pro-life debate). For the cult of faithful maidens and the complexity of female emotions involved, see Weijing Lu, *True to Her Word: The Faithful Maiden Cult in Late Imperial China* (Stanford, CA: Stanford University Press, 2008).

[42] Wang wrote: "A virtuous woman does not serve two husbands, but the ancient sages did not say she should not be *betrothed* to two husbands." He considered the keeping of chaste maidens no different than inviting them to be licentious. Yu Zhengxie's defense is especially heart-wrenching.

[43] Gui argued that "[b]efore the ceremony that makes her a wife, a woman is not tied to her husband. The betrothal pact is only an agreement between the parents; the woman herself does not know to whom her body belongs." This is the basis for Wang Zhong's reasoning. But scholars like Jiao Xun have tried to reject it as if it were a flood or menacing beasts.

- Liu Xi, *Explaining Terms* (Shiming): "Woman (*fu* 婦) is the homonym of being subservient (*fu* 服) in serving others. She serves by tending to duties at home."
- *Book of Rites*: "A woman does not speak of affairs outside."
- *Mao's Annotations to the [Book of] Songs*: "A woman has no affairs outside. Even for an empress, her duties are tending the silkworms and weaving."
- Zheng, *Annotations to the Mao Tradition of the Songs*: "A woman has no affairs outside. Her affair is being chaste and trustworthy."
- [This is repeated in] Zheng, *Annotations to Etiquette and Rituals*: "A woman has no affairs outside."
- Ditto [Zheng, *Annotations to Etiquette and Rituals*]: "A woman does not specialize in any duties at home. When errors occur, they are not women's fault; neither should women take credit when something good happens."
- Yang Zhen (59–124), "Memorial."[44] "The *Book of Documents* warns against a hen crowing. The *Book of Songs* satirizes crafty women who cause the downfall of their country. Duke Zhuang of Zheng indulged his mother's desires and spoiled his younger brother; the latter plotted to rebel and nearly brought down the country. The *Spring and Autumn Annals* criticized the duke for failing to bring up his brother properly. Indeed, women and mean people [as suggested in the *Analects*] are hard to deal with. If you let them get too close, they become too indulgent; if you keep your distance, they resent it. The *Book of Changes* makes it clear that a woman 'has nothing else to do beside preparing the wine and food.' Women should not meddle in political affairs."

These words make clear that women had responsibilities but not rights. Since the industry required to keep house was more than what men themselves could bear, they commandeered women to be their servants and slaves. And since men did not want women to meddle in their affairs, they invented such teachings as "women have no business in the outer sphere"

---

[44]Tr: Yang Zhen, a Later Han official, submitted this memorial to Emperor An (r. 106–125 C.E.) in 121 C.E. to warn him of the dangers of letting women meddle in political affairs. At the time, the emperor indulged his wet nurse and her daughter, who became powerful figures in the palace.

in order to deprive women of their natural rights (*tianfu zhiquan*). With respect to the argument [about women's responsibility], *men placed themselves in positions of leisure and admonished women to labor.* To follow up on the argument [about women's proper sphere], *men placed themselves in positions of intelligence and relegated women to stupidity.* Is this not injustice at its worst? The Han Confucian scholar Zheng Xuan, moreover, deemed managing the household a womanly task but also said that women should not specialize in any duties at home. Is this not oppression at its worst?

- *White Tiger Discourse*: "Wait three months after a woman marries into the house, and her goodness and badness will reveal themselves. After that they can partake in ancestral rites."
- *Book of Songs*: "The word *chuochuo* [in the poem "Grass Insect"] describes the mournful look [in *Mao's Commentary*] of a wife as she is being cast out and returned to her natal family."[45]
- [Kong Yingda (574–648),] *Commentary on the Zuo Commentary* (Zuozhuan zhengyi):[46] "The Rites: When a new bride is sent to her husband's family, she keeps the horse on which she comes to signal her modesty, that she would not take her husband for granted. If she were cast out, she would ride back."

---

[45]Annotations to the poem "Cao Chong." Tr: The commentator has given the love poem an allegorical moralistic reading. The stanza of the poem "Cao Chong" (Grass insects, no. 14) reads:

> I ascended that hill in the south,
> And gathered the turtle-foot ferns.
> While I do not see my lord,
> My sorrowful heart is very sad.
> Let me have seen him,
> Let me have met him,
> And my heart will then be pleased.

[46]Tr: The hermeneutic loop can get convoluted. Strictly speaking, a *"zhengyi"* is a commentary of a commentary, not of a canonical text (We have rendered the commentary of an original canonical text as *zhu* 注, "annotations."). Also, the *Zuozhuan* is in itself a commentary to the lost canon *Spring and Autumn Annals*. Hence, the most correct translation for *"Zuozhuan zhengyi"* should be this: "Commentary of the commentaries of the *Zuo Commentary to the Spring and Autumn Annals*." This self-referentiality, so central to the Confucian philologist's mindset, is exactly what He-Yin Zhen is trying to expose and debunk.

- *White Tiger Discourse*: "It was said, 'When a wife remonstrates with her husband, even if he doesn't listen he cannot cast her out.' But when a man marries a wife, he is not looking for someone to criticize him. And a wife should not leave her husband [just because he fails to listen] because the earth cannot leave the heaven."[47]
- *White Tiger Discourse*: "It was said, 'When a husband behaves badly, his wife cannot leave him.' This is because the earth cannot leave the heaven. Even when a husband errs, she cannot leave. Therefore, the Rites say, 'becoming one with him; remaining steadfast for life.'"

These constitute evidence that the power to determine the comings and goings of women rested in men. *The husband could cast off his wife, but the wife could not leave her husband.* Therefore, when men inflicted malicious behavior on wives, the latter had no recourse; but when women misbehaved, men charged them with the "Seven Causes" for divorce. Is it not clear that the ancients invented these causes to enhance and expand the power of men?

—◦◦◦—

- Preface to the *Mao Tradition of Songs*: "The wife who can extend favors to those beneath her is the one who will not be jealous."
- Ditto [preface to the *Mao Tradition of Songs*]: "The wife who is not jealous will prosper with multiple sons and grandsons."
- Ditto [preface to the *Mao Tradition of Songs*]: "A lady who is not jealous extends her favors to the lowly concubines. When she offers her [sexual service] to her lord, she still devotes herself [despite the concubines] because she understands that some are fated to occupy exalted positions and others are fated to be lowly."

---

[47]Tr: This is an abbreviated citation. He-Yin Zhen omitted the context, perhaps assuming that all her readers would know it. The saying refers to a poem, "Xiang Shu" (Rats, no. 52) in the *Songs*, which was sung by a wife to criticize her husband. The last stanza reads:

Look at a rat,—it has its limbs;
But a man shall be without any rules of propriety.
If a man observes no rules of propriety,
Why does he not quickly die?

- Ditto [preface to the *Mao Tradition of Songs*]: "During the reign of King Wen [of Zhou], in the area of Jiang and Tuo, there was a legal wife who would not let her designated concubines come with her [into a marriage]. The concubines met the suffering without complaint, and the legal wife came to regret her wrongdoing."[48]
- He Xiu, *Explications of the Commentary of Gongyang*: "In the court, [men] err by being jealous of those above them; women err by being jealous of those beneath."
- *White Tiger Discourse*: "The reason [the legal wife] brought her own nieces and younger sisters to her marriage [as the concubines] is because they would not be jealous of her."

Thus, women were forbidden from getting jealous of each other. The ancients established polygamy as the norm but worried that women were loath to serve a man with multiple wives. They thus made jealousy a vice and the lack thereof the proper way of women. Is it not self-evident that *men made up these teachings to give their licentiousness free rein?*

- *Zuo Commentary on the Spring and Autumn Annals* (Zuozhuan), the words of [Zhou minister] Xin Bo: "When concubines are elevated to a status on a par with the queen, that is the root of disorder."
- Zheng, *Annotations to Etiquette and Rituals*: "The concubine addresses her husband 'my lord' (*jun* 君) instead of 'husband' (*fu* 夫). This is

[48]Tr: In the Zhou period, aristocratic marriage was a form of political alliance and polygyny was a natural way to build such alliances. Specifically, the lord of a realm chose his legal wife (*di* 嫡) from another state. Two of the woman's consanguineous relatives of the same surname (niece or younger sister) from two other states would be designated concubines (*ying* 媵) and brought into the marriage. They could in turn bring their own "concubines." According to protocol, a *ying*-concubine was designated at age eight *sui*; began serving the legal wife at fifteen; and followed the wife into marriage at age twenty. The story cited here is based on a poem from the *Songs*, "Jiang You Si" (The Jiang Has Its Branches, no. 22):

> The Jiang has its branches, led from it and returning to it.
> Our lady, when she was married,
> Would not employ us.
> She would not employ us;
> But afterward she repented.

because she cannot be his equal and has to show extra reverence [more than even the wife]."

- *White Tiger Discourse*, on the "Instructions for Women" (*Neize*) chapter in the *Book of Rites*: "The concubine serves the wife with the same respect due to her parents-in-law. Respect for the legal wife [and the direct (*di* 嫡) line of descent she perpetuates] spells the end of jealousy."

- *Comprehensive Commentary of the Five Classics* (Wujing tongyi): "A concubine does not have a posthumous name because she is too lowly to be given one."

These make it clear that a concubine cannot match the wife in [legal and ritual status]. Although the wife and concubine are equally subject to male control, the two are differentiated into high and low. All the competition between concubines and wives is rooted in this. Surely concubines are of a lowly status, but wives should be more self-reflexive: Since you are lowly vis-a-vis your husband, how substantially different are you from the concubine?

- Zheng, *Annotations to the Book of Rites*: "A bereaved husband mourns his wife [for one year]. If his parents are still alive, he adopts the lesser rite of not holding a staff, and [he skips] the kneeling ceremony (*jisang* 稽顙). This is because in the presence of the revered parents, he dare not perform a private mourning rite to the extreme."

- *Commentary on the Han Tradition of the Book of Songs* (Hanshi waizhuan): "A man's filial respect for his parents is diminished by his having a wife."

Here is concrete proof that men have held their wives in extremely low regard. Since the ancients invented the theory [that a man's love for his wife is detrimental to his respect for parents], a couple who treat each other cordially could be accused of selfish indulgence. Thereafter, when husbands failed to get along with their wives, they could use the excuse of the wives' lack of filial piety as legitimate cause for divorce. Those like Wang Ji, Li Chong, and Miao Tong all found it entirely appropriate to do just this. The rotten Confucian scholars praised them for being high-minded, but I reprimand them for their extreme meanness. *They were mean because they disdained their wives.* As if this was not bad enough, they even used their disdain to garner a good name for themselves: men are indeed very adept in furthering their own interests.

--------⊸⊶⊸--------

- Master Zhou [Dunyi (1017–1073)]: "When family members fall asunder, the culprit is always women."
- Zheng Lian (fl. 14th century c.e.):[49] "The way to manage a family is none other than refusing to listen to a woman."

So the crime of family disorder is being planted on women. Domestic strife is actually rooted in the very fact of co-habitation: when people live together there are bound to be conflicts; it is only natural that families have fights. But people blame women for it. They blame women because husbands impute malicious intent to their wives, and there are some ignorant women who wallow in bad behavior. Households thus become more and more garrulous. Vulgar Confucian scholars ignore the real cause and only blame women. Are they not turning their backs on basic human feelings and reason?

--------⊸⊶⊸--------

- Du Qin, memorial [to Emperor Cheng of Han, r. 51–7 b.c.e.]: "A minister is yin [to the yang of] the prince; a son is the yin of his father; a wife is the yin of her husband; the barbarians to the east and west constitute the yin of China. The *Spring and Autumn Annals* records

---

[49]Tr: Zheng Lian (fl. 14th century c.e.) was the patriarch of an extended family, the Zhengs of Pujiang, Zhejiang Province, which managed to stay together for over seven generations. Legend has it that the first emperor of Ming summoned him to ask the secret of his family's success. His answer: Refusing to listen to a woman. Here, He-Yin Zhen departs from her pattern of citing from the original Confucian texts formulated in the Han dynasty. The case of the Zheng family, well known in China even today, demonstrates the power of culture in substantiating Confucian norms.

thirty-six solar eclipses and five earthquakes [both being symptoms of the decline of yang and flourishing of yin. The imbalance may manifest itself in] the barbarians invading China, the minister holding the reins of government, the wife riding the husband, or the minister rebelling against his lord-patriarch. As divergent as the symptoms may appear, they are of the same kind."

- Wang Ji (d. 48 B.C.E.), memorial [to Emperor Xuan of Han, r. 74–49/48 B.C.E.]: "The highest-ranked nobles of the Han house have a habit of marrying imperial princesses, and the countrymen[50] in the lesser domains favor the daughters of the lower princes. Men become lower than women and husbands less capable than their wives. The positions of yin and yang are thus reversed. No wonder usurpations by women prevail at court."

- Zheng, *Annotations to the Mao Tradition of the Songs*: "The man is yang, so when he plots and schemes he benefits the country. But the woman is yin, and when she schemes she disrupts the country."[51]

Here, women are being falsely accused of bringing disorder to the state. Granted that such ancient women as [the femmes fatale] Baosi, Feiyan, and Taizhen indeed brought disaster to their countries, the real culprit was the system of polygyny practiced by the ancient rulers—the people who caused disasters were all their favorites. If [from these few examples] we infer that all women are femmes fatale, how different is it from inferring from

---

[50]Tr: Countrymen (*guoren* 國人) refers to the residents in the metropoles of a domain, as opposite to rural residents (*yeren* 野人). To the extent that "countrymen" includes titled nobles and commoners attached to them, it is not a class designation.

[51]Tr: The commentator was referring to a poem in *Songs*, "Zhan Yang" (Looking up to great heaven, no. 264), which includes this stanza:

> A wise man builds up the wall [of a city],
> But a wise woman overthrows it.
> Admirable may be the wise woman,
> But she is [no better than] an owl.
> A woman with a long tongue,
> Is [like] a stepping-stone to disorder.
> [Disorder] does not come down from heaven; —
> It is produced by the woman.
> Those from whom come no lessons, no instruction,
> Are women and eunuchs.

the evil deeds of [last emperors] Jie, Zhou, You, and Li that there is not a single virtuous man among men? For men are eager to snatch power away from women but run out of excuses, so they single out one or two cases and extrapolate about women bringing down the country. Further, fearing that women's power might nonetheless grow, they view the subservience of husband to wife as a violation of the natural order. They let men embody yang and women yin and give all evil the attribute of yin and all goodness yang.[52] In this way, *women are made the most despicable and meanest people in the world; the worst epithets in the world are heaped onto them.* Is this not the biggest insult women have had to endure?

Now, have I made it clear that the [Confucian tradition of] scholarship has brought insult to women, tortured their bodies, and bound and restricted them? Those who promote these teachings are lucky enough to have been born male; if they happen to live in a woman's body, wear a dress, be confined in an empty room, be at the mercy of concubines, seek redress but without recourse, pray for a sudden death but to no avail, I am sure that they also would detest this kind of scholarship with all their hearts and minds. For even though in natural endowment males and females are different, they are both human beings. Even today people fabricate unjust teachings to rein in women. If there are still untrammeled conscience and universal justice left in this world, should one not *consider regarding others as if they were oneself and imagine oneself in their shoes?*

However, we should not be harsh on men categorically. Although men in general oppress women, there are some men who champion equality [between husband and wife].[53] The Later Han scholar Fan Ying, for example, was sick in bed one day. His wife sent her maid to pay her respects. Ying took the trouble of getting out of bed to return the bow. When asked why [he bothered], Ying explained, "A wife is an equal counterpart. In matters of stately sacrifices, [the principle is] to receive every offering with a proper

---

[52][Dong Zhongshu (179–104 B.C.E.)], *Luxuriant Dew of the Spring and Autumn Annals (Chunqiu fanlu).*

[53]*Etiquette and Rituals* states, "[H]usband and wife are one body." *Explaining Terms:* "It means that husband and wife are counterparts of equal weight." *Annotations to the Mao Tradition of Songs:* "The one who matches the husband is called 'wife.'" The *White Tiger Discourse:* "The wife (*qi* 妻) is an equal counterpart (*qi* 齊); she is one in body with her husband. This applies from the Son of Heaven down to the common men." The same can be found in *Rites, Explaining Terms,* and *Analysis and Explication of Characters,* which all gloss "wife" as "equal."

response [and it should be no different in conjugal rites]."[54] The late imperial scholar Tang Zhen (1630–1704) also discoursed on ethics and harmony in the inner chambers.

[Conversely, not all women embraced equality.] It is when women themselves choose to submit and prostrate themselves to men that the teachings can do the most harm. Take Nüzong, Bao Su's wife, for example. When Su served as envoy to the Wei state, he took in another wife (literally, outer wife). Nüzong's mother-in-law suggested that she leave him, but [Nüzong] replied, "A woman once married does not waver; even after her husband dies, she does not remarry. Moreover, I hear that there are 'seven causes' to divorce a wife, but none for divorcing a husband."[55] Another example is the wife of a man from Cai, whose husband fell seriously ill soon after marriage. Her mother wanted to marry her to someone else, but she said, "The husband's misfortune is my misfortune, how can I leave him? The Way of marriage is such that 'once having drunk from the same cup, there is no turning back.' She then wrote a poem to express her resolve."[56] There is also the wife of Duke Zhuang of Li. She was summoned into his palace, but the Duke never called for her since they had divergent desires and interests. Her mother pitied her, being so worthy yet dejected. Concerned that he had already sent her away but she wouldn't leave, the mother consoled her: "The way of husband and wife is such that you come together when there is the proper bond; when there isn't, you part ways. Now that you're so unhappy, why not just leave?" She cited a line from the *Songs*: "Reduced! Reduced! Why not go home?" The daughter responded, "The way of the wife is none other than [serving only] one. Although he doesn't come my way, how dare I depart from the proper wifely way?" She cited the next line from the same poem: "If it were not for his sake, why would I endure all the suffering?"[57] She remained steadfast in the wifely way and persevered in being chaste while awaiting a summons from her prince.[58]

---

[54] *History of the Later Han.* Tr: It should be emphasized that by "equality" He-Yin Zhen did not mean gender equality in general but equality in status between husband and wife.

[55] *Biographies of Exemplary Women*, chapter on worthy and enlightened women.

[56] *Biographies of Exemplary Women*, chapter on chaste and obedient women.

[57] Tr: The poem is "Shi Wei" (Reduced! Reduced! no. 36). It is noteworthy that both mother and daughter display rhetorical wit; they were conversant in the *Songs* and used this classic to express their own thoughts.

[58] *Biographies of Exemplary Women*, chapter on chaste and obedient women.

These persons (*ren* 人)[59] seem supremely content with their inferior position by taking subservience as their own calling. In their desire to garner the reputation of being the properly schooled ones in ritual and manners, they have no regard for others who are thus imperiled by their teachings. This is as if a minister decided to advocate that other offensive ministers be executed. Men in posterity have made use of these women's words: *they seize upon the teachings promoted by a few women to control the bodies of all women.* The situation is not unlike that of the Manchus pilfering the teachings of Confucius and Mencius and applying them to the suppression of the Han people. This is how the cult of female chastity has prevailed and spread far and wide, poisoning people's minds and unleashing so much harm in the world!

By the time we come to the Eastern Han period, we encounter the case of Ban Zhao, whose scholarship was unsurpassed before and after [in its toxic influence]; the teachings she promoted are particularly absurd. She opens her *Admonitions for Daughters* by championing lowliness and weakness, advising that a woman should behave in a humble and respectful manner, put others before her, swallow accusations and insults, and be constantly vigilant. She also opines that if a wife fails to serve her husband, the moral principles would falter; that those in a yin position get things done by passivity; that weakness is a woman's merit; that disrespecting the husband is strictly forbidden; and that chastity and quietude comprise fitting female deportment. Once these teachings took root, women began to consider their subjugation to men as their natural lot. What they call "rites and propriety" is nothing other than disgrace and insult; what is called "moral principles" is an embarrassing outrage. Does this not fit the description of what men denigrate as "the way of a concubine"?

In spite of being a woman herself, Ban the traitor was seduced by the seditious teaching of the Confucian tradition. She hacked at her own kind and brought shame onto womanhood in its entirety. In being a slave of men, she was an archtraitor to women. To have this person among womankind is like having [the traitor] Zeng Guofan among the Han people.[60] Ban the traitor actually said that "it is proper for a husband to

---

[59]Tr: Interesting that He-Yin Zhen used the unmarked gendered term "people" (*ren*) here to refer to women.

[60]Tr: Zeng Guofan (1811–1872) was a Han commander who subdued the Taiping Rebellion and restored Manchu rule.

remarry, but a woman must by no means serve two men." Since the husband is a woman's heaven and there is no escape from heaven, one cannot leave a husband. I truly did not expect these words to have come from a woman's mouth, even less the fact that they would be eulogized in the ages that ensued. That the rights and power of women failed to develop can be attributed to the fact that women are well versed in Ban the traitor's book; once her teaching becomes entrenched, nothing else could penetrate the mind. That Ban concocted these teachings in the first place was because she herself became so enamored with Confucian books that nothing else could penetrate her mind. Ultimately *the crimes of Ban the traitor were caused by Confucian teachings.*

It should be pointed out that the teachings championed by Confucian scholars are not only codes of behavior for men but also a creed women blindly adhere to. Not only are they detrimental to scholarship, they are also harmful to the law. Consider today's legal codes. Wives who kill their husbands are to be executed by slicing, and parents who have promised their daughter's hand to the point of accepting betrothal gifts but change their minds are to receive fifty lashes. Is it not true that lawmakers are guided by the Confucian hierarchy of superior men and inferior women? The law is rooted in scholarship, and scholarship is based on Confucian books. Without vanquishing the seditious teachings in Confucian books, the truth cannot come to light. Confucian scholarship is thus the third instrument of male tyrannical rule.

Translated by Dorothy Ko with Lydia H. Liu

PART 2: ATROCITIES OF MEN AGAINST WOMEN

My survey of the three forms of autocracy imposed by men on women makes it clear that women have long been trampled on. As women are so despised, they are robbed of all their rights, the most salient three being the right to bear arms and command armies, the right to hold political power, and the right to be educated.

Women Being Deprived of Three Rights

During his campaign against the Xiongnu, the Han general Li Ling (d. 74 B.C.E.) mused, "How come my men are lackluster and the drum beat sags? Could it be that there are women hiding in my army?" Having ferreted them out, the general cut them down with his sword. Referring to this incident, the Tang poet Tu Fu (712–770 C.E.) wrote: "Harboring women in the camp, the soldiers' spirits sagged." This kind of reasoning became entrenched in people's minds, making it inappropriate for women to join the army. So when Mulan took her ailing father's place, she had to cross-dress as a man as described in verse: "Comrades on the battlefield for twelve years, not knowing that Mulan was a girl." For a woman to have to disguise herself, does it not mean that having women in the military violated a taboo? This, then, is solid proof that women did not enjoy the right to bear arms or command an army.

As for political power, the Han Confucian scholars stated flatly, "Women have no business in the outer sphere." Elaborating on this command, the

"Preface to the Chronicles of the Empresses" of the *History of the Later Han* explained: "In the past even when the emperor was young and the times treacherous, they never appointed women to make momentous decisions of state. It was not until the Empress Dowager Xuan of Qin (r. 302–266 B.C.E.) in the Warring States period that women were made regents. During her rule [her half-brother] the Marquis of Rang exercised more power than King Zhao; her family enjoyed more wealth than the country. The Han dynasty continued this practice, knowing full well that it was wrong. The imperial line in the eastern capital in particular was broken repeatedly, with power falling into the hands of female rulers. Four emperors were installed from the outside, and six empresses ruled as regents. They made decisions from behind a screen and entrusted state affairs to their fathers and brothers. They favored infants on the throne to perpetuate their own rule and suppressed able ministers so as to remain uncontested."

From this we can surmise that empresses were not supposed to hold the reins of power. Those of the ilk of such Han Confucian scholars as Gu Yong and Du Gen saw the onslaught of natural calamities as omens of women having usurped power. Subsequent generations looked at the precedents of the Tang empresses Hu, Wu, and Wei and spoke of any woman seizing power as visiting a disaster like a flood or marauding barbarian hordes upon the country and its people. Surely a woman who made herself emperor [like Empress Wu] is condemned. But what is surprising is that even women who were made empresses were not allowed to have power. How can those who were not empresses ever dream of gaining it? This, then, is solid proof that women are deprived of the right to political power.

As for the right to an education, in the past women's education consisted of four elements: womanly virtue, womanly word, womanly deportment, and womanly work.[61] There were indeed provisions for teachers and instructors who taught unmarried daughters and wives alike.[62] But what they learned was no more than matters of etiquette and rites so as to perfect their skills in serving others.[63] Women never received an education that equaled men's.

---

[61] Tr: Often called "Four Virtues," these were first formulated in Ban Zhao's (ca. 45–116 C.E.) *Admonitions for Daughters*. See He-Yin's critique of Ban Zhao at the end of part 1 of this essay.
[62] Tr: The translator has omitted He-Yin Zhen's interlinear notes, such as the one citing the *Book of Songs*, the *Book of Rites*, and the *Gongyang Commentary* that introduces ancient terms used for female teachers and their respective meanings.
[63] *White Tiger Discourse*: "Why do women have teachers? What should they learn? The way to serve others."

In her official biography in the *History of the Later Han*, it was said that Empress Deng "became conversant in the histories at age six; at twelve she mastered the *Book of Songs* and the *Analects*. When her elder brothers studied the classics and biographies, she would query them in private. Her mind fixated on the classics and other books; she was profoundly disinterested in domestic matters. Her mother often chastised her: 'Why, I don't see you practicing your needlework to provide for your family's clothing needs. Do you really think that by studying you can become an erudite scholar?'" Does this not suggest that fathers and mothers at the time all regarded a learned daughter as a taboo?

Since then, generations of parents have upheld this line of thinking. When a daughter showed promise of talent, they saw it as a curse and worried that she would die young. Eventually, the very lack of talent became a sure sign of virtue for women. The equation in turn justified the denial of a path of learning to women. This, then, is solid proof that women were deprived of the right to an education.

Since women had no right to learning, those who managed to dabble in it tended to take excessive pride in their knowledge and became lax in their behavior.[64] In particular, those who learned to compose a simple verse with five characters to a line would boast of this minor skill. Instead of monitoring themselves, they were determined to follow their own sense of right and wrong.[65] And since women did not enjoy the right to political power, whenever they got hold of it, they allowed themselves to abuse it by

---

[64]Women who devoted themselves to philological studies—examples are Mother Wei from the ancient past and Madame Wang [Zhaoyuan (1763–1851)], wife of Hao Yixing, more recently—did not become lax in their behavior.

[65]There are two common errors of talented women in the past. One is meanness—witness the palace lady of the last ruler of Chen who stooped so low as to exchange poetry with his playmates. Another is licentiousness. All the talented women who appeared in the official histories and unofficial annals after the Six Dynasties are guilty of this. The Qing scholar Zhang Xuecheng (1738–1801) has an essay "On Women's Learning" in his *Wenshi tongyi*. In the afterword he opined that women who devoted themselves to poetry did so at the expense of adherence to the rites. He also listed the behavioral transgressions of "talented women." I completely agree with him. Witness those women poets who flocked to the door of such men as Yuan Mei, pledging themselves to be his "female disciples." And male scholars such as Yuan would thus call themselves "romantics." Is it not true that all women who have poetic talent are shameless to the utmost? No wonder Zhang Xuecheng said poetry and rites are incompatible. Tr: For Zhang Xuecheng's attitude on women's learning, see Susan Mann, "*Fu-xue* (Women's Learning) by Zhang Xuecheng (1738–1801): China's First History of Women's Culture," *Late Imperial China* 13, 1 (1992): 42–60.

indulging in sex and appointing members of their own families, unleashing catastrophes for the country, if not bringing it down altogether.[66] Those men who were brought to power by female rulers fared no better. Indulging in luxuries, sex, and other abuses, they ended up incurring the shame of history.[67] Likewise, since women did not normally have the right to possess military power, once they were in control, they unleashed cruelty onto the world, slaughtering innocent people at will to fan their noxious flames.[68]

---

[66]Only one female ruler deserves mention for avoiding these mistakes, Empress Dowager Xuanren of the Song dynasty who was esteemed as the Female [sage-ruler] Yao and Shun. But she is the exception. Empress Lü (r. 187–180 B.C.E.) of the Western Han favored the sexual services of Zhang Zixiang and Shen Shiqi. Empress Dowager Feng of the Northern Wei kept Li Yi as her favorite. Empress Dowager Hu was violent and odious. Empress Wu of Tang commandeered the sexual service of such men as Xue Huaiyi. Empress Wei followed her example and her sullied name traveled far and wide. One of her favorites, Wu Sansi, posted a broadsheet of her foul deeds on the Tianjin Bridge. These are all women who indulged in sex once they seized power. After Empress Lü became regent, she ennobled all her male relatives. Xiaoyuan, or Empress Wang of Han (71 B.C.E.–13 C.E.), enfeoffed five brothers in one day who succeeded her rule, opening the floodgates for usurper Wang Mang to end the Han mandate. The same is true for the Eastern Han. Historian Zhao Yi (1727–1814) wrote in his *Notes on the Twenty-Two Histories*: "There were many female regents in the Eastern Han. They had to rely on their fathers, brothers, or sons to ensure that they could be trusted. They thus acquired too much power. The unworthy ones came to be uppity, and even the worthy ones incurred envy from others who plotted to do the same. This vicious cycle led to the withering of the country." These examples constitute proof that women in power favored their own kin. Women are indeed liable to these shortcomings. Therefore the *Book of Songs* says: "Women who have long tongues, they are the root of disasters." Even the words of a mere woman are enough to bring down a country, [and thus] how much more so is it for those who have unmitigated power?

[67]Emperor Wu of Han appointed generals from men related to his empresses, such as Wei Qing, Huo Qubing, and Li Guangli. The five brothers ennobled by Empress Wang vied for luxuries. Treasures sent as bribes poured in from four directions, enabling grand mansions and giant harems. In the Eastern Han, men who owed their rise to women, such as Dou Xian and Liang Qi, stole from the people and persecuted the loyal, ending [their reigns] in the disgrace of their impeachments. In the Tang, Wu Sansi and Yang Guozhong both rebelled. Therefore historians are right in blaming the downfall of a country on men brought to power by women. Further, wet nurses rose to power during the reign of Emperor Ling of Han. The Mongol rulers also favored the husbands of wet nurses. Although the women themselves are to be blamed, the men they brought into the orbit of power caused much disruption.

[68]Tr: The translator has omitted the detailed rendition of the cruelties of Empresses Liu and Deng of the Han, Empress Jia of Western Jin, as well as Empresses Dowager Wenming and Hu of the Northern Wei. The remainder of He-Yin Zhen's interlinear note is as follows: Atrocities in the Tang are especially prevalent. Empress Wu Zetian strangled her own daughter to death to plant the blame on Empress Wang. After Wang and the consort of the prince were stripped of their titles, Wu had them caned two hundred lashes and threw their bodies into the brew,

The occasional women who commanded armies were particularly violent toward the people.[69]

Why is it that these extraordinary women who rose above their circumstances ended up causing so much damage and suffering? We have to realize that out of tens of thousands of women, only one or two gained access to an education. No wonder they regarded themselves as too special to abide by the normal expectations of discipline. So too, women who seized political or military control are so rare that it happened only once or twice in hundreds and thousands of years. Since they saw themselves as abnormal, they did not shy from a reversed course [from civilized behavior] in conducting their affairs. Although no doubt the individual women are to blame, we should also recognize that it was men who have long infringed on women's rights and deprived women of their rightful share. Therefore the occasional woman who did manage to gain power did not regard the situation as natural. No wonder they tended to overreach and abuse the power in their hands.

Without recognizing this fact, many critics have charged that women are by nature mean and cruel. They point out the apparent harm of women becoming educated, powerful, or in command of an army as the very reason that they should be barred from these things. Instead of analyzing the root cause of the situation, these critics' only solution is to guard women jealously day in and day out.[70] Even among women, many regard learning, exercising political power, and controlling military power as a shameful travesty.

---

saying that she wanted them to be drunk to their bones. Wu also murdered Tang officials who opposed her such as Zhangsun Wuji, Chu Suiliang, and Shangguan Yi. After Wu made herself emperor, she allowed her underlings to persecute the innocent, and not a day went by without an indictment or an execution. Scores of high officials lost their lives; almost a hundred lieutenants and generals died. Among those she exiled to Lingnan in the south as well as Jiannan and Qinzhong in the southwest, hundreds and thousands were killed. She also got rid of members of the Tang royal family and those in her own Wu clan; even her own son and lovers were not spared. Empress Wei had Emperor Zhongcong murdered. These are all insidious women in history; indeed, they are femmes fatale.

[69]The Ming female rebel Tang Sai'er was particularly cruel. In Shandong where she rose, not a single soul remained in sight for hundreds of miles. And a leader of the White Lotus Rebellion during the early years of Jiaqing (1796–1804), Qi Wangshi, indulged her army with slaughtering and looting. These are just two examples of women commanders who brought death to innocent people. In contrast, Empress Ma of the Ming can be said to have been more compassionate.

[70]That women are capable of these wrongs is because they have been suppressed for too long. It is like damming up a river: once the dikes break, the water is unstoppable. The same is true for women, who have been subjected to men's control for too many years to count. To expect them to not run amok once given a chance is to pretend that the dammed-up water could stay still forever.

Not only does this situation contradict the principle of equality between human beings, but it is also detrimental to women's lives. How so? Deprived of the right to be educated, women have become more and more ignorant; deprived of the right to hold political power, women have become more and more degraded; deprived of the right to bear arms, women have become weaker and weaker. Ignorance prevents women from establishing their independent selves; degradation prevents women from extending and expressing themselves; weakness prevents women from defending themselves. Not being able to become independent, increasingly women have died of hunger; not being able to express themselves, more and more women have died of depression; not being able to defend themselves, countless women have been seized and slaughtered.

May I suggest that it is in this sense that every single man from past and present has contributed to the oppression of women to the point of death? I have thus far mentioned the indirect methods men have used to murder us women. As for direct methods, there are six: death by cloistering,[71] by humiliation, by corporeal punishment, by kidnapping, by abandonment, and last, by defense of loyalty and chastity. Surely, also countless men lost their lives in these ways, but their deaths are different in nature from those of women, as this table makes clear:

MEN'S DEATH	WOMEN'S DEATH
Death by cloistering: only for prisoners who were proven guilty	Not restricted to prisoners; countless women died of being cloistered
Death by humiliation: Only for those who failed to develop their personalities	When women died in humiliation, they were victims of violence
Death by corporeal punishment: in most cases, men were responsible for the crimes for which they received the punishment	In most cases, women were punished by association with the men who committed the crimes
Death by kidnapping: normally only the old and infirm	Not restricted to the old and infirm

[71]Tr: Cloistering (*youbi* 幽閉): literally, being shut away from the light and locked up.

MEN'S DEATH	WOMEN'S DEATH
Death by abandonment: men abandoned by their lords usually won sympathy in public opinion	Women abandoned by their men were also rejected by society
Death in defense of loyalty and chastity: out of loyalty to the country	Out of loyalty to individual men

This overview amply demonstrates that the deaths of women are very different from those of men. Is this not the most tragic state of affairs for womanhood? Allow me now to enumerate the facts of the horrible deaths of women through the ages and hold them up as a mirror for all women to reflect upon.

Women Suffering Death by Cloistering

In ancient times, men of exalted status practiced polygyny. Particularly offensive to universal justice are two practices: in antiquity, paternal cousins often had to serve the same husband; in more recent times, one emperor can establish multiple empresses.[72] Furthermore, lords and sovereigns from successive dynasties never failed to cloister women in their harem. As early as the Warring States period, the sovereigns of the six states kept hordes of beauties and vied with each other in licentiousness. The first emperor of Qin staffed his Epang palace with beautiful women. In the Early Han, palace women were given such titles as Meiren, Liangren, Bazi, Qizi, Changshi, and Xiaoshi. The Emperor Wudi added to the roster Jieyu, Yine, Ronghua, and Chongyi, each with her own entitlements. He was also said to have recruited several thousand fair maidens into his harem.[73] The "Annals of Empresses" section in the *History of the Later Han* states, "In the Eighth Month, the court dispatched officials Zhong Dafu and Yi Tingcheng

---

[72]Tr: The translator has omitted here case-by-case examples of polygyny of dynastic rulers culled from the classics, official histories, and notations books.
[73]According to the *Gongyu zhuan*.

together with a physionomer to the countryside of [the capital city] Luoyang to inspect maidens from respectable families.[74] Those aged between thirteen and twenty and endowed with proper features in accordance with the rules of physiognomy were recruited into the harem." This is one example of the explicit mention of the institution of the recruitment of commoner women into the harem in the official histories.

The selection of commoner women into the harem means that there were plenty of lonesome women in the inner quarters. Hence, Later Han official Liu Yu wrote, "Nowadays the inner quarters are full of female entertainers and jesters, all replete with playthings and ornaments. They eat in vain in an empty chamber,[75] exhaust and dissipate the essence and vitalities of the body, thus falling prey to the six illnesses. This is an enormous waste for the whole country. Moreover, when we consider the nature of heaven and earth, yin and yang have to be correctly balanced. Blocking what should be kept flowing [i.e., the natural desires of women] would bring floods together with droughts. According to the *Book of Songs*, when a woman is lonesome she expresses her sorrows in songs that were recorded by Confucius. Even for a single man like Zhou Yin and a single woman like Qishi, [their pent-up emotions] brought forth such omens as collapsed walls, frost, and meteoroids. How much more so when it is the case with so many women—how can their collective sorrows fail to bring cosmic responses?"

Similarly, Han official Xun Shuang (128–190 C.E.) wrote in his memorial [to Emperor Huan of Han, 166 C.E.]: "I heard that as many as five to six thousand women are gathered in the harem, not even counting the attendants and servants. Hence, innocent subjects are taxed in vain to sustain a harem of women who serve no function. Outside the palace the people are impoverished; inside, the communion between yin and yang is blocked. The *qi* [vital energy] of harmony is disturbed, leading to frequent calamities and freakish omens. In the humble opinion of your minister, all women who were neither betrothed by the proper ceremonies nor consummated their unions should be released from the harem and matched with others. This would alleviate their forlorn sorrow and return yin and yang to harmony."

---

[74]Tr: "Respectable family" (*liangjia*) is a legal designation, referring to women who were not from the hereditary "mean" (lowly) families.

[75]Tr: *Gong* 宮—literally, "chambers of a palace"—is also a metaphor for the viscera in a human body. Both meanings are applicable here.

From these words it is clear that once selected into the harem, a female is subjected to cloistering that is no different from penal imprisonment. The unspoken sorrow must have destroyed countless lives. Who else other than women are imprisoned like this without any cause? No wonder women consider being selected for the harem as a major calamity.

The dynastic history of the Jin recorded that Emperor Wudi issued a comprehensive call for recruitment to staff his harem and asked Empress Yang to serve as the selector. Daughters from prominent families showed up in torn dresses and with decrepit looks to avoid being drafted. When Consort Hu was called up, she broke into tears on the spot. Those around her cautioned her to lower her voice, lest the emperor hear. She replied, "I'm not afraid of dying, so why should I be afraid of His Majesty?" Indeed, the women picked for the harem might as well be dead. No wonder that Consort Hu resisted to the point of death. That daughters from prominent families were so weary of the draft suggests that being selected is no different from a pronouncement of a death sentence.

In the Six Dynasties period, both the Song and Qi dynasties cast their nets widely for harem women. When it comes to Shubao (553–604 C.E.), the last ruler of the Chen dynasty, it is said that even counting only the beautiful ones, his harem boasted over a thousand women.[76] In the Tang dynasty, the "favorites of the inner palace" numbered five thousand. How can the number of women who died of such imprisonment be accounted for individually?

The actual lives of the women in the harem were often imperiled. As the dynasty fell, they could be kidnapped by marauding soldiers or raped by barbarian invaders, if they did not starve to death or wander in exile. Several hundreds if not a thousand palace women were reduced to digging for roots and trapping for fish in ponds when the Han collapsed. All eventually starved to death. During the rebellion of Li Cui in the Eastern Han, [Li Cui's] troops captured several thousand palace women, many of whom died in the cold outdoors or from drowning. Thus once [women were] selected into the harem, the lives of women were as precarious as an egg standing on its end. And this is not just from the imprisonment. What crime did women commit to warrant this calamity?

The precedent of drafting maidens was established by Chinese dynasties founded by the Han people. Later, the foreign dynasties also

---

[76]*History of the State of Chen (Chenshu)*.

emulated it.[77] Ruler Shi Hu (295–349 C.E.) of the Later Zhao, for example, inaugurated a hierarchy of "Female Palace" with twenty-four ranks and a hierarchy of "Eastern Palace" with twenty ranks. The nine ranks of lords and princes with feudatories in the provinces were given thirty thousand commoner women aged between thirteen and twenty. Using this as an excuse, he seized nine thousand women. His son Shi Xuan issued an unauthorized edict recruiting over ten thousand women, of whom three thousand resisted by hanging themselves. Other examples of alien rulers drafting maidens abound. During the reign of Taizong of the Mongols, for example, official Tuo Huan sent a memorial suggesting that he open a selection of all maidens from all corners of the empire. When Emperor Shizu ascended the throne, Yelu Zhu suggested that "the drafting of maidens can lead to abuses of the people. Why not mandate that every year large commanderies must submit three maidens [for inspection] and small commanderies, two. The parents of those deemed acceptable would be rewarded handsomely." Later, rumors raged among commoners that another draft was imminent. Hastily, all the young were married off.[78]

Even such neighboring tributary states as Korea elected maidens to send as tribute.[79] The Manchus, too, sent envoys during the Shunzhi reign to Tongzhou, barricading commoner boats to pluck their women away. A student, Jikai, remonstrated against it. When the alien people [i.e., Manchus] invaded China, no fewer than several tens of thousands of our women died from imprisonment. This may be written off as an atrocity of alien rule. Yet the Ming, a Chinese dynasty that chased away the Mongol barbarians of the Yuan, were even more relentless than the alien races in drafting maidens.[80]

It is recorded in the *History of the Ming* (*Mingshi*) that the founding emperor cautioned against admitting any women into the harem. He

---

[77]Tr: In an age of burgeoning racial consciousness, He-Yin Zhen's use of "Hanzu" (Han people or race) is significant. Her argument here amounts to one of gender trumping ethnic and racial differences. It can be seen as a continuation of her argument earlier in the essay about there being no difference between Manchus and Han because all equally oppress women.
[78]This proves that the people avoided the draft as a calamity.
[79]Tr: The translator has omitted the details about tribute women from Korea, culled from Zhao Yi's *Notes on the Twenty-Two Histories*.
[80]In recent times, [the Taiping ruler] Hong Xiuquan also kept countless women in his harem. From this we know that Han rulers—without exception—imperil us women. Tr: In the context of the revolutionary fervor of her times, He-Yin Zhen's critique of the Chinese Ming dynasty as even more objectionable than the alien Manchus was radical.

mandated that "the principal wives, concubines, and female attendants of the emperor and princes be carefully selected from daughters of upright commoner families." In other words, all empresses and imperial concubines were plucked from the rank-and-file in society. Whenever a new emperor ascended the throne, a new draft would have to be ordered.[81] The disturbances unleashed in the areas around the two capital cities of Beijing and Nanjing were particularly irksome.[82] After the Ming fell in 1645, the loyalist Southern Ming ruler Prince Fu was installed in the southern capital of Nanjing. He dispatched envoys into the countryside in four directions; whenever they came across families with women, they would seize the women on the spot, wreaking havoc in all the neighborhoods.

Sadly, women who died of imprisonment were not the only victims of the institution of selecting women for the harem after it was installed. Fathers and mothers also died of worry; neighbors died in the disorders unleashed. The ability of this system to persecute people to death surpasses that of the legendary tyrant kings Jie and Zhou. Since sovereigns and lords regarded women's lives so lightly, their ministers and subjects also held women in disdain, causing them to live lives of imprisonment unto death.[83]

The Western Han scholar Gongyu (124–44 B.C.E.) lamented that in the realm, [powerful men] vied to build excessive harems—even feudal lords had wives and concubines numbering in the several hundreds; rich officials and commoners kept scores of singers and entertainers. Hence, inside there were abundant unfulfilled women; outside, lonesome men abound. The "Treatise of Salt and Iron" in the *History of the Former Han* concurs: "In antiquity, one man was matched with one woman. But nowadays lords keep hundreds of women, courtiers scores, even attendants and wealthy commoners enjoy a roomful. Hence forlorn women lament the passing of time and men end up in exile without a mate." The official histories of the Former and Later Han are full of specific cases: The five marquises of the Wang clan, Liang Qi, and Dong Zhuo each kept several hundred concubines. Since the Three Kingdoms era, a trend developed that the more exalted a man's status,

---

[81]Tr: The translator has omitted cited examples from two notation books.

[82]All Ming empresses and imperial consorts are natives of Northern Zhili or Southern Zhili, the two regions surrounding the two capitals.

[83]Tr: Although here He-Yin Zhen's logic is weak, she makes an important rhetorical argument: that the lot of harem women—lifelong imprisonment unto death—is generalizable to *all* women.

the more wives he had; the richer the household became, the larger the number of concubines.

As for the women who became concubines, they died either of depression, jealousy, torture by the principal wife, or the cruelty of foster sons. The women would seek to end their own lives, pray for a quick end, or seek refuge in a nunnery. Is the lot of women not the saddest? We may say that the joys of living were denied the women of China, for rare is she who died a natural death. Worse still, in the Western Han when a lord died, all the women in his harem had to be sent away to guard gardens and tombs.[84] Even ministers at the time criticized the practice as being detrimental to the harmony of yin and yang as well as augmenting the circulation of forlorn sorrow. This is a case of harem women suffering indirect capital punishment. As for the first emperor of Qin, who was buried in Mount Li with many of his palace women, or the emperors and princes of Ming dynasty, who were accompanied to their graves by palace women as sacrifices,[85] these are cases of harem women suffering direct capital punishment. We thus know that despotic sovereigns committed against women heinous crimes of cruelty that reached to the high heavens. How can we women not regard all sovereigns as enemies so as to right these wrongs from the past? But those dead cannot be brought back to life again; hence, this regret and anger can never be quelled. This is one of the forces that has pushed women to the brink of death.

Women Suffering Death by Corporeal Punishment

A second, and direct, method of murdering women is death by prosecution and legal punishment. Women in the past and present are seldom sentenced to death in their own name, but innocent women are struck down without recourse to clear themselves because of the legal stipulations mandating that women follow their male relatives in their banishment. The "Gan" and "Tang" chapters in the *Book of Documents* both state, "I then *nu* (孥) kill you." The Han commentator Zheng Xuan thought that "nu" refers

---

[84]Tr: The translator has omitted cited examples from *History of the Former Han*.
[85]Tr: The translator has omitted cited examples from Zhao Yi's *Notes on the Twenty-Two Histories*, notation books, and He-Yin Zhen's own study notes.

to wives and slaves; this then constitutes proof that in ancient times, a man's crime was borne also by his wives and slaves. This marks the beginning of innocent women bearing the brunt of punishment by implication.[86]

Furthermore, the *Rites of Zhou* states, "His slaves and women are thrown in the cage." This shows that women were indeed incarcerated and tortured, but the classical books do not state clearly if the women were punished for crimes they themselves committed or on account of men.[87] On the one hand, the *Zuo Commentary* includes the line that "penal torture does not extend to women"; the *Gongyang Commentary*, too, states that "ill treatment stops short of her body." They thus seem to indicate that women in ancient times were not subjected to the rule of guilt-by-association. But on the other hand, the "Biography of Zhao She" in the *Records of the Grand Historian* records that the mother of Zhao Kuo sent a memorial to the king of Zhao, begging the latter to exempt her body from punishment after her son's army was vanquished. This shows that punishing the women of offending males is indeed a custom that reaches very far back.

The ancient institution of "nine *zu*" (nine degrees of familial relationship) included clansmen from the great-grandfather's generation to the great-grandsons. The "three *zu*," in turn, refers to a man's parents, wife, and siblings. The Qin dynasty established the precedent of punishing the three *zu*: when one man was impeached, his entire family would be executed. Hence it was said, "The Qin rule was so draconian that the crime of one person automatically extends to his three *zu*."[88] Similarly, when the Han emperor impeached Han and Peng, their parents, wives, and siblings were also destroyed along with them. Even those who followed Guan Gao and gave refuge to Ji Bu were executed along with their three *zu*. It was not until the reign of Han emperor Wen that death-by-association was abolished. Although the statute was taken off the books, later when general Li Ling (d. 74 B.C.E.) surrendered to the enemy and the thief-turned-official Wang Wenshu (d. 104 B.C.E.) was impeached, their entire *zu* perished.[89]

As women of China were ensconced in their inner quarters, they were no different from prisoners. Zheng Xuan wrote, "[W]hen there is goodness

---

[86]Tr: The translator has omitted He-Yin Zhen's discussion of a counterexample from *Zuozhuan*.

[87]Tr: The translator has omitted a cited passage from the *Book of Changes*.

[88.] "Biography of Yang Zhong" in the *History of the Later Han*.

[89]Tr: The word *zu* normally means "clan" or "lineage," but it is left untranslated here because as He-Yin Zhen's arguments in the following paragraphs make clear, the parameters of *zu* were subject to debate.

in the world, it cannot be credited to women; when there is evil, neither can women be blamed." But when one man is found guilty and his entire family, including women, are punished, are the jurists sending the message that the women should have said something when they noticed that the men had erred? Yet the Confucian scholars sternly warned that "women should not interfere in external affairs" and regarded "letting women into a plot" as an offense for men. If men were up to no good, how could their women have known? Were the women not being put to death although they were utterly innocent of any crime?

Or, could the jurists be saying, since the men committed a major travesty against the state, they must have been equally inept in "ordering the family,"[90] according to Confucian dicta,[and] therefore the entire family might as well perish with them? Little did they know that even with the sagacity of his empress, Jiang, King Xuan of Zhou was still incompetent in his official duties; even with the compassion of his empress, Ma, the Ming Taizu emperor remained cruel and despotic. When a man breaks the law and his women are held accountable along with him, does this not amount to a drummed-up charge fabricated out of nowhere?

We may say that from ancient times to the present, whenever a woman perishes from penal punishment, she dies on account of her men's crimes. Those who are men, not only do they denigrate all women in general as if it is in their nature, but they also inflict harm onto specific women in their own families, depriving them of a natural death. Do women owe something to men, or is it the case that men doubly owe something to women?

Let us consider the case of Chunyu Zhang, marquis of Dingling, whose rebellion against Emperor Cheng of Han brought punishment onto both elder and younger in his family. His principal wife, Naishi, and five minor wives had left him and married someone else before his plot was exposed. Zhai Fangjin and He Wu opined that since Naishi left Zhang while he was plotting the rebellion because she knew that as principal wife she would be punished as if she were the one committing the crime, she understood the law full well [and thus should be punished accordingly]. Kong Guang did not disagree with the law that when someone committed a major crime that offended the Way, his parents, wives, and siblings should be beheaded in public regardless of age. But he thought that the Way of husband and

---

[90]Tr: "Ordering the family" (qijia 齊家) is part of the ethical demand for the Confucian gentleman as stated in the *Great Learning*.

wife is such that they are united by righteousness and rent asunder by a lack thereof. Since Naishi left Zhang and remarried before the latter knew that he would incur punishment, she had already lost the title of wife. She thus should not be punished because she was no longer wife in name or in reality. Although Kong Guang appears to be more lenient than Fangjin, his reasoning suggests that when an official in the Han court committed a major offense, his mother, wife, and concubines could not escape punishment. How can we keep track of all those women who died on account of men?

The punishments in the Han were extended only to consanguineous relatives. Later, this was changed because of a misreading of a passage in the New Text version of the *Book of Documents* concerning the term "nine *zu*" in the *Canon of Yao*.[91] The misreading construes "the nine *zu*" as those who belong to the same clan but are of different surnames. By this reckoning, there are four *zu* on the father's side: (1) those within the five direct blood relationships, [namely, great-great-grandfather, great-grandfather, grandfather, father, and the self]; (2) married paternal aunts and their children; (3) married sisters and their children; (4) married daughters and their children. Then there are three *zu* on the mother's side: (1) those who share the surname of the mother's father; (2) those who share the surname of the mother's mother; (3) married daughters of the mother's sisters and their children. Finally, there are two *zu* on the wife's side: (1) those who share the surname of the wife's father; (2) those who share the surname of the wife's mother.

Those who followed this misreading extended the error in construing the "three *zu*" to mean those on the father's, mother's, and wife's sides.[92] Or, some argued that "three *zu*" refers to one's maternal grandparents, the sons of maternal aunts and the sons of one's wife's parents and her paternal aunts, and the sons of the children of one's sisters.[93]

---

[91]Tr: The New Text tradition of the Confucian classics acquires its name from two sources: first, from the versions of the Confucian classics written in the new script that prevailed at the beginning of the Former Han dynasty; and second, from a method of interpretation designed to elucidate the profundity and subtle language of the classics. The decree in 213 B.C.E. of the first emperor of the preceding Qin dynasty that all books of the ritual schools were to be burnt meant that pre-Qin Confucian classics (the "Old Text") were either destroyed or concealed. Dong Zhongshu's interpretations of the New Texts contributed greatly to the consolidation of Confucianism as the official ruling ideology of the Han. See http://www.philtar.ac.uk/encyclopedia/confuc/new.html.
[92]The reading of Ru Chun.
[93]The reading of Du Yu. Tr: The original word for "children" here is *zi* 子, which sometimes is gendered male ("sons") and sometimes remains unmarked ("children").

Despotic rulers and their abusive officers seized upon these misinterpretations to punish a wider net of people. Especially in the Wei and Jin periods, penal punishments became ever more draconian and inhuman. The "Biography of Cao Shuang of Wei" in the *Record of the Three Kingdoms* conveys that when [ruler] Sima Yi executed Shuang, he also eliminated Shuang's "three *zu*" and those of the members of his faction—male and female, old and young, married daughters of aunts and sisters, all were killed. Similarly, the "Biography of Guo Zhun" relates that Guo's wife is a younger sister of Wang Ling. When Wang was condemned, Guo's five sons beseeched their father by knocking their heads on the ground until they bled, begging him to intervene with Sima Yi so that their mother might be spared. Further, the "Treatise on Penal Codes" in the *History of Jin* mentions that when the Wei court impeached Qiu Jian, his son Dian and Dian's wife, Madame Xun, were expected to die with him, as was a daughter borne by Xun who had already married Liu Ziyuan. The daughter was spared from execution and was instead imprisoned only because she was pregnant at the time.

Clearly, when one man was imperiled in the Wei court, neither his sisters nor married daughters could escape punishment. Hence, the official Cheng Wei suggested in a memorial that married daughters [were doubly imperiled in that] if her parents committed an offense, the punishment would extend to her, *and* if her husband's side incurred a sentence, she would also have to be executed. Hence, the body of one woman was left vulnerable from both inside and outside.[94] A man would not be held responsible for the crimes committed by another *zu*, whereas a woman could be brought down by her association with two families (literally *men* 門, door). This situation was indeed unfair, Wei argued. From this memorial we know that before a daughter married, she had to "follow" her parent's [i.e., father's] offenses; after she married, she "followed" the punishments of both her marital and natal families.[95]

---

[94]Tr: In calling attention to the ambiguous location of a woman, He-Yin anticipated an important critique of Confucian patriarchy developed by feminist social historians in the Anglophone world. See, for example, the analysis by Susan Mann and Fangqin Du of the conflicting moral demands of filiality (to natal parents) and loyalty (to in-laws) in their "Competing Claims on Womanly Virtue in Late Imperial China," in Dorothy Ko, JaHyun Kim-Haboush, and Joan Piggot eds., *Women and Confucian Cultures in Premodern China, Korea, and Japan* (Berkeley: University of California Press, 2003), 219–247.

[95]Tr: The translator retains the slightly awkward formulation of "follow" (*cong*) because it is likely that He-Yin Zhen used this word intentionally to recall the famous Confucian dictum

The life of a woman was made as precarious as stacked eggs, and for what reason other than that she had to be subjected to punishment on account of her men? This is not even to mention the asymmetry that when a wife was being punished for her natal parent's transgressions, her husband remained unblemished; but when a husband offended the court, his wife was punished with him. This is another indignity beside the fact that women were being held liable for the crimes of both marital and natal families. The very laws that were being made were lenient to men and harsh on women. One may ask, since all those who violated the law were male, why should females be made sacrifices unto death?

The suggestion of Cheng Wei did change the law so that later, unmarried daughters were made to "follow" the banishment of parents only, and married daughters were liable only for the offenses of their husbands' families. But there is the case of Jie Jie. At the time he was condemned, his daughter was betrothed to the Pei family and was in fact to be wedded the following day. The Peis wanted to recognize her as an official wife so that she could be spared, but she said, "Since my family has come to this, what do I have to live for?" She thus met her death without complaint. This one example suffices to prove the cruelty of the law. We have lost count of the number of innocent women who died since the Qin and Han period because of such a law. Is this not what they call "killing people without having to justify it"?

The Northern Wei is particularly notorious for its harsh penal codes—there are cases of an entire tribe being executed, or of the men and women from a princely family supporting one another to meet their end. Coming in its wake was the institution of punishment that implicated the "five *zu*." The "Biography of Cui Hao" in the *History of the Northern Dynasties* records that when Cui was executed, all the Cuis from his native place of Qinghe, be they close or remote relatives, were eliminated. Also annihilated were the entire *zu* of his factional allies—the Lus of Fanyang, the Guos of Taiyuan, and the Lius of Hedong. Even the five *zu* of his attendants and butlers and the entire *zu* of those who served with him in the history compilation project were all executed. In other words, the law implicated not only kinsmen from the offender's own *zu* but also those affiliated with his mother,

for women—*sancong* (Thrice Following)—namely, before marriage she is to "follow" her parents; when married she is to follow her husband; when widowed she is to follow her son. It is noteworthy that He-Yin's critique of women's subservient positions in the family took the form of a radical critique of the gendered nature of state laws.

wife, and daughters as well as those from different surnames. In light of the fact that the law of inheritance followed only a patrilineal descent, is there a larger injustice than the law of execution-by-implication extending also to the bloodline of matrilineal descent? Since the offense concerned was committed by men, could there have been a more unjust law than this? When Gao Yang (529–559 C.E.) plotted to usurp the throne [and became Emperor Wenxuan of Northern Qi], he ordered that men and women from the twenty-five families of the former royal families surnamed Yuan be beheaded, regardless of age—a total of three thousand [*sic*] people killed.[96] These cases constitute proof that women lost their lives by implication.

Human lives were treated like dirt in the Five Dynasties period (907–960), when the execution of the entire *zu* became routine. Both clans of Wang Shifan in the Later Liang (907–923) and of Zhao Yan in the Later Tang (923–937) suffered from clanwide executions, and not one of their wives, children, or flesh-and-blood [relatives] managed to escape. The "Biography of Zhu Youliang" records that when Youliang was sentenced to death in the Later Tang, his wife, Madame Zhang, went to him with a contingent of two hundred family members, asking him to single out those who were truly his flesh-and-blood so that others could be spared from tragic death. Likewise, the "Biography of Wang Zhang" mentions that when Wang was executed as an official of the Han, his daughter, already married to Zhang Yisu, and who had been sick for years, was executed without pardon.

The laws of execution-by-the-*zu* in the Five Dynasties implicated the offender's wife, concubines, and married daughters—the rule of illegal punishment had by then reached its zenith. At the time, civil officials, military men, and commoners followed one another in succumbing to punishment. Over three thousand people perished when Zhang Jian and his faction were executed along with their *zu*. When Su Fengji was minister, he ordered execution-by-the-*zu* of entire populations who resided in the proximity of bandits. I do not know how the women who were born in those times managed to cope! This has to be the worst calamity visited upon women.

Besides these clanwide executions, there were other punishments meted out to a man in the Tang dynasty when his wife, concubines, sons, and daughters-in-law would all be banished into the palace as slaves and maids. The "Biography of Shangguan Yi" in the *History of the Tang* relates that when Yi and his son, Tingzhi, were found guilty, Tingzhi's wife, Zheng,

---

[96]Tr: He-Yin Zhen's source was inaccurate. The actual number of people put to death is 721.

and daughter, Wan'er, were dispatched into the palace. This is one example of the banishment of wife with daughter. The "Biographies of Wu Yuanji and Li Shidao" in turn records that when the plot of the two men failed, Yuanji's wife, Shen, and Shidao's wife, Wei, were sent into the palace. This is one example of the banishment of a criminal's wife. The "Biography of Cui Qun" adds that when Li Shidao was indicted, Emperor Xianzong told his prime minister that the wife of Li Shigu was an aunt of Shidao and that though she was considered a member of a rebellious *zu*, it was not appropriate to demote her status to that of a slave. Likewise, the wife of Li Zongshi also came from an aristocratic family, and it would be too harsh to demote her as well. Cui responded, Your Majesty has a compassionate heart. Henceforth, Madame Pei, the wife of Shigu, her daughter, Yiniang, and Zongshi's wife, Madame Wei as well as her sons and daughters were set free. This exception, however, proves the rule, whereby the wives and daughters of an indicted man's extended family were implicated in his sentence. The "Biography of Wei" relates how Censor Li Xiao, a member of the imperial family, was implicated in the affair of Li Xun and how his daughter was banished into the palace. The "Biographies of Empresses and Consorts" records that the daughter of Wu Linggui was sent into the palace when Wu was executed by implication. The eunuch Gao Lishi picked her out and presented her to the emperor; afterward, she gave birth to the future emperor Daizong and was crowned Empress Zhangjing.

These are cases of the daughters of indicted men, who were banished into the palace. The same "Biographies" records that when Li Qi was indicted for plotting a revolt, his concubine Zheng was seized and sent into the palace. Emperor Xianzong favored her; she gave birth to the future Suzong and became Empress Xiaoming. This is a case of the concubine of an indicted man being sent into the palace. The "Biography of Han" records a conversation with Liu Yuanzuo when passing by the city of Bianliang, saying that Li had better seek an audience with the Son of Heaven soon so that the lives of his mother, new daughter-in-law, children, and grandchildren could be spared. This is a case of the banishment of the mother of the indicted. The "Biography of Yuan Zai" records that Zai's daughter, Zhenyi, was tonsured at a tender age. After Zai was exposed, she was sent into the palace, and it was not until the reign of Dezong that she was told that Zai had died, whereby she wailed and collapsed onto the floor. Not even a nun was spared such punishment. What did it mean for a woman to be brought into the palace but to become a slave? A ruthless ruler would stop at nothing, as the pain of labor and the pain of humiliation were heaped on the woman's body.

There are even worse examples. When Yuanji was indicted in the Tang dynasty, Taizong made his concubines his own. When the innocent Wu Fujin was executed in public in the Five Dynasties period, his followers divided up his wives and children. The laws of the Song and Ming dynasties mandated that if a man committed an offense, his wives and daughters were to be sent to the Music Bureau and made into prostitutes. Hence, even loyal and chaste households became mired in shame. How can we count one by one all the calamities that befell women that were caused by men?

From the time of the Han dynasty, when a man ran afoul of the law, his wife was to be exiled to the frontier. The "Biography of Wang Jia" in the *History of the Han* records that the wife and children of Guardsman Zhang were all imprisoned; when Zhang died, they were exiled to Hepei. The "Biography of Xifu Gong" relates that when Gong died in the prison of Luoyang, over one hundred people were thrown into prison by implication; his wife, Chonghan, and family members were exiled to Hepu. The "Biography of Yang Bi" mentions that when Yun Yao was beheaded, his wife and children were exiled to Jiuquan. The "Biography of Chen Fan" in the *History of the Later Han* states that Fan was executed and his family members exiled to Bijing. All these persecutions of women were caused by association with what men had done. In the early Qing, political cases led to the execution of men by the hundreds and thousands; their wives and children were either exiled to Jilin Province or given to soldiers as slaves; they met their end by the tens and hundreds.[97]

The above discussion makes it amply clear that women in a country of despotic rule are deprived of their rights to life and freedom. There is no doubt that many of the prosecuted men were in fact innocent and that wrongful verdicts were not infrequently made, but at least an offense had to be named when men received their death sentences. When women were punished, no offense needed to be identified; punishment was inflicted on [a woman's] body simply because some man ran afoul of the law. In life, women did not enjoy the same rights as men; in death, women

---

[97]Tr: The translator and editors have retained the repetitious format of He-Yin Zhen's argument in the preceding paragraphs, which amounts to a long list of cases culled from the "Biography" sections of the official dynastic histories. The mind-numbing repetition itself supplies the rhetorical force of He's indictment: men caused women's suffering and downfall.

must endure the same punishment as men—how on earth could there be such unjust laws?! We may trace all of this to the fallacy of the Confucian dictum that "women follow men; men lead women." Women have been treated as appendages of men, and their rights to life and death are determined solely in accordance with the principle of whether men violate the law or not. We cannot but conclude that the death of women is effectively caused by men.

It makes me sad to review the annals of history from antiquity to the present, which are filled with despotic rulers and cruel officials, and I cannot even count the number of women whose deaths [the despostic rulers and cruel officials] have caused. In ancient times, all prominent families had numerous concubines; and when the winds of politics shifted, their men were liable to be executed in the public marketplace, whereupon their concubines could not help but follow them to death. It was unfortunate for a woman to be born in times of despotism, and even more unfortunate was for her to be born or marry into a prominent family. Surely, the main culprits were despotic rulers and their cruel officials, but also responsible is men's treatment of women as their private property. Men have caused many a woman's untimely death. If you are a man, would you not take a hard look and admit the extent to which you owe the women? In addition to polygyny in the harem, I argue, this [penal code] is the second force that pushes women to the brink of death.

Addendum

In recent times the law has slackened, and rarely are a wife and children sentenced with a man. But it is said that when Zhang Wenxiang assassinated Ma Xinyi (1821–1870, the governor-general of Liang-Jiang), Zhang's young daughter who had been adopted by her mother's brother was implicated and died a cruel death. The calamities also extended to Zhang's wife and the wife of his brother. Is this not new evidence that women are still suffering on account of men's offenses? When Xu Xiling's plot [to overthrow the Manchus] was recently exposed, the government sought to capture his wife and dispatched an order to Japan to do so. Even to this day, the law of guilt-by-association is not entirely eliminated. This unjust penal code—inflicting a guilty verdict upon an innocent woman by association with a man—must be rare in the world. Is there any further doubt that all despotic rulers and their allies are the enemies of women?

Originally published in *Tianyi*, no. 2 (June 10, 1907): pp. 1–13; no. 3 (July 9, 1907): pp. 7–23; no. 4 (July 24, 1907): pp. 1–6; no. 5 (August 9, 1907): pp. 65–70; and triple issue nos. 8–10 (October 29, 1907): pp. 19–25.[98] Signed Zhen Shu (authored by Zhen), with the name He-Yin Zhen listed in the journal contents. Reprinted in Wan Shiguo, pp. 663–691. Translated by Dorothy Ko from the Chinese original "Nüzi fuchou lun 女子復仇論."

[98]Tr: The title in this issue, "On the Revenge of Women," varies slightly from those of the previous and following issues. Instead of "revenge" (*fuchou* 復仇), it is "speaking of revenge" (*shuochou* 説仇). The variation could be attributed to a typo.

"On Feminist Antimilitarism"

He-Yin Zhen (1907)

In China today, those who are poorly informed fail to perceive any of the hardships that the peoples of Europe, the United States, and Japan are enduring. Rather, we only cower at their national strength, proposing to build up our own military forces while also spreading hawkish ideals. It is truly absurd that everyone boasts about becoming a militarized people. There are even a handful of women who ardently hope to become like Mulan or Liang Hongyu.[1] This is especially senseless. Today, in contrast to these sentiments, I will explain why women should be opposed to militarism. Below is an attempt to explain my thoughts.

In today's world, antimilitarism is flourishing in southern Europe. In France, Gustave Herve (1871–1944) has begun an antimilitarist movement, distributing pamphlets twice a year while also engaging in speeches.[2] Recently, he published a declaration with twenty-five comrades, which led to their punishment by arrest and fines. Over three thousand people have signed onto this declaration. Antimilitarism has also been prevalent in Switzerland, Italy, Spain, and Belgium. To the north, Karl Liebknecht

---

[1]Tr: Mulan, who joined the army in disguise on behalf of her ailing father, is the famous protagonist of the "Ballad of Mulan," which was first transcribed in the sixth century. Liang Hongyu (1102–1135) was a heroic female commander who led Southern Song forces against the Jurchens.

[2]Tr: Herve's antimilitarism was very short lived. Upon his release from prison in 1912, he turned into an ultranationalist, and his version of the National Socialists became the basis of French fascism and of collaboration with Hitler and Mussolini.

in Germany has been imprisoned for his opposition to militarism. Over two thousand Germans share the same sentiment. In Holland, Ferdinand Domela Nieuwenhuis proposed a general strike during times of war at the Socialist Party's general meeting. In Norway, [Einar] Li[3] has put into practice a movement to refuse military service. If you want evidence of protesters destroying warships, then look to the Americas. If you want evidence of soldiers deserting the army, then look to Japan. These are all instances of antimilitarist movements in the world.

Why do I claim that antimilitarism will benefit the common people? The people's revolutions of the past, based on the tactics of violent insurrection, built and defended barricades. The boulevards in cities today, however, have been widened and are now difficult to fortify. In addition, the armed forces have been reorganized to serve and protect the government and capitalists, making any resistance by the people difficult. Unless the people's party adopts a strategy of passive resistance—in the form of advocating the disbanding of armies—they will have little chance of success. Moreover, soldiers come from the common people, sharing in the quality of being subservient. These willing slaves allow the government and capitalists to take advantage of them. Day after day, they wage wars against the people both domestically and abroad, to the point of incurring their own deaths. They are the most pitiful of all humanity. We should by all means strive to make them see [the pathetic state they are in]. In this sense, antimilitarism can help the common people seize their own freedom; it can extend protection to all human lives.

Are not most women in the world today in the same position as the common people? Are they not a bona fide part of humanity? What if you were to ask the majority of women: Would they like to enjoy all the freedoms they wish for, or would they rather be oppressed, sinking into slavery forever? Would they rather enjoy their lives free from harm, or would they rather fall into disaster, suffering a wretched death? All women are familiar with enslavement and unnatural death and are disgusted by the experience. For that reason antimilitarism should be well received by women.

Military buildup and warfare harm women in more ways than one. If we examine the past, we see that troops are good for nothing but rape, kidnapping, looting, and murder. A poem by the abducted musician Cai

---

[3]Tr: Einar Li, editor of the newspaper *Social Democrat* in Oslo in the early twentieth century. Li and his co-conspirator, Lieutenant Puntervold, were the animators of an antimilitarist movement in Norway, for which they were imprisoned.

Wenji (b.177–?)[4] describes the carnage she saw after battle: "Severed heads of men hang from horses' sides; And in the back, women carried away [to the north]." Those words vividly convey the conditions of battle. In Chinese history, whenever warfare involved the besieging of towns and the robbing of land, all the women captured would be carried off by the invaders. When the Liao, Jin [Jurchens], and Mongols descended into southern China, they took millions upon millions of southern women. Even imperial clans-women and upper-class women could not avoid this fate, and many of them committed suicide or died by the roadside. In recent history we witnessed the Taiping Rebellion led by Hong [Xiuquan] and Yang [Xiuqing] and the Hunan Army that eventually quelled them; both sides acted like this. Even if a woman were to avoid the suffering of being a prisoner of war, she would have to flee her home instead and wander around as a refugee. Mothers who have lost their sons, wives mourning their husbands, and households that have been ruined, all of them are forced into starvation and the cold. According to a poem by Wang Can (177–217) of the Han dynasty, "As I walk outdoors I see nothing,/ White bones cover the flat land./ By the road there is a hungry woman,/ Who abandons her infant in the brush./ She looks back and hears the baby's cries,/ But wipes her tears without returning./ 'I don't even know where I will die,/ How can I look after both of us?'"[5] This paints a sobering picture of the miserable conditions of war. Is there any happiness to speak of with the kind of life women led in that age?

Some may object that what I have said above is applicable only to the military systems of barbaric ages. They may think that with the civilized nations of today imposing greater discipline on their troops, the calamities of rape, pillaging, and murder have subsided. Little do they know that during the Sino-Japanese War (1894–1895) and the Russo-Japanese War (1904–1905), large areas of the Liaodong Peninsula were shelled by cannon fire and stampeded by warhorses. Wherever they went, no women and children were able to escape the misfortune of a tragic death or the life of a refugee. As we turn next to the campaigns of the Armies of the Eight-Nation Alliance [in 1900, during the Boxer Uprising], there were untold numbers of

---

[4]Tr: Cai Wenji was a Han dynasty poet. Daughter of the musician Cai Yong, Wenji was captured by the Northwestern Xiongnu people and ransomed by the famous general Cao Cao in 207. Her poetry was widely known and appreciated for its expressiveness.
[5]Tr: Wu Fusheng, *Written at Imperial Command: Panegyric Poetry in Early Medieval China* (Albany: State University of New York Press, 2008), 28.

dead women around Beijing. Moreover, many of the women of Taiwan have become the playthings of the Japanese just because Japan has seized their land. As for the women of Annam, they are abused by the French on a daily basis. According to the "History of the Lost State of Annam,"[6] women from good families are accused of not being chaste, forced into prostitution, and then taxed. Is this not all because the French have taken their land? What enables the seizing of peoples and lands are armaments and military force. We can thereby conclude that the humiliation faced by Taiwanese and Vietnamese women is brought about by the expanding militaries of the great powers. Can we not gasp in horror?

Or, some may think that all I have said describes only those states that have been defeated in war. If a country were to embrace virile military values, then it would become strong and its women would not suffer like those under military attack. But then you may be unaware of the state of current-day Japan. Is that not a rich and powerful nation? Is that not the country that defeated China and Russia, two of the great powers, in war? Yet, ever since it began deploying troops in recent years, the number of prostitutes in the country has been growing by the day. What is the reason for this? It is because many of the country's able-bodied men die overseas in war and their families receive little in compensation. Wives who have lost their husbands and daughters who have lost their fathers cannot help but go into prostitution, for it becomes increasingly difficult to sustain a living. Of those who are prostitutes today, half of them belong to the families of servicemen. Regardless of whether or not a militarized nation has been victorious or is defeated, women have nothing to gain from the effects of war. There is clear evidence of this.

There is no happiness for a people but peace and security. But can women of a militarized nation expect any peace or security? If we heed the words of Chinese writers, there are countless works dedicated to the trials faced by soldiers' families. First, I would like to discuss the pain of parting. In "Rhapsody on Separation," Jiang Yan (444–505) writes:

And then, border commanderies are not yet pacified.
And a man, bearing plumed arrows, marches with the army.

---

[6]Tr: This book was written by Phan Boi Chao, an anti-French Vietnamese activist who was well known to Chinese intellectuals in Tokyo. Although the preface to the Chinese translation of his book was written by Liang Qichao, Phan was more in sympathy with Sun Zhongshan and the revolutionaries.

The Liao River stretched on without end,
Mount Yan soars into the clouds.
For the lady in her bedchamber, the breeze is warm.
And on the field paths, the grass is fragrant.
The sun rises, its beams brilliantly shining in the sky.
Dew falls, casting scintillating patterns over the ground.
In the reflected light, the glittering glare of vermillion dust.
Enveloping the air, the ethers of spring, thick and heavy.
Breaking springs of peach and plum, they cannot bear to part.
She sends off her beloved son, tears soaking her gauze skirt.[7]

The Tang poet Du Fu (712–770) writes in "Ballad of the War Wagons":

Rumble-rumble of wagons,
horses whinnying,
war-bound, bow and arrows at each man's waist,
fathers, mothers, wives, children running alongside,
dust so thick you can't see Xianyang Bridge,
snatching at clothes, stumbling, blocking the road, wailing, wailing
voices that rise straight up to the clouds.[8]

In the "Xin-an Officer," he writes: "The young men are so small, how will they defend the capital? The robust ones have mothers to send them off, whereas the frail ones have only themselves. Clear waters flow eastward all day as the green hills resound with wailing. Don't cry your eyes out! Save your tears! Even if your eyes were dried out, such that their sockets were exposed, both heaven and earth would still be merciless." And in the "The Newlyweds' Separation": "My hair adorned as your new wife, we have not even warmed our bed. Just married at dusk and already parting at dawn. Why must we be in such haste?" Later, Du Fu continues, "With you now off to a place of death, sorrow that breaks my heart." These poems indicate that as soon as dispatch letters are sent out, husbands and wives must painfully bid farewell to one another. Women everywhere know all too well the misery of snatching at clothes and stumbling.

---

[7]Tr: Xiao Tong, *Wen Xuan, or Selections of Refined Literature*, vol. 3, *Rhapsodies on Natural Phenomena, Birds and Animals, Aspirations and Feelings, Sorrowful Laments, Literature, Music, and Passions*, trans. David R. Knechtges (Princeton, NJ: Princeton University Press, 1996).
[8]Tr: Du Fu, *The Selected Poems of Du Fu*, trans. Burton Watson (New York: Columbia University Press, 2002), 8.

Second, I would like to discuss the pain of long separation. The poem "Dong Shan" [The hills to the east] in the Bin Feng section [of the *Book of Songs*] describes the thoughts of a man campaigning and his longing for his wife. There are not enough words to convey the miserable feeling of his visualizing the harvest at home in the section following the lines "The fruit of the heavenly gourd,/ Would be hanging about our eaves."[9] Cao Zhi's (192–232) *Miscellaneous Poems* proceeds thus:

Your handmaid now must keep her empty chamber,
her husband has gone marching off to war.
Although he swore to return in three years' time,
nine months of spring have now already passed.
A solitary bird goes winging round the trees,
its plaintive cry tells it has lost the flock.
I wish I were the sun that shines in the south,
to send my beams hastening to see my lord.[10]

Wang Can's (177–217) "Following Military Campaigns" says: "Man on the road longs for his relatives, / Who can avoid such deep longings? / . . . I grieve for those soldiers of 'Eastern Mountain,' / How I am moved by the crane's crying. / The sun and the moon never stay still, Who among

---

[9]Tr: The stanza reads thus:

We went to the hills of the east,
And long were we there without returning,
When we came from the east,
Down came the rain drizzlingly.
The fruit of the heavenly gourd,
Would be hanging about our eaves;
The sowbug would be in our chambers;
The spiders webs would be in our doors;
Our paddocks would be deer-fields;
The fitful light of the glow-worms would be all about.
These thoughts made us apprehensive,
And they occupied our breasts.

"Dong Shan" (The hills of the east, no. 156), trans. James Legge, http://etext.virginia.edu/chinese/shijing/AnoShih.html

[10]Tr: John Minford and Joseph S. M. Lau, eds., *Classical Chinese Literature: An Anthology of Translations* (New York: Columbia University Press, 2002), 428–429.

humankind can rest forever?"[11] According to Wang Hui's (d. 891) "Miscellaneous Poems":

> She looks out from the high terrace in longing.
> Recalling the past, she leans against the decorated banister.
> Her zither produces no music,
> there are only the bitter words of her elegy.
> Her basket and broom remain by the riverbank,
> while her husband has gone off to Yanmen.
> How could he ever recall not having enough clothing,
> now only knowing the warmth of fox hair?

A rhapsody by Emperor Yuan of Liang (r. 552–555) says: "I resent having to weave a circular text on brocade, / while you brood over the words of 'To the Frontier.' / Each thinking of the other and gazing into that direction, / realizing just how long the road is!" In addition, according to a poem by Gao Shi (d. 765] of the Tang dynasty: "Young women south of the city are nearly heartbroken. / The soldiers marching north of Ji turn their heads in vain." These poems suggest that women in the families of soldiers look into the distance besotted with grief and send off letters to faraway lands. [They wonder] Who will provide for them? Constantly on alert, their stomachs are in knots. Again, women know these feelings all too well.

Third, I would like to mention the pain of death notifications. In his "Admonition Against Attacking Min-Yue," the prince of Huainan, Liu An (177–122 B.C.E.), mentions what happened during the Qin: "Nearly half were dead before reaching the battlefield. Beloved wives and elderly parents wept while orphans cried aloud. Families and trades were ruined. With the corpses more than thousands of *li* away, only the skeletons were brought back in bundles. The air of sorrow did not pass for many years." According to Li Hua (715–766) of the Tang dynasty: "They may be alive or dead, the family knows not. And if one brings the news, they listen half doubting, half believing while their heart overflows with grief. Sleeping and waking, they seem to see the lost one's form. Sacrifices are made ready and libations poured, with tearful eyes strained toward the far horizon; heaven and earth, nay, the very trees and plants, all seeming to sympathize with their sorrow. And when in response to prayers and libations, these wanderers return not,

---

[11] Tr: Wu Fusheng, *Written at Imperial Command*, 30.

where shall their spirits find repose?"[12] Judging from these words, is there anything worse than the dismal situation faced by these wives? Let us consider a poem by Chen Lin (d. 217) of the Eastern Han: "On the border there are many strong boys, at home there are many widows." Another poem by Du Fu of the Tang dynasty says

> [Of three sons sent to defend Yecheng,] a letter came from one of them,
> the other two lost in the fighting.
> One alive, no more than a borrowed life,
> dead ones gone for all time!
> Here in the house not another soul,
> only a grandchild, still nursing at the breast.
> His mother stays to look after him, indoors or out,
> barely a skirt to cover her.[13]

From these poems we understand that when a country wages war, the pain of separation, in both life and death, affects women more than anyone else. Not only does warfare threaten [conjugal] love, it can bring women to impoverishment and death. Even if those troops who are deployed are victorious and return alive, the defeated nation will have a great number of casualties. Those casualties will come from the common people of that country, and those distressed from war will be their families. If our purpose is to help out our own compatriots but make widows and orphans out of the women and children of other countries, what honor and what glory is there for anyone to bask in? One way or another, warfare causes undeniable harm to women; women must therefore take the lead in protesting militarism.

That is not all. The reduction of women in the world today to a class of laborers (*gongnü*) means a life in the factory, and there must be a reason why it is so difficult for women to make a living (*shengji*). There may be no single cause for economic hardship, but soaring prices and increased rents and taxes have been crucial factors. And both of these increases can be attributed to the expansion of the military. If we take a look at any of the world's countries today, a large portion of public finance is allocated to national defense spending. In 1898, England spent over forty million pounds on their land and sea forces. Aside from paying indemnities, a large portion of funds gathered from

---

[12]Tr: Minford and Lau, eds., *Classical Chinese Literature*, 993.
[13]Tr: Du Fu, *Selected Poems*, trans. Watson, 50.

China's provinces goes toward revamping the military forces. The *lijin* taxes that were used in the past to finance armies have also increased. Therefore, just as armaments have grown by the day, so too has the tax burden shouldered by the people. This policy of unreasonably levying taxes has become the norm in one country after the next in the world. Moreover, with the growth of armaments, the numbers of people filling military-related positions have grown, turning them from gainful producers into mere parasites.[14] Aside from soldiers, there are also those people who manufacture military weapons, such as workers in armories, and those people who manufacture uniforms or national defense, such as workers in batteries. Those who in the past produced from the soil and provided the daily necessities of the people have left these positions instead to build weapons that harm people. The total amount of production can no longer meet all the people's needs—another reason for soaring prices. Taxes and high prices grow by the day, leaving too little income to care for the elderly or children. Scores of families suffer from starvation and cold. Women have no choice but to submit to the wage system, laboring in workshops to the benefit of the rich in exchange for sustenance in food and clothes. Below this class of women, there are those who are trapped in servility and prostitution. Alas! For what reason have women sunk into this situation? The reason is poverty, and the people are poor because of military expansion. If the military is not abandoned, I fear that women trapped in suffering and poverty will have no hope of ever being able to find relief.[15]

There is another thing that all women should know. In the past and present, the basis for the unequal distribution of rights between men and women has been the enlistment of men and not women [in the military]. Social

---

[14]Tr: The terms "producer" (*shengli* 生利; literally, those who make things of real value) and "parasites" (*fenli* 分利; literally, those who siphon off real value) is a distinction made in Liang Qichao, "On Women's Education," translated in this volume.

[15]Zhufu Yan (d. 126 B.C.E.) of the Han dynasty raised the example of the Qin in his "Admonition Against Attacking the Xiongnu," saying: "The men spared no efforts tilling the fields, but there was still not enough harvest for the provisions. The women spun an extraordinary amount of cloth, but there was still not enough fabric to cover the army tents. The people were exhausted, unable to care for orphans, widows, the elderly, and the sick. The dead could be found everywhere on the roads." This example is sufficient in illustrating the difficulties faced by the people amidst war. There have not been any wars in the past dynasties that have not been like this. Du Fu's "Ballad of the War Wagons" says: "Our Han land's two hundred districts east of the mountains, / a thousand villages, ten thousand hamlets gone to thorns and brambles. / Sturdy wives can handle plow and mattock, / but the rows of grain never come up right." Is it not clear that militarization impoverishes the people and causes them to neglect their proper livelihood?

hierarchies and classes are likewise structured. In ancient times, men stole and looted women, treating them as captives and extending the practice of concubinage—which was another outcome of war. The unyielding spirit of soldiers was so powerful that it was enough to subdue women. And women had no choice but to yield to men and become their inferiors. Over time, women became disposed to servitude and followed the commands of men. This is the true cause of inequality between men and women. The very origin of inequality between men and women lies in militarism. Those who speak out against women's rights point to the fact that women cannot become soldiers as proof why they cannot ever be equal to men. This ideology of male superiority and female inferiority originated in conscription and was passed on to later generations. Male conscription has had a history of thousands of years. Even if women wanted to share this duty today, they could not even out the score in a short period of time. Is it not better, then, to implement antimilitarism? Men would then be freed from conscription and return to being equals with women. They would no longer be able to use this empty talk of protecting the country to lord it over womanhood or indulge in their own power to force women into submission. This would in fact be a pivotal step toward equality between men and women and a crucial first step for women toward freeing themselves from the yoke of men. It follows that women who wish to stop supporting equality between men and women [may continue to be militarist]; but if they do want to achieve equality, there is no better course of action than antimilitarism. This is an unchanging truth.

To conclude, antimilitarism would be a great victory for weak nations [literally, "races or kind," *zhong* 種], the common people, and women. If antimilitarism thrives, weak nations would end the violation of their integrity by strong nations. Commoners would free themselves from oppression by the state. For women, it would mean giving up the yoke of men and winning independence. This would be a harbinger of world peace and happiness. I deeply hope that women all around the world will understand its significance and implement antimilitarism. It would be an extraordinary achievement to be able to save the world and relieve the people [of warfare], and such an achievement could rival the brilliance of the sun and the moon.

Originally published in the Editorial section (She shuo 社説), *Tianyi*, nos. 11–12 (December 20, 1907): pp. 25–32. Signed Zhen Shu 震述. Translated by Jeremy Tai from the Chinese original "Nüzi fei junbei zhuyi lun 女子非軍備主義論."

"The Feminist Manifesto"

He-Yin Zhen (1907)

M en and women have been unequal in this world for a very long time. In India, widows immolate themselves to sacrifice their lives for men; in Japan, women prostrate themselves in the service of men. In Europe and America, even though people practice monogamy and thereby proclaim equality, women are rarely able to partake in politics or vote. So, is there any substance to their "equal rights"? When we look back at China, our men practically treat women as subhuman beings. In ancient times, after a tribe defeated another group, they [the tribesmen] would truss up the women, bind up their bodies with pillories, and take them as concubines. This is how men became masters and women slaves. That period can rightly be called the age of [men's] plundering of women. In due time, since stealing other people's women was likely to induce conflicts, people developed the custom of sending deerskin as an engagement "gift." The ancient marriage rites that mandated the groom's family deliver betrothal gifts to the bride's side are remnants of this earlier kind of "property-marriage."[1]

---

[1]Tr: Two kinds of gifts are involved, conveyed in two distinct stages: *na cai* 納采 and *na zheng* 納徵 of the betrothal ceremony. As explained in the Confucian classic *Book of Rites* (in "The Meaning of Marriage"): "The ceremony of marriage was intended to be a bond of love between two families of different surnames, with a view, in its retrospective character, to secure the services in the ancestral temple, and in its prospective character, to secure the continuance of the family line. Therefore the superior men set a great value upon it. Hence, in regard to the various introductory ceremonies—the proposal with its accompanying gift (*na cai*), the inquiries about the lady's name, the intimation of the approving divination, the receiving of the special offerings (*na zheng*), and the request to fix the day—these all were received by the principal

Women were clearly regarded as a form of male property. Men are human, but women are merely chattel. That period can be called the age of [men's] trading of women. From these two root causes, inequality between men and women became entrenched. The specific forms this inequality has taken can be traced from the four institutions from the past.

The first is inequality in marriage. In ancient times, the more respected a man's position in society, the more wives he had. For example, during the Yin [Shang] dynasty (16th–11th century B.C.E.), the Son of Heaven could marry twelve women; his marquises, nine; high-ranking aristocrats, three; other titled men, two. During the Zhou dynasty (1046–256 B.C.E.), the Son of Heaven had one queen, three helpmates, nine consorts, twenty-seven women of family, and eighty-one ladies of honor. These constituted his wife and concubines.[2] Does this not indicate that in effect over one hundred women were married to one man? Since then, there have been no limits placed on the number of imperial concubines the emperor might retain. Honorable and illustrious families especially hoarded a lot of concubines. This is the first aspect of male-female inequality.

The second is inequality in status between husband and wife. Since men managed to expand their power, they became all the more vigilant against women. They invented the motto, "Once a woman becomes a man's wife, she remains so for life."[3] A woman is thus allowed to serve only one husband. What is more: "The husband is high as the wife is low; the husband is to heaven as the wife is to earth. The wife cannot do without her husband as the earth cannot do without Heaven."[4] As a result, a woman follows her husband's noble rank in life, and she takes her husband's family name, and she posthumously receives her husband's promotion to a higher rank. Women are made into men's subsidiaries. Song dynasty scholars followed this reasoning when they spoke of "shoring up the yang [male] and diminishing the yin [female]." This is the second aspect of male-female inequality.

The third is inequality in work and responsibility. The character for "woman" (fu 婦) is glossed as fu 服, or "to serve." The "woman" character is composed of a woman holding a broom. The Book of Rites ("Quli") makes

---

party on the lady's side." A version of these rites is still being practiced in China today. Translation adapted from James Legge, The Li Ki (The Book of Rites), http://ctext.org/liji/hun-yi.
[2]Tr: Book of Rites, cf. "Quli"; "Hunyi." Translation of the titles adapted from Legge's.
[3]Book of Rites.
[4]White Tiger Discourse (Baihu Tong).

it clear: "In presenting a daughter for the harem of the ruler of a state, it is said, 'This is to complete the providers of your spirits and sauces'; for that of a great officer, 'This is to complete the number of those who sprinkle and sweep for you.'"[5] It seems, in this way, ancient women considered serving and obeying to be their obligation. Furthermore, men concocted the teaching that women should not step out of the inner quarters so as to deprive them of their freedom. From then on, women did not have responsibilities aside from managing the household; being educated and talented was deprecated; [as a consequence,] they have taken being servile to be a natural state. This is the third aspect of male-female inequality.

The fourth is inequality in the system of rites. When a wife dies, the husband observes mourning for only one year, but a widow must mourn her husband for three years, and in the coarsest attire (unhemmed sackcloth). And she is to extend the same severity in mourning her husband's parents. But when she mourns her natal parents, she observes rites of the lesser grade (of one year and wearing sackcloth with even edges).[6] [The Confucian classic *Great Learning* says,] "It never has been the case that what was of great importance has been slightly cared for, and what was of slight importance has been greatly cared for."[7] But the mourning rites do exactly that! Even worse is that in ancient times, a daughter's mourning rites for her mother would be downgraded from three years to one if her father was still alive. This was most egregious. This, then, is the fourth aspect of male-female inequality.

Even from this cursory review it becomes very clear how men oppress and subjugate women. It is not hard to fathom why men would want to

---

[5]Tr: Adapted from Legge's translation, http://ctext.org/liji/qu-li-ii.

[6]Tr: The funerary and mourning rites, prescribed in the Confucian classic *Book of Rites*, constituted a major means of regulating and substantiating social and gender hierarchy according to the principle of patrilineal descent. There are five "mourning grades" varying in duration and attire. The most severe is *zhan cui* 斬衰 (three years; coarsest sackcloth with unhemmed edges). In ancient times it was mandated for a son mourning his father, a minister mourning his prince, and a wife for her husband. In Ming-Qing times (1368–1911 C.E.), a daughter-in-law also observed the most severe rite for her parents-in-law, as stated by He-Yin Zhen. Next in severity and importance is *zi cui* 齊衰 (three months, one year, or three years; coarse sackcloth with even or hemmed edges). A son was to observe three years of mourning for his mother if his father predeceased her, but only for one year if his father is alive. And so on. Also see "On the Revenge of Women," part 1 (translated in this volume), where He-Yin Zhen gives a more extended account of the gendered nature of these rituals.

[7]Tr: Adapted from Legge's translation, http://ctext.org/liji/da-xue. The "Great Learning" (Da xue), a part of the *Book of Rites*, was elevated to be a stand-alone classic.

bully women; but why, one might ask, are women so willing to submit? Could it be that the power of social customs and the teachings of pedantic scholars have come to bind and restrain women? Let me put it plainly so that all my companions in womanhood understand: men are the archenemy of women. As long as women fail to be men's equals, anger and sorrow will never be requited. Therefore, let me spell out all the things that women need to strive for one by one:

- The first is monogamous marriage. If a man has more than one wife, keeps concubines or mistresses, or is predisposed to whoring, then his wife can use the harshest laws to restrain him, so much so that he would die by women's hands. If a woman willingly serves a husband with multiple wives, the entire womenfolk would rise up against her. If a man only has one wife, but his wife has extramarital affairs, both men and women should rise up against her.

- The second is that after a woman marries, she should not take her husband's surname. Even if she retains her maiden name, it is still unfair because it is her father's surname but not her mother's. Therefore, women like us who are living in the present age should fashion our surnames from both the father's and the mother's [surnames]. After we overthrow the Manchus, neither men nor women should keep a surname. That would be the principle of supreme justice.

- The third is that parents should value sons and daughters equally. Daughters are no different from sons, and a daughter's offspring are full-fledged grandchildren. This way the entrenched custom of slighting daughters and valuing sons would end.

- The fourth is that soon after birth, daughters and sons should be raised without discrimination. As they grow, they should receive equal education. As grownups, they shoulder equal responsibilities. All affairs in society should be women's business.

- The fifth is that if a couple fails to get along after marriage, the man and wife can separate. Until then, neither should take up with someone else lest they violate the first goal above.

- The sixth is that first-time grooms should be paired with first-time brides. When bereaved, a man can remarry, but only to a woman who has married before. Likewise, a bereaved wife can remarry, but only to a man who has married before. If a first-time bride assents to marrying a man who has married before, womenfolk should rise to censure her.

- The seventh is to abolish all the brothels in the world and let go all the prostitutes under the sun to clean up the environment of lasciviousness.

We champion these seven goals, not because we women want to snatch power and rights into our hands, but because Heaven endows natural rights equally to men and women. Since men and women are both human, the lack of equality is unjust and contradicts the principles of nature; ultimately, what women strive for should not stop short of supreme justice for all.

But people may counter my suggestions by raising three common objections. The first is that women endure the toil of childbirth and afterward have to exhaust themselves in raising the children; thus a woman's work and responsibilities are by nature different from men's. Those who think so do not understand that what I am proposing is not merely a women's revolution but a complete social revolution. The women's revolution is but one aspect of the social revolution. After the social revolution is accomplished, after birth, all children would be raised in public child care facilities; accordingly, mothers would no longer have to raise their children by themselves. Once relieved of this task, women could assume responsibilities equal to men's.

The second objection may be that since there are more women than men in the world, it is unfair to mandate that one person can take only one spouse. But those who object thus do not know that women are more plentiful because they never fight wars. Active military duty is without fail a male prerogative; therefore their numbers dwindle by the day. Now, as women, would we rather not unleash destruction and die on the battlefield for posthumous honor than be oppressed to death as obedient concubines? If women indeed carried out the [social] revolution, after the violence ended, the number of women would certainly be the same as the number of men.[8]

The third argument one often hears is that since men have many wives, why shouldn't women have multiple husbands as a form of redress? The misunderstanding here is that we women desire equality and will get it, not by [the passive means of] reform or boycotting, but by the application of brute force to coerce men to make us equal. But polygyny is a major male

---

[8]Tr: He-Yin Zhen is not necessarily issuing a call to arms but is suggesting that revolutions are violent and women's participation in the revolution would cull the female population into balance with the male population. For He-Yin Zhen's pacifist views, see her essay "On Feminist Antimilitarism," translated in this volume.

transgression. If women choose to emulate them, how are we to defend ourselves when men accuse us [of transgressing]? A woman who has multiple husbands is virtually a prostitute. Those women who are now advocating multiple husbands use the pretext of resisting men, but their real motivation is to give full rein to their personal lust, following the path of prostitutes. These women are traitors to womanhood.

In sum, men and women are both human. By [saying] "men" (*nanxing*) and "women" (*nüxing*) we are not speaking of "nature," as each is but the outcome of differing social customs and education. If sons and daughters are treated equally, raised and educated in the same manner, then the responsibilities assumed by men and women will surely become equal. When that happens, the nouns "men" and "women" would no longer be necessary. This is ultimately the "equality of men and women" of which we speak.

People in China have recently come to believe that for women to reach this goal, they must apply themselves to herald—even ahead of men— racial, political, economic, and other revolutions; they must not allow themselves to lag behind men again. According to their view, the revolution between men and women should proceed side by side with racial, political, and economic revolutions. [They believe] if they succeeded, women could establish the first real regime of "women's rights" in the world. If they failed, women would perish *with* men, never to be subjugated by them again. I think this is a narrow-minded view. Whether people agree with me or condemn me is not my concern here.[9]

Original published in *Tianyi*, no. 1 (June 10, 1907): pp. 1–7. Signed He-Yin Zhen. Reprinted in Wan Shiguo, pp. 654–656. Translated by Meng Fan and Cynthia M. Roe; edited by Dorothy Ko from the Chinese original "Nüzi xuanbu shu 女子宣布書."

---

[9]Tr: He-Yin Zhen's expression "*zhiwo zuiwo* 知我罪我" connotes her self-image as the moral judge of history. The expression comes from the Confucian classic *Mencius* and is supposed to be uttered by Confucius himself: "Again the world fell into decay, and principles faded away. Perverse speakings and oppressive deeds waxed rife again. There were instances of ministers who murdered their sovereigns, and of sons who murdered their fathers. Confucius was afraid and made the *Spring and Autumn*. What the *Spring and Autumn* contains are matters proper to the sovereign. On this account Confucius said, 'Yes! It is the Spring and Autumn that will make people know me, and it is the *Spring and Autumn* that will make them condemn me.'" Adapted from Legge's translation, http://ctext.org/mengzi/teng-wen-gong-ii/zh?en=on

Liang Qichao in Australia, 1900, from *Liang Qichao yu yinbing shi* [Liang Qichao and the Ice Drinker's Studio], ed. Guo Changjiu. Tianjin: Tianjin guji, 2003.

Liang Qichao 梁啓超 (aka Liang Rengong 梁任公,

1873–1929) was the foremost modern intellectual of China in the first two decades of the twentieth century. He was born in Xinhui, Guangdong Province, and became a disciple of the New Text Confucian scholar Kang Youwei. Liang was involved in the Hundred Days' Reform led by the young Guangxu emperor in 1898. Following a coup d'état by Empress Dowager Cixi's powerful conservative opponents, he and the other leaders of the movement were forced into exile in Japan, where his iconoclastic journalism and scholarly searchings began to shape the minds of a whole generation of Chinese students.

Liang was the first modern intellectual in China to achieve public stature through a systematic exploitation of journalism. While still in China, he founded and was editor of two prominent newspapers, *Sino-Foreign News* (*Zhongwai gongbao*) and *The Chinese Progress* (*Shiwu bao*), which advocated sweeping reforms to China's society and polity. While in exile, he was editor-in-chief of *Journal of Pure Critique* (*Qingyi bao*) and *New Citizen Miscellany* (*Xinmin congbao*), where he published many of his influential political essays and translations and inspired young Chinese with progressive new ideas in the last decade of the Qing dynasty (1644–1911).

Liang's essay "On Women's Education" was first published in *The Chinese Progress* in Shanghai in 1897. It was one of a dozen essays Liang wrote in response to China's defeat in the Sino-Japanese War (1895). He called for revamping the country's education system and the need to enlighten women and children. These essays form a single collection called "On Institutional Reform" (*Bianfa tongyi*), which spearheaded the country's school reform, modern education programs, and national self-strengthening. An important historical document, "On Women's Education" represents the voice of progressive male intellectuals who sought to put women on the agenda of national salvation. It is translated in this volume for the first time.

"On Women's Education"

Liang Qichao (1897)

I t was said in *Mencius*, "[But men possess a moral nature; and if they are well fed, warmly clad, and comfortably lodged,] without being taught at the same time, they become almost like the beasts."[1] Such pithy and truthful words! If any man were treated like an animal, we would certainly expect him to be enraged. Yet if what Ziyushi [Mencius] said above is true, then there are innumerable people today who are like beasts.

In this great wide world, there are some four hundred million people who have round heads and square toes [and are thus Chinese].[2] Among them, nearly one hundred and ninety million are peasants, artisans, merchants, and soldiers, who have lived their entire lives without being educated. Among those who are called officials or scholars, several million actually have no learning although they claim to have. And in China, there are also nearly two hundred million who have round heads but bent toes [i.e., women],[3] among whom there are no officials, scholars, peasants, artisans, merchants, or soldiers; since ancient times, they have never been educated. What is more, those officials, scholars, peasants, artisans,

---

All notes are translator's notes.

[1]The passage is an apology for the establishment of Confucian moral education by the sage King Shun. "Teng Wen Gong I," *Mencius*, trans. James Legge, http://ctext.org/mengzi/teng-wen-gong-i/zh?en=on (accessed August 17, 2012).

[2]In Chinese mythology, heaven is a dome-shaped canopy over the square earth. Embodying this perfect cosmic pattern, a human being is said to have a round head and square toes.

[3]By "round heads but bent toes," Liang refers to the harm that footbinding inflicted on the natural bodies of Chinese women.

and merchants whose lives are almost like those of beasts are nevertheless ashamed of that fact; but women who are not officials, scholars, peasants, artisans, or merchants and are almost like beasts feel no such shame! Not only is this so, but all of humanity simply takes this state of affairs to be the natural, fixed order of things. Alas! How painful it is! How painful it is!

Liang Qichao says that if one were to bring up the problem of women's education in China today, the reply would certainly be that there are innumerable issues that are of greater urgency now.[4] The listener would respond that with so many other important reforms having yet to be implemented, the discussion of women's education is a distraction from the most pressing and fundamental problems. However, when I seek out the root causes of national weakness, I find that they inevitably lie in women's lack of education. Please allow me to offer [four] reasons why I believe this to be true.

The first reason is that philosophers (*gonglijia*[5] 公理家) say that it is necessary that everyone in a country have his own occupation and be able to support himself. Only then will the country prosper. Indeed, the strength of a nation is directly related to the proportion of its people who are without work. Why is this so? People without work must be supported by people with work. If they are not supported, then people without work are endangered; yet if they are supported, then those with work are themselves imperiled. Translated Western texts have referred to this idea as the principle of profit making and profit sharing (生利, 分利), which is similar to the principle found in our [classic] *The Great Learning* (*Daxue*): "[T]hose who produce should be many, while those who consume should be few" [*to consume is to eat and to deplete*]. It is said in *Guanzi* that "if a man fails to plough, someone will starve; if a woman fails to spin, someone will freeze." These are not empty words; instead, it is the practical conclusion reached by considering the nation's labor force and material production as a whole and as they relate proportionally to national profit. In China, even if we consider only the men, the number of those who only consume comes to roughly half of those who produce. According to the philosophers, this situation alone already makes a stable national government impossible, let

---

[4] A convention of the time was to write in the third person. The author, Liang Qichao, does so here.

[5] This term's individual components are as follows: *gong* (公), typically translated as "public"; *li* (理), variously meaning "reason," "principle," or "logic"; and *jia* (家), literally, "expert" but in this context meaning "philosopher." The most direct translation might render this term "experts of public principle"; we translate it here simply as "philosopher."

alone when we consider the nation's two hundred million women, among whom all are consumers and none are producers. Owing to women's inability to support themselves and their dependence on other people, men raise women as livestock or slaves. Thus women live harsh lives. Since women are wholly dependent and men have no choice but to support them, even those men who work for the entire year cannot afford to care for their wives and children. Men [thus] also live harsh lives. Based on what I have observed, regardless of social status, neither upper-class officials, nor middle-class scholars, nor lower-class peasants, artisans, merchants, or soldiers can ever enjoy a time without panic and anxiety. And it is even more difficult to count the number of those who suffer from poverty—those who endure cold and hunger and whose dead bodies are discarded in ditches. In fact, based simply on the aforementioned principle of proportion, there would be no possibility of poverty if everyone worked with his own body to provide for his own sustenance.

Today, everyone worries about poverty in China. Poverty is caused when one person is forced to support several people. Although there are indeed several factors that have caused multiple people to become dependent upon one person, I would argue that the lack of employment of women is the original factor. Men and women are equally human—how is it that one works and the other does not? For all professions, there are necessary principles and practices that cannot be acquired without learning. We can see this clearly in the experience of men—an educated man who is conversant with the nature of things can easily find a job, whereas the less learned have much greater difficulty seeking employment. We might conclude, then, that education is the mother of occupations. The reason for women's lack of employment is not rooted in any natural principles or reason. Instead, it is a relic from the chaotic time in our past when humans struggled for power and to dominate each other by force. These values accorded with the natural abilities of men; women were unable to compete. As a result, women were seen as insignificant and were not to be educated. And without education, it was not possible for women to have occupations. After such a long time, the origins of women's lack of employment have gradually been forgotten by most people. It is now taken for granted that women are born without occupation and that they should depend on other people. Hence, men have become superior while women have become inferior. Women sit in idleness while men toil. But leading a life of leisure and being despised as inferior is by no means a naturally happy life, nor is being taken as superior while leading a life of toil.

How, then, would it be if we were to balance out this relationship of superiority and inferiority between men and women? How would it be if we were to make equal their proportions of work and leisure? This solution is consistent with principle but contrary to reality in current practice. One might ask: How can a country become strong? It is strong when its people are wealthy. How can a country's people become wealthy? They will be wealthy when everyone can support himself or herself and only himself or herself rather than several people. If the number of employed people doubles in a country, then the amount of the local products and goods produced will quickly double as well. This increased quantity is exactly that which had previously gone wasted or unrealized. It is very appropriate and profitable indeed to take what was once wasted property and to use it to enrich the people. Hence, there is no reason to reject women's education.

The second reason is that what has commonly been said of women's virtue—namely, that "in women, lack of talent is a virtue"—is entirely untrue. Our shortsighted scholars have held fast to this notion and have dedicated untold efforts toward keeping all women illiterate and unschooled. These scholars claim that such ignorance is the very foundation of women's virtue, when it is in fact the path to national disaster. In ancient times there were so-called talented women whose best achievements were nothing more than several stanzas of ditties upon the beauty of the wind and moon, verses describing the flowers and the grasses, or poems lamenting the passage of spring or the loss of a friend. Such activities cannot be called learning. Even a man would be despised as frivolous and trifling if he knew nothing else and were to pursue fame in this kind of writing, let alone a woman.

What I mean by education is twofold: it should open one's inner mind while also teaching a person skills to earn his or her livelihood (*shengji*). In this one pursuit, multiple good results are achieved, and I see in it no harm posed to women's virtue. If one says that ignorance is women's virtue, then why do illiterate women in the remote villages, of whom there are no fewer than several million, never become more virtuous because of their ignorance? Instead, all that we see is their quibbles and quarrels, which surely make them less virtuous than women from the official-scholar families. What do you say to this? Common people's quibbles and quarrels inevitably come from the narrow scope of their minds. In their daily lives, they are trapped within this extremely small and limited world. If they are made to know the ten thousand years of history, the five continents of the world, the way people get along with each other, and the way countries become prosperous or weak, their minds will be busy attending to the needs of all the people under heaven and will have no time for quibbling over family chores or affairs of women and children. Today most women are disadvantaged because they know nothing about the world and therefore devote all their energy to fighting daily over trivial matters. As a result, women all cultivate the same ugly habits without even having to learn them or having to consult one another. Because of this, among hundreds of millions of people and tens of millions of families throughout the land, there is not one family that is at peace inside and out, and where the conduct and speech of its members reflect harmony. And all these family conflicts begin with women—the mothers-in-law, daughters-in-law, and sisters-in-law. Some cynics have even gone as far as to suggest that all women should be killed.

Are women evil by nature? If you throw together a bunch of untamed, uncivilized hollow bodies and lock them up in one room, do you expect them to get along with each other? Unable to provide for themselves, these women become men's burden by wearing men down bodily and physically. Even worse, if the family is in chaos all day, causing a man to become agitated and upset as soon as he enters the room, the degree to which this undermines and exhausts his spirit and aspirations cannot be underestimated. Hence, even for an outstanding and charismatic hero, the mundane trivialities of domestic life can scarcely fail in a short time to confine and to undermine his ambition and talent. If so, women really are poison and men should not be united with them. Instead of ingesting and enjoying this poison, perhaps men should pay some attention to finding the antidote.

The third proof [for my claim that women's education is necessary for national survival] is that for Westerners, out of a hundred tasks involved in educating young children, over seventy are borne by the mother. A small infant is naturally closer to the mother than to the father, [and] therefore only the mother can take advantage of this propensity to guide him. Consequently, if the mother is a good teacher, it is easy for the child to grow upright; if the mother is a bad teacher, then the child is not likely to turn out well. According to *The Family Instructions of Master Yan* (*Yanshi Jiaxun*):[6] "[C]hildren's education should begin at infancy. Before [the children begin] going to school and studying under a mentor, the children's character and

---

[6]Refers to a sixth-century text compiled by Yan Zhitui (531–591). It became an influential and commonly referenced source of Confucian perspectives on the family and education.

ambition have generally been established. The future development of the children's character will follow the one that is formed at a very young age." This is indeed the foundation of pedagogy. If the mother understands the fundamentals of education and is skilled in applying them, then even before ten years of age, her children will be able to comprehend the rudimentary principles of scholarship, and they will already have established their ambitions and aspirations.

Today, children's primary education is not established in China. When a child studies under a tutor outside the family, the teachers are shallow, ignorant, and careless, having nothing valuable to teach the pupil. Such tutelage is no different from the experiences of early childhood; [the child] is used to feeling satisfied at home in the care of the wet nurse, immersed daily in nothing but the most tedious and scandalous domestic trifles. Even a better teacher merely educates the child to admire success in the imperial examination and the accumulation of wealth, while admonishing the child to safeguard family property and to produce more progeny. This is the best education these teachers can muster. Therefore, in the child's mind as he grows up, there is nothing in the world more important than these achievements. In thousands of homes in all places, people commiserate in their ignorance, which results in the shallow, shameless, ignorant, and savage world in which people vie to pursue their private interests. Although people complain about the barbaric and degenerate ways of the world, they have no idea how it came to be this way; and even worse, people seem content with this state of affairs just as it is. If we were to have a small schoolboy from the West walk side by side with our majestic and aged official-scholars, the boy's varied knowledge and ambitions would certainly exhibit features with which our scholars could not compete. Is this because the Westerners belong to a special species or race (*zhong* 种), different from us entirely? No, the difference is that when young, our people grow accustomed to our erroneous methods of education.

In short, it has been said that there are two fundamental principles of governance: the first is to instill an upright heart, and the second is to recruit talented people from far and wide. Children's education establishes the foundation of both principles. Children's education begins with the mother's teaching, which is itself rooted in women's education. Therefore women's education fundamentally determines whether a nation will survive or be destroyed and whether it will prosper or languish in weakness.

The fourth reason is that prenatal education, discussed thoroughly in [the ancient texts] *Rites of Dai Senior* (*Da Dai Li*)[7] and *Discursive Weighing* (*Lun Heng*),[8] has long been forgotten by later generations. Nowadays, Westerners certainly pay a lot attention to the issue. In their investigation of the principle of the transformation and evolution of animals and human species, Western philosophers think that inside any living organism (human beings, birds, insects, fishes, and grasses and trees are living organisms; metal, stone, water, and soil are inorganic substances), some parts are dead, whereas others are not dead. For example, the root, trunk, fruit, flower, and leaf are all dying parts of a plant. Those parts that do not die leave the mother and cling to the seed, thereby continuing the life of the species to the next generation. This is called propagation. The same process is true for human beings. Even so, there are gradual changes that occur between the two kinds of changes that can cause the species to develop from monkeys to human beings, from a savage and backward species to a civilized and noble one. The changes are slight and imperceptible in the beginning, but they will be enormous by the end of the process. It is for this reason that Western scholars who study the science of race have taken prenatal education as a top priority. They have given much thought to the various ways of improving their own species. Countries intending to strengthen their military power also order their women to practice physical exercises. They recognize that only in this way will their children have plush skin and strong, powerful tendons and muscles. This is also a fundamental concern in girls' schools.

Nowadays, for people who have foresight and who are concerned about the world, there are three important matters: to protect the nation, to protect the species, and to protect education. How are we to protect the nation? Only by strengthening it can it be protected. How are we to protect the species? Only by improving it can it be protected. To advance from deceit to loyalty, from selfishness to public spirit, from division to unity, from ignorance to intelligence, from savagery to civilization, this is the way [to improve the species]. Men's education constitutes half [of the nation] and women's education the other, but the education of men necessarily begins with that of women. As such, the protection of the species necessarily begins with and pivots on the education of women.

---

[7] *Da Dai Liji* refers to a set of descriptions of Zhou dynasty rituals.
[8] *Lun Heng* is a Han dynasty text (ca. 80 C.E.) comprising a set of philosophical essays by Wang Chong.

Nowadays, when I discuss the necessity of women's education with people, they hardly take it as a practical and appropriate step to save the species. They think it is like saving people from starvation by teaching them how to plow or rescuing people from thirst by teaching them how to dig a well. They do not realize that the necessity of women's education has been carefully discussed, thoroughly interrogated, and avidly pursued by both our own ancient sages and the learned scholars of the West.

(According to *The Treatise on Fetal Education* [*Taijiao Pian*], "[I]t is said in the *Book of Changes* that '[when one] grasps the fundamentals, the myriad things would naturally fall into place. Even a minor lapse can lead to a major mistake. A learned man is therefore conscientious of the repercussions of his actions.' When he selects for his children the spouse who will carry his descendents, he will choose a family known for its benevolence and uprightness for generations. In this way, their offspring will be benevolent and filial, and they will not fall into debauchery and violence. Everyone they associate with will be benevolent, and the members of their three clans [the clans of the father, mother, and wife] will assist them. Therefore people say that the offspring of the phoenix are born with kindness, whereas those of the tiger and the wolf are born to be greedy and ruthless. The difference between the two stems from the characters of their mothers. There is in this statement a profound and obvious truth." It is also said that "the ways of prenatal education should be carved on the jade board, hidden in the golden casket, and placed in the ancestral temple as admonition for later generations. The seriousness with which the ancients treat this issue is not without reason."[9] Mr. Yan Youling [Yan Fu] translated *Evolution and Ethics* [*Tian Yan Lun*],[10] in which it is said that "inorganic substances cannot die because it never had life to begin with. The living organism, however, has some dead parts and also some live parts in its body. The live parts are not the so-called spirit or soul, and the parts that will die and those that will not

---

[9]This text from the Tang dynasty (7th century C.E.) laid out the argument that women's behavior while pregnant would affect their child, so that quarreling, food and drink, and so on, were all to be monitored strictly. For more on this issue, see the introduction to Tina Phillips Johnson, *Childbirth in Republican China: Delivering Modernity* (New York: Lexington Books, 2011).

[10]Yan Fu (1854–1921), was a reformer and translator during the late-Qing and republican periods. In particular, he was known for his translations of Adam Smith's *The Wealth of Nations* and Herbert Spencer's social evolutionary text *Evolution and Ethics* 天演论. For Yan Fu's importance at the time, see Benjamin Schwartz, *In Search of Wealth and Power: Yan Fu and the West* (Cambridge, MA: Harvard University Press, 1964).

die are two absolutely different things. The root or the trunk of the plants is the part that will die. The part that remains alive leaves the mother and clings to the filial generation. It may undergo slight modification, but it will not die; or part of it may die, but it will not die entirely. Animals and plants all follow this principle." Thus, one person will carry with him the immortal aspect that is transferred to him from his grandfather. When one is endowed with life and form, the immortal part of his forebears is passed on in evolved form to today; this is the reason for the need for prenatal education. In his correspondence with me, Mr. Yan has said that "the principles of biology [*shengxue*][11] hold that when a person is born, his mind, talent, physical figure, disposition, and character are inherited within the body. He is born with the mind and life experiences that were accumulated and stored by the grandparents from tens of hundreds of generations ago, and these experiences will change according to his own exposures, the influence from his teachers and friends, and his life experiences in the future." This insight is very profound. If one is concerned about the protection of the human species, one has to pay attention to the two above factors. The first factor explains the root of the advantage of prenatal education, whereas the second factor elucidates the even deeper basis for that truth. This theory will certainly be understood by everyone within a few decades, but now hardly anyone believes it to be practical or useful.)

A Western scientist (*gezhi jia*)[12] has said that "women are generally not as good as men in comprehending abstract knowledge such as arithmetic and science. But when these theories are rendered into such practical specializations as medicine and manufacture, men are generally not as good as women." In terms of learning and education, men and women each have their strengths, but neither is inherently superior or inferior. People may claim that for thousands of years, men have brought forth significant scholarship and accomplished great tasks, so much so that our ancient annals are full of records of them, but none whatsoever about women. This may lead them to conclude that even if women were educated, their achievements would amount to very little.

---

[11]Shengxue is generally termed *shengwu xue* today.

[12]*Gezhi* can be rendered as "natural studies"; it was accepted at the time as equivalent to "science." Today, *kexue* is the accepted term for "science." For a recent study of the shifting meanings of *gezhi* and the introduction of modern Western science to China, see Benjamin Elman, *A Cultural History of Modern Science in China* (Cambridge, MA: Harvard University Press, 2006).

Let us consider these arguments in light of the principles of biology. In the hierarchy of living things, plants which grow upward from the earth are utterly lacking in intelligence. Animals that crawl about the surface of the earth are more intelligent than plants. But if these creatures could walk upright and perceive the world through our eyes, there would be no major differences among the various intelligences. Whatever difference in intelligence there might be is determined solely by the degree of enlightenment in living creatures. Let us consider two illustrations of this principle. During the reigns of Qianlong and Jiaqing emperors (1735–1820), Han Learning scholars of the Jiangzhe [Jiangsu-Zhejiang] region were both accomplished and numerous, whereas in my Yue [Guangdong] region there was not even one.[13] Since the reigns of Xianfeng and Tongzhi emperors (1850–1875), however, the Yue region witnessed a sudden proliferation of scholars who could not stop discussing Ma Rong and Zheng Xuan or clinging to their copies of *Analysis and Explication of Written Characters* (*Shuowen Jiezi*), and they were as numerous as carp in the river.[14] The reason for this change is not that people in the Yue region were dumb in the eighteenth century but became intelligent in the nineteenth century. Similarly, before the Meiji

---

[13]Liang is sketching out a history of the geographical shifts in Confucian schools of learning here. Jiangzhe (encompassing present-day Shanghai and parts south of there in Jiangsu and Zhejiang Provinces) was a traditional stronghold of Song Learning prior to the eighteenth century, when Han Learning was rediscovered and elevated to a form of critique of the Qing imperial state. The differences between the schools are technical, but also political. What Liang is pointing to here, in the first place, is the spread of Han Learning (also known as New Text Confucianism) to Guangdong in the south from its birthplace in Suzhou. Second, he is pointing to the political import of Han Learning as a critique of the imperial state and the state's alleged addiction to abstract rather than concrete, "statecraft" learning. For more on these issues, see Benjamin Elman, *Classicism, Politics and Kinship: The Ch'ang-chou School of New Text Confucianism in Late Imperial China* (Berkeley: University of California Press, 1990).

[14]Han Learning relied upon a philological authentification of which Confucian texts were the actual ancient texts. Thus, the philological dictionary was of primary importance to this school of thought.

Ma Rong (79–166) was a classicist and writer of the Eastern (Later) Han dynasty. He was born in Fufeng Maoling (now Guangping in Shaanxi Province). Scholars in the Ming dynasty (14th–17th century C.E.) edited *The Anthology of Ma Jichang*, thus contributing to the revival of his form of learning. Zheng Xuan (127–200), a classicist of the Eastern (Later) Han dynasty, was born in Beihai gaomi (now it is Gaomi in Shaanxi Province).

Shuowen Jiezi was written by Xu Shen in the Eastern (Later) Han dynasty. It sums up six categories of Chinese character construction and is the most famous work of philology in China. It is the basis of the New Text (Han Learning) school of Confucianism.

period (1868–1911) in Japan, people were unenlightened and the quality of their manufacture was poor. Since the vast and rapid change brought about by the Meiji Restoration, the achievements of the Japanese have been astonishing.[15] This is not because they were stupid in the past and smart at present. When the mind is stiff and unexercised, the intelligence is blocked. But if properly instructed and guided, the mind is activated just like flipping a switch, when all the strings will start to move. Through thousands of years, women did not acquire fame in learning because they were never guided to that path. If women were to begin learning, they would have two advantages over men: first, they have fewer social entanglements and obligations; second, they are spared the difficulty of the official examination.[16] Women live quiet lives and have meticulous minds. Therefore, women can often perceive principles that men cannot, and they can invent new methods that could elude men.

According to an account in Western historiography, Mohammed's mother, who was the daughter of Muttalib and the aunt of Zaynab bint Jahsh, attained scholarly achievement that held its own in comparison to that of the men of her time. There are also young Chinese women, such as Kang Aide or Shi Meiyu,[17] who went abroad to study and then returned to China after they completed their studies. Such women are praised even by prestigious scholars in the West. In light of all this, how can we possibly say that women are born without the ability to learn? These are two hundred million human beings who walk upright and perceive the world with their

---

[15]The Meiji Restoration refers to the period around 1868, when Tokugawa rule was deposed and a new emperor and reign, named Meiji, was established. Under the Meiji regime and the compulsion of threatened Euro-American invasion, Japan quickly modernized and within several decades became an Asian imperialist power, defeating China in the 1894–1895 Sino-Japanese War, through which Japan acquired Taiwan, and defeating Russia in the 1904–1905 Russo-Japanese War, thus proceeding toward the annexation of Korea. Such Chinese intellectuals as Liang were both admiring of and threatened by Japan's rise.

[16]The official examination refers to the civil service exams, established in the tenth century and abolished in 1905, which were restricted to men only and served to recruit educated people for the dynastic bureaucracy. These were highly competitive, and men whose families could spare their labor prepared for decades to take them, with little hope of success.

[17]Kang Aide (aka Ida Kang, 1873–1931) and Shi Meiyu (aka Mary Stone, 1873–1954) were among the first four Chinese female students to study abroad. Shi received an MD at the University of Michigan in 1896, and Kang received her MD there in the same year. For more on Liang's version of Kang and Shi, see Hu Ying, "Naming the First 'New Woman,'" in *Rethinking the 1898 Reform Period: Political and Cultural Change in Late Qing China*, ed. Rebecca E. Karl and Peter Zarrow, 180–211 (Cambridge, MA: Harvard University Press, East Asian Monographs, 2002).

eyes, yet they are treated as though they were barbarians and discarded as though they were plants and beasts. There is no denying that such treatment is cruel and contrary to benevolence.[18]

It is certainly a good thing that all schools of thought have come to be concerned about the problem of equality! (Mr. Nanhai [Kang Youwei], in fact, claims that Confucian doctrine already contains the basic principle of equality.[19]) Where does inequality come from? It stems from the worship of power. Where does equality come from? It comes from the love for benevolence. Although all belong to the same species of human beings, those who are named "the people" [min] are made to obey the ruler like servants and concubines; those who are named women [nü] are made to obey men like slaves. They are not just called servants, concubines, and slaves, but their ears and eyes are sealed, their hands and feet are bound, their minds are frozen, their path toward learning is blocked, their livelihood is cut off, and so they have no choice but to be totally subservient to those with power. As millennia passed, they grew accustomed to being servants, concubines, and slaves, taking their status as natural without any self-awareness. If anyone expressed the slightest doubt and questioned his or her unfair treatment as servant, concubine, or slave, others would rise up and ridicule him or her. For several thousands of years, therefore, no man has articulated the necessity of women's education for the proper governance of the empire. Nor has there been any woman who has endeavored to rally her own kind to fight for the cause. It is not because women are inherently lacking in talent but because they are faced with formidable forces of oppression.

Today if you tell people that "education is necessary to strengthen the nation," most are convinced. Yet, if you tell them that "women's education is necessary to strengthen the nation," most will be skeptical. [Besides what I have already argued,] there is another reason for this deluded view. In China today, people wave their arms and waggle their tongues with talk of "strengthening the nation"; they are stunned by Westerners and desire to

---

[18]Liang is shaming his fellow men by drawing upon one of the cardinal principles of Confucian social behavior: benevolence.

[19]Kang Youwei (1858–1927), Liang's teacher, a Confucian scholar and the leader of the reformers, led the petition movement and the Hundred Days' Reform (1898). His works includes *Xinxue weijing kao* [A study of the "New Text" forgeries], *Kongzi gaizhi kao* [A study of the reforms of Confucius], and *Datong shu* [The book of great unity]. See "The Historical Context," in this volume, for more on the 1898 reforms.

emulate their successes—the grandness of their ships, the sharpness of their weapons, the speed of their railways, and the spectacular growth of their mining industries. Of these pursuits, there is not one in which women are of any consequence. Hence, those who are concerned with the nation claim that "to educate women is not urgent." They are not aware that though the strengths of Westerners are manifested in the manners listed above, the root of Western strengths resides somewhere else altogether. Men can succeed in agriculture, handicrafts, medicine, business, science, law, and academia, but so can women. Men and women are the same in that education can make them useful to the nation. Today, education is considered the foundation of successful governance. Is it not because the nation rests on the foundations of its talented people? Is it not because the talents with which the people of China are already endowed can be developed only through education? Why, then, should we assume that at most only two hundred million people have talent and dismiss the other two hundred million as being without talent?

Of all the nations of the West, America is by far the most prosperous. Of all the ascendant nations in the East, Japan is the strongest. The idea of equality between men and women was first advocated in America and was gradually practiced in Japan. Women's education in Japan generally consists of thirteen subjects: first, moral cultivation; second, education (i.e., how to teach and raise children); third, national language (i.e., Japanese); fourth, *Kanbun* [classical Chinese writing]; fifth, history (including foreign history); sixth, geography; seventh, mathematics; eighth, science; ninth, household management; tenth, calligraphy; eleventh, painting; twelfth, music; and thirteenth, physical education. Only a few of these subjects differ at all from the curricula used in men's education. They diverge only when it comes to military affairs and politics, which remain central concerns for men in a world obsessed with power.

Even as Westerners have set about building their nations, they have yet to make the world peaceful. In a peaceful world, no matter whether big or small, far or near, all places under heaven would be the same. There would exist no borders between nations or races; nor would there be any wars, weapons, or military conscription. For the true progress of nations to occur, only such occupations as agriculture, commercial business, medicine, law, science, and manufacture are to be encouraged. No matter whether one is a man or a woman, all people in the nation should engage in their own line of work and be able to support themselves, eliminating the division between those who can provide for themselves and those who cannot. Toward this end, men and women must receive comparable education. Today, America is closest to this ideal. We may therefore conclude that a country with the best women's education is also the strongest. Such a nation can "win a war without a fight," such as America has done. Next in strength are those countries where women's education is less developed [than that of America], such as England, France, Germany, and Japan. Finally, in those countries where women's education has declined and where even the education of mothers has been lost, the unemployed are numerous and intelligent people are rare, having survived only by luck. Among such unfortunate nations are India, Persia, and Turkey.

It is for all the above reasons that I claim that women's education is truly an urgent matter in China today.

Although "women's education" has not yet come into existence in China, [what we mean by] education cannot be attained by hunching over one's desk and studying from dawn to dusk; nor does it come from mumbling a text aloud to oneself. One's intelligence should be inspired by studying with teachers and friends; one's talent should be increased through travel in China and abroad. Only through these complementary experiences can one's education be said to be complete. In China today, women live secluded in their inner chambers, never going out; for their entire lives they never encounter one single wise person nor visit one metropolitan city. They study alone without any friends, ignorant of any news of the world beyond their chambers. This manner of study cannot even allow them to learn how to write the frivolous poetry that entertained women of previous generations much less master the practical studies that are useful to the nation.[20] I recognize that that this is really a tall order even for the most extraordinarily talented few.

Beyond this, I am aware of another form of hardship to which woman is subjected—a hardship by which her limbs are broken and her flesh made to fester. By this means of torture her body is crippled merely for the pleasure of another. As long as footbinding remains in practice, women's education can never flourish. When the rule of the Qing began, the emperor ordered

---

[20]These are stereotypes of women that became popularized at the time. For a more historically complete view of nineteenth-century women's lives, see Susan Mann, *Talented Women of the Zhang Family* (Berkeley: University of California Press, 2007).

all men to shave their foreheads and grow the Manchu queue.[21] As soon as order was restored in the nation toward the end of the reign of the Shun-zhi emperor (1644–1661), footbinding was publicly banned; but alas, the ban has not been enforced for a long enough time, so the old habit remains unchanged.[22] The power of one ruler cannot change the hearts of the igno-rant masses, and the heads of our strongest men are no match for the feet of our most vulnerable women. And so this terrible practice persisted and spread for hundreds of years, becoming more entrenched by the day, such that it now endures even under the opprobrium of the emperor and the scorn of foreign nations. Women suffer in plain sight from the bitterness of this terrible poison, but in truth it is our entire race that is left with the greatest injury.

Is it as punishment that Heaven has left our four hundred million people saddled with this terrible sin, or does it persist because our rulers have for so long averted their eyes to it?

This essay was first published in the late-Qing journal Liang Qichao him-self edited, *Shiwu Bao* [*The Chinese progress*] 23 (March 11, 1897): 1a–4a, and *Shiwu Bao* 25 (April 11, 1897): 2b–4a. Reprinted in *Jindai Zhongguo nüquan yundong shiliao*, ed. Li Yu-ning and Chang Yu-fa, 549–555. Trans-lated by Robert Cole and Wei Peng; edited by Dorothy Ko from the Chinese original "Lun nüxue 論女學."

---

[21]One way the Manchu Qing dynasty enforced visible fealty to their rule was through the sarto-rial requirement of a male queue. By 1911, with the revolution against the dynasty, many elite men began to cut their queues; during the high Qing, the absence of a queue was taken as sedi-tious and punishable by death. For the Shunzhi edicts on footbinding, see Dorothy Ko, "The Body as Attire: The Shifting Meanings of Footbinding in Seventeenth-Century China," *Journal of Women's History* 8, 4 (Winter 1997): 8–27.

[22]For the Shunzhi edicts on footbinding, see Dorothy Ko, "The Body as Attire: The Shifting Meanings of Footbinding in Seventeenth-Century China," *Journal of Women's History* 8, 4 (Winter 1997): 8–27.

Jin Tianhe, 1914, from *Tianfanglou shi wen ji* [Collected poems and essays of the Freedom Tower], ed. Zhou Luxiang, vol. 1. Shanghai: Shanghai guji chubanshe, 2007.

Jin Tianhe 金天翮 (aka Jin Songcen 金松岑, Jin Yi 金一, 1874–1947) was a writer, educator, and political figure. Born to a wealthy family in Anhui Province, he received a traditional education at elite local academies. After failing an attempt at the imperial civil service examinations, he turned to the "statecraft" (*jingshi*) learning that had gained popularity among elites in the years after the Opium Wars. His early work was published in such journals as *Women's World* (*Nüzi shijie*), *Jiangsu*, *The Weekly Independent* (*Duli zhoubao*), and *The Grand Magazine* (*Xiaoshuo daguan*). Jin helped fund the publication of *The Revolutionary Army* (*Geming jun*) by Zou Rong (1885–1905), an important tract that called for the overthrow of the Qing court, and paid for (ultimately unsuccessful) attempts to defend Zou Rong from prosecution. After the 1911 revolution, Jin served in education-related government posts and as a parliamentary representative for Jiangsu Province. In 1932, he worked with Zhang Taiyan (1868–1936) and others to found the Society for National Learning (Guoxue hui).

The Women's Bell (*Nüjie zhong*) was published in Shanghai by Datong Shuju in 1903 and quickly appeared in subsequent editions reprinted in China and Japan. It was little known in the late twentieth century until feminist historian Li Yu-ning issued a facsimile reprint of the 1903 edition with an extended scholarly commentary (published by Outer Sky Press) in 2003. In the same year, Shanghai Guji Chubanshe published a punctuated edition to celebrate the one-hundredth anniversary of this key text. The translation in the present volume is based on both editions.

"The Women's Bell"

Jin Tianhe (1903)

Preface

The muggy rainy season with its endless drizzle is stifling. Lotuses droop in the torpid hot breeze. The trees are listless and the distant hills dormant. On the eastern end of the continent of Asia, in a country that knows no freedom, in a small room that knows no freedom, my breathing is heavy, my mind has gone sluggish. I want to let in the fresh air of European civilization, draw it in to restore my body.

I dream of a young, white European man. On this day, at this hour, with a rolled cigarette in his mouth, walking stick in hand, his wife and children by him, he strolls with his head held high and arms swinging by his sides through the promenades of London, Paris, Washington. Such happiness and ease! I wish I could go there myself; [although I cannot,] I do know of that world indirectly.

In the eighteenth and nineteenth centuries, the drums of vicious battle sounded, the bells of liberty rang out, the flags of independence unfurled, and memorial towers were built, giving rise to a dozen thrilling life-and-death dramas of revolution. At their completion, everyone had the right to freedom; everyone was made equal. This created a majestic, resplendent, and magnificent new world in Europe. If we seek to understand the reasons behind these revolutions, we find that they were inspired by people like Rousseau, Voltaire, Hegel, John Stuart Mill, Huxley, and Spencer.

Today the sky moves, the earth spins, and the wind drives the clouds. The ideas of these thinkers, crated in steamships, have crossed the Pacific and reached China. My two hundred million brother compatriots were slumbering in a world of darkness. Now, a ray of sunlight pierces the curtains, opens their eyes, pricks their nostrils and reaches straight into their brains; all of them let out a collective sneeze in unison. They arise and walk around in the courtyard, and run their hands along the tree of liberty, and water the flowers of civilization. They say, "Natural rights." They say, "Give me liberty or give me death." They say, "The greatest good for the greatest number." Each day they nurture these ideas in their hearts and keep them on their tongues.

My two hundred million sister compatriots, however, are still kept as ignorant as before, in chains and fetters, obsessed with dreams in winter and wallowing in melancholy in spring, knowing nothing of the ideas of equality between men and women or ideas of women's participation in politics that are held by free people in civilized nations. If they did know something of these ideas, they would surely think them strange. Thus I bathe and anoint myself three times, straighten my brush, and pay respect to Heaven. On a raft of benevolence, I will ferry the afflicted across the sea of suffering, light a lamp in a pitch-dark chamber, speak of the dharma with a humble and patient heart until my throat grows hoarse,[1] and write this *Women's Bell*.

---

[1] Tr: The raft, sea of suffering, and lamp are all Buddhist imageries. Here, Jin presents himself as a Buddhist savior of women in China.

PART 1: INTRODUCTION

When people occupy a higher position relative to others, enjoying the spoils of tyranny, they will certainly see equality as a detestable thing, an evil word, and summon every bit of energy to drive it away and secure their own position. Therefore, the idea of limited monarchy is something for which millions of ordinary people gave their lives, not something that monarchs gladly offered.

In our world, there is not a single man who does not enjoy the triumph of lording over women like a tyrant. If women are not treated as mere playthings, then they are seen as colonial possessions. For this reason, although people like John Stuart Mill and [Herbert] Spencer advocated the rights of women, the idea met with resistance, just as Napoleon's proclamation of liberty and rights for the people encountered the united opposition of European monarchs. In nineteenth-century Europe, women began to take action on their own to fight with men for the rights that had been lost. Although women have not yet been allowed to climb to the highest levels of civilization, the seeds of women's rights sailed on the spring winds, and their first sprouts have begun to rise from the ground. Alas! In our wondrous land, my jadelike compatriots are weak in spirit and character. I want to rescue them from the bottom of the sea and place them high in the heavens, but my knowledge and strength fall short. My heart is filled with dread!

Today I want to straighten my garments, sit down, and offer advice to my two hundred million women compatriots; but I must not proceed too directly. First, I will cry out to my male compatriots and say: anyone who has experienced the bitter horrors of tyranny must hate oppressive forms of government with their entire being and must not stand to let them exist in the world. Thus one French person said, "May the world turn red from the blood of tyrants."[2] As for monarchies, may I ask how many have survived in this world, with shame on their faces? The Buddha said, "If I do not enter hell, who will?" How many people are in these hells in our world today? To rescue all beings from a sea of suffering—this should be our lofty

---

[2]Tr: The source of this quotation is unclear, but it may refer to the famous saying, "The tree of liberty grows only when watered by the blood of tyrants" or the "blood of patriots and tyrants," which in turn was spoken by such figures as Bertrand Barère (1755–1841) and Thomas Jefferson (1743–1826).

wish; to treat all as my equal—this is our duty. The rights of the people and women's rights are intimately linked together, like a cicada molting on a branch. The one leads to the other; they cannot be suppressed. I say this not only for the benefit of my two hundred million sisters but for all of China's four hundred million people. Let me try to explain: a nation (*guo*) must have a base on which to establish itself between heaven and earth; this base is called the people of the nation (*guomin*). And women are the mothers of the nation's people.

There is no proper way to name "the people of the nation" in China today. The closest we come is the "ten thousand surnames." This shows that our people are dull, weak, and fit only to appear in the *Dictionary of Historical Surnames*.[3] Although a person's character may change according to external influences and stimuli, he or she is also formed by internal natural characteristics passed down across the generations. The transmission of this character occurs between mother and child. The yang (mother) gives and the yin (child) receives; some children are quick to learn, whereas others are slower. Therefore, although the people appear to have no teacher, women are in fact their teachers. My people! For two thousand years, you gentlemen with fine brows, none of you can match those found in Wang Can's *Lives of Heroes* or Plutarch's discussions of heroes;[4] you beautiful ladies, not only are you no match for the likes of *Jeanne d'Arc*,[5] Mary Queen of Scots,[6] *Vera Sassouhitsch*,[7] *Sophia Perovskaia, Pethias*,[8] and *Florence Nightingale*,

---

[3]Tr: *Shi xing yun bian*, ed. Wang Huizu, a dictionary cataloging surnames that appeared in the twenty-four dynastic histories.

[4]Tr: Wang Can (117–217), one of the "Seven Masters of Jian'an" during the Wei period, wrote the *Han mo yingxiong ji*. Here, Jin Tianhe, perhaps as a result of a translation he encountered, also considers Plutarch's *Lives* to be a record of heroes.

[5]Tr: The italicized names in this list are reproduced exactly as they were written in the Chinese text, which included both Chinese characters and the names spelled out in the Roman alphabet.

[6]Tr: Also known as Mary I of Scotland (1542–1587), beheaded for her alleged involvement in an attempted assassination of Queen Elizabeth I.

[7]Tr: Probably refers to Vera Zasulich (1849–1919), famous for her failed assassination attempt of the then-governor of St. Petersburg, General Theodore Trepov (1812–1889).

[8]Tr: Here the English in the original text reads "Pethias," but the corresponding characters, *Picha*, are a transliteration for the name of Harriet Beecher Stowe, who was held up by intellectuals as an exemplary female intellectual and activist. See Xia Xiaohong, "Ms. Picha and Mrs. Stowe," in *Translation and Creation: Readings of Western Literature in Early Modern China, 1840–1918* (Philadelphia: John Benjamins, 1998), 241–252.

even such [legendary heroines as] Ban Zhao,[9] Pang E,[10] Ti Ying,[11] Mulan,[12] and Feng Liao[13] cannot come close to these [foreign] heroines. Has our red brush run dry? Will the annals of our history hold no new glories? Will our "Wondrous Land" (*shenzhou*) never achieve success and prosperity? Will our yellow race never gain fame and honor?! Alas! There are no true men in the state! There are no true men in the state![14]

China suffered terribly in the nineteenth century's rough currents of worldwide competition, but it stands to reason that in the twentieth century China will rise again to the front of the stage. If this is true for men, then how can it not be true for women? When the women of ancient Sparta prepared their sons for battle, they said, "I hope that you come back carrying your shield, or that you come back carried on a shield." When Mary Queen of Scots was in prison, she said, "I may not be able to save myself, but as long as I live and breathe, I must fight on to save the nation." How magnificent these words are! If there were one such person among my two hundred million compatriots in China, I would pay her homage with precious gold, the finest silk, and fragrant flowers in the belief that this person could bring about the new China and create its new people, that this person would lead the revolutionary army of women with an embroidered battle flag, and from atop a white horse speckled with red dots speak with elegant words to awaken women cloistered in the inner chambers from their nightmares. Gu Tinglin[15] once said, "The common man has a hand in all the affairs under heaven." Why should it be only the common man? The common woman, too, has a hand in these affairs.

---

[9]Tr: Ban Zhao (45–116 C.E.), younger sister of historian Ban Gu (32–92 C.E.). She completed Ban Gu's *History of the Former Han* (*Han shu*) and wrote the "Instructions for Daughters" (*Nü jie*) quoted below.

[10]Tr: Pang E, also known as Zhao E'qin, avenged the death of her father by beheading his murderer.

[11]Tr: Ti Ying, daughter of Han dynasty official Zhun Yuyi. When her father was imprisoned, she petitioned the emperor and won his release.

[12]Tr: Hua Mulan (aka Fa Mulan), legendary woman of the Northern Wei dynasty (386–534), who donned men's clothes so that she could take her father's place in the army.

[13]Tr: Feng Liao, an attendant of a Han dynasty princess of Chu known for her knowledge of foreign affairs who was consulted personally by Emperor Xuan of Han (91–49 B.C.E.).

[14]Tr: This last sentence alludes to the conclusion of Qu Yuan's "Encountering Sorrow" (*Li sao*), "There are no true men in the state: no one to understand me." Translation borrowed from David Hawkes, trans., *Ch'u T'zu: Songs of the South* (Oxford: Oxford University Press, 1959), 34.

[15]Tr: Gu Tinglin is the courtesy name of Gu Yanwu (1613–1682), scholar, philologist, and critic of orthodox Neo-Confucian thought.

PART 2: WOMEN'S MORALITY

"In women, lack of talent is a virtue"—such evil words. They are the means by which two hundred million men have poisoned the rest of the world, through imitating the ways of the first emperor of the Qin, who kept the people ignorant and buried scholars alive. Although common "morality" sees itself as far removed from the behavior of slaves and beasts, they are in fact two sides of the same coin. [Followers of this morality] quote the classics chapter and verse but keep their minds set on the status and rewards of an official post. When they look up at the sky, they cannot distinguish the eight constellations; when they look down at the earth, they do not recognize the five continents. They only kneel before the Eastern Hu and revere them as the Heavenly Emperor,[16] serving them as if they were their ancestors and taking pride in themselves for virtue that rivals the worthies and sages of the past. If they were right, then my compatriots might as well look up to the old women tending the stove and the servant girls from the villages, or they might as well regard the estrangement or rupture of natural familial bonds as eternal law.[17] But I will not bother to discuss in detail what is called lack of talent. I will speak only of what relates to women's morality.

I will discuss women's morality as it concerns the ethics of human relations; this can be separated into three main areas:

The first issue is women's morality and virtue regarding the self. Women's virtue is commonly equated with the "admonitions for daughters." Ban Zhao wrote, "As to women's attainments, a woman need not be extraordinarily intelligent. [She should be] gentle and sedate, constant and quiet, chaste and orderly, be careful in her conduct, and adhere to rules in all her actions."[18] These words, why do I refute them? As civilization advances around the world, women's education is changing along with men's education: studying, going to school, making friends, and

---

[16]Tr: Here Jin refers to the Manchu rulers of the Qing dynasty.

[17]Tr: The original text alludes to Jia Yi (201–169 B.C.E.), who attacked the failings of the legalist-based Qin dynasty (221–206 B.C.E.) in the perversion of morals through the estrangement of parents and their children.

[18]Tr: Translation of Ban Zhao's "Admonitions for Daughters," also translated as "Women's Precepts" (*Nü jie*), amended from R. H. van Gulik, *Sexual Life in Ancient China* (Leiden: Brill, 1974), 100–101.

---

traveling are means for women to expand their knowledge and improve their moral character. Morality and knowledge are a natural part of the individual, with no distinction between men and women. Light emanates from the mind constantly, yet when this light does not shine in the right direction, it will shine in another. Therefore, when women's desire for education is not satisfied, they turn to writing silly poems and lyrics about idle pursuits. When women cannot go to school, hordes of them will set up prayer altars, visit monasteries, hand out alms, and hang prayer flags. When women cannot make true friends, they fall in with the people they have always known, their favorite servant girls and old grannies and aunties. When they wish to travel but cannot, then they indulge in the theater and go on outings on Tomb-Sweeping Day; or they dream of India and the Potalaka, of presenting flowers to the Buddha, and of making pilgrimages to Buddhist temples so they can enjoy the spring scenery. Some women become so used to the limitations placed on them that they have no knowledge of it and stay near the stove or in the ladies' quarters, fussing over their trifles while the husband's family praises them for their remarkable uprightness and the clan marvels at them as an example for the ages.

Oh! Such is the character of China's women that we see before us. The most embarrassing thing in the world is to compare one's own situation with another's and discover which is superior and which is inferior. If we compare the development and prosperity of women in Europe today to that of women in China, would Chinese people be ashamed? Or would they shamelessly defend themselves, condemning European women under their breath?

The second issue is morality in relation to men. A woman's moral obligation to men is commonly thought to involve aiding her husband. Man and woman is each one half of the whole; this is demonstrated by the world around us and is a great blessing for humans and for nature. The harmonization of yin and yang, establishment of love, intermingling of personal character, discussion of learning, and upholding of morality—all stem from conjugal relations. Therefore a civilized couple manage their home together, handle affairs with others outside the home appropriately, take different paths in their studies, and travel together. They know no worry, no terror of one another, no wild dreams that spring from their separation, and thus there is no dependency between them.

Chinese women, however, often hear evil sayings about the "three fol-
lowings" (*sancong*) and the "seven grounds for divorce" (*qichu*) and hold
themselves to these standards without ever letting themselves free.[19] Guarding themselves in fear and trembling, they do not dare to go astray even
one small step. They have no other hopes except for the blessed wedding
night, when, like a candidate who has passed the imperial examinations,
[the wife] kneels thrice and kowtows nine times, thanking the emperor
for his munificence, as if she has been given an official post—as if the most
important event of her life has been achieved. As for men, they have "the
bow of mulberry wood and arrows of the wild raspberry" and "arrows in
four directions."[20] They should go forth, sword in hand, with no worries
about troubles at home. But if a man must comfort his wife at night as she
sings and weeps at the bedchamber curtains, his concerns for the affairs of
the state will be exhausted, his spirit and ambition dampened. When I read
the poems of young wives from the inner chambers, not once have I not
closed the book and sighed three times in regret. Even then, however, these
are the good cases. As for the bad cases, poverty causes quarreling, and the
wife and mother-and-law hurl curses at each other. In the worst cases, the
woman is a servant, not a wife. There are so many of these awful happenings
and terrible habits between husband and wife that my mouth cannot bear
to speak of them, and my brush cannot bear to describe them. I have not
heard that the encouragement Madame Roland and Queen Mary the First
received was from a jealous husband; and I have not heard that the comfort
Garibaldi and Mazzini[21] received involved a flood of tears. There is no gate
or door to happiness, only what people make for themselves. Do my compatriots know this?

---

[19]These are not the words of Confucius. Confucius did transmit them, and in this sense his
knowledge and understanding were not the wisest.

[20]Tr: This refers to the importance of archery in ritual texts. According to "The Meaning of the
Ceremony of Archery" (*Shenyi*) in the *Classic of Rites*, "When a son is born, a bow of mulberry
wood, and six arrows of the wild raspberry plant (are placed on the left of the door), for the
purpose of shooting at heaven, earth, and the four cardinal directions. Heaven, earth, and the
four points denote the spheres wherein the business of a man lies." See *The Li Ki* [*Li Ji*], trans.
James Legge, in *The Sacred Books of the East* (reprint, Delhi: Motilal Banarsidass, 1968), 27: 452.

[21]Tr: Both were leaders of the Italian reunification in the late nineteenth century. For more on
their depictions in China, see Xiaobing Tang, *Global Space and the Nationalist Discourse of
Modernity: The Historical Thinking of Liang Qichao* (Stanford, CA: Stanford University Press,
1996), chap. 3.

The third issue is morality toward the family. Women's moral obligation to the family involves what is commonly referred to as "women's propriety" (*kunfan*). The meaning of women's propriety is twofold: first, education; and second, household management.

Education

Education can subsequently be divided into two parts. The first of these is fetal education (*taijiao*). The fetus is the egg at the stage that it begins to change into a human. It begins as a tiny egg only one-three-hundredth of an English inch but undergoes multiple changes. In a few days, it changes into a shape resembling a fish; in a few more days, it resembles an animal with webbed feet; after six weeks it begins to look like a mammal; in another eight weeks it resembles a small dog, and from this it turns into a human. Therefore, humans are created beings: from a beginning as the lowest form of animal and changing into the highest form of animal. An evil nature or good nature [in the child] is created by people's own actions. Every time a child's mother worries or laughs, it can be passed on and appear in the child. Thus it is said: "[W]hen a phoenix is born, it tends toward benevolence and righteousness, but when a tiger or wolf is born, it has a greedy, fierce heart. The difference between them comes from their mothers." Nowadays Western books on care of the fetus usually focus on matters related to hygiene (*weisheng*) such as how to move and carry oneself, food and drink, arrangement of the house, and clothing. They are much more detailed than such Chinese works as "Regulations for the Inner Quarters" (*Neize*), "Proceedings of Government in the Different Months" (*Yueling*), the "Luxuriant Dew" (*Fanlu*), or *Discursive Weighing (Lun heng)*, except that they do not discuss how to nurture a fetus of good moral character. The *Biographies of Exemplary Women* says, "In ancient times, when a woman became pregnant, [it was prescribed that] when sleeping, she did not lie on her side; when sitting, she did not lean to one direction; when standing, she kept her feet straight; she did not look upon evil colors, did not hear improper sounds, did not eat foods with strange flavors. At night she was to have a blind person recite poetry for her and speak of proper matters."[22]

---

[22]Tr: Here Jin's text slightly abridges the "Three Mothers of Zhou" (Zhoushi sanmu) entry of the *Biographies of Virtuous Women* (*Lienü zhuan*). See Zhang Jing, ed., *Lienü zhuan jinzhu jinyi* (Taipei, Taiwan: Shangwu yinshuguan, 1994), 13–14.

These are the essentials of caring for the fetus. To give birth to children that are strong and healthy, clever and brilliant, enthusiastic about public morality (*gongde*), and who will be known for their moral character, then one's efforts must be based on the noblest and purest care of the fetus.

Second, there is the mother's behavior. Westerners divide the education of children into a hundred different areas; 70 percent of these are taught by the mother. A child's mind is like a clean, blank sheet of white paper: the spot you touch with cinnabar will turn red, and the spot you touch with ink will turn black. The child's mind has no independent perspective of its own. If you speak to the child about universal love (*bo'ai*), martial spirit, colonization, sea navigation, republicanism, and revolution, then [the child's mind] will absorb them. If you speak to the child about stealing from the people, toadying to authority, treachery and lawbreaking, or loving money and sex, then [the child's mind] will also absorb them.

In today's China, education of children in the home is low and vulgar. From the time they are wrapped in baby's clothes until their hair is braided and they are sent to school, in their daily lives they learn nothing but how to compete for the examinations and civil service posts; how valuable stealing and calculating advantage can be; how hilarious lustful hags, filthy servant girls, and their crafty arguments are; how frightening ghosts, buddhas, fairies, fox-spirits, gods, and demons are. These things all nurture the unspeakable morals of our people. They make the children stupid, devious, and low, and if they [the children] are even sent to a teacher, the teacher himself may not be much better. Alas! I need not discuss how Napoleon's and Washington's mothers taught their sons or mention the mothers of Meng Ke, Fan Pang, Xu Shu, Liu Zhongying, and Ouyang Xiu.[23] Everyone knows about them, but mothers' behavior in raising their children has become so depraved! Raising sages, worthies, emperors, kings, heroes, and gallant knights-errant is the work of virtuous mothers and not extraordinary beings.

---

[23]Tr: Here Jin cites stories of virtuous mothers from ancient and medieval history. According to legend, the mother of Mencius [Meng Ke] moved three times to ensure that he had a proper environment for his education. Fan Pang was an official from the Eastern Han executed during factional infighting. Before his death, his mother assured him of the righteousness of his cause. In an incident from the *Romance of the Three Kingdoms*, Xu Shu's mother, incorrectly believing that Xu Shu had betrayed Liu Bei for Cao Cao, hanged herself in anger. Liu Zhongying's mother gave him pills made from the gall of a bear to aid in his study. Finally, because of their relative poverty, Ouyang Xiu's mother was said to have educated her son largely on her own.

Household Management

Household management has both broad and narrow definitions. What is commonly referred to as household management is complicated and difficult, and [the commonly accepted explanation] is in fact the narrow definition of the term. What I refer to as household management—the broad definition—is straightforward and simple. What is commonly referred to as household management is limited to worrying about the minutiae of measuring out salt and rice, much as when the Qin emperor ruled the land and set and enforced even the smallest units of measurement. Instead, what I call household management involves a few simple, clear areas, from raising children and [ensuring] hygiene to [managing] economics, law, employment of personnel, and administration. It is much like a miniature of the state. When the principles are clear, all details fall into place. And when the slaves plant the fields and the servant women spin the silk,[24] things are much as when Yao and Shun simply folded their hands, let their garments drape, and ruled the land. As for embroidery, this work was originally a form of art. Westerners once included it in their schools alongside singing and physical exercise, but now such work is performed by machines, producing results vastly superior to pieces made by Chinese women. Who decided that women should borrow strings of cash or pecks of grain in order to sew a new pair of slippers every ten days and make a new embroidered jacket every month? Why should they spend their days worrying and toiling over such things? If my plan is followed, then happiness in the household is created by women alone. One can either bolt the door and go outside to travel and study away from home. Or, one can stay in and invite guests home to dance and make merry, or one can open books and study alone. A nation has never been weak when women produce and do not just consume, when women stand on their own and are not dependent.

Generally speaking, for three thousand years Chinese women have been focusing on private morality while seeming to have never heard of public morality. They will say "maintain your body like jade" or "guard vigilantly against selfishness" but see such ideas as equality between men and women, women entering schools, and freedom of marriage as tools to destroy private morality. Great disasters often evade the attention of the watchful few,

---

[24]Tr: In other words, when all people perform their appointed duties.

appearing where they are not expected. The Qin emperor dug the grave at Lishan, burned the books, and slaughtered scholars,[25] and yet Chen [Sheng] and Wu [Guang], Liu [Bang] and Xiang [Yu] all arose from tilling the fields [to challenge the Qin].[26] Wary of the troubles once caused by the devolution of military power to provincial governors during the Tang, the Song tried to reign in the power of military generals; the Ming emperors guarded vigilantly against powerful members of the royal family, but ultimately the people who destroyed the Song and Ming lineages and became the rulers of the country were not Chinese aristocrats but, rather, goatish ruffians and specimens of an inferior race. Who made sacrosanct women's bodies, which should have been protected from violation, unable to keep their essence of purity? I acknowledge that not all European women can be as highly developed as I have praised them, but I can say with certainty that their society is civilized, that their morality is advanced, and that all in their society desire to be honorable. Now the morals of our society are deteriorating every day, yet most of us do not trace the problem to its origins but seek instead to deprive ordinary individuals of their rights as a way to ward off these problems. How closely this resembles the perverse and wrong opinions of the monarchs! Indeed, they share the same sickness at the source of the problem.

What is women's morality and virtue? It includes filial piety, high moral integrity, great talent, and shrewdness. All these are subordinate to public morality, which comes before all others. Public morality is patriotism and [national] salvation. Men are cool and detached, whereas women are enthusiastic; men esteem those who are firm and unbending, whereas women are more gentle and yielding. Patriotism and salvation, then, are the duties of women. For this reason, Ti Ying's pure and filial conduct was a thousand times greater than Cao E's,[27] and Mulan's remarkable deeds were ten thousand times greater than those of Ying'er of the Northern Palace.[28] My compatriots! Women! I hope that you will travel the world with bright

---

[25]Tr: King You (r. 781–771 B.C.E.) of the Western Zhou dynasty died at Lishan; his defeat marked the end of the Western Zhou.

[26]Tr: All four of these individuals were involved in rebellions against the Qin. Liu Bang, known as the founder of the Han dynasty, has been held up in many phases of Chinese history as an individual who rose to power from the peasant class.

[27]Tr: Cao E, a young woman from the Eastern Han period, searched for her father's body for many days after he drowned in a river. Eventually, she, too, drowned herself.

[28]Tr: Mentioned in the *Zhanguo ce*, Ying'er of the Northern Palace was a woman from the kingdom of Qi who did not marry so that she could take care of her parents in their old age.

eyes, that your delicate hands will uphold the nation. Women! My compatriots! I hope you will summon your clever tongues to follow in the path of Beecher,[29] that you will raise your wise swords and march with Sophia, that you will set your mind to push forward with Nightingale. Do not make skirts, hairpins, and headdresses into symbols of shame, and do not let the female heroes and soldiers of ancient times go down in history without successors. This is the bright light of morality and virtue.

---

[29]Tr: Harriet Beecher Stowe (1811–1896).

PART 3: WOMEN'S CHARACTER

Women in today's China have a unique character. Those qualities that win praise and worship are called "elegance and auspiciousness." I, too, love and value this character, but nowadays a refined quality is as rare as a unicorn or phoenix. As for auspiciousness, this is commonly found, to be sure. For this reason, it is better to flatter women with words about their magnificent, showy beauty than it is to praise them for their hard work and good deeds. Rather than praise them for their great talent and unmatched beauty, it is better to pay tribute to them with words about wealth, long life, and many sons. In the morning, women look for fortune-tellers; and at night, they chant spells to ward off evil. On the first and fifteenth of every month, they abstain from meat in gratitude to their parents. On the Lantern Festival, they turn to fortune-telling to predict whether their husbands will succeed in the civil service examinations. Shy and coquettish, they give one another all kinds of "help," every move controlled by superstitious rules, none of which leads to anything. Because their minds are clouded and their spirit sapped, four hundred million people are about to fall into a deplorable state. It is ironic that women would like to avoid inauspicious signs but in fact contribute to an unfortunate reality. For this reason, today women in China should take the following to be the most important parts of character: liveliness, perceptiveness, charisma, the destruction of superstition, and escape from oppression. Second to these are study and learning. If they can accomplish this, then the creation of a new citizenry will be halfway complete.

I would like to compare the levels of education and learning among Chinese women but have no standard by which to do so. For women in the area where I live, five out of ten can tell the different shapes between characters; six out of twenty can explain their meaning and distinguish their tones; ten in one hundred can write simple but imperfect essays or letters; and only one in three thousand understands major events in the world and can keep up in discussions on affairs ancient and modern. As for a woman whose erudition can reach the aims of the work of Cang Jie and Kharosthi,[30] who can contemplate the happiness of the nation's people, she is perhaps one in two hundred million, but I cannot survey such a great number of people! It was once said that "[a] shallow mind is a poor match

---

[30]Tr: Legendary inventors of Chinese and South Asian writing systems.

for a beautiful face; a golden pavilion cannot hold a wordless stele."[31] Let us, for now, set aside those [with wordless steles]. The majority of our citizens subscribe to antiforeign ideas and detest the ideas of women's rights. They indulge in frivolous entertainment, which only makes their own enslavement worse. They close off the harbors and dam the rivers that lead toward civilization, and their immediate concerns and individual actions do not go beyond simple pleasures. In my view, their minds are closed against all intelligence. If today we have our compatriots read books by Western thinkers and go to listen to learned men's ideas, it would increase their knowledge and inspire their spirits, stimulate their minds, and wash out their stomachs. Then, I know that when they close their eyes, a new world and a new China will appear in their dreams: such beauty, reflected on the clouds; gorgeous women in their splendor, the fragrant flowers of the season; pagodas and terraces of gold and jade where beauties play the mouth-organ; it is like ascending the heavens, like traveling among the immortals. Oh, why don't you come to join me!

Nevertheless, I have discussed character only as it relates to inner qualities. As for the way character relates to exterior qualities, Chinese women face several obstacles, including [these]:

1. The evil of footbinding. Such sorrow! A punishment from Heaven! In fact, punishments from Heaven are tolerable, but how can we justify such a punishment from humans? Women had the misfortune of being born on this earth, where they not only must go through the trial of bearing children and suffering much harder work than men but also must suffer this pain of binding and cutting. The men of this world are heartless! The practices of skull flattening seen among women in Africa and the use of corsets by women in the West are enormously cruel, but they do not rise to the cruelty of footbinding in China. The cap can be torn, but shoes cannot be removed; the skulls [of males and females] are similarly rounded, but the toes are not similarly square. It is said that [humans with their caps have] their head touch the sky and [with their shoes] their feet walk the earth, yet [women] are left with these things that, crushed and folded into a few square inches, could never touch the earth. If you do not believe what

---

[31]Tr: "Golden pavilion" refers to extravagant quarters built for a wife or concubine. "Wordless stele" refers to the Tang empress Wu Zetian (625–705 C.E.), who ordered that a blank stele be placed before her tomb.

is said about the inequality in China between the ruler and the people and between men and women, then you only need look to caning and foot-binding. She cries and longs for death; the dried blood and flesh begins to rot; and her limbs are mangled. I would bring the person who started this practice to justice, but I regret that I cannot summon Li Sheng[32] from hell to hang him by his ribs from the ceiling as punishment. I worship Zhang Xianzhong's heroism as if he was the second Napoleon.[33] What good deeds did Temüjin and Nurhaci[34] perform, that their sons and grandsons ruled China for generations? Simply by promoting natural [i.e., unbound] feet, they invited Heaven's protection for a good several centuries.

Nonetheless, we cannot speak only of these crimes committed against women. We must ask, why do Chinese women wound and poison them-selves like this? Because they think it is beautiful? There is nothing dignified about a crippled exterior and a corrupted interior. Moreover, the body is nei-ther a bird-and-flower painting nor jewelry nor ornament. How can women make themselves up and mold their bodies into an artificial form so that they are nothing more than a plaything? Because they think it is an old cus-tom? The Japanese are reforming the practices of eyebrow shaving and tooth blackening; tattooing and nose-piercing have been eliminated even among primitives. Why should ladies of elegance and high standing have limbs cruelly shrunken and paralyzed, so that they cannot stand tall and support themselves as do their servant girls, who keep their feet in a natural form?

Since ancient times, the annihilation of a race or destruction of a nation begins as a self-inflicted act; it is not something that can be accomplished by outsiders. Nowadays opium smoking, footbinding, and separation of men and women are turning China into a land of beasts and demons; we are speeding up the loss of our spirit and soul and putting an end to the sacrifices to our own ancestors. Think of it, my compatriots! To escape oppression, you must first remove these bonds. When the body and mind are natural and healthy, the race will be strong; when the race is strong, the nation will rise. I hope that thirty years from now, the evils of footbinding and other

---

[32]Tr: Li Sheng (r. 937–942), first ruler of the short-lived Southern Tang dynasty. According to legend, the practice of footbinding originated among the ladies of his court.
[33]Tr: Zhang Xianzhong (1606–1647), a rebel who conquered Sichuan Province and tried to establish his own dynasty but was quelled by the Manchus.
[34]Tr: Temüjin was the birth name of Genghis Khan (1162?–1227). Nurhaci (1558–1626), or Qing Taizu, was considered to be the founder of the Manchu state that formed the Qing dynasty.

backward customs will come to an end, their remnants existing only among a minority of courtesans and actresses, and will eventually disappear completely. If we want to avoid the disaster of completely disappearing, then we must first unbind women's feet.

2. The evil of ornamentation. If I say that the clothing and accessories Chinese women wear should be annihilated, would that be going too far? When European women bind their waists, push up their breasts, and stick flowers in their hats, I do not know what good it does for hygiene or why this should be regarded as a kind of civilized decoration. In recent years Chinese women's clothing has become quite suitable in terms of width and length. If they suddenly begin imitating Western clothes, I cannot approve of them. As for embroidered collars with piping, necklaces of jade and pearls around the neck, and the latest fashion from head to toe, although such things are related to an individual's economic situation, they expend all of a person's energy on useless things. As for hair ornaments, arm bangles, tourmalines, "kingfisher" jade, coral, agate, gold, and pearls, their craftsmanship grows more sophisticated with each day, and women treasure them like temple cauldrons and holy relics. Poor or rich, they treat jewelry like antiques worthy of collecting. With so much attention devoted to these playthings, how could they have any time left over for reading from classics and histories, for discussing the affairs of the day?

Even worse, among all these things are cosmetic pastes and powders. Humans get the color of their skin from Heaven, and beauty and homeliness cannot be forced or changed. For women born beautiful, it is as Song Yu said: powder makes them too white, rouge makes them too red, and both red and white ruin their beauty. For women born homely, unless they are what in Western countries are called painters of the skin or have what the Chinese call false masks for the face, then there is no way to cover it up. Moreover, lead and mercury can easily injure the blood vessels, causing them to atrophy when applied. Have we not heard how Cromwell admonished his portrait painter? He said, "Do not lose my true appearance."[35] I ask you, my compatriots, how could you lose your true appearance? Have you also not heard of the poems and lyrics of Li Bai

---

[35]Tr: Cromwell is reputed to have said, "I desire you would use all your skill to paint my picture truly like me, and not flatter me at all; but remark all these roughnesses, pimples, warts, and everything as you see me, otherwise I will never pay a farthing for it."

and Tang Linchuan [Xianzu]? They say, "Lotuses stand in autumn water, all natural and without ornaments,"[36] and "I have loved nature my entire life."[37] If my compatriots love themselves, then I hope they will treasure their natural selves and natural rights equally.

Even worse than the use of makeup are ear piercing and putting hair up in elaborate buns. Although ear piercing may not be as harmful as footbinding, such a small piece of skin with a tiny hole will also endure pain with heavy earrings hanging and swinging from them. Moreover, ear piercing is a form of punishment among soldiers. Along with rings and cuffs, it serves as a sign and evidence that in primitive times men forced women to submit to them. And now it is seen as an honor? As for putting hair up in buns and arranging it on the temples, women use this as a way of enhancing their beauty; for if their hair is messy and their clothes coarse, even their own family would laugh at them. I believe, however, that the source of women's dissipation and corruption arises from and is made worse by the experience of footbinding and making elaborate hairdos. When they awake in the morning, even before washing their faces or cleaning their teeth, they spend the better part of an hour on nothing but fretting over all the fine details of putting up their hair. Then they spend another two or three hours making up in front of the mirror, ordering about their underlings until they reach a subtle perfection that no wind can ruffle—the hairpins' glint, shadows on the temples, so dazzling to the eyes. By the time they are finished, half the day is gone. Because of this, when women go to school, they should at least for the time being adopt the braided hairstyles of the northern tribes, if only for the sake of saving time. In today's customs and in our society, is the hair braid not sacred and inviolable, as if the spirits of countless ancestors were held in it? Although our bodies are said to be the progeny of our parents, for the sake of beauty, we think nothing of subjecting the ear or feet to severe punishment; but we take such meticulous care of our tiny length of hair, and when ends are cut off, they are treasured for safekeeping. "When sable tails are gone, dog tails are used," and some will spare no expense to buy them. Nowadays the knowledge of men of ambition from all places is evolving, and they are cutting their hair in the name of good hygiene. I believe that the evolution

---

[36]Tr: This line is misquotation of a poem from Li Bai, which reads, "Lotuses stand in clear water, all natural and without ornaments."

[37]Tr: This line appears in Tang Xianzu's *The Peony Pavilion*.

of women should also begin by cutting their hair. I do not say this simply to shock others. Once they use the sword of wisdom to cut their hair, tender sentiments will be curtailed, freedom will not die, and all troubles in the mind will be driven out. Some [women] may be mistaken for *bhik-khuni*,[38] but as long as they do not behave as Wu Zhao [Zetian], I see no harm in it to our morals. Freemen in the fifteenth century used this type of sign to distinguish themselves. I dare not expect the average woman to use it. However, there are immortals in this world who can influence and reform mortals. They have incredible power and technique. They will probably agree with me on this matter.

3. The evil of superstition. How does superstition develop? It starts from humans' feelings and hopes, and women are factories of feelings and hopes. In barbaric times, women were mentally weaker than men, and so they became accustomed to depending on men. They counted on men to deliver those feelings and hopes they wished for and could expect to obtain. And they counted on the gods to grant them those things that were out of their control. Superstition began, then, in prehistoric times. Children are not as superstitious as adults, and adults are not as superstitious as the elderly. An elderly person's mind has been habituated; no wonder her superstition becomes more entrenched as she lives by it day after day.

Yet superstition itself has no rules, and thus if it is questioned, the mind simply cannot comprehend it. Followers of Sakyamuni will defend their Sakyamuni,[39] followers of Daoism will defend their Daoism, followers of divination will defend their divination, and followers of Jesus will defend their Jesus. They will discuss Sakyamuni, Kuan-yin, the patriarch Laozi, King Wen, and the Master of Ghost Valley in one breath; they pay homage to Guan Yu,[40] Yue Fei, Wutong,[41] and Qisha as if there were no difference among them; they are filled with dread when they hear Jesus' words; sweat pours down their bodies when they see the Cross, and they kneel down to the ground. They believe that the sun and moon are brother and sister, that thunder and lightning are like husband and wife, and when they see a tiny snake, they pay obeisance to it and say: "This is my ancestor!" They speak with great seriousness, and those who listen are deeply moved. If you tell

---

[38] Tr: Sanskrit, Buddhist nun.

[39] Tr: Siddhārta Gautama, regarded as the founder of Buddhism.

[40] Tr: Guan Yu, a god of war; Yue Fei, general and warrior known for his superhuman strength.

[41] Tr: Wutong, god of wealth and, in some traditions, male sexual prowess.

them that a duck's brain holds the spirit of Qin Kuai or that an eagle is the son-in-law of the god of the underworld, they will believe you. If you tell them about the inventions made and knowledge gained through the study of electricity and steam, they will doubt you. But if you tell them that the sixty-eight chemical elements were made by the gods or that the technology of printing was created by demons, they clap their hands and say, "It's true! It's true!" Alas! With the people's learning in this state, what else can I say?

Superstition is an inauspicious thing. Nuns, witches, geomancers, and astrologers are inauspicious people. I do not understand why for an auspicious matter like marriage people defer to the monastery and ask for strips of paper? Or why for an auspicious matter like moving house do people go to a geomancer to choose the proper directions? Parents take their infant son to be rubbed on the head by a freakish nun, who they hope will take the baby as her "foster son." In doing business, merchants will look to the skies for a sign and offer food and wine in thanks. Even a stout, strong man will bow down before a sorcerer, and even a tight-fisted miser will give alms to a monk. When old people's spirits have grown weak and they wheeze with each breath, their minds are filled with thoughts of the end of life and hopes for the next life; therefore they burn incense and chant the Buddha's name, seeking fortune in their next life. Buddhism is most suited to the simple minds of the elderly. As they gain experience, young people have all kinds of plans and thoughts about the past and the future and struggle every day to reconcile their feelings and hopes. Their minds are embroiled in endless complicated matters that create limitless openings for superstition to enter. As for children, they have a wealth of feelings and limitless hopes, like rushing spring waters, like brilliant flowers bursting into bloom. Their religious thinking is undeveloped by nature; but when religious ideas are transmitted through racial character and through the teachings of clergy to students, young people cannot but believe in them. Thus when personal problems arise, they blame [their problems] on fate. From childhood to old age, what is commonly called fate always follows the material body; nothing between heaven and earth can escape it. Superstition among Chinese women has more than one source. I will sum it up in two sentences: the daily talk of fate is the warp, and Buddhist talk of the field of merit[42] and blessings from the Buddha are the woof. All other extraneous things only support these two and carry out their work.

---

[42]Tr: *Futian*: the Buddha, Sangha, and the dharma.

Can we say that women have no sense of patriotism or concern for the world? Every day I see such words as "May the wind blow gently and the rain fall in time; may the country be prosperous and the people live in harmony" pasted on the gate lintels of humble homes. As for prosperity for the people, it is undoubtedly something that can be brought about only through human efforts. And wind and rain change according to the climatic conditions and not by human or divine intervention. The ability of the type of thinking found in the couplets to confuse and do harm to the people is little better than those who worship [at temples] during solar and lunar eclipses, pray during drought, and cower in fear of rainbows. I want to destroy superstition in women, reverse its course, and use their talents and apply them to a sense of patriotism and concern for the world. Reading every day about Columbus and Magellan is not as good as carrying out the work of Columbus and Magellan; praising Confucius and [Jesus] Christ every day is not as good as carrying out the work of Confucius and Christ; chanting every day for the Master of the Universal Gate[43] or Saintly Mother of Mei Island is not as good as carrying out the work of a master or saintly mother for oneself. With willow sprig in hand, spread the nectar of the gods across the three thousand galaxies;[44] let down your hair, carry a sword, and travel the seas, and see with knowing eyes the sufferings of all sentient beings. Good women, good women, use my words to determine whether you are honest or not, believers in the Way or not.

Is superstition an enemy of the development of human society? If a society of humans is to develop, it must break through any and all limitations and obstacles. When superstition holds on, however, nothing can be accomplished, not even the smallest step can be taken, and in three hundred years China will be the same as it is today. In the seventeenth century, science in Europe became more sophisticated, and in these countries the people's spirit became solidified and their willpower grew stronger. The revolutions of the eighteenth century followed. Today we cannot wait for China to meet its "fate"—I want to take extreme measures, use sulfuric acid and gunpowder to wipe it out and wash it away, slash the gnarled cloth with one swipe of the knife blade, break the chain with an awl. I will smash the Yellow Crane Tower to pieces for you, and you can give Parrot

---

[43]Tr: *Pumen dashi*, refers to Guanyin.
[44]Tr: The willow sprig is one of the eighteen items a Buddhist monk should carry. The "three thousand galaxies" comprise the domains of the Buddha.

Island a good kick and turn it upside down for me.[45] How wonderful! When superstition is rooted out, oppression will be driven out; when oppression is driven out, a civilized nation and a free people will appear in China. For good men and honest women, the results of their efforts can yield something this remarkable.

4. The evil of restriction [to the home]. Chinese women's character is that of stuffy, decrepit people. They are shy and speak awkwardly, and they run away at the sight of strangers, just like a small child. When we search for the source [of this behavior], we find that it lies in their restriction to the home. A young and ignorant ruler will not be able to distinguish between beans and barley. When he hears that a famine is occurring, much like the French princess, he will say, "Why don't the people eat porridge cooked with minced meat?"[46] This is the result of people living in splendid isolation.

Chinese women have the dignity of kings but are lower than prisoners. Cloistered in their chambers, they see nothing of the world. As for the limitations on their rights, for their entire lives they dare not inquire into anything more than a few dozen steps outside their gate; if they go more than half a *li* beyond their front door, they are lost; and they are ignorant of everyday concerns of the world. They are not born ignorant. Deep in the gilded inner chambers and lavish boudoirs, words from inside do not travel out, and words from outside do not travel in, and many things isolate them so that they cannot make judgments and distinctions and gain knowledge.

China and foreign lands were once isolated from one another, and then they traded with one another. The ruler and the people were once isolated from one another, and then revolutions began. [Authorities] worked to restrict knowledge, resulting in the works of Martin Luther, Kossuth's newspapers, and the banned books of Russian youth—none of them could be cordoned off. Those who discuss the isolation of Chinese women believe it is related to morality and character and do not realize that such women of the highest morals and character as the daughter of Fu Sheng or Ban Zhao taught the classics and read the canonical histories, and they exchanged ideas and conducted business with people [from outside their family]

---

[45]Tr: Yellow Crane Tower, on the banks of the Yangtze River, is a site that often appears in literati poetry. Parrot Island, across the Yangzi from Wuchang, also appeared in numerous stories and poems.

[46]Tr: These famous words, spoken by Emperor Hui of Jin (Jin Huidi, reigned 290–306), can be thought of in the same way as Marie Antoinette's "let them eat cake."

without any fear of shame. None of this caused any harm. Lady Wei passed her mastery of calligraphy on to [Wang] Xizhi,[47] and Xie Daoyun debated with [male] guests and answered their questions while separated only by a thin screen—acts that earned her praise in the historical record.[48] Even when locked behind heavy gates beyond which they are never to take a single step, women will still hear the "Song of the Male Phoenix Seeking His Mate" and run off in the middle of the night to elope.[49] [Zhuo] Wenjun's scandalous conduct represents some of the flaws in [women's] character—how can such flaws be repaired by isolation? Moreover, should women alone be praised or blamed for all acts in history of low morality and character? If Qiu Hu, when he stepped down from his chariot, behaved so lewdly toward his wife, how must he have behaved toward other women?[50] Men, then, should be the ones undergoing the punishment of banishment, perhaps by exile to the eastern or western edges of the Asian continent in complete isolation. Moreover, I see that the isolation of women only keeps them from discussing learning and current events with men. However, they sit with men shoulder to shoulder in Buddhist temples and theaters. Why do the moralists not think this strange instead of taking it for granted, then? If one does not treat people in a civilized way, then those people will allow themselves to be uncivilized. Today the world is made anew, barbaric customs are being swept aside, and "my father has seen the aspect of my nativity"[51]—this is women's rights in the twentieth century. She enjoys a life equal and holds the value of a thousand pieces of gold. Her countenance reveals her brilliance, her speech direct and excellent. With bejeweled sword and beautiful brows, the dragon-god appears before us. Who is it? The woman of new China!

---

[47]Tr: Wei Shuo (Lady Wei, 272–349), taught the famed calligrapher Wang Xizhi (303–361).

[48]Tr: Xie Daowei (also Daoyun), known as a prolific poet from the Eastern Jin period. For a brief account, see Richard B. Mather, trans. and ed., *Shih-shuo hsin-yü: A New Account of Tales of the World* (Minneapolis: University of Minnesota Press, 1976), 412.

[49]Tr: This passage alludes to the famous romance of Sima Xiangru (179–117 B.C.E.) and Zhuo Wenjun. Upon hearing Sima Xiangru play the "Song of the Male Phoenix Seeking His Mate" on the zither, Zhuo Wenjun, recently widowed and living in her parents' home, fled in the middle of the night to marry Sima Xiangru.

[50]Tr: Qiu Hu left his wife at home for five years to take up an official post. On his return, he saw a beautiful woman in the fields and stopped his chariot so that he could speak in lewd terms to her and try to take her as his concubine. When he arrived at his home, he realized that the woman from the fields was his wife. See "Hu Qiu jie nü," in Zhang, ed., *Lienü zhuan*, 190–191.

[51]Tr: See Qu Yuan's "Encountering Sorrow," translation borrowed from Hawkes, *Ch'u T'tzu*, 22.

The four areas discussed above are the limitations and obstacles inflicted [on women] from the outside world. When these are eliminated, the character of Chinese women will be wholesome and complete. Nevertheless, in the past, social customs have reversed themselves, depriving people of their freedom and casting them into a world of darkness. If there are those whose behavior is unique, then people will gather and shout at them. For this reason, those who are limited by old-style customs are the most inferior. Those who have escaped old-style customs fare better. And those who have escaped old-style customs and can reform and create new customs are superior.

To escape old-style customs and improve and create new customs, nothing is better than going abroad to study in Europe and America. When their studies are complete and they return, my compatriots can choose whether to serve in political parties, in parliament, in medicine, as lawyers, or as news reporters. As for women in Japan, they are slight and obedient; there is nothing to be learned from them. I have looked through their histories of women's rights and see how plain and lusterless they are. I have heard that according to their customs, when they see a man, they must kneel; when they see guests, they must kneel; that they serve men as playthings in the house; and that they bathe together with men in the same pool. Lower-class people in China would not do such things, but this is how most women in Japan behave. Those who study in Japan should be concerned only with scholarship and technical learning and not allow these evil customs found among women there to return home and taint others.

PART 4: WOMEN'S CAPABILITIES

Do women have capabilities? This question has been debated and researched by dozens of European psychologists and philosophers. The extent to which a person's capabilities can flourish depends on the inborn talents and how they are structured within the person but can also be assisted through education. Bad education, however, can destroy what has already been formed in a person. Some people may blame the result on the person's lack of natural gifts, but that is not reasonable. Little children, boys and girls, may differ slightly in their character, but there is no difference in the degree of their capabilities; this is proof that they have not been subjected to barbaric education. If boys are subjected to barbaric education today, some will have an underdeveloped character well into old age. They will profess to follow in the footsteps of [sage-rulers] Yao and Shun, but in their heads and hearts they are like Tyrant Jie and Robber Zhi.[52] If they see the machinery of civilization, they will be shocked and run away in fear. For this reason, women's abilities should be judged by whether or not they have been educated.

The "Admonitions for Daughters" reads:

> In olden times when a daughter was born, on the third day she was cradled on the floor below the bed, and she was given a loomwhorf as a toy. She was cradled on the floor to show her low estate and subservience. She was given a loomwhorf as a toy to show she was destined for labor and dedicated service. And her parents' solemn report of her birth to the ancestors signified her duty of continuing the lineage of her lord.[53]

What criminal writing! Offering sacrifices is the teaching of the ancestors in China. It is a sacred ritual, and yet many people have women, whom they treat as lowly servants, perform the offerings. Why not, then, allow tattooed convicts and castrated officials to offer wine to the ancestors? Among the most disgusting and utterly barbaric things in this world, nothing is worse

---

[52]Tr: King Jie, the last ruler of the Xia dynasty, was an infamous tyrant. In *Zhuangzi*, Robber Zhi was a notorious bandit who overwhelmed Confucius in a debate; see Burton Watson, trans., *The Complete Works of Chuang Tzu* (New York: Columbia University Press, 1968), 323–331.

[53]Tr: Translation amended from van Gulik, *Sexual Life in Ancient China*, 98.

than to take something ancient people commonly said and treat it as holy writ or to use one person's self-satisfied, smug words to deny everything in the world. Ming Taizu[54] said, "I would kill all women, if a woman had not given birth to me." Muslims said, "Women have no souls." These words sound no different to me than sounds made by wild beasts. Yet they lead to such evil practices as drowning infant daughters and give rise to the saying that raising girls means pure financial loss, until women have no place in the world to stand on their own. My compatriots, women, are you willing to accept this ill fame and suffer it for all time? If not, then there must be a way to wash away this shame.

Abilities are the fruits of intelligence, and intelligence is the flower of the brain. Biology has been used to measure capabilities of human brains and thereby to determine the superiority and inferiority of different races of people; this is the pinnacle of European scholarship. Nowadays women do not match up to men in terms of body size, but it is recognized worldwide that their mental capacities are no different from men's, and in some cases they are superior to men's. The ratio of the brain size to body size is fixed for various species. To wit, the larger the body, the smaller the brain is. Thus a whale's brain is 1/3,300 of its body, an elephant's is 1/500; a dog's is 1/250; a bird's is 1/27; the New World monkey's is 1/29 to 1/13; and a human's is 1/45 to 1/46. Birds and monkeys do not match up to humans, only because there are many shortcomings in their physical structures; they still possess high intelligence and sharp senses. Women's small body frame, then, is clear evidence of the potential to develop their abilities. There is no reason to cultivate them [i.e., women] like flowers in hothouses and then blame them for their apparent uselessness.

Head circumference measurements [in millimeters] of European newborn boys and girls taken by *Ke-wu-cai* (Francis Galton?) and *Kai-de-lai* (James McKeen Cattell?)[55] produced the following results:

$$\text{Men} \begin{cases} 353 \\ 335 \end{cases} \qquad\qquad \text{Women} \begin{cases} 352 \\ 341 \end{cases}$$

---

[54]Tr: Zhu Yuanzhang (1328–1398), founder of the Ming dynasty.

[55]Tr: It is not clear to whom these transcribed names refer (Galton). For contemporary information on this type of measurement, see World Health Organization, "Child Growth Standards," http://www.who.int/childgrowth/standards/en (accessed June 3, 2011).

The same measurements of Japanese newborns as performed by *Pei-lu*,[56] combined with the above measurements, are shown as follows:

$$\text{Men} \begin{cases} 338 \\ 336 \\ 344 \end{cases} \qquad \text{Women} \begin{cases} 352 \\ 353 \\ 372 \end{cases}$$

From the above numbers it can be seen that Nature has made girls superior to boys. The males of European civilization are not able to rival females for intelligence until they have accumulated a great deal of thinking and their cerebral cortex expands. One day, when women's education has made progress, there is no doubt that the capacity of their brains will expand further. For those lucky children born at the end of the twentieth century, women will be at the forefront. I love my compatriots and praise China's children, for they will bring the ideas of equality and freedom to fruition! This work lies not in ideals in words but in the ability to transform. Abilities are the fruits of intelligence that come out of waves in the brain. If we wish to make the world anew, turn events in a new direction, restore rights [to the people], change social customs, and make parents around the world have a preference for female children over male children—women should see that they themselves can accomplish these goals, that they do not have to wait for some exceptional individuals to deliver these changes.

It is certainly true that women's abilities tend toward literature and fine arts. In the past few centuries, Europe has been home to a multitude of talented women. The scholarly works of [Mary] Somerville, Miss [Caroline] Herschel, and [Rosina Maria] Zornlin have gained applause around the world. The plays of Joanna Baillie; the novels by women like [Jane] Austen, [Fredrika] Bremer, [Catherine] Gore, and Madam Dudevant [George Sand]; the poems of [Felicia] Hemans, [Letitia] Landon, [Mary] Tighe, and [Elizabeth Barrett] Browning;[57] and the painting passed on by a certain

---

[56]Tr: It is not clear to whom this name, *Pei-lu*, refers.

[57]Tr: In the original text, many of the aforementioned names printed in romanized form contain typos, which make them illegible. We have identified the English source in which these names originally appeared and have restored them accordingly. The English source on which Jin relied was a book entitled *Eliza Cook's Journal* (London: John Owen Clarke, 1849). The information contained in Jin's paragraph is based on a loose translation of a paragraph from this

princess called *The Momentous Question* are all equal to or better than the work of men and deserve to be called masterworks.[58] These women are truly ladies of great learning and broad literary ability. Moreover, the philosophy of Madame de Staël, the economic thought of Miss Martineau, and the political thought of Madame Roland also exhibit highly refined talent and quick wit to win fame in the realms of politics and letters and one worshipped by men. How is this possible? Women in those times were said to be unworthy of high-level education, and even though their scholarship and thinking were not well-developed, such a large number of talented women still came to the forefront. Today, if we promote [women's education], the fields will be filled with an endless harvest.

Chinese women are infamous around the world for their lack of education. But when I read what is described in the old histories, what is held in collections of women's writings, I see that in the classics and histories there were such women as Lady Fu;[59] in literary writing, there were the achievements of Han Yu,[60] Lady Zuo,[61] Lady Xie,[62] and Sister Bao;[63] calligraphy saw the innovations of Wei Heng, Wei Shuo,[64] and Wu Cailuan;[65] in painting, Xue Yuan,[66] Lady Guan;[67] in music, Han E,[68] the wife of Huo Li, Cai Yan,[69] Lady Lu;[70] in

---

book. Mary Somerville (1780–1872) was a Scottish science writer; Caroline Herschel (1750–1848), younger sister of the astronomer William Herschel was known for her discoveries of several comets; Rosina Maria Zornlin, science writer; Joanna Baillie (1762–1851), Scottish poet and dramatist; Frederika Bremer (1801–1865), Swedish writer and feminist activist; Catherine Gore (1799–1861), English novelist and dramatist; Felicia Hemans (1793–1835), English poet; Letitia Landon (1802–1838), English poet; Mary Tighe, nee Blackford or Blanchford (1772–1810), Anglo-Irish poet.

[58]Tr: This appears to be a cavalier translation of the original text from *Eliza Cook's Journal*, which goes, "In sculpture, fame has been acquired by a princess; a picture like 'The Momentous Question' is tolerable proof of female capacity for painting," p. 144.

[59]Tr: The daughter of Fu Sheng, a scholar from the Western Han dynasty.

[60]Tr: Also Han Jieyu, Han dynasty poet.

[61]Tr: Daughter of Zuo Si (250–305).

[62]Tr: Xie Daowen, poet from the Eastern Jin dynasty (317–420).

[63]Tr: Bao Linghui, younger sister of the famed poet Bao Zhao (414–466).

[64]Tr: Wei Heng and Wei Shuo, both figures from the Jin dynasty.

[65]Tr: A woman from the Tang period known for using her calligraphy to support her family.

[66]Tr: Also Xue Susu, famed courtesan of the Ming dynasty.

[67]Tr: Also Guan Zhongjie (or Daosheng), wife of famed painter Zhao Mengfu (1254–1322).

[68]Tr: A legendary singer mentioned in early texts.

[69]Tr: A poet from the Jian'an period (196–220) known for her talent for playing the zither.

[70]Tr: A woman in the palace of Cao Cao (155–220), also known for playing the zither.

other arts, Ruolan and Lingyun.[71] Like grass growing without roots, like a stream flowing without a spring, these women made lasting achievements that are remarkable in their own right. Some went even further: to save the world, Ti Ying; in patriotism, Mulan; in chivalric justice, the sister of Nie Zheng[72] and Pang E; in sword fighting, the Lady of Yue and Hong Xian;[73] in courage and bravery, Tong Bana[74] and Li Bomei;[75] in military strategy, the mother of Yu, Xun Guan,[76] Lady Liang, Sha Lizhi,[77] and Qin Liangyu.[78] Feng Liao [in the Western Han dynasty] was charged with diplomatic missions because she understood international relations, and Empress Zhao's [ca. 300–265 B.C.E] discussion with the ambassador proclaimed the rights of the people.

These women's abilities were granted to them by Heaven and could not be matched by others. Nonetheless, that which is granted by Heaven may be taken away; it is far better, and far less difficult, to develop and promote human abilities. In early times, there were no lineages or castes of kings, lords, generals, and ministers of state; people simply chose what they would like to do. The same principle of choosing one's own calling should also be applied when it comes to things as trivial as scholarship and skills. Can my compatriots do this? If not, they will be like the cereus, which blooms and falls to the ground in only a few moments.[79] Thus, as for the Muslim saying that "women do not have souls," if those who claim this had in fact experienced it as truth, I would not dispute their contention—in fact, I would treat it as the truth.

---

[71]Tr: Su Ruolan and Xue Lingyun, from the Jin dynasty and the Kingdom of Wei, respectively, known for their skill in weaving and needlework.

[72]Tr: The sister of the assassin Nie Zheng, who after his death sacrificed her own life to ensure that he would be recognized for his work in service of his kingdom. See the biography of Nie Zheng in the "Biographies of the Assassin-Retainers" (*Cike liezhuan*) in the *Shiji*.

[73]Tr: The Lady of Yue (*Yue nü*) was a famous swordswoman from the kingdom of Yue during the Spring and Autumn period. Hong Xian, famous female knight-errant whose story is told in Tang dynasty *chuanqi* tales.

[74]Tong Bana is a filial daughter from the Song dynasty who saved her mother from the jaws of a tiger.

[75]Tr: Li Bomei is a sixth-century woman archer who could shoot from both left and right sides on horseback. She was immortalized in a poem by Empress Hu of the Northern Wei.

[76]Tr: During the Jin dynasty, Xun Guan led cavalry against troops surrounding her city.

[77]Tr: Sha Lizhi, mentioned in the "Virtuous Women" biographies of the *History of the Jin* (*Jin shi*), led local men and women into battle to fend off invading troops.

[78]Tr: Qin Liangyu (1574–1648), famed female general and supporter of the Ming Empire against the Manchus.

[79]Tr: In Buddhism, the cereus, especially the night-blooming variety, symbolizes a rare opportunity that must be seized quickly.

Another common saying, that "beauties are ill-fated" is quoted almost as often as "lack of talent in women is a virtue." It implies that the Creator of All Things is jealous of talent and beauty and will steal the lives of those women who possess them. Given the popularity of this view I am all the more puzzled how women could shun what is called talent and turn to rely even more heavily on what is called beauty. Physical beauty is an ax that harms nature; sentimentality is a prescription for saddening the spirit. To focus unswervingly on a single thing was forbidden by those who nourished life and sought immortality, and [thereby] days of happiness are followed by desolation. I have no way to alleviate the problem, no prescience, but if I use reason to assess the situation, I can reject all their obsessions in one stroke, without any hesitation, and all becomes clear to me.

There is a perfect way to develop women's abilities in today's China: through education. Alas! The barbaric education in China in days past suffered from all kinds of viciousness and corruption. When I think of them, it pains my heart; when I speak of them, my hair stands on end; when I see them, I grind and gnash my teeth, and my eyelids are rent apart. When they unfurl their mat to lecture, stuffy countryside Confucian schoolteachers act as if they were the Sage himself, and they use their unlimited legal power to punish their students. The worst of them fine their students or put them in shackles. The children smile and laugh as they leave for school but cry and weep when they return home. Their parents also scold them but then console and encourage them, believing that the sacrifice the children make in flesh-and-blood will one day be rewarded with fame and wealth—that this is the price to pay for an *optimus* and prime minister. Yet when I see older, trained students read aloud what they have memorized, they sound like nothing more than the cries of begging urchins or the babbling chants of wicked monks. Thus we hope to reform education but have no means to reform it and no people to undertake the reforms.

If anyone can undertake the reforms, it is women. Placing women in charge of education would have several benefits. First, women's personalities are closer to those of children. Second, they can lead others step by step.[80] Third, they will not unjustly beat children and can play well with them. Fourth, they have an eye for detail and will not be sloppy in their

---

[80]Tr: "[Yan Yuan said of Confucius:] 'The Master is good at leading one on step by step. He broadens me with culture and brings me back to essentials by means of the rites.'" See D. C. Lau, trans., *Confucius: The Analects* (Hong Kong: Chinese University Press, 2000), 9: 11.

work. Fifth, their minds are not ruined by absurd dreams of passing the examinations and taking official titles. Sixth, they are well suited to teaching basic, introductory aspects of such subjects as geometry and physics. With these six points in mind, I argue that China must immediately begin establishing teachers' colleges for women. When these colleges are established, they should take over the entire nation's education, and no child under the age of ten, boy or girl, should be placed in men's hands. In Japan's kindergartens, the women who work there have amazing ability to provide complete and sensitive care to the children, and [the caregivers] never show any difficulty in meeting the children's every request. Alas! If power were in my hands, I would cast out these self-appointed sages and establish a republican government [in the field of education] and make women its leaders. This is my most serious and heartfelt wish in advocating women's rights—but will my compatriots hope for it, too?

The greatest potential women hold for the world is found in their magical ability to move people's hearts and minds. This magical power uses a core of stillness and beauty to lead others without their conscious knowledge; it uses lofty thoughts to inspire indescribable adoration; it appears to do so effortlessly, when in fact its achievements are deeply difficult. This magical power is like both a magnet and a diamond. The best way to use this magical power to attract people is through public speeches. Although hundreds of men might talk themselves hoarse before a crowd, they cannot match one woman's voice speaking to society. With subtle words and gentle spirit, women can both move others' hearts with ease and shame them into taking action. It is said that reform (*bianfa*) begins from below; are women not the lowest among us? When students from Russia "*go among the people*," many of these movements are led by women, which shows how women's character is suited to gaining the trust and love of laborers in society. As they [women] spread the seeds of freedom from the West among the fields, people old and young gather to listen to their gentle words. As they speak, they explain cause and effect and teach by "stick and shout"[81] until they reach their listeners' hearts, moving them to tears. No man can match this ability in women. Not to harness this potential to change the direction of the world is a waste of women's talents. If women wish to use their talents well, then they must be employed in these two tasks [i.e., teaching and public speaking]!

---

[81]Tr: "Stick and shout" refers to a method of teaching by Chan masters. Here, too, "cause and effect" (*yinguo*) in the text refers to a fundamental principle of Buddhism.

Children have abilities, as when the boy from Waihuang outsmarted Xiang Yu.[82] Even the great Napoleon was once bested by a seven-year-old girl. Once a person's abilities are applied, it is no coincidence that unimaginable consequences will follow. When an old woman plays the bamboo flute, the Hui and Qiang peoples weep; the cries from the wife of [Fan] Qiliang brought down part of the Great Wall. A woman's ability might even startle the wind and the rain or make ghosts and gods weep. In the West, it is said that "[w]omen are weak, but when they become mothers, they are strong." These words describe their ability to protect and defend [their children]. But are women only the mothers of individuals? Because they also give birth to and raise the people of the nation, they pray that the people will avoid death and disaster and support one another. Now they can only sit and watch as tigers and wolves devour their children, as flames and floods engulf their children, as children from other lands gang up together to insult their children, as their property and, too, their lives are taken from them. Can they know no sorrow? Can they take no action?!

In ancient times there was a remarkable man in China called Sun Wuzi,[83] who used his abilities to train the beauties of the Wu Palace for battle. Do court beauties really have the ability to face the raging fires of battle? This achievement [by Sun Wuzi] cannot match the way Lycurgus trained the women of Sparta. Be that as it may, I do not have any wild hopes. Women should, however, take part in sports and exercise. Sports and exercise help to develop the body and keep it healthy. It is often said in the West that "to be prosperous, one's body must be healthy." Rousseau said, "When the body is weak, the spirit is weak." The world is a scene of competition and natural selection. Superior races may win out in natural selection, but those with the strongest, healthiest bodies must take the final victory. Today the Chinese race has lost its superior position, becoming a giant hospital specimen; it is no surprise to hear people say that "nine out of ten men have piles, and nine out of ten women have [unhealthy] vaginal discharge."

---

[82]Tr: When Xiang Yu (232–202 B.C.E.) led his army into Waihuang, he met stiff resistance from the local people. To penalize them, Xiang Yu planned to bury alive all men in the area under the age of fifteen. The unnamed thirteen-year-old boy, however, convinced Xiang Yu to spare the people of Waihuang. See "The Basic Annals of Xiang Yu," in Sima Qian, *Records of the Grand Historian*, trans. Burton Watson, rev. ed. (New York: Columbia University Press, 1993), 42–43.

[83]Tr: Another name for Sun Zi (544?–496? B.C.E.), reputed author of *The Art of War*.

Nonetheless, women suffer in greater degree from all types of illnesses and maladies. Although the source of these illnesses lies in footbinding, the sedentary ways and abnormal daily lives caused by their confinement in the home are also to blame. If they could exercise, how could they end up like this? In the diary she kept while observing the education of women in Europe, the Japanese Shimoda Utako[84] wrote:

European women have both gentle and strenuous forms of exercise, which can be divided into three types. The first is the formal *jimunasuchikku*[85] (*the name of a type of exercise*), which resembles military training for men. The second type is *jimunasuchikku* dance, and the third type is games. At a girls' school in Scotland, the clothes worn during exercise were better than those worn by boys. Their physical ability seemed stronger than the boys'. I asked the school's director whether having the girls exercise too much caused any public health problems, and she replied, "This is what makes Scotland unique. Our women's bodies are strong and healthy, and their spirits are lively, which makes them better than [any woman in] Great Britain."

Shimoda also wrote: "Women in this country value physical education so much that those who receive poor grades in exercise class are seen to be just as bad as those with poor grades in moral education. Some are even treated as outcasts." Alas! Now we realize how important physical education and exercise are to them![86]

Today Chinese women must seek out forms of exercise. Exercise makes the body strong. When the body is strong, the spirit will be lively and happy, giving them more than enough energy to go about their daily tasks. People with all kinds of medicines and books of cures, with every variety of worry and illness can barely accomplish what needs to be done in the home. As soon as they exert themselves in thinking or in performing physical labor, they fall into bed from distress, and in three days they take ill and in another

---

[84]Tr: Shimoda Utako (1854–1936), Japanese scholar and educator.

[85]Tr: Here the Chinese text reproduced in Japanese the katakana transliteration of the word "gymnastics."

[86]As I write this, I must mention something in passing. Once there was a Chinese person who saw a foreign woman playing tennis. He quietly said to his valet: "How much does this woman get paid for playing ball? Why does she work so diligently every day?" I cannot but laugh at this question.

seven days are at death's door. A poem by the Chinese thinker Gong Zizhen says, "I hope to find the secret of a jadelike body and long life." Another poem reads: "I'm forever finished with youthful beauty and 'Sorrow for Troth Betrayed.'"[87] These two lines seem to complement one another. I present these lines to my compatriots so that they may know my intention.

In sum, abilities follow inborn knowledge. Inborn knowledge is granted by Heaven, and everyone possesses it. The structure of the body is the same [in all people], and therefore the system of the brain is the same. If the system of the brain is the same, then the various types of intelligence and talents are the same; the only differences are in terms of degree. In a time when tyrants and traitors rule the land, the people are called nothing but ignorant and base, whereas all praise the man on the throne as a sage and saint, no matter how childish or ignorant he may be. It makes me ill for days on end to hear about the wonders of [our] government. If our people do not wish to tolerate the names of ignorance, baseness, and evil placed on them, why should they give such names to women? Do they think that women are stupid, that they do not know any better? Will women accept this?

What abilities do women have? More than one can describe. By expanding on what is already available to us, if we extend our lines of force, then all kinds of shapes will take form according to our will. As the pace of change in the world speeds up, the demand for talent increases. My female compatriots! It is time to gather up your gowns and ride your horses on to the stage of the twentieth century! When the flutes and drums sound, when the banners and flags unfurl, the people of the five continents will take notice, clap their hands, and sigh in wonder. They will lower their head in reverence and say, "Do not say there are no worthy people in Qin." Talk of "the Yellow Peril" will become a reality. People will think, "If the women are like this, then how can we be any match for the men?"

---

[87]Tr: See poems no. 260 and no. 2 from Gong Zizhen's *Jihai zashi*, in Liu Yisheng, ed., *Gong Zizhen Jihai zashi zhu* (Beijing: Zhonghua shuju, 1980), 324–325, 2. "Sorrow for Troth Betrayed" (*Xi shi*) is a piece commonly attributed to Qu Yuan.

PART 5: METHODS FOR EDUCATING WOMEN

We can understand the state of education in a country by examining the character of its people. An Englishman once said, "Schools in other countries may produce countless doctorates and other degree-holders, but England's schools produce only one thing: self-respecting, self-reliant people." How his words fill me with sorrow! If self-respect and self-reliance are nurtured in the English, then that makes them unique. The English are Heaven's chosen people! China and other countries, then, can only submit to and obey England, becoming her slaves, or the slaves of her slaves. Our state will be taken over by outsiders, and our race will die off. On the Asian continent, where rivers flow and magnificent mountains rise, twilight retreats across wilting grass; we have herded and penned ourselves into this land like animals. Some wonder and ask, if we are content to make this our home, why should we concern ourselves with education? Yet this kind of thinking is wrong.

What is the state of education in China? I dare say that it is slave education. Alas! Now I realize that the Star of Slavery has shone down on China's people for three thousand years; that trees rooted in slavery have spread across our continent of East Asia for three millennia. The Six Classics and Three Histories are the writings of mere servants, and the Hundred Schools of Thought are contracts drawn up for slave boys. The other so-called teachers, great women, famous ministers, and virtuous women are all just the talented slaves of clever gentry, the poetic slave girls of Kangcheng.[88] They are slaves to wealth, to clothing, to food, and to their houses. They are slaves to expensive curiosities and all types of social customs. They are slaves to placing high in the imperial examinations, to winning official promotions and getting rich, to following orders from above. They are slaves to their lords and slaves to ministers, slaves to the sages, heroes, and gallants, to such major figures as King Wen, King Zhou, and Confucius, and to such lesser figures as Zhang [Zai], Cheng Hao, Cheng Yi, and Zhu Xi,[89] as well as other characters in the *Book of Ghosts* from barbaric times. Although their slavery may take different forms, it all originates from education that does not teach self-respect and self-reliance. As I say this, I believe even more that there is no hope for China.

---

[88]Tr: Kangcheng was the style name of the Han dynasty scholar Zheng Xuan (127–200 C.E.). The female servants in his household were said to be so well educated that they could recite pieces from the *Classic of Poetry*.
[89]Tr: Major thinkers associated with Neo-Confucianism.

Women, then, are the slaves of slaves. They are not even allowed to receive the education of slaves. Although in a strict sense they are not slaves, they commonly refer to themselves as "slave" (*nu*) instead of "I." "By [our] placing women under heavy repression, their slavelike nature will only become more deeply established, and the people of the entire nation will become nothing more than groups of slaves. Countries that do not support women's rights are nearing destruction." Who wrote these words? It was the self-respecting, self-reliant eighteenth-century Englishwoman Dame [Millicent Garrett] Fawcett.[90] Yet the slavelike nature of women in eighteenth-century England was no less strong than that in China, but they have changed into who they are today because of Fawcett. Isn't Dame Fawcett the bright star of the world of women? Isn't she the savior of women? Alas! My heart is filled with the desire to save Chinese women from the world of slavery, to issue an Emancipation Proclamation. As a man, today let me take up the role of Garrison;[91] if tomorrow I were to change into a woman, I would swear to become Beecher;[92] the next day, if I were to be made emperor, then I would take Lincoln as my model. What is the method for liberating slaves? Only education.

It is said: "The ten thousand things are nourished together without their injuring one another."[93] It is also said: "If humans are well fed, warmly clothed, and comfortably lodged without being educated at the same time, they become almost like beasts."[94] Alas, how little there is to separate uneducated people from wild beasts and the ten thousand things! It pains me to see how uneducated Chinese women, when they have the unlucky fate of coming into this world, are the first to suffer and the last to enjoy any reward. If they cannot rescue themselves soon from the world of slavery, then they will truly be beyond all hope. If people lack self-respect and self-reliance, they will fall into slave education. If they do not allow themselves to become slaves, then I am certain that they can establish a form of education based on self-respect and self-reliance.

---

[90]Tr: Dame Millicent Garrett Fawcett (1847–1929), British suffragist and feminist. The reason for Jin Tianhe's description of her as an "eighteenth-century" woman is not clear.

[91]This is an American who established a newspaper to debate slavery. Tr: William Lloyd Garrison (1805–1879), founder of the abolitionist newspaper *The Liberator*.

[92]Tr: Harriet Beecher Stowe.

[93]Tr: "Doctrine of the Mean," in James Legge, ed. and trans., *The Chinese Classics* (rpt. Hong Kong: Hong Kong University Press, 1960) (hereafter CC), 1: 427.

[94]Tr: *Mencius*, trans. Legge, CC 2: 251, translation emended.

Education is a machine for manufacturing a national people. Women and men each compose one half of the national people, and therefore education should be spread widely among both women and men. I have never heard of a situation where a half-paralyzed educational system did not pass its illness on to the nation as a whole. It is the same with the body: if the left side is numb and incapacitated, the right side will also suffer along with it.

Education is like a storehouse of spirit. An education that neglects spirit is as wrong as forbidding people from eating grain and serving up sparrows and rats as food. Alas! Our world of education is starving.

Recently I saw the book *Lively Youth* by the Japanese [writer] Suzuki Tengan.[95] On the very first page the book makes statements about the different characteristics of men and women so odious and absurd that they could convict the author of high crimes against women. I give a sample of his writings here:

Men belong to yang, and women to yin. Men value bone (*gu*), essence (*ti*), martial skill (*wu*), substance (*zhi*), directness (*zhi*), firmness (*gang*), absolutes [in judgment] (*duan*), spirit and vigor (*qi*), guiding principles (*gang*), and physical strength (*zhuang*). Women tend to the flesh (*rou*), function (*yong*), ornament (*wen*), emptiness (*xu*), indirectness (*qu*), pliability (*rou*), relativity [in judgment] (*lüe*), talent (*cai*), detail (*mu*), and physical beauty (*mei*). One is active, the other, passive; one is self-directed, the other, dependent. Thus it is the responsibility of men to ascend the commanding heights, to break open the mysteries of Heaven, to strike out on their own, to establish the basis for all matters, and to set boundaries and limits; and it is the duty of women to follow calmly within established organizational boundaries, to follow what is customary and, acting in accordance with principles, to make themselves valuable by using the abilities granted them. Men are made to travel the seas, to make great journeys on their own, to perform great deeds and make a name for themselves that resounds across the ages; they are not made to fuss over the trifles of the women's quarters. It is the duty of women to move about indecisively, to focus all their feelings on one area, to stay shyly off to the side, and to devote their moral goodness to one person. Thus a good government minister cannot fail to have some of the character of a general, but a good general must not have the character of a minister;

---

[95]Tr: See Suzuki Tengan, *Katsuseinen* (1891).

the work of the general is what men were made to perform. (*Confucius said, "In one's household, it is the women and the small men that are difficult to deal with."*[96] *There must be some truth in these words, but I cannot say so based on my own experience, though there is nothing unusual in that.*)

These words, aside from all the inconsistencies in its overwrought comparisons, are unethical words; their scorn for women's rights is a crime against half of the nation. Even so, these words represent the character of women's education in Japan and should merit attention from those interested in the larger situation in the country. Nevertheless, what he says about men is correct. The men of China who are following in the footsteps of Suzuki are what he calls "dead youth." Why don't they come alive first?

Women's education in Europe is astonishing! Their science is so profound, their thought so developed, and their character so respectful and noble—I cannot discuss it all fully but will give two examples that can represent the whole. Holland is a country in Europe that gained independence from Spain in the eighteenth century. Normally there are no girls there who do not begin school by the age of six, and none who do not graduate from upper-level schools by the age of fifteen. In everyday society, women who do not speak such languages as English, French, and German are said to be uneducated. I ask my fellow Chinese, how many men in China today know the language of any other country? I know of a Japanese person who studied in Germany for several years and boarded with some local people. His landlady, an old woman, would talk with him in her free time; she knew by heart the length of the coastlines of Germany and Japan and their ratio. Our people should ask themselves, how many people who claim to be learned scholars know the length of China's coastline? I bring this up not to place on women's shoulders the enormous burden of making up for all of our learned scholars' shortcomings but, rather, to show the great difference between the new and old national people. *Women's China* (*Nü Zhonghua*), written by a native of Guangdong, said:

Nowadays men in China behave like women, and Chinese women are ashamed of men and dare not act like them! I see that from now on China will be a China that is not made up of men, but rather of women. On whom can China depend except on its two hundred million women? I love men, but I love women even more who have the substance to create a new China!

---

[96]Tr: *Analects* 17: 25, in Lau, trans., *Confucius*, 180.

If women want to have the substance needed to create a new China, education is the only way.

"Matronly Models," "Exemplars of Female Conduct," and "Female Ancestors"[97] such as the Wife of Bao of Song are not simply women who wore their clothes and hair in unique ways, but women who had the qualities needed to lead others by their example. Therefore establishing women's schools is the most important task at hand. Women between twenty and thirty years of age who dedicate themselves to hard work and who show intellectual promise can graduate in three years and be given an appropriate work position. Those who wish to study in Europe or the United States should be sent out in groups. A three-year curriculum for the schools is as follows:

FIRST YEAR	SECOND YEAR	THIRD YEAR
Writing	National language [Chinese]	National language, history, geography
Elementary history	Intermediate history and geography of China	Ethics
Elementary geography	Elementary history and geography of foreign countries	Psychology
Mathematics and bookkeeping	Geometry	Chemistry and biology
Elementary physics and chemistry	Ethics	Basic philosophy
English	Psychology	Basic economics
Singing	Intermediate physics and chemistry	Basic law
Calisthenics	English	Map-making
	Drawing	English
	Singing	Art
	Calisthenics	Singing
		Calisthenics

[97]These phrases refer to the categories used in the *Biographies of Virtuous Women*.

Are you convinced, reader? Some may ask, why is home economics not included? As a subject, home economics is simple and easy and can be taught orally and by example over a few days. Moreover, China's clan system has become highly developed over the last two thousand years. Take, for example, the revered saviors, the gallant women heroes Ti Ying, Pang E, and Mulan, I dare say it is not out of sincere patriotism, a desire to save the world, or noble thoughts, that they performed brave deeds but because they were stimulated and forced by the clan itself. This is true time and again, as in the case of Mother Lü from Haiqu, a citizen of the early Eastern Han. She changed her name, joined a group of bandits, gave away untold riches, brewed liquor, and bought knives, swords, and clothing for young men—much in the style of the Russian nihilists.[98] If we examine her underlying intentions, however, we find that she only wanted to kill the prefect of Langya to avenge the death of her son and nothing more. Even worse, when the woman from Qi wept, her concern for the people and the nation only came from her own worries about her family's fields.[99] Thus I would rather use economics, law, and philosophy to shape women's ideals and use physics, chemistry, and map-making to put them into practice. As for ethics, it also includes home economics. History, geography, and mathematics are basic general subjects. Psychology is for use in education. And education is a calling very naturally suited to women! They could put their education to use in the following positions:

1. Elementary school teachers
2. Kindergarten teachers
3. Management of schools
4. Studying in Europe and the United States

Can women put their education to use only in these occupations? Women have strong sentiments and critical thought. They have a

---

[98]Tr: See the biographies of Liu Xuan and Liu Penzi in the *History of the Later Han*. This story is often cited as an early example of citizen uprisings against corrupt officials.

[99]Tr: Because she placed her worries for the state above her own concern for having her parents arrange her marriage, this woman from the Qi family in the state of Lu during the Warring States period was often held up as an example of female patriotism; an entry for her ("Lu Qi shi nü" 魯漆室女) is included in Liu Xiang's *Biographies of Virtuous Women*. See Zhang, ed., *Lienü zhuan*, 121–122.

mind for detail and complexity but have less of the physical strength to endure demanding adventures. They could take part in the following affairs:

1. Women's educational associations
2. Women's discussion associations
3. Industrial experimentation and testing associations
4. Arts associations
5. Women's exercise associations
6. Women's unity leagues
7. Preparatory parliamentary association

Nowadays one of the most difficult roadblocks to Chinese women's rights and education is the question of whether friendships should be allowed between men and women. The associations discussed above only mention women simply pursuing education. The mixing between men and women, between outer and inner, however, remains an unquestionable prohibition for fusty Confucians. Now I say unequivocally: given how slavish, stupid, and feeble-minded Chinese men are today, even if they have the credentials needed to communicate with women, I would erect higher, stricter barriers between them in the name of the Confucian ethical code. If, however, some of these men followed the new morality, engaged in civilized thinking, and sincerely pursued the exchange of ideas [with women], then I am willing to bet with my own body and everything that there would be no harm in their becoming friends.

Those fusty Confucians do not know what morality really is; with the words "colonized plaything" written across their chests, they hope to monopolize morality for their own benefit. Men and women have the same form and vital force, have the same capacity for knowledge; to discuss morality at their leisure, to share joy with one another, to discuss topics covering thousands of years and ten thousand miles, "to appreciate marvelous writings and parse difficult passages," these are the benefits of friendship. What could be wrong with presenting oneself and behaving with proper decorum in the presence of the opposite sex? Why must we always fear that they will lead to secret trysts, hidden passion, and other immoral and scandalous acts? Indeed, education is the only way to make women value reputation and morality.

Jin Tianhe

What I have described, however, is friendship in the short term. As to the question of coeducation, educators in both the East and the West hold different opinions. Those who support coeducation argue:

> If boys and girls are brought together and provided with an appropriate education, the boys will be influenced by girls to develop more moderate, gentle personalities, and the girls will be driven by the boys to become more independent. Generally speaking, boys like deep, difficult scholarship, whereas girls prefer simple, plain techniques; if boys and girls are not brought together [in the classroom], then they will be too unbalanced. Coeducation, then, must be put into practice.

Those who oppose coeducation argue:

> Girls' qualities, habits, and ways of associating with people have always been different from those of boys, and thus the methods used to educate them must also be different. Otherwise, their characters will suffer and their health will be harmed. (*Note: This probably refers to physical exercise.*) According to current Japanese laws, at standard elementary schools, if the number of girls of the same school-year is large enough to form a class, then boys and girls of the same grade are placed in separate classes. (*This rule does not apply to first and second grade.*) At upper-level elementary schools, all the girls in the school are placed into a class, with the boys' and girls' classes separate from one another. These rules are in place because of the benefits and drawbacks of coeducation.

According to the Japanese scholar Ikunojō Yamataka:

> No detrimental effects have been seen from coeducation in standard elementary schools, but peculiarities do emerge in the upper-level elementary schools. When the numbers of male and female students are lopsided, one has no choice but to teach all of the female students together. There are benefits and unavoidable drawbacks, however. When one is forced to place all the female students into a separate grade, although the results in teaching may be much better than in coeducational settings, the deleterious feelings that form between the female students will make group education difficult. This is a problem in women's education that requires substantial attention.

This may be true, but I have a way of quickly explaining the coeducation problem. Speaking of students up through the completion of upper-level elementary school, feelings that develop between classmates in coeducational settings are stronger than usual, but the students still lack maturity in their moral character. Therefore, coeducation in this case can be an obstacle to learning. This must be distinguished from other situations.

At this point, has my discussion on educational methods come to a conclusion? Let me offer a few more words for my compatriots: what is the center of gravity for this kind of education? Guan Yiwu and King Goujian of Yue, concerned with expanding their populations, established houses of ill repute and gave themselves over to pleasure, and thus there were many evil customs in the states of Qi and Yue.[100] Duke Wu,[101] wary of and irritated by the high morals common among scholars at the end of the Eastern Han, brought lawless, shameless men into the court, whose wicked influence persisted until the Eastern Jin, when the northern tribes wrought havoc in Chinese lands. Ming Taizu led the common people and hoped to maintain permanent order under heaven, but weakened the literati with the eight-legged essay until none could prevent the fall of the dynasty. Now the people serve under the yoke of an alien race, weakened and nearly dead. Saigō Takamori,[102] displeased with the reform government's fawning view of the West, founded a school in Kagoshima that educated the spirit of its students. Within a few years, fifteen thousand strong young men raised their voices for revolution and died together for their cause. The German emperor William I, seeking vengeance, conscripted all the people of certain provinces. He emphasized military education, and soon he crushed Austria and France. To this day, their army is the finest in the world.

Thus education has been an indispensable part of society, an essential factor in creating results in the future. Education is a microcosm of society. What I call for in women's education is as follows:

1. Teach women to be noble people who can fully realize their natural talents.

2. Teach women to be free, happy people who have shaken off oppression.

---

[100]Tr: van Gulik, *Sexual Life in Ancient China*, 65n.

[101]Tr: Cao Cao, (155–220 C.E.).

[102]Tr: Saigō Takamori (1827–1877), often called the "last samurai," led an armed rebellion against the Meiji government in 1877.

3. Teach women to be forward-thinking people with the character of men.
4. Teach women to be enlightened reformers of social customs.
5. Teach women to be strong in body and give birth to healthy children.
6. Teach women to be people with pure morality who act as a model to the nation.
7. Teach women to be people who promote public morality and show empathy for the troubles of the world.
8. Teach women to be people who are steadfast, unyielding, and fierce advocates of revolution.

Even though we might set these goals, are women capable of achieving them? I am certain that they can. If a minority can establish their resolve, it will become popular among the majority, as is the nature of most women. The key is foresight! Foresight! I burn incense in prayer for it. Far away on the mountain of Gushe lives a holy man.[103] Those who hear about him must doubt his existence. Yet he is not just a legend. If those who gather up their robes and follow him tell him that the women of China are enslaved, he will also doubt it.

---

[103]Tr: See Watson, trans., *The Complete Works of Chuang Tzu*, 33–34.

PART 6: THE RIGHTS OF WOMEN

The eighteenth and nineteenth centuries were the era of revolutions against monarchy; the twentieth century is the era of revolutions for women's rights. One cannot but feel a profound sadness for women! Today women are cast into the waves of revolution, swords thrust into their hands, yellow robes placed on their shoulders,[104] [and] floodwaters lap at their feet, bullets and cannon shells rain around their heads—and they still do not see it? Since the situation cannot be avoided, their only choice is to charge into battle. The clouds of war gather, the battle drums sound, the banners unfurl, and both great revolutions approach China—and Chinese women still do not see it? I know it—how can I not cry out?

A small number of women participated in the French Revolution. They did so for revolution against monarchy, not for women's rights. Many more women participated in the revolution in Russia;[105] but this, too, was for a revolution against monarchy, not a struggle for a revolution for women's rights. Did they think revolution was a mere game, an exercise? Blood rained down on the earth, winds of slaughter spread death and terror, and the sun was blotted out from the sky. The executioner's platform, the fortresses of Siberia—even now, when I speak of them I go pale and my knees quiver. Did they take any joy in this? There must be a greater goal behind these events. What is that greater goal? Rights.

In the destruction of a nation, rights are first to fall; in the enslavement of a race, rights are an omen of what is to come. When humans can give up all their rights, then they are not far from becoming slaves and wild beasts. Thus it was not out of line for the Romans to see slaves and animals as equal in status. When England conquered India, it first employed tens of thousands of pound sterling in the East India Company to wrest away India's rights. When India did not resist, England conquered it with the flick of a wrist. England and France brought Egypt to ruins when they spent a trillion dollars[106] to open the Suez Canal and trample [Egyptians'] rights. When Egypt did not resist, England and France conquered the country in one fell swoop. When England controlled America, it used taxes on such items as sugar, tea, and printed papers to violate the rights of the thirteen colonies.

---

[104]Tr: In imperial times, yellow robes were worn exclusively by the emperor.
[105]Tr: Here the author refers to the strikes and revolutionary agitations up to 1903.
[106]Tr: Here Jin does not specify to what currency he refers.

The thirteen colonies rose to the occasion, and the democratic republic of the United States of America was brought into the world.

Even so, these are only tangible rights. As for intangible rights, one example can be found in the case of Ireland, which is a colony of England. On the sixtieth anniversary of Queen Victoria's ascent to the throne, the flag of the British Empire flew high in celebration, while the Irish shocked the English by using a black flag to show their patriotic sentiments.[107] When Hungary belonged to Austria, the Austrians often tried to trample the Hungarians' "Golden Bull." Despite all his efforts, even the illustrious Austrian minister Metternich, who was revered by the leaders of all the great nations, could not take away the Hungarians' hereditary right, passed down across the generations, to "take up arms in resistance to government." When the third call for revolution went up in France, the enemy of the people Metternich fled to England, where he died in isolation.[108]

The children of the Yellow Emperor and China's aristocracy have been colonized by the Manchus. The Manchus issued a single order, and [the Chinese] immediately had pigtails hanging from their heads and thought it not the least bit ugly. From then on, each new generation was enslaved, and Western peoples entered China and used indirect methods to make them fall in with the slaves of slaves. Thus, because the Chinese had cast aside their rights, they had arranged their own suicide without knowing. Alas! The Chinese people have been cynical and sick of life for so long!

Rights bring happiness. When, at times, happiness cannot be attained, then hardship must be required to attain it; this is true in international legal rights and even more so in civil law for individuals. Rights inhere in everything from property and marriage to housing, clothing, and food; therefore, rights comprise another way of nurturing life (*weisheng*). What the law does not protect, I will protect myself; what cannot be explained by mathematics, I will explain myself. If another person wants to trample on any part of my rights, I must throw my whole body into battle to defend those rights; thus rights come from hardship; one may call them the happiness born of

---

[107]Tr: This probably refers to protests by Irish nationalists against the jubilee celebrations of Queen Victoria's rule. See James Loughlin, *The British Monarchy and Ireland, 1800–Present* (Cambridge: Cambridge University Press, 2007), 244–245.

[108]Tr: Austrian diplomat and politician Prince Klemens Wenzel von Metternich (1773–1859), who was famous for his role in the Congress of Vienna of 1814–1815. Here Jin Tianhe's narrative is inaccurate: although Metternich fled to England with his family in 1848, he returned to the Continent in 1849 and died in Vienna, not England, in 1859.

hardship. Of all the things under heaven granted to humans, none are more important than their most personal, most beloved, most precious rights! When I think of this, and realize that my people still have not launched a revolution, I see how pitiful they truly are!

It is well known that I try to be as moderate as possible when discussing the violation and abuse of the people's rights in today's China. As for the violation and abuse of women's rights, they result partly from the teachings of sages and worthies handed down from barbaric times and partly from laws established by tyrants around the world. But rights can never be obtained by begging sages, worthies, and tyrants to hand them over. Rights that have been lost can be taken back only by fighting with all one's strength, even if it means sacrificing peace and moving toward violence. Look at the abolition of slavery [in the United States]. The deaths of millions of soldiers and officers who fought under the flags of the North and South were not enough; only after the blood of Lincoln was spilled was abolition achieved. If we look at the histories of liberty for farmers, artisans, and the religious, we realize that they are a succession of vicious battles and grim drudgery. If women today hope to recover, maintain, and protect their rights, how will they go about it?

Why and how does one struggle for rights? Rights are to humans as air is to heaven and earth. Yet if I end my own life and do not take another breath, people will not pay me homage or preserve a few hundred cubic feet of fresh air as a monument to me that is never to be breathed. What I call a lack of rights occurs when others expand the boundaries of their rights so far that they encroach on my own domain. This encroachment becomes difficult to reverse and eventually leads to tyranny. Alas! "The heavens are high, but I dare not but stoop under them; the earth is thick, but I dare not but walk daintily on it."[109] "Fearing for its head and fearing for its tail, there is little of the body left [not to fear for]."[110] When their rights have been thoroughly exploited and violated, this useless bit of human is still left behind. What do Chinese women think when they see this?

"People suffer from never knowing when to be satisfied. When they capture *Long*, they cast an eye on *Shu*."[111] When thought on rights becomes

---

[109]Tr: See the poem "Zheng Yue" in the "Minor Odes of the Kingdom" (*xiaoya*) section of the *Book of Songs*. Translation borrowed from Legge, CC 4: 317.

[110]Tr: See *The Ch'un Ts'ew, with the Tso Chuan*, trans. Legge, CC 5: 278.

[111.] Tr: This is an allusion to a remark allegedly made by Cao Cao in 215 C.E. when his army conquered Hanzhong in the Three Kingdoms period.

developed, it is like the steam engine: its ever-increasing speed cannot be contained. The rights of women in Europe are thousands of times greater than the rights of women in China. Once they reached this goal, however, new questions arose related to their equal right to participate in politics. If suffrage cannot be obtained, then it must be taken by force—and thus the twentieth century is the era of revolutions for women's rights. Seeking equal rights peacefully is like hoping to have a child while avoiding the pain of giving birth. Is that possible?

Now that I have said this, have I crushed the flowerlike spirits of all women? My words may shock some, but they are not the subjective words of one individual. Simply put, rights are a way of referring to sovereignty. The opposite of the master is the slave; but our women do not recognize themselves as slaves. In ancient Greece, the god of justice held a scale in one hand to show how it balanced rights. In the other hand, the god held a sword to show its intention to carry out justice. Therefore, a sword without a scale is only brute force; but with only a scale and no sword, rights will be useless. Only with balance between the sword and scales can the law be complete. Yet for women in China, obtaining those rights is still not the most difficult problem. Their [i.e., Chinese women's] hopes and wishes are far lower than those of women in Europe. If they do not put themselves forward, even if these rights were to fall to them like a gift from the heavens, they would be hard put to make use of them!

The rights that women should recover are as follows:

1. The right to schooling. Chinese people take no pleasure in schooling, and some see education and schooling as the most painful part of taking control of their rights. But people without education are ignorant, and ignorant people accomplish nothing; talk of "aiding the husband" in the inner chambers is empty prattle. Moreover, one's thinking on rights can be developed only through study, although rights do not reside in the books themselves. Study, then, is the beginning [leading] to all other efforts.

2. The right to establish friendships. An understanding of rights can grow in the home only in part; the rest must be stimulated outside the home. Lazily sitting on a stool, gazing up at the sky and sighing, lamenting some lost companion— these actions represent the bitterness of having no friends. Birds seem to need friends to live; how can people stand to be shuttered away in their homes? Moreover, if women are to be molded through study and schooling, establishing friendships is even more important!

3. The right to do business. Without rights, [women] cannot do business; without doing business, women rely on others and lack any independence; lacking independence, they consume without producing and [thus] everyone within and outside the home, in both the private and public realms, suffers losses. Nowadays in Europe, some businesses run by women have challenged men's dominance and achieved a surprising state of development. Despite their love for one another, it is unavoidable that husband and wife would erode each other's rights; it is even more true for businesses run by men and women. Yet women are not uncomfortable with it, and in fact this kind of affair [i.e., competition with men] is very beneficial to women.

4. The right to own property. Chinese women possess great ability to own and manage property. When their husbands are weak, or when some live alone, they manage households on their own effortlessly. Sometimes, their behavior is apparently characteristic of someone possessing the right; therefore, we cannot say this right does not belong to women. This right, however, is not recognized by law, and the occasional, exceptional cases of women owning property have not been enough to establish precedent.

5. The right to leave and return home freely. Have I been given liberty? If I am not given liberty, am I given death instead? Since antiquity, one way to violate a person's rights has been not to take the individual's life or property but to seduce the person into limiting his or her movements. Pearl-stringed curtains and embroidered chambers may look like palaces in the heavens, but in fact they are worse than prisons. The nightingale is imprisoned in a filigreed cage; the tree that inspired the chaste woman [of Lu] to sing grew from a prison of thorns.[112] Without the freedom to leave and return home, what other freedoms are left?

6. The right to freedom of marriage. Freedom of marriage is a flower of liberty that has yet to bloom in China, both for men and women. Men, however, have some right to choose whom they prefer other than their principal wives, whereas women are not only forbidden to speak their preferences but also denied any sexual desire. What should have been a natural happiness for humans is treated as something unspeakable, like the faithful pairings of quails and vigorous couplings of magpies.[113] It is as

---

[112]Tr: See note 102.

[113]Tr: *Book of Songs*, "Chun zi ben ben": "Boldly faithful in their pairings are quails; vigorously so are magpies." See *The She King, or the Book of Poetry*, trans. James Legge, CC 4: 80–81.

if beautiful sentiments on a fine spring day were covered over and finally blotted out by frigid clouds. Marriage in China is synonymous with a bitter lack of rights! With the loss of these rights, eight or nine out of ten people cannot know happiness.

As for the six rights described above, will women obtain them without difficulty? They could be demanded by a new constitution, without the trouble brought by revolution. I believe that if women truly want these rights, then they surely can obtain them. If they cannot be obtained, then we must use the scales of the god of justice to weigh their importance and support [this judgment] with the sword. Although Saturn devoured his children as they were born, I still approve of his deeds.[114]

Rights and law depend on one another, protect one another, and gain stability in one another. To seek rights without laws, Chinese women have had to resort to the strange practice of controlling their husbands. The Lioness of Hedong, the Rouge Tiger[115]—who compared women to lions and tigers? Aren't women given a bad name because they have misrecognized their rights and exercised them without knowing the proper way? Reputation, too, is a type of right. Women are deprived of their good name but still have these [improper] "rights," and what results is the poor character of the Chinese people that we see today.

Rights emerge together with freedom. All who cry out for freedom must extend their love to their group (qun), for I have never heard of an individual's freedoms reaching development while the group to which they belong remains undeveloped. Freedom of thought, freedom of speech, freedom of the press—these are the rights of individuals, but freedom of assembly is the right of a group. Previously I have laid out the main ideas behind freedom of assembly;[116] what I wrote was a call to arms, summoning my compatriots to struggle for freedom. Will my compatriots celebrate the freedom of assembly? My gift to them would be a wreath of civilization, and I would unfurl the banners Independence, Liberty, and Equality to wish a long life

---

[114]For the story of Saturn, see *The Struggle for Law*. Tr: This refers to Rudolf von Jhering, *Der Kampf ums Recht*. For an English version, see *The Struggle for Law*, trans. John L. Lalor (Chicago: Callaghan, 1915). Von Jhering began his treatise with the words "The end of the law is peace. The means to that end is war."

[115]Tr: Nicknames for famously pugnacious women from the Song dynasty.

[116]Tr: This could refer to one of Jin's articles published in the journal *Jiangsu* he edited.

of ten thousand years for the rights of Chinese women. If tyrants and enemies of the people play tricks to suppress and disperse them, then I will raise the sword of Byron[117] and use all my power to defend my compatriots. When hares die, foxes suffer; people are saddened when others of their own kind meet misfortune. I, too, am a person who has lost his rights, who is oppressed, and I am willing to die for my closest friends.

In my dreams, I still hope for women's right to vote and elect political representatives. I hope even more for the day that my compatriots have the right to be representatives in government. Admittedly, my words sound like a beggar discoursing on gold doubloons. However, the greatest obstacle to carrying out things is the lack of qualifications (*zige*). Those who have the qualifications of slaves will become slaves; those who have the qualifications of kings will become kings; those who have the qualifications needed to establish a constitution will establish a constitution; those who have the qualifications needed to make revolution will make revolution; those who have the qualifications needed for representative government will create representative government. Qualifications do not appear overnight; they are built up over time. I think of my compatriots, those unhappy legions; they toil all year round; as always, they must depend on others. I hear the buffeting wind and rain, the rooster's plaintive call; I look out and see my country, weakened and shattered. How can we stand to see natural rights sacrificed for tyrants and enemies of the people? Heroic men and women, raise up your hands together and make an oath to one another to combine your strength.

How does the establishment of private law come into conflict with public law [public international law]? It is common for people to ask this question if they are not interested in the scholarship on law and politics. They do not know that it is only when the people's rights are strengthened that sovereign rights can flourish and national sovereignty can go uncontested. They might also ask, is it not true that the development of thought on people's rights is, in the end, only to the benefit of individuals?

[I reply:] A nation is made up of individuals. If national sovereignty suffers, it has a direct effect on me. In today's world, every plant and stone falls

---

[117]An English poet who died in Greece's war for independence; I have written a biography of him and Lafayette, a gallant French prince who, upon hearing of the American war for independence, picked up his sword and went to offer help. Tr: Jin's note may refer in an exaggerated way to the Marquis de Lafayette (1757–1834).

under someone's claim to ownership and authority. Only our people while away their time on trifles, not knowing if one day they will be a slave in the Zhang household or a concubine in the Li household. Tyrants and enemies of the people try every day to wipe out our sense of shame, and our vigorous and fierce thought on rights grows small, cold, weak. These tyrants do this not only to trample private law and wrest sovereignty away from the people but probably also to make it easier for them to hold the people at their beck and call, to pawn the people off or give them away to others, all without risking the people recognizing their poisonous behavior. Now the god of justice has entered the people's dreams, saying, "To eat, you must toil; to earn fame, you must compete." The new private law they create will be based on the words of Jhering! As for the uses of toil and competition, none can be greater than taking back the rights of the people. In battling tyrants from home and abroad, even though they may be outnumbered, surrounded on all sides by the songs of Chu,[118] the spirit of my people will not give way. If they cannot take back these rights, then the blood from the skulls, hearts, and throats of millions of our men and women will not be too high a price to pay for them. Otherwise, it will still be conceivable to trade a beloved concubine for a horse, and beauties from Handan will be married to lowly men; how heartless these men from the northern tribes are! For each day they live, I suffer a thousand years of shame. I fear we will be like the flower falling in the duckweed, falling again and again, while these rights are buried for thousands of years like jade in an ancient tomb, never to come again into the light. I want the women of our nation to fight in the courts of private law, and our people to do battle in the wilds of public international law. Is my determination surprising? Will my dogged determination be understood? Those who understand me will be my honored, beloved female compatriots. Now that they have heard the call from Europe of the first revolution for women's rights, let them rise up!

---

[118]Tr: Referring to the state of "being surrounded by one's enemy" who mimic one's own folk-songs; an allusion to the defeat of the king of Chu Xiang Yu in 202 B.C.E.

PART 7: WOMEN'S PARTICIPATION IN POLITICS

The question of women's rights in the twentieth century is a question of political participation. Political participants are charged with the two great tasks of forming and supervising the government. In China, where there is no national assembly, no political parties, no elections, and no political representation, two hundred million men slumber in the examination halls, lulled to sleep by the government's siren song. Even the most shocking nightmares will not awaken them. Is it too early, then, for me to encourage women to seek the right to participate in politics? To speak of walking after taking a few steps, to speak of running after just beginning to walk—this is nothing unusual. But to talk of flying after learning just a few steps—would that get you anywhere? Well, let me write for women about tasks that can easily be accomplished. My discourse will be practical, not lofty and abstract.

To understand the morale of a nation's people, one must look to its form of government. In countries where the rights of the people are growing stronger, women's rights will develop more and more quickly in ways that are not completely dependent on the people's education and scholarly learning. Education of women in Germany was far superior to that of [women in] France, and early arguments by the Russian People's Party[119] for equality between men and women were no less forceful than those in America. France and America, however, are democratic republics. In other words, a nation's people's knowledge and learning are developed through education, but their wishes and hopes hinge on their form of government. Women's rights in constitutional monarchies, then, must be less developed than what is found in democratic republics. If one were to plant the elegant, beautiful flowers of French and American civilization in the bleak darkness of China, their petals would be covered in tears until they withered away, sacrificed in vain. These days women in China focus on questions related to education and make no mention of political participation.

China is a country ruled by an autocratic monarchy. All the problems of inequality found in European societies have appeared across China, but none to this day has been solved. Yet, if anyone claims that the common people should be prohibited from speaking of what goes on in the imperial

---

[119]Tr: This term could refer to any number of socialist, nihilist, and revolutionary parties in turn-of-the-century Russia.

palace and that these matters should be monopolized by men who kneel and pay obeisance [while speaking to the emperor], my people will rebuke them. As for the idea of equal rights for men and women, my people agree on this matter, so why do we tip the scales so that women are not treated equally? Moreover, precisely because the evils of autocracy are so grave, we have to set the methods and goals for the way forward to tunes and songs and sing them everywhere so that even women and children will know them. This is called the popularization of education. Even though we have no national assembly or political parties, no elections or representative system, my people cannot afford not to prepare for their establishment.

The political participation of women is one of the greatest problems facing European governments. In general, the idea that people are born naturally with rights is not valued by governments, just as a feral child will be cast out by society. It is more common for governments to let a few ambitious men seize power and wreck peace and order by giving weapons to bandits and succor to thieves than it is for them to plan ahead and willingly give away power.

It is not only governments but also many of the most powerful political philosophers in the world who reject the idea of people's natural rights out of hand. Women's rights are a case in point. In the nineteenth century even men like Bluntschli, the Mount Tai and North Star of his nation's learning, opposed women's rights. If the brilliance and righteous anger of John Stuart Mill and [Herbert] Spencer had not swept aside detracting arguments, then women would still be under a pall of darkness. Even when the flowers of civilization and freedom have sprouted and spread their seeds around the earth, there are those who hope to keep them at bay, those who would burn zithers for fuel and boil cranes for food; their evil influence extends in every direction. Here, then, I will list a few of the arguments made against women's right to political participation:

1. Men rule the outer sphere; women rule the inner sphere. Nature intends women to manage the affairs of the home, not the affairs of the nation. If women are allowed to intervene in national affairs and to contend with and come into conflict with men in politics, then they would shed the purity of their morality, their essential qualities of kindness and gentleness—all that is noble in women would be lost. This would be a disaster for both the home and the nation.

2. A nation should be an autonomous entity. Sovereignty, therefore, is crucial. Simply put, the nation has a masculine spirit. Although we have seen examples of women serving as rulers and government leaders, these were aberrations; no female ruler has ever been superior to a male ruler. When the female rulers of England, Austria, and Russia were in office, their nations grew wealthy and their armies grew strong, but these successes surely resulted from the efforts of fine and worthy [male] officials who were charged with these tasks and given unlimited trust.

3. Women are, by nature, highly sensitive, often overcome by emotion. If they participate in government, then conflicts and battles between parties and cliques will rise to a fever pitch, to the point where [the women] will pay no consideration to the benefits or drawbacks of proposed laws and policies but will simply follow their emotions. Male legislators, too, suffer from this flaw. Indeed, if women are allowed to intervene in politics, religious beliefs will take over, until politics and religion become inseparable and the nation becomes locked in a downward spiral.

4. In our world today, no nation that calls itself civilized does not uphold justice and revere morality. The fact that they do not give [rights] to women must be the result of an unchanging principle and not the product of partiality or bias. For this reason, all the nations of Europe agree that women do not have the rights of citizens.

In another example, the German scholar Bluntschli, in his *Study of the Modern State*,[120] argued that five types of people do not have citizenship:

1. Women
2. The young and the infirm
3. Heathens
4. Those without religion
5. Slaves and the poor

---

[120]Tr: *Lehre vom modernen Staat* (1875–1876), by Johann Caspar Bluntschli (1808–1881), legal scholar, jurist, politician, and co-founder of the Institute of International Law at Ghent. See the historical introduction to this volume for his presence in Chinese debates at the time.

Even so, I hold the view that the statements described above are all based on the realities of the past and present times. If our methods are focused on creating a national people of the future, how can we seek moral character and ethics in their broken tablets and fallen-down temples, or write new textbooks based on moth-eaten histories and catalogues of laws? I find such behavior detestable and must oppose it.

By bringing together various schools that advocate women's rights and adapting them to my own judgments, I refute the aforementioned arguments as follows:

1. It is ignorant to say that women should have the same rights as children. If one argues only that [both children and women] are easily ruled by government, then it may appear that there are no differences between them; but many men, too, are ruled by their governments. Furthermore, children are not whole and complete people. They lack complete feelings, wishes, self-consciousness, and ideas. The way they flail about, weep, laugh, sleep, and eat is like a portrait in miniature of primitive humans. When has the state ever ruled them with laws? Only women have ruled them. If primitive people rule primitive people, then how will our world ever free itself of its barbaric ways? If a nation sees its sons evolve every day and gives them power to participate in government when they are grown, yet keeps women forever under the yoke of tyranny, can such a country be called civilized?

2. If systems differentiating between public and private are not reformed, then women's rights will still not be equal. [Under these systems,] although a woman serves her husband like a guard, she at least has the right to manage his property for him. As for public rights, [the state] collects taxes from women but tramples on their rights, forcing them to pay a high price for nothing in return. Under republican governments, it is often said that "taxes are insurance for the people" and that "taxes are the raw materials for creating happiness and wealth." To pay taxes without demanding rights, to cater to government's every greedy whim, to be eaten whole and have the marrow sucked from your bones, and then still pay out for official titles and lottery tickets, all while never bothering to ask where the money goes—only Chinese people would do these things. Such behavior is never seen in Europe. But to demand that women who have no right to participate in government pay taxes is what I call stealing or establishing a government of thieves.

3. Some say that women lack the talent needed to participate in government, or that those women who do have this talent cannot exceed that of men. I have not noticed that all men in the world are sages of great learning, courage, uprightness, wisdom, and sensitivity, whereas all the women of the world are people of utter weakness, ineptitude, stupidity, and lowliness. How can there be no women of great courage and ability? How can anyone take hold of the brush and deny women's ability in one stroke? Indeed, at times women have exercised their rights out of public view, only slightly revealing themselves within the political realm, such as Napoleon's wife, Josephine, or Bismarck's wife, Johanna. From time to time these women were able to control their iron-willed husbands, acting as both their advisers and their supporters, and thus showing their own superiority. Moreover, the rights of men and women must in every case be considered based on their talent and knowledge. However, I am afraid that even if we have the appropriate means for measuring the talents of men and women, the measurements cannot be entirely accurate or precise.

4. Some say that although women are gentle and nurturing, they may use emotions to influence men. But I ask: Are gentleness and nurturing not virtues? Or are they evils? If they are evils, then why do we use something that is disallowed in the outer sphere to govern the inner sphere? Moreover, the problem of political participation is a question of rights, not of psychology. If we deprive women of rights as citizens for the reason that they have emotions, then the distribution of public rights is based on whether or not one possesses emotions; guarded against like this, emotion becomes a filthy thing! As to the theory that women's emotionality will lead to fierce fighting between political parties, I reply: even men are unable to avoid struggles between political parties and cliques, so why not strip men of their rights, too? This will surely allow the restoration of an untouchable, complete, and mature *autocracy*! In sum, although our world is moving toward republican government, the vicious disease of tyranny over women has not yet been cured.

5. Some argue that if one looks at the history of nations, it becomes clear that women have never gained rights to political participation—so why should they hope for them now? What is so surprising, however, is that even when all women have been forbidden from the political arena, some women have still been able to reach the pinnacle of government and

be called "empress" and "queen." The earliest example of these women is the mother of Elagabalus,[121] whom he allowed to serve in the Senate. Since then, female rulers have been seen many times throughout history, in England, Austria, Russia, Spain, and Portugal. Although the compositions of their governments were different, none of these women was known as "empress." More recently, Queen Victoria ruled an empire for decades. How is it that this old woman could enjoy such success and happiness while both refusing to allow women around the world to participate in high public office and herself alone holding the throne, fixing the eyes of all women on her single person? I know that one day those who contend for and covet the scepter and throne will be not men but women bedecked in rouge and powder. If the female demon of tyranny Catherine the Great[122] were alive today, could the women of the Nihilist Party be any quicker to take action?

In sum, the question of women's participation in politics cannot be avoided in today's world. The French king Louis XIV advocated the divine right of kings, but the brilliant commoner Rousseau attacked these ideas in everything he did, driving them away like so many wild dogs. If rights are not granted by Heaven, then how can [women] not be allowed to participate in politics? John Stuart Mill, Spencer, *La-pu-le* (French scholar), Bebel[123] (German scholar) and *Ke-lei-tong*[124] (Swiss scholar), were all strong advocates of women's rights, but I believe that women would still move forward without these men. The tide of women's rights is washing across the East. Although women do not possess phoenixes' wings, one day they will soar. Given their great intelligence, they will take their case to those who rule this world. Women are making their own plans, standing up for themselves, and creating a new citizenry!

When I read the history of the Socialist Party, I learned of their philosophy of equal rights for men and women. I was amazed, envious, and sympathetic toward them. At the congress held in 1891 in Brussels, the

---

[121]Tr: Short-lived Roman emperor, also known as Marcus Aurelius Antonius (203–222 C.E.).

[122]Tr: The name *Jia-tuo-li* most likely refers to Catherine the Great (1729–1796).

[123]Tr: August Ferdinand Bebel (1840–1913), one of the founders of the Social Democratic Party of Germany.

[124]Tr: The references to *La-pu-le* and *Ke-lei-tong* could not be determined.

Belgian capital, the declaration made at the meeting followed the same principles:

> At this Congress, we ask socialist parties around the world to adopt language regarding the equality of men and women. All members of our party recognize the equality of rights of citizenship and political participation for men and women and will make every effort to abolish the laws of various countries around the world that do not grant equal rights to women.

Arguments for women's rights in Europe reached a point of maturity in these words. By comparison, similar ideas in China are still in their infancy, still germinating. When I discuss the ideas, I am elated; yet very few can sing along to the tune of "Spring Sun and White Snow": the waning moon, the breeze at dawn, where will I be when I awake after my wine?[125] Perhaps my discussion will make an impression on the minds of our people only like flowers in the mirror and mirages on the water! Nonetheless, I must dare to believe that my hopes will be realized.

Do China's women realize that they live in an autocratic monarchy? Women's rights do not exist in autocracies, and women suffer in silence. Some women, however, have heard a great deal about nonautocratic countries. Political participation certainly involves the two major tasks of overseeing government and organizing government. When efforts to supervise government are turned back, why not demand the right to do so? When efforts to organize government fail for lack of talent [in that government], then it will do no harm to break up that government. To demand these rights and bring women into government—this is a duty men must work tirelessly to fulfill. To tear down and rebuild—this is the shared duty of men and women. To demand these rights will test the brain, mouth, and writing-brush. When the brain is exhausted, the mouth is parched, the brush is worn to a stub, and you are driven to tears; when tears run dry and turn to blood, when the blood flows and swords are taken up, when every sword is taken up and followed by mortars and chlorine gas shells,[126] then the work of breaking

---

[125]Tr: "Spring Sun and White Snow" (*Yangchun baixue*) was a tune named in a text by Song Yu (3rd century B.C.E.) that only a few could sing along with. "Waning Moon," and so on, refers to "The Rain-soaked Bell" (*Yu lin ling*) by Lin Yong, a famous poem that lamented parting. Translation borrowed from Wu-chi Liu, *An Introduction to Chinese Literature* (Bloomington: Indiana University Press, 1966), 106.
[126]Tr: Used by the Eight-Nation Alliance during the Boxer Rebellion (1899–1901).

up [the government] has begun. "Women, be steadfast": this is the magical creed that will drive you to seize these rights and liberty for your compatriots. The eighteenth-century English lady Millicent Garrett Fawcett said, "This punishment would kill off more than half of the English people." In a speech, she also said, "The status of the women of England is worse than [that of] wild animals." Living at the level of wild animals, oxen, and horses is even worse than the foolishness of those who commit suicide in a ditch.[127]

A China where women participate in politics is an ideal country. Ideals are made up of two parts: philosophy and fiction. Chinese works of fiction may be corrupt, but some works contain high ideals. Who has not read about characters employing their honed rhetorical skills in palace debates? Who has not read about handsome men who serve as both strong generals and trusted ministers of state? Who has not read about heroes clashing, bringing honor to their country on the battlefield? Who has not read of characters sneaking into the palace, a dagger hidden in their simple gowns, to exact revenge for their father or husband? My compatriots are all completely familiar with these stories. "They are human. . . . I am also human . . . supervision and organization . . . demand and tear down!" In sum, if in the twentieth-century the government of the new China is not led by the hands of women, I will die with my eyes open, and I hope that my compatriots, too, will die with their eyes open!

Conventions must be organized to prepare for new government. My detailed discussion of this matter in the past did not assume women and men working together. If we put them together, then the people must establish a consultative committee that allows both men and women as members. Men and women should also be elected for administrative, deliberative, and investigative positions; and either a man or a woman may serve as director. The numbers of male and female members should not be equal, for if they are equal, then there will still be separation between men and women, just as to this day the distinctions between Manchu and Han have never been eradicated. These committees will resemble the European socialist and nihilist parties; they will carry out revolution with the goal of establishing a republic. The rules and bylaws of these organizations can be discussed later, so I will not go into them here.

---

[127]Tr: See *Analects* 14: 17, in Lau, trans., *Confucius*, 137. Committing suicide in a ditch "without anyone noticing" is the result of petty, unthinking loyalty, as opposed to a more enlightened loyalty to the well-being of the people.

How strange! The common Chinese people have a unique character (*texing*) that, I argue, guarantees that women will reach new levels of development; this is called female character [personhood] (*nüxing*). A French historian wrote, "The peoples to the north of France spread female character among women of the country, and thus women gained uniquely prominent positions." What is in the female character? It consists of the beauty of literature, the depths of philosophy, the towering heights of technology, the confluence of religion, the intricacy of poses, the suppleness of language, the hidden complexity of illness, and the attachment of love. In the past, our people have usually received the positive aspects of female character, and now they acquire the negative aspects; taken together, they make up the female character. When we gain a sense of the depths of feminine qualities, we understand women's great ability to influence people, and we see that one day women will undoubtedly take on positions of prominence. Will women participate in politics? There can be no question. I hope that women will serve as legislators and that they will leave their mark on China's navy and army, on the Ministry of Finance,[128] among advisers to government, and on the Ministry of Foreign Affairs.[129] Even more, I hope that the women of China will muster their morals, erudition, reputation, and experience and credentials to gain the office of president. When merit and virtue reach their highest levels, so, too, do the honors won by women.

How is the world made? It is made in our heart-mind (*xin*). How is a nation formed? It is formed through the desires of the people. When the mind becomes enlightened and is filled with far-reaching aspirations, then equality and republicanism, which were thought of as freakish things before the eighteenth century, are now sacred and beyond reproach. Who created this situation? It was not created by Heaven. If I hope to create a new world for women, then I must rely on my heart-mind and desires; indeed, if one does not ferry across all sentient beings, one will never become a bodhisattva.

With its hexagrams, the *Book of Changes* (*Yijing*) is a book of divination that promotes the heretical doctrine of repressing yin. Of the hexagram *kun*, it says: "Hidden lines. One is able to remain persevering. Some may follow

---

[128]Tr: Here Jin refers to the *Ōkura-shō* (Ch: *Da zang sheng*), the Ministry of Finance in Meiji Japan.
[129]Tr: Here Jin refers to the *Gaimu sho* (Ch: *Wai wu sheng*), the Ministry of Foreign Affairs in Meiji Japan.

in the king's service."[130] This is a sign that women will appear in the realm of politics. [It also reads:] "Dragons fight in the meadow. Their blood is black and yellow." This refers to [women's] unavoidable path toward seizing rights and winning liberty. Its final comment reads: "When the lines are all sixes, it means: lasting perseverance furthers."[131] Referring to this trigram, one commentator wrote: "What is yielding cannot preserve [its passive nature] permanently; if it turns to yang, then all six lines [of the hexagram] change to solid lines." This hexagram means, then, that women will ascend the heights of leadership.

Such goodness! Such goodness! If I could move [Queen] Victoria to America, or Wilhelmina (*the female ruler of Holland*)[132] to Switzerland, I would be following the intention of the *Book of Changes*. A herd of dragons rises together, so strong that no one leader is needed—this day will come to pass in China. Who would oppose what I am speaking of? The admonitions of the Four Sages[133] planted the seeds three thousand years ago. If China's women finally reap their fruits in our times, then how can I be blamed for it?

---

[130]Tr: Translations from passages in the *Yi jing* are borrowed and amended from *The I Ching, or Book of Changes: The Richard Wilhelm Translation*, trans. Cary F. Baynes, 3rd. ed. (Princeton, NJ: Princeton University Press, 1967), 14–15.

[131]Tr: Wilhelm's commentary reads: "When nothing but sixes appears, the hexagram of THE RECEPTIVE [i.e., *kun*] changes into the hexagram of THE CREATIVE [i.e., *qian*]. By holding fast to what is right, it gains the power of enduring." Ibid., 15.

[132]Tr: Wilhelmina of the Netherlands (1880–1962), who assumed the throne at an early age.

[133]Tr: Shun, Yu, the duke of Zhou, and Confucius.

PART 8: ON THE EVOLUTION OF MARRIAGE

When heaven and earth came into existence, there began to exist the ten thousand things. When the ten thousand things came into existence, male and female then came into being. From the existence of male and female came husband and wife.[134] The interactions between husband and wife are the great invariable relations of humankind.[135] How are these relations maintained? Not through marriage, which is simply a ceremony, but through the spirit of the ceremony, which is love. Love, how mysterious and divine! Love, how clean and pure!

How great is love's power in the world! What drives the heavens and planets, all the living things on earth, organic and inorganic matter, to rotate, toss about, live and die, and assemble into structures? What drives them to burgeon, proliferate, and become fully developed; to have joy of meeting and sorrows of parting; to feel greed, rage, and naïve love; and to experience suspicion, jealousy, fighting and struggle, violence and killing, terror and fear? It is love. "Although the earth is destroyed, the flowers of love still bloom"—these are the words of Flammarion, angel of genuine love![136] Even so, in love there are both deduction and induction. What is induction? Marriage.

Marriage is the ignition point for the world's most sacred, purest power of love. In physics, all objects with opposing characteristics have powers to attract and influence one another; while in psychology, those of the same type have the most sincere and enthusiastic affection for one another. The main element of love is *Inspiration*[137] transformed through heat and friction. Although they may differ in many ways, the teachings of the [Confucian] classics and the Buddhist discussions of cause, effect, and fate all work to define the true meaning of love. When it is cast into form and regulated, then marriage is born into the world, and the groundwork for civilization is established.

---

[134]Tr: Echoing the conclusion to the previous section, here Jin quotes from "The Orderly Sequence of the Hexagrams" (*Xu gua zhuan*) appended to the *Classic of Changes*; see *The I Ching*, trans. James Legge, *Sacred Books of the East* (1899, reprint. New York: Dover, 1963), 16: 435–436.

[135]Tr: This sentence follows the *Doctrine of the Mean*. See Legge's translation, CC 1: 429–430.

[136]Tr: Nicolas Camille Flammarion (1842–1925). Flammarion's *La Fin du Monde* was translated by Liang Qichao under the title *Shijie mori ji* and serialized in Liang's journal *New Fiction* (*Xin xiaoshuo*) beginning in 1902.

[137]Tr: This English word is transcribed in the text as *Yanshipilichun*.

Now that I have discussed the principles of marriage, I will now turn to its history. Marriage is a discovery of the civilized era and cannot be found among primitive early peoples. The history [of human relations] before marriage can be divided roughly into three eras:

1. The era of plunder. How dim those early people were! With no real knowledge, their physical desires were the same as eating and drinking. In these times, people separated even by small distances formed separate tribes that fought with and raided one another. Women were like any other prized possession to be fought over such as livestock or provisions. When a few women were obtained, the chief would monopolize the best among them, assigning the rest to other men of the tribe. When they were stolen, then the tribe would steal women and girls from another tribe. Practices seen today of stealing women and forcing them into marriage are left over from this early period.

2. The era of supervision and control. Among primitive peoples, women's strength and courage were often equal to men's, and some women resisted the humiliations brought on by their captors, which in turn led [elites] to use force to suppress them. Those who in earlier dynasties were called "[palace] musicians" or those whom the Manchus forced into the slave class had no hope of improving their lot once they had been placed in such a low position.

3. The era of providing [for both men and women]. Where the era of supervision and control was ruled by suppression, the era of providing was ruled by compulsion and regulation. By this point women had become more submissive, men had become less severe, and divisions of labor began to appear, with men hunting and doing battle outside the home and women cooking and sewing inside the home. Their labor was put to use in virtually every area, from food to clothing to shelter; the remnants of this model are still seen in today's society. No wonder when Africans first saw oxen working hard in the fields, they mistook them for white men's wives.

The preceding three eras are all stages passed through by primitive people. It is a mysterious fact of history that the roles assigned to "man" and "woman" should have transformed so radically into "husband" and "wife." Still, a gulf remains between these words and [what occurred later in] the evolution of marriage. I separate the events that came to pass into two historical periods:

1. The era of mixed lineages. Marriage brings together two families and passes on one lineage's bloodline. However, over time bloodlines get mixed and become impure, for which there are various reasons. Generally speaking, the mixing and impurity are brought about by primitive nature. Even to this day the era of mixed lineages has not completely disappeared, a fact that I must discuss before proceeding further.

1.1. The sale of wives. Primitive peoples originally saw their wives as currency, like gold or animal skins. Thus, when they were short on gold or animal skins, they used women in their place, the same way that nowadays some men will try to sell their wives after they have gambled away all their money. When there is the sale of wives, it is unavoidable that the continuation of X's lineage is sometimes intercepted and that his progeny is transferred to Y's lineage.

1.2. Keeping another woman. I was shocked to learn that it is a common custom in Japan for men to keep another woman outside of the home. I am nauseated by stories of men who, because they are tired and lonely when they are away from home on business or studying abroad, buy sex from someone else's mistress. They foolishly take comfort in another woman, whereas the women wreck their husbands' bloodlines for the sake of a little money. These women behave no differently from geishas, so how can any of this be worth the trouble?

1.3. Remarriage by women. Before the system of monogamous marriages was implemented, the ancient sage-kings did not forbid remarriage by women, which was completely fair and reasonable. Upper-class European society sees nothing wrong with remarriage by women. Only China looks down on people who engage in this behavior; this is one area where China is completely correct and is superior to the rest of the world.

1.4. Polyandry. The practice of polyandry is one of the greatest stains on humankind! Taken objectively, however, there are original causes [behind this practice]. The three original causes are [these]: (1) Nomadic tribes are constantly at war, and the work of moving their supplies, provisions, and family members presents many difficulties. For this reason, men had no choice but to share the same wife in order to adapt to the needs of their situation.

(2) Smaller tribes who had been robbed or had their women stolen needed to increase their numbers, even as women made up a minority in their tribe. Agreements were made to share wives as a way of remedying the problems the tribe faced. (3) Occasionally an ambitious and ruthless woman, perhaps using the power of her former husband, seized leadership over the group and, unleashing her lascivious urges, selected a few men to attend to her. In primitive times, it was also quite common for women to rebel against men's domination. All this is part of the history of polyandry. This behavior almost certainly has not died out among the Miao, Yao, Zhuang, and Luo,[138] or among the primitive people of Australia and Africa. Plato from Greece often advocated polyandry, which was a case of a worthy man taking too much delight in strange ideas.

1.5. Polygamy. How powerful men were in primitive times! The *Book of Documents* speaks of "sending down two daughters,"[139] and the *Book of Rites* speaks of "nine court ladies"[140]—these are absurd customs passed down to the present day, where men simply treat women as playthings and take pride in owning their beauty. Do they not know that when one man has several wives, many other men cannot marry? A man may have several wives and concubines in order to have many heirs and maintain their bloodline. They do not understand, however, that it is disgraceful for women to be wives sharing a husband; aside from dishonorable women, who will want to attach themselves to a man with multiple wives? As for concubines, they are usually singing girls and servants of poor stock and low character. Although they may mimic the behavior of a wife, in the end they will not match [the wives]. Indeed, China sees marriage not as a place of divine purity but as a marvelous amusement. People say that they revere the teachings of their ancestors, but most give no thought to their bloodlines, behaving instead like lewd swine in a nasty sty.

Because of such factors as these, the civilization of marriage has taken one step forward and three steps backward. Moreover, some of the factors affecting marriage come not from primitive times but from the past thousand years.

---

[138]Tr: "Minorities" and border peoples in the Chinese Empire.

[139] Tr: According to the "Canon of Yao" (*Yao dian*), the legendary ruler Yao gave his successor, Shun, two daughters to take as his wives. See *Shoo King* [*Shu jing*], trans. Legge, CC 3: 25–27.

[140]Tr: Members of the imperial harem, as recounted in the *Book of Rites*. See *The Li Ki*, in Legge, trans., *The Sacred Books of the East*, 28: 432–433.

2. The era of same-surname marriages. When men and women from the same lineage marry, they will not have many children; this was seen as far back as the Spring and Autumn period.[141] Yet I notice that in Europe, this practice has been common in recent times, but I am not sure when China reformed its own system. When I read Dr. Katō's *One Hundred Essays on the Principles of Evolution*,[142] I see that one heading is titled "My Ancestors 990 Years Ago." If mother and father are represented as "2," maternal and paternal grandparents as "4," then if one traces back in this fashion, the number of ancestors becomes incredibly large. If a generation is counted as lasting thirty years, then thirty-three generations will have passed over this period, which I will lay out in the following chart.

Parents	2	Grandparents	4
Great-grandparents	8	Great-great-grandparents	16
5th-generation grandparents	32	6th-generation grandparents	64
7th-generation grandparents	128	8th-generation grandparents	256
9th-generation grandparents	502	10th-generation grandparents	1,024

In these 300 years, then, the number of ancestors would be 1,024.

11th-generation grandparents	2,048	12th-generation grandparents	4,096
13th-generation grandparents	8,192	14th-generation grandparents	16,384
15th-generation grandparents	32,768	16th-generation grandparents	65,536
17th-generation grandparents	131,072	18th-generation grandparents	262,144
19th-generation grandparents	524,288	20th-generation grandparents	1,048,576

[141]Tr: Roughly 77–476 C.E.
[142]Tr: *Tensoku hyaku wa*, by Katō Hiroyuki (1836–1916), a text about which Liang Qichao wrote in detail; see Liang's "Jiating boshi 'Tianze bai hua,'" *Xinmin congbao* [New people's miscellany] 21 (1902).

In these 600 years, then, the number of ancestors would be 1,048,576.

21st-generation grandparents	2,097,152	22nd-generation grandparents	4,194,304
23rd-generation grandparents	8,308,608	24th-generation grandparents	16,777,216
25th-generation grandparents	32,554,432	26th-generation grandparents	65,108,864
27th-generation grandparents	130,217,728	28th-generation grandparents	260,435,456
29th-generation grandparents	520,870,912	30th-generation grandparents	1,041,741,824

In these 900 years, then, the number of ancestors would be 1,041,741,824.

31st-generation grandparents	2,083,483,648	32nd-generation grandparents	4,066,967,296
33rd-generation grandparents	8,033,934,592		

In these 990 years, then, the number of ancestors would be 8,033,934,592.

Taking these calculations into account, what if all people in China were in fact marrying those with different surnames? If the number of my parents' surname would be 1, then my paternal and maternal grandparents' surnames would be 2. Following the above calculation reduced by one-half, after 990 years, aside from my own surname, I would have 41,516,967,296 surnames [in my family background]. If we make the same calculations for China's four hundred million people, then one-half of 166,000,007,704,400 hundred million would be the number of China's historical surnames. Although some overlap would mean that these numbers are not completely accurate, the number of surnames would be far more than just several hundred. China's population, however, only began to grow to its current number of four hundred million people after it had done away with the system of same-surname marriages.

Nowadays the Manchus have been within our borders for over 260 years, yet over this long period of time their numbers have only reproduced fivefold, whereas the Han race has increased twentyfold. At first I was unable to find a reason for this [difference in birthrates], but now I see that there were few partners of other surnames for those Manchus dispatched to garrisons and defensive sites. Marriage between people of the same bloodlines has caused them to become weak and inferior; gradually they are being eliminated through the processes of evolution, and one day they will disappear entirely. This testifies to the length of the history of same-surname marriages.

After reviewing the history of marriage, what do we find when we turn to look at the world of the present day? The sky is clear, and the day is warm; birdsong and flowers' fragrance fill the air. The nuptial wine-cup is raised in praise of equality, and the bride and groom share in the joys of liberty. Nothing can improve on this human happiness—marriage has advanced to a highly evolved state indeed! However, this is the state that Europe has advanced to, whereas China's evolution still lags behind. In what [evolutionary] stage do we find marriage in China? It is still in the stage of matchmakers, the stage of fortune-tellers, and the stage of the power of money.

What is meant by "the stage of matchmakers"? Matchmakers are a fine method for solving the problems of the times. The ancients understood problems in marriage practices and promoted matchmakers as a way to limit those problems. They said:

> In hewing the wood for an axe-handle, how do you proceed?
> Without another axe, it cannot be done.
> In taking a wife, how do you proceed?
> Without a go-between, it cannot be done.[143]

Matchmakers function as witnesses. They pass messages between families and evaluate and compare their talent, wisdom, and moral character, ensuring that they will not fall into disputes. In fact, matchmakers have the power to spread humaneness and remake the world. Matchmakers poison society,

---

[143]Tr: Translation borrowed from Legge's translation of the *Classic of Poetry*, see CC 4: 240.

however, when they do not spread humaneness; when they do not evaluate talent and wisdom but are concerned, rather, about making every little bit of money they can; when they knowingly lavish praise on the undeserving. People often criticize marriage as an unfair practice produced by the tyranny of parents over their children, but I never fail to insist that such statements are unjust. Why, I ask, give matchmakers the same tyrannical powers as held by the nobility? Those who cheat, deceive, and play evil tricks—only they can be held responsible. With a chattering magpie as his go-between, Qu Yuan knew only disappointment.[144]

What is meant by "the stage of fortune-tellers"? Matchmakers exert influence as people, whereas fortune-tellers invoke ghosts and spirits for their powers. When ghosts and spirits are allowed to control marriage, their power is great indeed. The phrase "a match made by Heaven"[145] resembles the way Westerners give thanks to the Savior; but this cannot be used as a standard [for judging matches]. Allowing ghosts and spirits to control marriage would lead to disaster: the river god would be allowed to take a wife,[146] and Dan Zhu[147] would be able to impregnate the wife of King Zhao of Zhou. The year, month, day, and hour on which I was born were a coincidence, yet according to my horoscope I am fated to live out my life as a widower. How is it that the tortoise shell has a spirit, but it cannot tell me what will happen in the distant future? When you ask fortune-tellers what the shell says, they will certainly reply, "Auspicious events and good fortune." However, if you observe what actually happens later, there will often be many frustrations and separations. This is not because there are random disasters but because fortune-tellers pretend to decipher the future. A fine match makes for a happy couple, but a poor match makes husband and wife into enemies. Ghosts and spirits, then, should not be allowed to come between men and women when they marry!

---

[144]Tr: See Hawkes, trans., *Songs of the South*, 30, 120–121.

[145]Tr: See "Da ming," in *She king*, trans. Legge, CC 4: 434.

[146]According to one famous story, the official Ximen Bao prevented villagers from sacrificing young women in a ceremony where the river god "took a wife." See the biography of Ximen Bao in the *Shi ji*.

[147]Tr: This line alludes to an anecdote in the *Discourses of the States (Guoyu)*. See the Sibu Bei-yao edition of the *Guoyu* (Shanghai: Zhonghua shuju, 1936), 21b–22a. Dan Zhu was known in Chinese myth as the stupid and cruel son of the sage-emperor Yao. For a brief description, see Mark Edward Lewis, *The Flood Myths of Early China* (Albany: State University of New York Press, 2006), 82–83.

What is meant by "the stage of the power of money"? This is a major problem for marriage today. In poor and weak countries around the world, the people worship gold. When one's own clothes are tattered, one will envy other people's embroidered gowns; when one can eat only coarse food, one will be jealous of other people's enjoyment of fatty meat and fine grain. If one envies something but cannot get it on one's own, then one will try to seek it through the marriage of one's children. In taking a wife for their son, parents hope for a rich dowry; and when they marry off a daughter, they ask to see the prospective husband's books that record his property. If they do not receive what they hoped for, some couples cannot get along with one another, and some of these couples divorce. When the parents do get what they hoped for, they will unhesitatingly make their daughter agree to the marriage even if the man is old like a dry willow tree or is only a peddler of silk. We cannot say that in this process there are no young men and women with high aspirations who seek out happiness in this world and are not will-ing to rashly commit themselves to another person for the rest of their lives. These young men and women will, however, certainly be sternly scolded by their parents, some of whom greedily seek out cash gifts for their daughter's hand, as if they were hawking a piece of fine jade. This is the inexorable fate of those caught up in this stage of marriage. With each passing day, the harm created by competition between individuals worsens: people fail to set their homes in order, society degenerates, education declines, moral-ity falls into disarray, and the human race cannot be improved. How could things become so bad? Because of the power of money.

"Soon after I wore my hair covering my forehead/ I was plucking flow-ers and playing in front of the gate,/ When you came by, walking on bam-boo-stilts/ Along the trellis, playing with green plums./ We both lived in the village of Changgan,/ Two children, without hate or suspicion."[148] How remarkable! The call for equal rights and liberty in China was beginning to form over a thousand years ago! How could things have fallen into the state of decline we see today? What I have discussed above are the elements of unfree marriage. In the twentieth century, the people of tyrannical states all make it their goal every day to gain their liberty. If they cannot gain even this minor freedom of marriage, then it is certain that their cries to the masses for revolution will only end in failure. A lack of freedom in marriage

---

[148]Tr: Li Bai, "Changgan xing," in Arthur Waley, trans., *Poetry and Career of Li Po* (Melbourne: Arthur & Unwin, 1951).

arises from restrictions on and suppression of individuals. Although it may be possible to escape physical restriction and suppression, it is much harder to escape the restriction and suppression of ideas, which attach to the body like scabies. When a person understands the joy of equality and liberty and desires to pursue it but dare not speak of that desire, the situation is like that of someone who feels the painful itching of scabies but dare not seek treatment for fear of revealing his illness.

Here, then, I will cry out to the women of our country:

"Freedom of marriage!"

What is marriage? It is the source of human morality. In their conduct of ethics, fathers and sons, elder brothers and younger brothers, and friends all gain feelings of love and respect for one another because of longtime familiarity with one another. When their morals and ethics accord with one another, when their characters complement one another, when their knowledge and learning are at similar levels, when their talents and interests match one another, then people will naturally develop feelings for one another. Moreover, in relations between husband and wife, the seeds of happiness are planted in the inner chambers. What is called "a perfect match" cannot be forced with money but must arise from the combination of [the couple's individual] refinement, like the intermingling of water and milk. Nowadays it is also common to treat marriage as a precious, serious affair, but most do not understand that if we make two people who yesterday were still "strangers on the road" to each other share a quilt today, the situation potentially places every stranger on the road in the place of a woman's husband and lord. In other words, society may hope to ennoble its women's character by isolating them from men before marriage, only to force them into lowly and wretched deeds. In a coincidence, two sparrows may fall into a happy match. Their evil fate is sealed, however, when one is beautiful and the other is ugly, or when one is clever and the other is dull. Little can be done to alleviate a lack of feelings [between a couple], but who is responsible for the countless cases since ancient times of "broken mirrors" and tales of "souls leaving the body"?[149] The lack of freedom in marriage is responsible for these things. When a poem reads, "My beloved now belongs to

---

[149] Tr: The "broken mirror" commonly refers to separation of husband and wife. "Souls leaving the body" refers to the Tang tale "Li hun ji."

Shazhali, there are no more righteous men such as the Lackey Gu,"[150] what is responsible for these events? The lack of freedom in marriage is responsible. When a woman's beauty and elegance is not given freely to a friend but instead is made a possession of her enemy, could the affairs of the world be in greater disarray? How strange are the things of which I have heard!

When Chinese people speak of "love," their meaning is different from what is meant when Europeans speak of love. When Chinese people speak of love, its meaning is frivolous; it is affection without honor,[151] and thus they designed ceremonies to set models for love and to guard against love becoming too forceful and causing low behavior. These ceremonies, however, are left over from primitive times. Bowing, kneeling and paying obeisance, and kissing are all forms of expression from primitive times. Whereas Chinese people find honor only in victory on the battlefield, Europeans find happiness in love that comes from friendship—this is how [the two] differ from one another.

After much effort, I still cannot understand marriage in China. People who are utterly separated from each other, having no prior interactions, can still look each other in the eye and perhaps even size up or make fun of each other without thinking it the least bit strange. But once they are arranged to marry each other, they are filled with fear for each other; if their eyes should meet, they run away shouting, as if they've seen a demon. On the night the man welcomes the bride into his home, he bows thrice to the east and thrice to the west, kneeling, paying obeisance, and standing back up, like a circle with no beginning or end. As the wedding attendants drone out incantations, he stands there like a fool while everyone snickers at him. As for the woman, her face is covered with a red cloth, and she is filled with shame. Although she suffers no illness, others help her walk; although she should smile and laugh, she can only weep. She closes her eyes in concentration,

[150] Tr: According to one Tang story, Shazhali was a general from northern tribes who carried away Lady Liu, the beautiful wife of Han Yi. See Xu Yaozuo, "Liu shi zhuan." Later the story was used to refer to one's wife or desired partner being stolen by another man. The "Lackey Gu" refers to a highly righteous and loyal official. See Xue Tiao, "Wushuang zhuan."

[151] Tr: Here Jin refers to the *Record of Rites*, which states: "Here is now the affection of a father for his sons; – he loves the worthy among them, and places on a lower level those who do not show ability; but that of a mother for them is such, that while she loves the worthy, she pities those who do not show ability: – the mother deals with them on the ground of affection and not of showing honor; the father, on the ground of showing them honor and not affection. See *The Li Ki*, in Legge, trans., *The Sacred Books of the East*, 28: 341.

and on the third day she washes her hands and enters the kitchen to make the new bride's soup. I have no words to explain any of these things.

As for marriage among Europeans, although they pay respect to their parents, they do not allow them to interfere in too many matters. This most important choice in their life must be made from among fellow students and friends, and the bride's and groom's talents, intelligence, and appearance should be well matched. Once they know each other for a few years, their love for each other grows, and they promise themselves to each other in marriage with an exchange of rings. On the night of their marriage, they go together to a church, where the elders serve as witnesses. Family and friends are overjoyed as the two ride off together in the same carriage, holding hands as they return home. They pay respect to the groom's parents in the main hall of the house and hold a gala party. What a romantic and joyous occasion! This is why the trees with branches intertwined and the birds that fly wing to wing can be found only in the West but not in China. I want to move these birds and trees to the continent of Asia, for if these forty million square *li* of land are to become a paradise, if my four hundred million compatriots are to enjoy true happiness, we must begin with freedom of marriage. "May all those who feel love in their hearts be united in marriage"[152]—this is my great hope! And I hope that my compatriots will work to achieve this.

Freedom and equal rights are twins, though freedom was born first. Therefore, when freedom arises, equal rights will be established; when equal rights are established, a system of monogamy will be implemented, and the way of the superior man (*junzi*) will begin in its simple elements, from the interactions of common men and women.[153] The shameless, animal behavior of ancient times was created by the early sages, worthies, and kings. It is said, "If Lady Zhou had penned the *Odes*, there would not have been anything like 'foregoing jealousy' found in the 'Guan Ju' and 'Zhong Si.'"[154] The union of marriage is created by a contract between two people that leaves no space for interference by a third party, just as a secret treaty

---

[152.] This famous line is sung by Du Liniang in *The Romance of the Western Chamber*.

[153.] For this conversation between Grand Tutor Xie and Lady Liu, see the "Record of Jealousy." Tr: "The way of the simple man may be found, in its simple elements, in the intercourse of common men and women; but in its utmost reaches, it shines brightly through Heaven and Earth." See *Doctrine of the Mean*, trans. Legge, CC 1: 393.

[154.] In this famous story from the Six Dynasties, Xie An (320–385) was rebuffed by his wife when he tried to convince her that the virtues espoused in the *Book of Songs* allowed for him to set up separate quarters for concubines.

between two countries cannot tolerate manipulation by a third. It is absurd for men to play women off one another, just as Zhang Yi manipulated the enemy states of Qin, and it is equally absurd for wives to use diplomatic tactics against one another![155] It is now fashionable among the idle rich to keep several concubines who compete for favor by backstabbing and conniving against one another. The husband wears himself out trying to solve the disputes and invariably ends up in a dilemma. When the Eight-Nation Alliance [who came to suppress the Boxer Uprising] demanded that their common enemy be rooted out, the ruler of China went into hiding, fearing for his life. I have frequently seen the wives and concubines try to expand their powers, just like the eight allies trying to expand their extraterritorial rights so that they might all have a share of the loot. Is there anything saintly or pure about such a situation? If my compatriots hope to establish socialism, they can do so only on the basis of monogamous marriages.

[I see] red perfumed sleeves, couplets written in a fine hand as she sits against a tree in a park in the morning, rides in the carriage of liberty in the evening. Discussing the future of the nation, giving birth to a child for the wondrous revolution. The fruits of marriage—can they be greater than these things? When I look to the West, my eyes are dazzled, my heart and mind are enthralled. My beloved has given me a perfect jade, how shall I repay her?[156] With liberty and equal rights!

Alas! The river and sky glow like a dream, the moon shines bright as a pearl; the wind and rain are showing no mercy, and even before spring passes, I know the flowers will scatter. My compatriots, women, hear my words and recognize the truth. If you follow them, you will be new citizens of the nation; if you do not, you will die in slavery. My words end here—what else can be done?

---

[155] Zhang Yi, a minister in the Kingdom of Qin, was known for playing rival states against one another.
[156] Tr: Alludes to the "Four Poems on Sorrow" (*Si chou shi*) by Zhang Heng (78–139 C.E.).

PART 9: CONCLUSION

Jin Yi [Jin Tianhe] concludes:[157] How remote are the things I have spoken of! When I look to the society of China's women, I see how bad their situation has become. When I look to the society of China's men, I see that their situation is even worse. Alas, when I speak, who will listen to my words? When I sing, whose voice will join in unison with mine? Remote, indeed, are the things I have spoken of! Whereas thousands may sing along with a folk tune; and "when the villagers hear the popular melodies of 'The Breaking Willow' or 'Bright Flowers,' grinning from ear to ear,"[158] I am probably one of those who will be ridiculed. Wang Qiang and Xishi were ancient women of unparalleled beauty, but upon seeing them, fish would hide in the depths, birds would take flight, and wapiti elk would lower their horns [for battle].

I am probably one of those at whom others will lower their horns. If women put my words into action, they are bound to encounter even more opposition. Nevertheless, my body is one that has survived great misfortune; my words are words that will remain valid even after great calamities. In China today the fire of revolution burns like the stars, and the floodwaters of China's division[159] grow stronger. The government's tyranny weighs down like rocks of tens of thousands of pounds, while the people's hundred thousand well-honed swords flash in the air. When we climb the Himalayas and look to the west, we see the Eiffel Tower of France; how high it stands! When we take a ship across the Pacific Ocean and step ashore, we hear the clear ring of America's Liberty Bell. Look east to the land under the Changbai Mountain and next to the Yalu River, and all variety of freaks and monsters are to be found there. The wings of the Vermillion Bird constellation are about to fall. To the west, when we seek the sword and bow at Qiaoshan and the dragon's whiskers at Dinghu,[160]

---

[157]Tr: It was common for an author to refer to himself in the third person.

[158]Tr: "Great music is lost on the ears of the villagers, but play them 'The Breaking Willow' or 'Bright Flowers,' and they grin from ear to ear. In the same way, lofty words make no impression on the minds of the mob. Superior words gain no hearing because vulgar words are in the majority." See *The Complete Works of Chuang Tzu*, trans. Watson, 140.

[159]Tr: Here the text refers to fears that China would be "carved up like a melon" (*guafen*) into different territories or colonial possessions.

[160]Tr: Places associated with the mythical Yellow Emperor.

the spirit of the Yellow Emperor, our sacred forefather, weeps and cries. The feud of nine generations burned in the heart of Duke Huan of Qi; Luo Binwang cried loudly to condemn Wu Zhao.[161] Alas! If women touch off these disasters, then women will be the ones to save this world; if women are the ones who betray this country, then women will also love this country.

But the women of our country have yet to stir! Thunderclaps shatter heaven and earth. Gods cry out, ghosts weep, mountains collapse, and trees split in two. Wolves rush into the city, and snakes and dragons come out of hiding. Alone, no help in sight, and weak, [the people] cower in fear. Such misery! The drama of revolution is tragedy, the drama of the loss of the nation is no less tragic, and the drama of enslavement is an even greater tragedy. The dramas that took place in the capital, in Tianjin, and in Lüshun[162] were tragedies, but the "ten days of Yangzhou" and "three massacres of Jiading"[163] were greater tragedies. Imprisoned by people who wear animal skins, forced to have sex with people who drink milk and eat cheese; serving as officials to a foreign race; serving as concubines of a foreign tribe. Such misery! When I think about how [Cai] Wenji (177 C.E.–?) returned home to the Han after being a captive in foreign territory for twelve years, and how [Wang] Zhaojun (52–21 B.C.E.) had to exit the barriers on the border to be sent to a barbarian king, I think of these incidents as stains on the world of women that the water of the five oceans could not wash away! "Singing girls, with no thought of a perished kingdom,/ Gaily echo 'A Song of Courtyard Flowers.'"[164] Slaves know their own kind of pride, and servant girls know their own kind of happiness, but I do not understand their pride and happiness—such misery! [And yet I hope they] rise up and love liberty, esteem equal rights,

---

[161]Tr: Luo Binwang (640?–684), one of the "four eminences" of the early Tang dynasty, wrote the famous parallel-prose "Dispatch on Behalf of Xu Jingye Condemning Wu Zhao," which attacked then-empress Wu Zetian.

[162]Tr: Lüshun, formerly called Port Arthur, was the site of massacres by Japanese troops following the First Sino-Japanese War.

[163]Tr: Yangzhou and Jiading were the sites of widespread killings of Chinese civilians by Manchu armies during the Manchu conquest of the Ming Empire and founding of the Qing in the seventeenth century.

[164]Tr: Du Mu, "A Mooring on the Qin Huai River," translation borrowed from *The Jade Mountain*, trans. Witter Bynner (New York: Anchor, 1964), 144.

and establish a republic of men and women that will take the creation of a new national people as its starting point and the organization of a new government as its ultimate goal.

Good women, vow to be like Ti Ying and Mulan; vow to be like Nie [Zheng's] sister and Pang E; vow to be like Mother Lü from Haiqu; vow to be like Feng Liao; vow to be like Xun Guan, like the mother of Yu [Ji],[165] like Lady Liang, like Qin Liangyu; vow to be like the Lady of Yue, Hong Xian, and Nie Yinniang.[166] Good women, vow to be like Beecher, vow to be like Nightingale, vow to be like Dame Fawcett, vow to be like Anita,[167] Mary Queen of Scots, Joan of Arc, and Vera Sassouhitsch [sic]; all are your teachers and masters. Good women, your eyes are eyes of wisdom,[168] your wrists are wrists of great sensitivity and dexterity, your sentiments are passionate sentiments, your hearts are compassionate hearts, your tongues are tongues of great eloquence, your bodies are bodies that possess natural rights, sacred and inviolable, your value is a thousand pieces of gold. You are the mothers of the nation's people—how long our people have placed their hopes on you! The bird called the Jingwei one day will fill up the sea;[169] the beauty will rise up with a sword like a rainbow. Thus my words are not spoken in vain. If one does not carry across all sentient beings, one will not become the Buddha; by carrying across women; one carries across China. Good women, I would spill my own blood for your benefit. Even as I traverse the void and the autumn wind filled with endless dust and sand, each grain of sand has within it a body; each body has a tongue; each tongue makes a sound with which to create an infinite chorus to awaken China's women. In my next incarnation, as the spring wind blows across the void, bringing brilliant flowers, each flower has within it a body; each body has a tongue; each tongue makes a sound with which to create an infinite chorus

---

[165]Tr: Yu Ji (1272–1348), famed literatus of the Yuan dynasty.

[166]Tr: Both Hong Xian and Nie Yinniang ("Cloaked Woman Nie") were famous female knights-errant whose stories were told in Tang dynasty tales of marvels.

[167]Tr: Anita Garibaldi, who, along with her husband, played a major role in the nineteenth-century Italian reunification.

[168]Tr: In Buddhism, "eyes of wisdom" (huiyan) are the eyes of sages.

[169]Tr: The reincarnation of a daughter of the Flame Emperor (Yandi) who drowned at an early age, the Jingwei bird vowed to exact revenge on the sea by filling it up one stone at a time. See Anne Birrell, Chinese Mythology: An Introduction (Baltimore: Johns Hopkins University Press, 1993), 214–215.

to praise China's women. Long live women's rights! Long live my compatriots! And long live China!

In my youth I wielded the sword and played the flute,
But gone are my swordlike valor and flutelike heart.
Who could have foreseen this desolation upon my boat's return,
When a myriad of joys and sorrows will converge upon me tomorrow morn-
ing? Forsaking rivers and mountains, I play autumn sounds on the flute,
There is no place in this world without sorrow.
Suddenly I hear an infinite green of the sea,
And appoint myself little lord of the southeast.[170]

Translated by Michael Gibbs Hill; edited by Tze-lan D. Sang from the Chinese original "Nüjie zhong 女界鐘."

---

[170] Tr: This final line pieces together two poems by Gong Zizhen, poem no. 96 from "Miscel-laneous Poems of the Year Jihai" (*Jihai zashi*) and "Composed in a Dream (No. 1)" (*Meng zhong zuo*). Translations borrowed from Shirleen S. Wong, *Kung Tzu-chen* (Boston: Twayne, 1975), 96, 40.

Bibliography

Bacchetta, Paola. "Sur les spatialités de résistance de lesbiennes 'of color' en France." *Genre, Sexualité & Société*, no. 1 (June 2009): 2–18.

Barlow, Tani E. *The Question of Women in Chinese Feminism*. Durham, NC: Duke University Press, 2004.

Birrell, Anne. *Chinese Mythology: An Introduction*. Baltimore: Johns Hopkins University Press, 1993.

Butler, Judith. *Undoing Gender*. New York: Routledge, 2004.

Chan, Ming K. and Arif Dirlik. *Schools Into Fields and Factories: Anarchists, the Guomindang, and the National Labor University in Shanghai, 1927–1932*. Durham, NC: Duke University Press, 1991.

Chang, Hao. *Liang Ch'i-ch'ao and Intellectual Transition in China, 1890–1907*. Cambridge, MA: Harvard University Press, 1971.

Chin, Tamara. "Defamiliarizing the Foreigner: Sima Qian's Ethnography and Han-Xiongnu Marriage Diplomacy." *Harvard Journal of Asiatic Studies* 70, 2 (2010): 311–354.

Chin, Tamara. "Orienting Mimesis: Marriage and the *Book of Songs*." *Representations* 94, 1 (2006): 53–79.

Chinese Text Initiative. University of Virginia Library. http://etext.virginia.edu/chinese/ shijing (accessed February 15, 2012).

Crenshaw, Kimberlé. "Demarginalizing the Intersection of Race and Sex: A Black Feminist Critique of Antidiscrimination Doctrine, Feminist Politics and Antiracist Politics." *University of Chicago Legal Forum 1989*, 139–167.

De Bary, Wm. Theodore and Richard Lufrano, comp. *Sources of Chinese Tradition: From 1600 Through the Twentieth Century*. 2nd ed. Vol. 2. New York: Columbia University Press, 2000.

Dirlik, Arif. *Anarchism in the Chinese Revolution*. Berkeley: University of California Press, 1991.

Bibliography

Dooling, Amy. *Women's Literary Feminism in Twentieth Century China*. New York: Palgrave, 2005.

Dooling, Amy and Kris Torgeson, eds. *Writing Women in Modern China*. New York: Columbia University Press, 1998.

Du, Fu. *The Selected Poems of Du Fu*. Trans. Burton Watson. New York: Columbia University Press, 2002.

Du, Mu. *The Jade Mountain*. Trans. Witter Bynner. New York: Anchor, 1964.

Edwards, Louise. "Chin Sung-ts'en's *A Tocsin for Women*: The Dextrous Merger of Radicalism and Conservatism in Feminism of the Early Twentieth Century." *Research on Women in Modern Chinese History* (Jindai Zhongguo funushi yanjiu), no. 2 (June 1994): 117–140.

——. *Gender, Politics, and Democracy Women's Suffrage in China*. Stanford, CA: Stanford University Press, 2008.

Elman, Benjamin. *Classicism, Politics, and Kinship: The Ch'ang-chou School of New Text Confucianism in Late Imperial China*. Berkeley: University of California Press, 1990.

——. *A Cultural History of Modern Science in China*. Cambridge, MA: Harvard University Press, 2006.

Fong, Grace S. "Alternative Modernities, or A Classical Woman of Modern China: The Challenging Trajectory of Lü Bicheng (1883–1943): Life and Song Lyrics." *Nan Nü: Men, Women & Gender in Early & Imperial China* 6, 1 (2004): 12–59.

Frankenberg, Ruth. *White Women, Race Matters: The Social Construction of Whiteness*. Minneapolis: University of Minnesota Press, 1993.

Gates, Hill. *China's Motor*. Ithaca, NY: Cornell University Press, 1996.

George, Henry. *Progress and Poverty*. New York: Robert Schalkenbach Foundation, 1955.

Grewal, Inderpal. *Transnational America: Feminisms, Diasporas, Neoliberalisms*. Durham, NC: Duke University Press, 2005.

Gulli, Bruno. *Labor of Fire: The Ontology of Labor Between Economy and Culture*. Philadelphia: Temple University Press, 2005.

Hawkes, David, trans. *Ch'u T'zu: Songs of the South*. Oxford: Oxford University Press, 1959.

He-Yin Zhen [Zhen Shu]. "Economic Revolution and Women's Revolution" (*Jingji geming yu nüzi geming*). *Tianyi*, double issue nos. 13–14 (December 30, 1907): 9–12.

He-Yin Zhen. "The Feminist Manifesto" (*Nüzi xuanbu shu*). *Tianyi*, no. 1 (June 10, 1907): 1–7.

He-Yin Zhen [Zhen Shu]. "On Feminist Anti-Militarism" (*Nüzi fei junbei zhuyi lun*). *Tianyi*, nos. 11–12 (December 20, 1907): 25–32.

He-Yin Zhen [Wei Gong]. "On the Question of Women's Labor" (*Nüzi laodong wenti*). *Tianyi*, no. 5 (July 10, 1907): pp. 71–80; *Tianyi*, no. 6 (August 10, 1907): 125–134.

He-Yin Zhen [Zhen Shu]. "On the Question of Women's Liberation" (*Nüzi jiefang wenti*). *Tianyi*, no. 7 (September 1907): pp. 5–14; and *Tianyi*, double issue nos. 8–10 (October 1907): 187–192.

He-Yin Zhen [Zhen Shu]. "On the Revenge of Women" (*Nüzi fuchou lun*). *Tianyi*, no. 2 (May 1907): 1–13; no. 3 (June 1907): 7–23; no. 4 (June 1907): 1–6; no. 5 (July 1907): 65–70; and double issue nos. 8–10 (October 1907): 19–25.

Hu, Ying. "Naming the First 'New Woman.'" In *Rethinking the 1898 Reform Period: Political and Cultural Change in Late Qing China*, ed. Rebecca E. Karl and Peter Zarrow, 180–211. East Asian Monographs. Cambridge, MA: Harvard University Press, 2002.

Hu, Ying. "Writing Qiu Jin's Life: Wu Zhiying and Her Family Learning." *Late Imperial China* 25, 2 (December 2004): 119–160.

Huang, Alex. *Chinese Shakespeares*. New York: Columbia University Press, 2009.

Huang, Philip. *The Peasant Family and Rural Development in the Yangzi Delta, 1350–1988*. Stanford, CA: Stanford University Press, 1990.

The I Ching, or Book of Changes: The Richard Wilhelm Translation. 3rd. ed. Trans. Cary F. Baynes. Princeton, NJ: Princeton University Press, 1967.

Internet Sacred Text Archive. http://www.sacred-texts.com.

Jenks, Edward. *History of Politics*. London: Macmillan, 1900.

Jin Tianhe. *Nüjie zhong* [The women's bell]. Annotated by Bernadette Yu-ning Li. New York: Outer Sky Press, 2003.

Jin Tianhe. *Nüjie zhong* [The women's bell]. Annotated by Chen Yan. Shanghai: Guji chubanshe, 2003.

Jones, Andrew. *Developmental Fairy Tales: Evolutionary Thinking and Modern Chinese Culture*. Cambridge, MA: Harvard University Press, 2011.

Judge, Joan. "Talent, Virtue and the Nation: Chinese Nationalisms and Female Subjectivities in the Early Twentieth Century." *American Historical Review* 106, 3 (June 2001): 765–803.

Kang, Wenqing. *Obsession: Male Same-Sex Relations in China, 1900–1950*. Hong Kong: Hong Kong University Press, 2009.

Karl, Rebecca E. *Staging the World: Chinese Nationalism at the Turn of the Twentieth Century*. Durham, NC: Duke University Press, 2002.

——. "The Violence of the Everyday in Early Twentieth-Century China." In *Everyday Modernity in China*, ed. Madeleine Yue Dong and Joshua L. Goldstein, 52–79. Seattle: University of Washington Press, 2006.

—— & Peter Zarrow, eds. *Rethinking the 1898 Reform Period: Political and Cultural Change in Late Qing China*. East Asian Monographs. Cambridge, MA: Harvard University Press, 2002.

Ko, Dorothy. "The Body as Attire: The Shifting Meanings of Footbinding in Seventeenth-Century China." *Journal of Women's History* 8, 4 (Winter 1997): 8–27.

——. *Cinderella's Sisters: A Revisionist History of Footbinding*. Berkeley: University of California Press, 2005.

——. "Gender." In *A Concise Companion to History*, ed. Ulinka Rublack, 203–225. Oxford: Oxford University Press, 2011.

Lau, D. C., trans. *Confucius: The Analects*. Hong Kong: Chinese University Press, 2000.

Bibliography

Legge, James, trans. *The Chinese Classics*. [With a translation, critical and exegetical notes, prolegomena, and copious indexes.] Taipei, Taiwan: Wenxing shudian, 1966.

——. *The Li Ki*. http://ctext.org/liji (accessed February 15, 2012).

Le-Mons Walker, Kathy. *Chinese Modernity and the Peasant Path: Semicolonialism in the Northern Yangzi Delta*. Stanford, CA: Stanford University Press, 1999.

Lewis, Mark Edward. *The Flood Myths of Early China*. Albany: State University of New York Press, 2006.

Li, Yu-ning and Chang Yu-fa, eds. *Jindai Zhongguo nüquan yundong shiliao* [Documents of the modern Chinese women's movement]. Taipei, Taiwan: Biographical Literature, 1975.

Liang, Qichao. "Jiateng boshi 'Tianze bai hua.'" *Xinmin congbao* [New people's miscellany] 21 (1902).

——. "On Women's Education" (Lun nüxue). *Shiwu Bao* [*The Chinese progress*] 23 (March 11, 1897): pp. 1a–4a; and *Shiwu Bao* 25 (April 11, 1897): 2b–4a.

Liu, Huiying. "Cong nüquan zhuyi dao wuzhengfu zhuyi—guanyu He Zhen yu Tianyi" [From feminism to anarchism: He Zhen and *Natural Justice*]. *Zhongguo xiandai wenxue yanjiu congkan*, no. 2 (2006): 194–213.

——. "Feminism: An Organic or Extremist Position? On *Tien Yee* as Represented by He Zhen." *Positions* 11, 3 (Winter 2003): 779–800.

Liu, Jen-p'eng. "'Zhongguo de' nüquan, fanyi de yuwang yu Ma Junwu nüquanshuo yijie" ["China's" feminism, translation's desire, and Ma Junwu's translation of feminism]. *Jindai zhongguo funüshi yanjiu* [Research on women in modern Chinese history] 7 (August 1999): 1–42.

Liu, Lydia H. *The Clash of Empires: The Invention of China in Modern Worldmaking*. Cambridge, MA: Harvard University Press, 2004.

——. *Translingual Practice: Literature, National Culture and Translated Modernity— China, 1900–1937*. Stanford, CA: Stanford University Press, 1995.

Liu, Wu-chi. *An Introduction to Chinese Literature*. Bloomington: Indiana University Press, 1966.

Liu, Yisheng, ed. *Gong Zizhen jihai zashi zhu* [Annotated poems of Gong Zizhen composed in 1839]. Beijing: Zhonghua shuju, 1980.

Loughlin, James. *The British Monarchy and Ireland, 1800–Present*. Cambridge: Cambridge University Press, 2007.

Lu, Weijing. *True to Her Word: The Faithful Maiden Cult in Late Imperial China*. Stanford, CA: Stanford University Press, 2008.

Ma Xulun. "Ershi shijizhi xin zhuyi" [The new "ism" of the twentieth century]. In vol. 1 of *Wuzhengfu zhuyi sixiang ziliao xuan* [Selection of materials on anarchist thought], ed. Ge Maochun et al., 1–13. 2 vols. Beijing: Beijing daxue chubanshe 1984.

Mann, Susan. "*Fu-xue* (Women's Learning) by Zhang Xuecheng (1738–1801): China's First History of Women's Culture." *Late Imperial China* 13, 1 (1992): 42–60.

——. *Talented Women of the Zhang Family*. Berkeley: University of California Press, 2007.

—— and Fangqin Du. "Competing Claims on Womanly Virtue in Late Imperial China." In *Women and Confucian Cultures in Premodern China, Korea, and Japan*, ed. Dorothy Ko, JaHyun Kim-Haboush, and Joan Piggott, 219–247. Berkeley: University of California Press, 2003.

Mather, Richard B., trans. & ed. *Shih-shuo hsin-yü: A New Account of Tales of the World*. Minneapolis: University of Minnesota Press, 1976.

McCall, Leslie. "The Complexity of Intersectionality." *Signs* 30, 3 (Spring 2005): 1771–1800.

Minford, John and Joseph S. M. Lau, eds. *Classical Chinese Literature: An Anthology of Translations*. New York: Columbia University Press, 2002.

Munro, Donald J. *The Concept of Man in Early China*. Stanford, CA: Stanford University Press, 1969.

Nash, Jennifer C. "Re-thinking Intersectionality." *Feminist Review* 89 (2008): 1–15.

Ono, Kazuko. *Chinese Women in a Century of Revolution, 1850–1950*. Stanford, CA: Stanford University Press, 1989.

Oyewumi, Oyeronke. *The Invention of Women: Making an African Sense of Western Gender Discourses*. Minneapolis: University of Minnesota Press, 1997.

Park, Katharine. *Secrets of Women: Gender, Generation, and the Origins of Human Dissection*. New York: Zone Books, 2006.

Pomeranz, Ken. *The Great Divergence: China, Europe and the Making of the Modern World Economy*. Princeton, NJ: Princeton University Press, 2000.

Pusey, James. *China and Charles Darwin*. Cambridge, MA: Harvard University Press, 1983.

Nanxiu Qian, Grace S. Fong, and Richard J. Smith, eds. *Different Worlds of Discourse: Transformations of Gender and Genre in Late Qing and Early Republican China*. Leiden: Brill, 2008.

Schneider, Helen. *Keeping the Nation's House*. Vancouver: University of British Columbia, 2011.

Schwartz, Benjamin. *In Search of Wealth and Power: Yan Fu and the West*. Cambridge, MA: Harvard University Press, 1964.

Scott, Joan W. "Gender: A Useful Category of Historical Analysis." *American Historical Review* 91, 5 (1986): 1053–1075.

Sima Qian. *Records of the Grand Historian*. Trans. Burton Watson. Rev. ed. New York: Columbia University Press, 1993.

Spivak, Gayatri Chakravorty. "French Feminism in an International Frame." *Yale French Studies*, 62 (1981): 154–184.

Stoler, Ann Laura. *Race and the Education of Desire: Foucault's History of Sexuality and the Colonial Order of Things*. Durham, NC. Duke University Press Books, 1995.

Sudo, Mizuyo. "Concepts of Women's Rights in Modern China." Trans. Michael Hill. *Gender & History* 18, 3 (November 2006): 472–489.

Tang, Xiaobing. *Global Space and the Nationalist Discourse of Modernity: The Historical Thinking of Liang Qichao*. Stanford, CA: Stanford University Press, 1996.

Bibliography

Tian Yi (*Tien Yee*). Facsimile reproduction of nos. 3, 5–6, 8–12, 15–19 (1907–1908). *Early Chinese Socialist Documents*. Book 2 of vol. 6, Chinese Materials Series. Tokyo: Dai'an, 1966.

Van Gulik, R. H. *Sexual Life in Ancient China*. Leiden: Brill, 1974.

Volpp, Sophie. "The Male Queen: Boy Actors and Literati Libertines." PhD diss., Harvard University, 1995.

Von Jhering, Rudolf. *The Struggle for Law*. Trans. John L. Lalor. Chicago: Callaghan, 1915.

Von Sivers-Sattler, Gabriele. "He Zhens Forderungen zur Namensgebung von Frauen im vorrevolutionären China: Untersuchungen zur anarchistischen Zeitschrift Tian Yi ('Naturgemäße Rechtlichkeit') (1907–1908)." In *Cheng—In All Sincerity*, ed. Denise Gimpel and Melanie Hanz, 275–284. Festschrift in Honour of Monika übelhür. Hamburg, Germany: Hamburger Sinologische Gesellschaft, 2001.

Waley, Arthur. *Poetry and Career of Li Po*. Melbourne: Arthur & Unwin, 1951.

Wan Shiguo, ed. *Liu Shenshu yishu buyi* (Supplementary additions to collected works of Liu Shipei). Yangzhou, China: Guangling Press, 2008.

Watson, Burton, trans. *The Complete Works of Chuang Tzu*. New York: Columbia University Press, 1968.

Wiegman, Robyn. *American Anatomies: Theorizing Race and Gender*. Durham, NC: Duke University Press, 1995.

World Health Organization. "Child Growth Standards." http://www.who.int/childgrowth/standards/en (accessed February 15, 2012).

Wu, Fusheng. *Written at Imperial Command: Panegyric Poetry in Early Medieval China*. Albany: State University of New York Press, 2008.

Xia, Xiaohong. "He Zhen de wuzhengfu zhuyi 'nüjie geming' lun" [On He Zhen's anarchist "Women's Revolution"], *Zhonghua wenshi luncong* 83 (2006): 311–350.

——. *Wanqing wenren funü guan* [Late-Qing elite views of women]. Beijing: Beijing daxue chubanshe, 1995.

Xiao, Tong. *Wen Xuan, or Selections of Refined Literature*. Vol. 3, *Rhapsodies on Natural Phenomena, Birds and Animals, Aspirations and Feelings, Sorrowful Laments, Literature, Music, and Passions*. Trans. David R. Knechtges. Princeton, NJ: Princeton University Press, 1996.

Yan, Fu. *Shehui tongquan* [translation of Edward Jenks, *History of Politics*]. Beijing: Shangwu yinshuguan, 1981.

Zarrow, Peter. "He Zhen and Anarcho-Feminism in China." *Journal of Asian Studies* 47, 4 (November 1988): 796–813.

Zhang, Jing, ed. *Lienü zhuan jinzhu jinyi* [Biographies of eminent women, with annotation and translation in modern Chinese]. Taipei, Taiwan: Shangwu yinshuguan, 1994.

Index

abilities of women, 231–240
accessories for women, 223
active calls for women's liberation, 59
"Admonition Against Attacking Min-Yue" (Liu An), 175
"Admonition Against Attacking the Xiongnu" (Zhufu Yan), 177n15
Admonitions for Daughters (Ban Zhao), 145, 212, 231
America: economic reasons for marriage in, 97–103; education of women in, 202; factory workers in, 77–82; He-Yin Zhen's opinion of, 38; marriages in, 57–59, 86; oppression by government in, 67; prostitutes in, 83, 87, 88; slave system in South, 76n7
Analysis and Explication of Characters, 135
Analysis and Explication of Written Characters, 114–115
analytical category, translating *nannü* as, 10–13
anarchism: currents of at turn of twentieth century, 39–41; of He-Yin Zhen, 23–24; promotion of in "On the Revenge of Women", 106–107
ancestral worship, 121
ancient world, marriage in, 108–109

Annam, 172
Annotations to Etiquette and Rituals (Zheng), 130, 136, 139–140
Annotations to the Book of Changes (Zheng), 129, 131
Annotations to the Book of Rites (Zheng), 129, 131, 135, 140
Annotations to the Mao Tradition of the Songs (Zheng), 130, 132, 136, 142
Annotations to the Rites of Zhou (Zheng), 130, 135
antimilitarism, feminist, 169–178
archery, in ritual texts, 214n20
aristocratic marriage, Zhou period, 139n
aristocratic women in political office, 65–67, 69
armies, women's right to command, 147
arranged marriages, 56–57
assembly, freedom of, 256–257
"Atrocities of Men Against Women" section, "On the Revenge of Women": addendum, 167–168; death by cloistering, 153–158; death by corporeal punishment, 158–167; overview, 147; rights deprived of women, 147–153
attire, mourning, 119–120n, 181n6
auspiciousness, 220

Index

Austria, Hungarian resistance against, 252

authority, as reason for support of
women's liberation by men, 60

autocracy, 259–260

autonomous labor, 25

bachelor tax, 100, 100n15

Baillie, Joanna, 234n57

"Ballad of the War Wagons" (Du Fu), 173,
177n15

banishing of women for crimes of men,
164–166

Ban Zhao, 145–146, 211n9, 212, 231

Bao Linghui, 234n63

bear arms, women's right to, 147

beauty, 236

Bebel, August Ferdinand, 264n123

Beecher Stowe, Harriet, 210n8

betrothal gifts, 179–180n

Biographies of Exemplary Women, 125,
125n21, 133–134, 134n35, 215

bloodlines, mixed, 271–272

Bluntschli, Johann Caspar, 261, 261n

bond servitude, 72–76

Book of Changes, 124, 126, 267–268

Book of Documents, 161

Book of Rites: betrothal ceremony,
179–180n; chastity of women, 131;
cloistering of women, 53–54; docility
as desirable in women, 130; gender
inequality, 125; inequality in work and
responsibility, 180–181; responsibilities
of women, 136

Book of Songs, 113, 113n, 137, 174

book publishing, 46–47

brain size, 232

Bremer, Frederika, 234n57

bride kidnapping, 116–118

brute force, control of women by, 92–93

Buddhism, 226–227

business, women's right to do, 255

Butler, Judith, 21

Cai Wenji, 170–171, 171n4

Cai Yan, 234n69

Canon of Yao, 126, 161

Cao Cao (Duke Wu), 249, 253n111

"Cao Chong" (Grass insects) poem, 137n45

Cao E, 218n27

Cao Shuang, 162

Cao Zhi, 174

capabilities of women, 231–240

capitalism, as reason for women's
involvement in labor, 78–82

casting out of wives, 137–138

cereus, 235n79

character of women, 220–230

chastity of women, 131–135

Chen Fan, 166

Cheng Wei, 162

Cheng Yi, 133, 133n

Cheng Yichou, 118

Chen Li, 129n

Chen Lin, 176

Chen Xiefen, 45

child bride marriage, 94

children: discrimination between sons
and daughters, 113; education of by
mother, 193–194, 215–216; feminist
goals regarding, 182; women as having
same rights as, 262

China, late-Qing, 28–35

Chinese feminism: early, 4–8; overview,
1–4

Chinese patriarchal discourse, *nannü*
concept and, 17–18

Chunyu Zhang, 160–161

civil service exams, 199n16

class: versus livelihood, 76n6; *nannü* as,
17–18

classical learning, gender inequality in,
122–146

Classic of Rites, 214n20

cloistering: and education, 202; evil of,
228–229; overview, 54–57; women's

right to move freely, 255; women suffering death by, 153–158
clothing, of women, 223
coeducation, 248–249
command armies, women's right to, 147
Commentary of Guliang, 128
Commentary on the Han Tradition of the Book of Songs, 140
Commentary on the Zuo Commentary (Kong Yingda), 137, 137n46
Commentary to the Book of Changes (Jing Fang), 129
committees, political, 266
commodified labor, 25–26
commoner women, recruitment into harems, 153–157
communal husbands and wives, 92, 108–109
communally owned property, 90–91, 107–108
The Communist Manifesto, 5–6
competition between wives and concubines, 281
The Complete Works of Chuang Tzu, 282n158
Comprehensive Commentary of the Five Classics, 140
concubinage, 96; competition between wives and concubines, 281; era of mixed lineages, 272; inequality in marriage, 180; overview, 82–90; status of concubines, 139–140
confinement of women. *See* cloistering
conflict, wives as to blame for, 141
Confucian tradition: critique of, 15, 35–36; gender inequality in, 122–146, 122n; geographical shifts in, 198n13; New Text tradition, 161n91
conscription, inequality in, 177–178
constitutional reform, 62
consumers, principle of proportion, 190–191
control, era of, 270
corporeal punishment, women suffering death by, 158–167

cosmetics, 223–224
Cui Hao, 163
Cui Qun, 165
Cui Yingying, 56n11
curriculum, for schools for women, 245

Da Dai Liji, 195n7
Dan Zhu, 276n147
death: by cloistering, 153–158; by corporeal punishment, 158–167; of men versus women, 152–153
death notifications, pain of, 175–176
Deng, Empress, 149
dependence, mutual, 90–91
despotism, 107
Dictionary of Historical Surnames, 210n3
differentiation between man and woman, 53–54
Differing Meanings in the Five Classics (Xu Shen), 129
Discourses of the States, 276n147
distinction, *nannü* as category of, 20–22
divorce, 86
docility, as desirable in women, 130–131
domination, and *nannü* concept, 21–22
"Dong Shan" poem, 174, 174n9
Dong Zhongshu, 128n27
Dooling, Amy, 27
drafting of women into harems, 153–157
Du Fu, 173, 176, 177n15
Duke Wu (Cao Cao), 249, 253n111
Du Mu, 283n164
Du Qin, 141–142
dynastic reform, 29

ear piercing, 224
Economic Evolution, 77, 79
"Economic Revolution and Women's Revolution" (He-Yin Zhen): marriage for love, 103–104; marriage in China, 92–97; marriage in Euro-America, 97–103

economics, as reason for support of
    women's liberation by men, 60–61
economic thinking of late-Qing period,
    30–33
economy, burden of warfare on, 176–177,
    177n15
education: and capabilities of women,
    231–240; and character of women,
    220–221; of children by mothers,
    193–194; in late-Qing China, 33–34;
    methods for educating women, 241–250;
    and morality, 212–213; "On Women's
    Education", 189–203; prenatal, 195–197,
    215–216; reasons for support of women's
    liberation by men, 61; of Western
    women, 59; and women's morality,
    215–216; women's right to, 148–153, 254
Elagabalus, 264n121
emotions of women, and involvement in
    politics, 261, 263
Emperor Hui of Jin, 228n46
Emperor Wu, 106
Emperor Xianzong, 165
Emperor Yuan, 175
employment. *See* labor
Empress Deng, 149
empresses, 148, 149, 150n66
Empress Wu Zetian, 150–151n68, 221n,
    283n161
Empress Xiaoming, 165
Empress Zhangjing, 165
Empress Zhao, 235
England, abuse of rights of other nations
    by, 251–252
enlistment, inequality in, 177–178
equality: antimilitarism and, 178; as
    championed by some men, 143–144; of
    education, 200–201; versus freedom,
    23; as goal of women's liberation, 59;
    of men and women, Socialist Party's
    recognition of, 264–265; in Western
    society, 59

equal labor, 90–91
equal rights, 70
etiquette, gender inequality in, 121
Etiquette and Rituals, 117, 125, 125n20, 129
Euro-America: economic reasons for
    marriage in, 97–103; education of
    women in, 244; factory workers in,
    77–82; He-Yin Zhen's opinion of, 38;
    marriages in, 57–59, 86, 280
Evolution and Ethics (Spencer), 196–197
execution of women, 158–167
exercise, by women, 238–240
exiling of women for crimes of men, 166
Explaining Terms (Liu Xi), 136
*Explications of the Commentary of
    Gongyang* (He Xiu), 125, 129, 132–133, 139

factory workers, 77–82, 88, 89
faithful maidens, 133–135, 134n41
faithfulness of women, 131–135
family, women's morality in relation to,
    215–219
family conflict, wives as to blame for, 141
The Family Instructions of Master Yan
    (Yan Zhitui), 193–194
family members: appointment of by
    women in power, 150n66; corporeal
    punishment of, 158–167
family names, 108–113, 182
Fa Mulan. *See* Mulan
Fan Pang, 216n
Fan Ying, 143–144
fate, 226
Fawcett, Dame Millicent Garrett, 242,
    242n90, 266
Fei Nianci, 56n10
female-embodied labor, 25–26
female rulers, 261, 263–264
female slaves, 72–76
female writers, 43–46
feminine qualities, 267
feminist antimilitarism, 169–178

"The Feminist Manifesto" (He-Yin Zhen), 14, 179–188
Feng Liao, 211n13, 235
fetal education, 195–197, 215–216
fiction, 46–47
filial piety, 140–141
Finland, women's movement in, 64, 67, 69
Five Dynasties period, 164
"five *zu*", 163
Flammarion, Nicolas Camille, 269n136
"Following Military Campaigns" (Wang Can), 174–175
footbinding, 34n10, 202–203, 221–223
fortune-tellers, 276
France, oppression by government in, 67
freedom: of assembly, 256–257; versus equality, 23; as goal of women's liberation, 59; of marriage, 255–256, 277–281
French Revolution, 251
friendships: between men and women, 247; women's right to, 254
Fu, Lady, 234n59
Fu, Ming Prince, 157
fu character, 108–109, 114
Fukuda Hideko, 44
funeral rites, 118–122, 181, 181n6
Fu Xi, 117n11

Gao Shi, 175
Gao Yang, 164
Garden of Persuasions, 131, 131n
Garibaldi, Anita, 284n167
Garrison, William Lloyd, 242n91
Gautama, Siddharta (Sakyamuni), 225n39
gender: as analytical category, 12–13; sexual difference concept, 21; *shengji* concept as critique of political economy of, 22–26; "social constructivist" view of, 14–15
"Gender: A Useful Category of Historical Analysis", 12–13

gender inequality: as caused by militarism, 177–178; in classical learning, 122–146; forms of, 179–181; in social institutions, 116–122; in writing, 114–116
George, Henry, 42
global world, late-Qing China in, 28–35
goals for women, 182–183, 249–250
Goldman, Emma, 40n19
Gongyang Commentary, 159
Gongyu, 157
Gong Zizhen, 285n170
Gore, Catherine, 234n57
Goujian, King, 249
governments. *See* anarchism; state
The Great Learning (Daxue), 181, 190
Guan, Lady, 234n67
Guangdong (Yue) region, 198
Guan Yiwu, 249
Guan Yu, 225n40
Guanzi, 190
guilt-by-association, 158–167
Gui Youguang, 135n43
Guo Zhun, 162
Gu Tinglin (Gu Yanwu), 113, 211n15

Haggard, H. Rider, 99n10
hairstyles, 224–225
Han dynasty: corporeal punishment of women, 159–161; empresses in, 148; gender inequality under, 122n, 124, 128n27; system of multiple wives in, 112
Han E, 234n68
Han Learning, 198n13, 198n14
Han people: family names of, 110n; rule over women by, 106–107
Han Tradition of the Book of Songs, 117–118
harems, 112–113, 153–158
head circumference, 232–233
health, of women, 238–240
Hemans, Felicia, 234n57

Index

Heng hexagram, 126n22

Herschel, Caroline, 234n57

Herve, Gustave, 169, 169n2

He Xiu, 125, 129, 132–133, 139

He-Yin Zhen (He Zhen): basic tenets of feminist theory, 8–10; biography, 51; comparing to other Chinese feminists, 7; critique of contemporary male feminists by, 2; "The Feminist Manifesto", 179–188; intersectionality, 18–22; "On Feminist Antimilitarism", 169–178; overview, 2–4, 7; *shengji* concept, 22–26. *See also* "On the Revenge of Women"

—"Economic Revolution and Women's Revolution": marriage for love, 103–104; marriage in China, 92–97; marriage in Euro-America, 97–103

—*nannü* concept: beyond sex-gender problematic, 13–18; critique of, 19–22; translating as analytical category, 10–13

—"On the Question of Women's Labor": equal labor, 90–91; factory workers, 77–82; prostitution and concubinage, 82–90; slave girls, 72–76

—"On the Question of Women's Liberation": cloistering of women, 54–57; goal of women's liberation, 70–71; men's role in liberation, 59–63; overview, 53–54; Western women, 57–59; women's role in liberation, 63–69

—worlds of thinking: general discussion, 47–52; late-Qing China in global world, 28–35; media worlds of thinking, 42–47; overview, 27–28; textual and ideological worlds, 35–42

historical context, 6–7; general discussion, 47–52; late-Qing China in global world, 28–35; media worlds of thinking, 42–47; overview, 27–28; textual and ideological worlds, 35–42

historical grounding of *nannü* concept, 20

History of Jin, 162

A History of Politics (Jenks), 108, 116–117

"History of Prostitution", 87

History of the Former Han, 157

History of the Han, 166

History of the Later Han, 148, 149, 153–154, 166

History of the Northern Dynasties, 163

History of the State of Wei, 114

History of the Tang, 164–165

Holland, education of women in, 244

home economics, 246

Hong Xian, 235n73, 284n166

household management, 115–116, 217–219

housemaids: abuse of, 96; prostitution by, 88–89

Hua Mulan. *See* Mulan

Huang, Alex, 98n9

Hu Chenggong, 129n, 134

Hui of Jin, Emperor, 228n46

"Humble Voices of the Miserable", 89

Hundred Days' Reform period, 29

Hungary, resistance against Austria, 252

husbands: communal, 108–109; evolution of marriage, 269–281; gender inequality in Confucian tradition, 124–128; inequality in marriage, 180; mourning period for, 119; women's morality in relation to men, 213–214. *See also* marriage

Ibsen, Henryk, 93, 93n2

ideological world, of He-Yin Zhen, 35–42

ignorance, as virtue of women, 192–193

Ikunojō Yamataka, 248

independent employment of women, and marriage as mutual prostitution, 97–98 inequality, gender: as caused by militarism, 177–178; in classical learning, 122–146; forms of, 179–181; in social institutions, 116–122; in writing, 114–116

infidelity, 271

inheritance of property by women, 97

injustice, in writings of He-Yin Zhen, 8–9

inner qualities, of women, 220–221

"Instruments of Men's Rule Over Women" section, "On the Revenge of Women": classical learning, 122–146; family names and rise of patriarchy, 108–113; overview, 105–108; social institutions, 116–122; writing, 114–116

intelligence of women, 197–200, 231–240. See also education

international legal rights, 251–252

intersectionality, 18–22

Ireland, patriotic sentiments in, 252

isolation of women. See cloistering

Japan: concubinage and prostitution in, 87, 88–89; education of women in, 201; effects of war on women, 171–172; feminists in, 44; He-Yin Zhen's opinion of, 38; Jin Tianhe's opinion of women from, 230; Meiji Restoration, 198–199, 199n15; oppression of women in, 55n7; women laborers in, 80

jealousy, as forbidden in women, 138–139

Jenks, Edward, 108, 116–117

Jiading, 283n163

Jiang Yan, 172–173

"Jiang You Si" (The Jiang Has Its Branches) poem, 139n

Jiao Xun, 134

Jia Yi, 212n17

Jie, King, 231n52

Jie Jie, 163

Jing Fang, 129

Jingwei bird, 284n169

Jin Tianhe, 1–2, 7, 204, 205. See also "The Women's Bell"

Joan Haste (Haggard), 99n10

journals, Chinese-language, 42–46

Kaneko Kiichi, 79, 86

Kang Aide (Ida Kang), 199n17

Kang Youwei, 200n19

Kanno Suga, 44

Katō Hiroyuki, 273, 273n142

kidnapping, bride, 116–118

kin: appointment of by women in power, 150n66; corporeal punishment of, 158–167

King Goujian, 249

King Jie, 231n52

Ko, Dorothy, 34n10

Kong Guang, 160–161

Kong Yingda, 137

Kuang Heng, 131

Kun hexagram, 126n22

labor: as basic human activity, 24–26; and education of women, 190–192; equal, 90–91; factory workers, 77–82; independent employment of women, and marriage as mutual prostitution, 97–98; inequality in, 180–181; in late-Qing China, 30–32; occupations for women, 246–247; prostitution and concubinage, 82–90; slave girls, 72–76; of women, and women's liberation, 55

"Lackey Gu", 279n150

The Lady from the Sea (Ibsen), 93, 93n2

Lady Fu, 234n59

Lady Guan, 234n67

Lady Lu, 234n70

Lady of Yue, 235n73

Lady Zuo, 234n61

La Fin du Monde (Flammarion), 269n136

Landon, Letitia, 234n57

land redistribution advocacies, 41–42

Index

late-Qing China, 28–35
law, bondage of, 58–59
learning, gender inequality in, 122–146.
    See also education
legal punishment, death by, 158–167
Li, Einar, 170n
Liang Dingfen, 56n9
Liang Hongyu, 169n1
Liang Qichao, 24, 39, 186; biography,
    187–188; "On Women's Education",
    189–203
Li Bai, 277n
liberalism, 36–39
Li Bomei, 235n75
Li Chaoluo, 135
Li Hua, 175–176
Li Ling, 147
lineages, era of mixed, 271–272
Lin Shu, 46
Lin Yong, 265n125
Lin Zongsu, 45
Li Qi, 165
Li Sheng, 222n32
Li Shidao, 165
literature, 46–47
Liu An, 175
Liu Bang, 218n26
Liu Jen-p'eng, 37
Liu Shipei, 32n, 51
Liu Xi, 136
Liu Xiang, 125
Liu Yu, 154
Liu Yuanzuo, 165
Liu Zhongying, 216n
livelihood: concubinage and prostitution
    as problem of, 86; as reason for
    women's involvement in labor, 77–81;
    slavery as problem of, 74–76
Lively Youth (Suzuki Tengan), 243–244
Li Xiao, 165
love, 103–104, 269, 279, 279n151
loyalty, of women, 131–135

Lu, Lady, 234n70
Lü, Mother, 246
Lü Bicheng, 46n26
Lun Heng (Wang Chong), 195n8
Luo Binwang, 283n161
Luo Yanbin, 45–46
Lüshun, 283n162

magical power of women, 237
maidens, faithful, 133–135, 134n41
maids: abuse of, 96; prostitution by, 88–89
makeup, 223–224
male origins of Chinese feminism, 36–39
male queues, 203n21
Manchus: colonization of China by, 252;
    rule over women by, 106–107; slavery
    under rule of, 73
Mao's Annotations to the Songs, 130, 132,
    136
Mao Tradition of Songs, 132, 138–139
Ma Rong, 125, 198n14
marriage: in ancient world, 108–109;
    arranged, 56–57; ceremonies,
    279–280; child bride, 94; in China,
    economic reasons for, 92–97; era of
    mixed lineages, 271–272; in Euro-
    America, economic reasons for,
    97–103; evolution of, 269–281; family
    names and rise of patriarchy, 108–113;
    freedom of, 255–256, 277–281; gender
    inequality in, 116–118, 180; for love,
    103–104; for purchase, 93–97, 117–118;
    same-surname, era of, 273–275;
    Western, 57–59, 86; women's morality
    in relation to men, 213–214
Marxism, 41
Mary Queen of Scots, 210n6
matchmakers, 275–276
maternal line, mourning period for, 119
matrilineal descent, 109–110
media worlds of thinking, He-Yin Zhen,
    42–47

Meiji Restoration, 198–199, 199n15
"Memorial" (Yang Zhen), 136, 136n44
men: brought to power by female rulers, 150n67; corporeal punishment of women belonging to, 158–167; death of, versus of women, 152–153; differentiation between women and, 53–54; effect of Western intellectual developments on, 6; marriage as prostitution by, 98–100; mourning period for, 120; numbers of women versus, 84–85; queues, 203n21; role of in women's liberation movement, 59–63; women's morality in relation to, 213–214. *See also* husbands
—atrocities of against women: death by cloistering, 153–158; death by corporeal punishment, 158–167; overview, 147; rights deprived of women, 147–153
—instruments of rule over women: classical learning, 122–146; family names and rise of patriarchy, 108–113; overview, 105–108; social institutions, 116–122; writing, 114–116
Mencius, 184n, 189
Mencius (Meng Ke), 216n
The Merchant of Venice (Shakespeare), 98n9
"Methods for Educating Women" section, *The Women's Bell*, 241–250
Metternich, Prince Klemens Wenzel von, 252n108
militarism, opposition of women to, 169–178
military power, women with, 150–151, 151n69
Mill, J. S., 36–39
Ming dynasty, 73, 156–157
Ming Taizu, 249
Miscellaneous Poems (Cao Zhi), 174
"Miscellaneous Poems" (Wang Hui), 175
mistresses, 271. *See also* concubinage

mixed lineages, era of, 271–272
money, marriage for: in China, 92–97; in Euro-America, 97–103; marriage for love, 103–104
money, power of, 277
Mongol conquest of China, 73
monogamy, 58–59, 111–112, 182, 183–184, 280–281
"A Mooring on the Qin Huai River" (Du Mu), 283n164
morality: bondage of, 58–59; friendships between men and women, 247
—of women: education, 215–216; household management, 217–219; overview, 212–215
Mother Lü, 246
mothers, education of children by, 193–194, 215–216
mourning attire, 119–120n, 181n6
mourning practices, 118–121, 181, 181n6
Mulan, 147, 169n1, 211n12
multiple wives, 111–113. *See also* concubinage
mutual dependence, 90–91
mutual prostitution, marriage as system of, 97–103

Naishi, 160–161
names: era of same-surname marriages, 273–275; family, 108–113, 182; pen-names, 42–43
nannü concept: beyond sex-gender problematic, 13–18; critique of by He-Yin, 19–22; overview, 9; translating as analytical category, 10–13
nanxing concept, 15–17
nationalist-feminist analysis, 35
national rights, 251–252
native feminism, 37
Natural Justice (*Tien Yee* or *Tianyi bao*), 4–6, 35n13, 51
natural rights theory, 39

neologisms, sex and gender related, 16
"The Newlyweds' Separation" (Du Fu), 173
New Text Confucian tradition, 35–36,
    161n91, 198n13, 198n14
New York City, prostitutes in, 83, 87
Nie Yinniang, 284n166
Nie Zheng, 235n72
"nine *zu*", 159, 161
Norway, suffrage of women in, 64,
    65–66
nu character, 115
nü concept, 109n4
nüquan, 63n23
Nurhaci (Qing Taizu), 222n34
nüxing concept, 15–17
Nüzong, 144

occupations. *See* labor
official examination, 199n16
*One Hundred Essays on the Principles
    of Evolution* (Kato Hiroyuki), 273,
    273n142
"On Evolution of Marriage" section, *The
    Women's Bell*, 269–281
"On Feminist Antimilitarism" (He-Yin
    Zhen), 169–178
"On the Question of Women's Labor"
    (He-Yin Zhen): authorship of, 43;
    equal labor, 90–91; factory workers,
    77–82; prostitution and concubinage,
    82–90; slave girls, 72–76
"On the Question of Women's Liberation"
    (He-Yin Zhen): cloistering of women,
    54–57; critique of contemporary
    male feminists in, 2; goal of women's
    liberation, 70–71; men's role in
    liberation, 59–63; *nannü* concept,
    13–14; overview, 53–54; Western
    women, 57–59; women's role in
    liberation, 63–69
"On the Revenge of Women" (He-Yin
    Zhen):

—atrocities of men against women:
    addendum, 167–168; death by
    cloistering, 153–158; death by corporeal
    punishment, 158–167; overview, 147;
    rights deprived of women, 147–153
—instruments of men's rule over women:
    family names and rise of patriarchy,
    108–113; gender inequality in classical
    learning, 122–146; gender inequality
    in writing, 114–116; inequality in
    social institutions, 116–122; overview,
    105–108
On the Subjection of Women, 36–37
"On Women's Education" (Liang Qichao),
    187–188, 189–203
oppression of women, 200. *See also*
    cloistering; rule over women,
    instruments of
ornamentation, evil of, 223–225
Ouyang Xiu, 216n

pacifism, 169–178
Pang E (Zhao E'qin), 211n10
Pan Xizi, 99n10
parents: discrimination between sons
    and daughters by, 113; feminist goals
    for, 182
Paris-based anarchists, 40
parliamentary representation, 64–69
Parrot Island, 228n45
passive calls for women's liberation, 59–60
paternal line, mourning period for, 119
patriarchal discourse, *nannü* concept and,
    17–18
patriarchy, rise of, 108–113
penal punishment, death by, 158–167
pen-names, 42–43
Phan Boi Chao, 172n
philological grounding of *nannü* concept,
    20
philosophical grounding of *nannü*
    concept, 19–20

physical beauty, 236
physical education, 239
pierced ears, 224
pin character, 114
pinfei, 115
plundered marriage, 92–93, 270
plundering of women, age of, 179
political concept, *nannü* as, 21–22
political economy of gender, *shengji* concept as critique of, 22–26
political power: women's right to hold, 147–148; women with, 64–67, 69, 149–151, 150n66
political upheavals, late-Qing China, 28–30
politics: equal rights in, 70; women's participation in, 259–268
polyandry, 271–272
polygamy/polygyny: death of women by cloistering, 153–158; era of mixed lineages, 272; jealousy as forbidden in women, 138–139; overview, 111–113; Zhou period, 139n. *See also* concubinage
poststructuralist feminists, 14–15
poverty: concubinage and prostitution, 82–90; and employment of women, 79–80, 191; resulting from warfare, 176–177, 177n15; slavery as problem of, 74–76. *See also* money, marriage for
power: bondage of, 58; of money, and marriage, 277; *nannü* concept as mechanism of, 21; as reason for support of women's liberation by men, 60
prenatal education, 195–197, 215–216
primitive people, marriage among, 270–272
The Principles of Sociology (Spencer), 109
print media, Chinese-language, 42–46
private property, 22–23, 92–97
private prostitutes, 87

privilege, bondage of, 58
producers, principle of proportion, 190–191
professional independence, 70
profit: bondage of, 58; making and sharing, 190–192
promiscuity, sexual, effect of cloistering on, 55–57
property: communally owned, 90–91, 107–108; inheritance of, for women, 97; women as, 92–97, 114–115; women's right to own, 255
property-marriage, 92–97, 179–180
property relations, 22–23
proportion, principle of, 190–192
propriety, women's: education, 215–216; household management, 217–219; overview, 215
prostitution: feminist goal regarding, 183; marriage as system of mutual, 97–103; overview, 82–90; as result of war, 172
providing, era of, 270
pseudonyms, 42–43
public morality, 217–219
public speaking, women in, 237
punishment: corporeal, women suffering death by, 158–167; slavery as, 72
purchase, marriage for, 93–97, 117–118

Qi, woman from, 246, 246n99
Qian Daxin, 134
Qian hexagram, 126n22
Qin dynasty, 159
Qing Taizu (Nurhaci), 222n34
Qin Liangyu, 235n78
Qiu Hu, 229n50
Qiu Jian, 162
Qiu Jin, 35
Qi Wangshi, 151n69
qualifications, 257
quanli, 58n13

Index

Queen Victoria, 264
queues, male, 203n21

race, as analytical category, 18–19
"The Rain-soaked Bell" (Lin Yong),
    265n125
"Record of a Woman's Lot", 79
Record of Rites, 279n151
Record of the Three Kingdoms, 162
Records of Rites by Dai Senior, 128, 130
Records of the Grand Historian, 159
recruitment into harems, 153–157
reform of education, place of women in,
    236–237
relatives, appointment of by women in
    power, 150n66
religion, 225–227, 261
remarriage, 182, 271
republicanism, socialism as fulfillment of
    promise of, 41–42
responsibilities: inequality in, 180–181; of
    women, 135–137
revolutionary movement in China, 29
revolutions, 251–252
"Rhapsody on Separation" (Jiang Yan),
    172–173
rich women, in political office, 65–67, 69
rights: deprived of women, 147–153;
    participation of women in politics,
    259–268; of women, 251–258
"The Rights of Women" section, *Social
    Statics*, 37
"The Rights of Women" section, *The
    Women's Bell*, 251–258
rites: ancestral worship, 121; funerary,
    118–122; inequality in, 181; marriage,
    116–118
Rites of Zhou, 159
Robber Zhi, 231n52
rule over women, instruments of:
    family names and rise of patriarchy,
    108–113; gender inequality in classical

learning, 122–146; gender inequality
    in writing, 114–116; inequality in
    social institutions, 116–122; overview,
    105–108
rulers, female, 261, 263–264
rural economy, in late-Qing China, 31–32
Russian Revolution, 251
Russo-Japanese War, 171

Saigo Takamori, 249, 249n102
Sakyamuni (Siddharta Gautama), 225n39
sale of wives, 271
same-surname marriages, era of, 273–275
scholastic tradition, gender inequality in,
    122–146
Scott, Joan W., 12–13
self, women's morality and virtue
    regarding, 212–213
self-comfort, as reason for support of
    women's liberation by men, 61–62
self-distinction, as reason for support of
    women's liberation by men, 60
self-gratification, versus liberation, 63–64
self-indulgence, versus liberation, 63–64
self-interest: bondage of, 58; as reason for
    support of women's liberation by men,
    60–62
separation: after marriage, 182; of soldiers
    from family, 172–175
servitude, 72–76
sex, indulgence in by women in power,
    150n66
sex-gender problematic, *nannü* concept,
    13–18
sexual difference concept, 21
sexual self-gratification, versus liberation,
    63–64
sexual transgression of women, effect of
    cloistering on, 55–57
Shakespeare, William, 98n9
Sha Lizhi, 235n77
Shangguan Yi, 164–165

Shao Feifei, 97, 97n
Shazhali, 279n150
shengji concept, 9, 22–26
Sheng Xuanhuai, 56n10
Shen Qinhan, 134
Shi Hu, 156
Shi Meiyu (Mary Stone), 199n17
Shimoda Utako, 239
Shi Xuan, 156
Shun, King, 106
Shuowen Jiezi (Xu Shen), 198n14
Sima Xiangru, 229n49
Sino-Japanese War, 171
Six Classics, 127n26
slaves, female: abuse of, 96; and education, 241–242; as evidenced in writing system, 114–115; overview, 72–76
Smith, Adam, 42
"social constructivist" view of gender, 14–15
Social Democratic Party, 68–69
social etiquette, gender inequality in, 121
social institutions, gender inequality in: funerary rites, 118–122; marriage, 116–118; overview, 116
socialism, 41–42
Socialist Party, 264–265
social revolution, feminist, 183
Social Statics, 37
society, effects of education on, 249–250
socioeconomic thinking of late-Qing period, 30–33
sociopolitical upheavals, late-Qing China, 28–30
soldiers, suffering of family of, 172–176
Somerville, Mary, 234n57
Song dynasty, gender inequality under, 124
Song Learning, 198n13
Spencer, Herbert, 36–39, 109, 196–197
sports, participation of women in, 238–240

"Spring Sun and White Snow", 265n125
state: form of government, relation to women's rights, 259–260; late-Qing period, 28–30, 32–33; liberal, 39; socialist view of, 41–42; Tokyo anarchist critique of, 40–41; women as bringing disorder to, 141–143. *See also* anarchism
statism, 39
Stone, Mary (Shi Meiyu), 199n17
strikes, by female laborers, 80
Study of the Modern State (Bluntschli), 261
"Study of Wealth and Power" (*Fuqiang Xue*), 30–31, 82, 82n10
subjugation of women. *See* rule over women, instruments of
submission, as desirable in women, 130–131
suffrage, 33, 64–69
suicide, by widows, 95, 95n5
Sun Wuzi, 238
Sun Zhongshan (Sun Yatsen), 39, 41–42
supersigns, 12n
superstition, 220, 225–228
supervision and control, era of, 270
surnames, 182, 273–275
Su Ruolan, 235n71
Suzuki Tengan, 243–244
Syntactic and Semantic Analysis of the Han Tradition of the Book of Songs (Xue), 132

talented women, 149–151, 149n65, 192–193, 233–236, 263
tang character, 115
Tang dynasty, 112–113, 164–165
Tang Sai'er, 151n69
taxes, payment of by women without rights, 262
Tazoe Tetsuji, 77, 79
teachers: mothers as, 193–194; women as, 236–237

Index

textual world, of He-Yin Zhen, 35–42
"Three Obediences", 128–130
"three *zu*", 159, 161
"Thrice Following", 128–130
Tighe, Mary, 234n57
Ti Ying, 211n11
Tokyo anarchists, 39–41
Tong Bana, 235n74
totemic societies, 108–110
trading of women, age of, 179–180
translating *nannü* as analytical category, 10–13
translation of Western literature, 46–47
The Treatise on Fetal Education, 196
Tu Fu, 147
tyranny, 209–210

Undoing Gender, 21
unions, women's, 80
United States, oppression by government in. *See* America
universal suffrage, 66–67, 68–69
upper-class women, in political office, 65–67, 69

Victoria, Queen, 264
Vietnam, 172
virtue, of women, 131–135, 192–193, 212–219

waged laborers, women as, 77–82
Wang Can, 171, 174–175, 210n4
Wang Chong, 195n8
Wang Hui, 175
Wang Ji, 142
Wang Shifan, 164
Wang Zhang, 164
Wang Zhong, 135n42
warfare, effects of on women, 170–178
wealth, women as instruments of. *See* women's labor
wealthy, 82–86, 89. *See also* money, marriage for

Wei Heng, 234n64
Wei Shuo, 229n47, 234n64
well-field system, 72–73
Wen, King, 106
Wen Tingshi, 56n9
Western marriages, 86
Western origins of Chinese feminism, 36–39
Western women: education of, 201, 202; liberation of, 57–59
White Tiger Discourse: casting out of wives, 137, 138; docility as desirable in women, 130, 131; gender inequality, 125; jealousy as forbidden in women, 139; matrilineal descent, 109; overview, 124n16; status of concubines, 140; subservience of women, 129
widows: chaste, 133; suicide by, 95, 95n5
Wilhelmina of the Netherlands, 268n132
William I of Germany, 249
wives: as to blame for family conflict, 141; casting out of, 137–138; communal, 108–109; competition between concubines and, 281; evolution of marriage, 269–281; filial piety, 140–141; gender inequality in Confucian tradition, 124–128; inequality in marriage, 180; jealousy as forbidden in, 138–139; mourning period for, 119; multiple, 111–113; sale of, 271; women's morality in relation to men, 213–214. *See also* marriage; women
wo character, 114
"woman", in writings of He-Yin Zhen, 8–9
women: acceptance of inferior position by, 144–146; antimilitarism of, 169–178; cloistering of, 54–57; concerns of in late-Qing China, 34; death of, versus of men, 152–153; differentiation between men and, 53–54; education of, 189–203; "The Feminist Manifesto", 179–188; goals for, 182–183; labor by in

late-Qing China, 32; magical power of, 237; marriage as prostitution by, 100–102; mourning period for, 120; numbers of men versus, 84–85; property inheritance for, 97; remarriage by, 271; rights deprived of, 147–153; rights of, 251–258; as rulers, 261, 263–264; writers, 43–46
—atrocities of men against: death by cloistering, 153–158; death by corporeal punishment, 158–167; overview, 147; rights deprived of, 147–153
—instruments of men's rule over: classical learning, 122–146; family names and rise of patriarchy, 108–113; overview, 105–108; social institutions, 116–122; writing, 114–116
"women of color" concept, 18–19
The Women's Bell (Jin Tianhe), 1–2, 7, 205; Conclusion, 282–286; On Evolution of Marriage section, 269–281; Introduction, 209–211; Methods for Educating Women section, 241–250; Preface, 207–208; Rights of Women section, 251–258; Women's Capabilities section, 231–240; Women's Character section, 220–230; Women's Morality section, 212–219; Women's Participation in Politics section, 259–268
"Women's Capabilities" section, *The Women's Bell*, 231–240
"Women's Character" section, *The Women's Bell*, 220–230
Women's China, 244
women's journals, 43
women's labor: equal labor, 90–91; factory workers, 77–82; prostitution and concubinage, 82–90; slave girls, 72–76
women's liberation: cloistering of women, 54–57; goal of, 70–71; men's role in,

59–63; overview, 53–54; Western women, 57–59; women's role in, 63–69
"Women's Morality" section, *The Women's Bell*: education, 215–216; household management, 217–219; overview, 212–215
"Women's Participation in Politics" section, *The Women's Bell*, 259–268
women's propriety: education, 215–216; household management, 217–219; overview, 215
work. *See* labor
worlds of thinking, He-Yin Zhen: general discussion, 47–52; late-Qing China in global world, 28–35; media worlds of thinking, 42–47; overview, 27–28; textual and ideological worlds, 35–42
writing, gender inequality in, 114–116
Wu, Duke (Cao Cao), 249, 253n111
Wu, Emperor, 106
Wu Cailuan, 234n65
Wu Fujin, 166
Wu Linggui, 165
Wutong, 225n41
Wu Yinsun, 56n8
Wu Yuanji, 165
Wu Zetian, 150–151n68, 221n, 283n161

"Xiang Shu" poem, 138n
Xiang Yu, 238n82
Xian hexagram, 126n22
Xianzong, Emperor, 165
Xiaoming, Empress, 165
Xie An, 280n154
Xie Daowei (Daoyun), 229n48
Xie Daowen, 234n62
Xie Feng, 134
Xifu Gong, 166
Ximen Bao, 276n146
"Xin-an Officer" (Du Fu), 173
xing character, 109–110

Index

xing concept, 15–17

Xue Han, 132

Xue Lingyun, 235n71

xueshu, 122n

Xue Yuan, 234n66

Xu Gan, 74

Xun Guan, 235n76

Xun Shuang, 126, 127–128, 154

Xunzi, 124

Xu Shen, 129, 198n14

Xu Shu, 216n

Xu Xiling, 167

Yan Fu, 196–197, 196n10

Yang Zhen, 136, 136n44

Yangzhou, 283n163

Yan Zhitui, 193–194

Yao, 272n139

Yellow Crane Tower, 228n45

Yellow Emperor, 106

Yelu Zhu, 156

Ying'er of the Northern Palace, 218n27

yin-yang cosmology, 128n27, 141–143, 154

You, King, 218n25

youbie, 53n

Yu, Han, 234n60

Yuan, Emperor, 175

Yuan History, 74

Yuanji, 166

Yuan Zai, 165

Yue (Guangdong) region, 198

Yue, Lady of, 235n73

Yue Fei, 225n40

Yu Ji, 284n165

Yun Yao, 166

Zasulich, Vera, 210n7

Zeng Guofan, 145n60

Zhangjing, Empress, 165

Zhang Wenxiang, 167

Zhang Xianzhong, 222n33

Zhang Xuecheng, 149n65

Zhang Yi, 281n155

"Zhan Yang" (Looking up to great heaven) poem, 142n51

Zhao, Empress, 235

Zhao Kuo, 159

Zhao Yan, 164

Zheng, 129

Zheng Lian, 141, 141n

Zheng Xuan, 198n14; chastity of women, 132; concubinage, 139–140; corporeal punishment of women, 159–160; docility as desirable in women, 130–131; education of servants, 241n88; mourning rites for wives, 140; responsibilities of women, 135, 136, 137; women as subsidiaries of men, 129; yin-yang cosmology, 142

Zhi, Robber, 231n52

Zhou Dunyi, 141

Zhou dynasty: polygamy during, 139n; system of multiple wives in, 112

Zhufu Yan, 177n15

Zhuo Wenjun, 56n11, 229n49

Zhu Youliang, 164

Zhu Yuanzhang, 106, 232n54

Zornlin, Rosina Maria, 234n57

zu, 159n89

Zuo, Lady, 234n61

Zuo Commentary on the Spring and Autumn Annals, 139, 159

WEATHERHEAD BOOKS ON ASIA

WEATHERHEAD EAST ASIAN INSTITUTE, COLUMBIA UNIVERSITY

LITERATURE

David Der-wei Wang, Editor

Ye Zhaoyan, *Nanjing 1937: A Love Story*, translated by Michael Berry (2003)

Oda Makato, *The Breaking Jewel*, translated by Donald Keene (2003)

Han Shaogong, *A Dictionary of Maqiao*, translated by Julia Lovell (2003)

Takahashi Takako, *Lonely Woman*, translated by Maryellen Toman Mori (2004)

Chen Ran, *A Private Life*, translated by John Howard-Gibbon (2004)

Eileen Chang, *Written on Water*, translated by Andrew F. Jones (2004)

Writing Women in Modern China: The Revolutionary Years, 1936–1976, edited by Amy D. Dooling (2005)

Han Bangqing, *The Sing-song Girls of Shanghai*, first translated by Eileen Chang, revised and edited by Eva Hung (2005)

Loud Sparrows: Contemporary Chinese Short-Shorts, translated and edited by Aili Mu, Julie Chiu, and Howard Goldblatt (2006)

Hiratsuka Raichō, *In the Beginning, Woman Was the Sun*, translated by Teruko Craig (2006)

Zhu Wen, *I Love Dollars and Other Stories of China*, translated by Julia Lovell (2007)

Kim Sowŏl, *Azaleas: A Book of Poems*, translated by David McCann (2007)

Wang Anyi, *The Song of Everlasting Sorrow: A Novel of Shanghai*, translated by Michael Berry with Susan Chan Egan (2008)

Ch'oe Yun, *There a Petal Silently Falls: Three Stories by Ch'oe Yun*, translated by Bruce and Ju-Chan Fulton (2008)

Inoue Yasushi, *The Blue Wolf: A Novel of the Life of Chinggis Khan*, translated by Joshua A. Fogel (2009)

Anonymous, *Courtesans and Opium: Romantic Illusions of the Fool of Yangzhou*, translated by Patrick Hanan (2009)

Cao Naiqian, *There's Nothing I Can Do When I Think of You Late at Night*, translated by John Balcom (2009)

Park Wan-suh, *Who Ate Up All the Shinga? An Autobiographical Novel*, translated by Yu Young-nan and Stephen J. Epstein (2009)

Yi T'aejun, *Eastern Sentiments*, translated by Janet Poole (2009)

Hwang Sunwŏn, *Lost Souls: Stories*, translated by Bruce and Ju-Chan Fulton (2009)

Kim Sŏk-pŏm, *The Curious Tale of Mandogi's Ghost*, translated by Cindy Textor (2010)

The Columbia Anthology of Modern Chinese Drama, edited by Xiaomei Chen (2011)

Qian Zhongshu, *Humans, Beasts, and Ghosts: Stories and Essays*, edited by Christopher G. Rea, translated by Dennis T. Hu, Nathan K. Mao, Yiran Mao, Christopher G. Rea, and Philip F. Williams (2011)

Dung Kai-cheung, *Atlas: The Archaeology of an Imaginary City*, translated by Dung Kai-cheung, Anders Hansson, and Bonnie S. McDougall (2012)

O Chŏnghŭi, *River of Fire and Other Stories*, translated by Bruce Fulton and Ju-Chan Fulton (2012)

Endō Shūsaku, *Kiku's Prayer: A Novel*, translated by Van Gessel (2013)

Li Rui, *Trees Without Wind: A Novel*, translated by John Balcom (2013)

Abe Kōbō, *The Frontier Within: Selected Writings of Abe Kōbō*, translated by Richard Calichman (2013)

Zhu Wen, *The Matchmaker, the Apprentice, and the Football Fan: More Stories of China*, translated by Julia Lovell (2013)

The Columbia Anthology of Modern Chinese Drama, Abridged Edition, edited by Xiaomei Chen (2013)

HISTORY, SOCIETY, AND CULTURE

Carol Gluck, Editor

Takeuchi Yoshimi, *What Is Modernity? Writings of Takeuchi Yoshimi*, edited and translated, with an introduction, by Richard F. Calichman (2005)

Contemporary Japanese Thought, edited and translated by Richard F. Calichman (2005)

Overcoming Modernity, edited and translated by Richard F. Calichman (2008)

Natsume Sōseki, Theory of Literature *and Other Critical Writings*, edited and translated by Michael Bourdaghs, Atsuko Ueda, and Joseph A. Murphy (2009)

Kojin Karatani, *History and Repetition*, edited by Seiji M. Lippit (2012)

CPSIA information can be obtained
at www.ICGtesting.com
Printed in the USA
FSHW011254270820
73354FS